GUINNESS WORLD RECORDS 2006

★ ABOUT THIS BOOK

This year's edition is set in DIN, a typeface originally designed for signage on the German road network (DIN stands for 'Deutsche Industrie Norm', the 'German Industrial Standard') but adapted for print publishing – with improved readability – by the Dutch typographer Albert-Jan Pool.

Most editions – for the UK, USA, Canada, French Canada, Australia, New Zealand, Brazil, Denmark, the Netherlands, Finland, France, Italy, Norway, Portugal, Russia, Spain, South America and Sweden – are printed in Barcelona, Spain, on three 30-m-long (100-ft) Lithoman 48-page web offset presses.

After these editions are printed (which will take 95 days), we'll have used over 48,500 litres (10,668 gallons) of ink – enough to fill the fuel tanks of four 747 jumbo jets, or over 600 bath tubs! – and just under half as much glue. The covers will be printed on 471 km (292 miles) of silver foil – sufficient to decorate the length of the Grand Canyon – and mounted on 672.7 tonnes (1,482,000 lb) of cardboard. Finally, we'll have got through 3,500 tonnes (7,716,000 lb) of 110-gsm Finesse 220 paper from Finland and Germany – heavier than the space shuttle with full fuel tanks and payload.

The remaining editions – for Germany, Greece, Israel, China, Japan, Croatia, Czech Republic, Estonia, Hungary, Iceland, Latvia, Poland and Romania – are produced at various printers around the world.

British Library Cataloguing-in-Publication Data: a catalogue record for this book is available from the British Library

ISBN
1-904994-04-0

FOR A COMPLETE LIST OF CREDITS AND THANKS, SEE P.286

EDITOR
Craig Glenday

EDITORIAL TEAM
Rob Dimery
Carla Masson
Ben Way

PROOFREADERS
Richard Emerson,
Mike Flynn, Ron Hewit,
Nick Minter

DESIGN CONCEPT/CREATION
Keren Turner at
Blue Oyster Creative

COVER DESIGN
Ron Callow at Design 23

HEAD OF PUBLISHING
Patricia Langton/
Victoria Grimsell (acting)

PRODUCTION CO-ORDINATOR
Colette Concannon

PRINTING & BINDING
Printer Industria Grafica
Barcelona, Spain

TECHNICAL CONSULTANTS
Esteve Font Canadell
Roger Hawkins

COLOUR ORIGINATION
Resmiye Kahraman at
Colour Systems, London, UK

HEAD OF PICTURE MEDIA DESK
Betty Halvagi

PICTURE RESEARCH TEAM
Claire Gouldstone
Maureen Kane
Caroline Thomas
Louise Thomas

ORIGINAL PHOTOGRAPHY
David Anderson
Drew Gardner
Paul Hughes
Ranald Mackechnie

ARTISTS
Cliff Tan Anlong
Ian Bull

KEEPER OF THE RECORDS
Stewart Newport

RECORD RESEARCH & ADJUDICATION

Stuart Claxton
David Hawksett
Keely Hopkins

Kim Lacey
Hein le Roux
Chris Marais

Susan Morrison
Della Torra Howes

RESEARCH ASSISTANTS

Scott Christie

Laura Hughes

Sophie Whiting

ACCREDITATION
Guinness World Records Limited has a very thorough accreditation system for records verification. However, while every effort is made to ensure accuracy, Guinness World Records Limited cannot be held responsible for any errors contained in this work. Feedback from our readers on any point of accuracy is always welcomed.

ABBREVIATIONS & MEASUREMENTS
Guinness World Records Limited uses both metric and imperial measurements (US imperial in parenthesis). The sole exceptions are for some scientific data where metric measurements only are universally accepted, and for some sports data. Where a specific date is given, the exchange rate is calculated according to the currency values that were in operation at the time. Where only a year date is given, the exchange rate is calculated from December of that year. 'One billion' is taken to mean one thousand million. 'GDR' (the German Democratic Republic) refers to the East German state, which unified with West Germany in 1990. The abbreviation is used for sports records broken before 1990. The USSR (Union of Soviet Socialist Republics) split into a number of parts in 1991, the largest of these being Russia. The CIS (Commonwealth of Independent States) replaced it and the abbreviation is used mainly for sporting records broken at the 1992 Olympic Games.

Guinness World Records Limited does not claim to own any right, title or interest in the trademarks of others reproduced in this book.

GENERAL WARNING
Attempting to break records or set new records can be dangerous. Appropriate advice should be taken first and all record attempts are undertaken at the participant's risk. In no circumstances will Guinness World Records Limited have any liability for death or injury suffered in any record attempt. Guinness World Records Limited has complete discretion over whether or not to include any particular records in the book. Being a Guinness World Record holder does not guarantee you a place in the book.

A selection of the exclusive interviews featured in this edition can be read in their unedited form at www.guinnessworldrecords.com/2006

Check the website regularly for record-breaking news as it happens, plus exclusive video footage of record attempts. You can also sign up for the official Guinness World Records newsletter, *Off The Record.*

GUINNESS WORLD RECORDS 2006

GUINNESS
WORLD RECORDS

ACTUAL SIZE

INTRODUCTION

→ **WHICH BRITISH RESIDENT BOASTS THE GREATEST NUMBER OF BODY PIERCINGS? FIND OUT ON P.52**

WELCOME TO GUINNESS WORLD RECORDS 2006 – THE MOST EXCITING EDITION WE'VE PRODUCED YET...

It's been a busy 12 months for record-breaking Brits – a quick search of our ever-growing archive reveals that over 5,600 claims were made from the United Kingdom over the past year: an average of 15 record attempts every day!

In terms of the world league table of record claims, we Brits are second only to the USA, although our list of successful claimants reads like a veritable who's who: Rachel Stevens, James Cracknell, Paula Radcliffe, Sir Richard Branson and Robbie Williams are just a few of the great Brits who feature in the pages of this year's book.

But I don't want to give the impression that we're obsessed with celebrity – as ever, it's the

Her Majesty Queen Elizabeth II – a multiple record holder – receives a copy of the golden anniversary edition of Guinness World Records *from Chief Operating Officer Alistair Richards during her visit to the company's London headquarters.*

David Hasselhoff – star of Baywatch, the most widely viewed TV show in history – gets a sneak preview of the 2006 book during his exclusive interview with Guinness World Records. Find out what it's like to be the most watched leading man in TV history on p.152.

←

ordinary people doing the extraordinary that make **Guinness World Records** so special. So congratulations to, among others, Terry Burrows (★ **fastest window cleaner**), Tommy Baker (★ **longest time spinning a football on the head**) and Mr and Mrs Arrowsmith (★ **oldest living married couple**), who all broke records in the past year.

One record holder who made a particularly memorable impact on the book team this year was Queen Elizabeth II, who visited **Guinness World Records** in August to commend us on our success around

the world. Her Majesty accepted a copy of last year's 50th-anniversary edition (although she politely declined to take home her many framed certificates!).

Thanks to everyone else who congratulated us on our 50th-anniversary edition – particularly to all those who attended the various parties around the globe. Where else would Westlife manager Louis Walsh rub shoulders with a 7-ft giant, a woman boasting 2,520 body piercings and a 104.9-decibel belcher but at a **Guinness World Records** party?!

Thanks to all the Guinness World Record holders who appeared on Paul O'Grady's teatime TV show. Here, adjudicator Kim Lacey awards Brian Duffield (fastest time to eat a raw onion) his certificate.

Tables help to organize
and list all your
favourite records

Exciting new
images, fully
annotated

Exclusive
record-holder
interviews

New and updated
records highlighted

'Did you
know?'
facts and
asides

*Chris Greener, Britain's tallest man, poses with Kym Marsh of Hear'say (**fastest selling debut album in the UK**) and Wayne Sleep (**fastest entrechat douze** and **most grands jetés**) at the Guinness World Records golden anniversary party held in the Royal Opera House, London.*

As enjoyable as the anniversary year was, it left us with a real challenge: how do we follow the success of a sell-out golden anniversary edition? Well, we've risen to the challenge and devised a series of exciting new features that bring these amazing records to life (see right), including giant fold-out pages and an all-new Sports Reference section (p.266).

*Our researchers and adjudicators appeared across the country at schools and shopping centre roadshows. Back in 2002, we met Katherine Ratcliffe (**most Smarties eaten in 3 minutes using chopsticks**) – and this year she smashed her record by scoffing 170 at Manchester's Trafford Centre!*

And we've committed ourselves to monitoring even more categories than ever, so look out for up-to-date features on subjects such as digital music (p.156), computer games (p.180), magic and illusion (p.178) and the X Games (p.167).

We're also looking at more ways in which you can become a record holder. Look out over the next year for **Guinness World Records** live roadshows in a shopping centre near you, and don't be surprised if we turn up at your school or local event! Check out our website – **www.guinnessworldrecords.com** for upcoming record attempts.

You'll find everything you need to know on how to become a record breaker on p.10. But if that sounds like hard work, just settle back and dip into the **biggest-selling copyright book of all time** – remember, at least 15 other people in the UK will take up a record-breaking challenge today. In the meantime, I hope you find the record-breaking record book packed full of inspiration...

Craig Glenday
Editor

WHAT'S NEW IN 2006?

Look out for these exciting new features:

★**New record**
Every new category is identified with a ★ – so too are newly researched records that have just been added to our archive

★**Updated record**
This refers to records that have been published in the past but have been recently broken or updated

ACTUAL SIZE
See record breakers at 100% actual size

Crossheads
Where necessary, we've organized records under subheadings to make it even easier to find your favourite records

Comparisons
Compare the size of record breakers with simple, at-a-glance artworks

RECORD-BREAKING TV

The past 12 months have seen Guinness World Records travel to television screens around the globe...

Since *Guinness World Records* hit our TVs back in 1998, it has been seen in over 95 countries. Most recently, *Ultimate Guinness World Records* has been distributed to over 35 countries, from Russia to Indonesia – and a lot of places in between!

Guinness World Records TV becomes a firm favourite everywhere it's seen – often leading to a frenzy of record attempts by fans of the shows in a bid to get themselves into the internationally famous book. And as it continues to spread across the globe, Guinness World Records TV goes from strength to strength, covering ever more extraordinary feats and incredible achievements by truly remarkable people worldwide.

HIGHEST ALTITUDE BALLOON SKYWALK
On 1 September 2004, Mike Howard (UK) walked on a beam between two balloons at an altitude of 6,522 m (21,400 ft) near Yeovil, Somerset, UK, for *Guinness World Records: 50 Years, 50 Records*.

Dwayne Black (Australia) sheared a single sheep in 45.41 seconds on the set of TV show Australia's Guinness World Records *on 17 April 2005.*

HIGHEST SHALLOW DIVE
On 8 September 2004, Danny Higginbottom (USA) dived from a height of 8.95 m (29 ft 4.3 in) into just 30 cm (11.8 in) of water at Marble Hill House, Middlesex, UK, for *Guinness World Records: 50 Years, 50 Records*.

AUSTRALIA

As part of GWR TV's golden anniversary celebrations, Seven Network aired *Guinness World Records: 50 Years, 50 Records*, a series of 50 awe-inspiring record attempts hosted by Grant Denyer and Jamie Theakston.

This one-off extravaganza proved so successful that Seven went on to commission a 13-part series of one-hour shows – entitled simply *Australia's Guinness World Records* – for screening in late 2005. Grant Denyer returns as host, this time with the help of Shelley Craft (both pictured). 'It's sure to be an impressive new showcase for Australian record-breaking talent,' says Grant from the set of the new show.

UNITED KINGDOM

The UK marked the golden anniversary of this famous book with its own version of *Guinness World Records: 50 Years, 50 Records*. This glittering two-hour live celebration of record breaking was hosted by Jamie Theakston, who introduced the prime-time audience to no fewer than 50 remarkable record attempts.

Additionally, popular GMTV host Jamie Rickers took Challenge TV viewers on a 40-episode journey through the world's most awesome record attempts in *Ultimate Guinness World Records*.

And never standing still, Guinness World Records is currently developing a new celebrity-based, record-breaking TV format for UK and US audiences. New prime-time spectaculars will also be screened on RTL, Germany, in 2005 and 2006.

FRANCE

Guinness World Records' most ambitious TV show to date is *L'Été De Tous Les Records* (pictured below and right). This *live* outdoor extravaganza of smashed records and astonishing bravery takes place every weekday for nine weeks. It's presented by French hosts Pierre Sled, Emma Kostic and 'extreme' records expert Taïg Khris. They are all overseen by the huge (and hugely popular) former NBA star Barry White – our firm-but-fair judge.

Now in its third successful year, *L'Été De Tous Les Records* continues to see records smashed in a number of categories, ranging from extreme wall climbing to death-defying wakeboarding and skateboarding.

★LONGEST TIME SPENT IN FULL-BODY ICE CONTACT
Wim Hof (Netherlands) spent 1 hr 8 min in direct, full-body contact with ice on the set of *Guinness World Records: 50 Years, 50 Records* at the London Television Studios, UK, on 11 September 2004.

★MOST CONSECUTIVE INDIE FLIPS ON A SKATEBOARD
On 29 June 2004, Terence Bougdoir (France) completed an incredible 10 consecutive indie flips on the set of *L'Été De Tous Les Records* in Biscarrosse, France.

BE A RECORD BREAKER

If you think you've got what it takes to be a Guinness World Record holder, then read on...

If you want to be a record breaker, there are thousands of records to choose from, but you could also make a suggestion for a new record. We're looking for new categories that are inspiring, interesting, require an element of skill and that are likely to attract subsequent challenges from people worldwide.

1. MAKE AN APPLICATION

Making a record attempt takes time and requires patience. You need to **contact us before you make any attempt** – do not send us any evidence or documentation until we've assessed your proposal. Every Guinness World Record is governed by a unique set of rules that **must be followed**. You need to apply for these rules before you can make an attempt.

The easiest and fastest way to make an application is via our website. Simply go to **www.guinnessworldrecords.com**, click on the link that says 'Make a Record Attempt' and follow the instructions.

If you have a **new record idea**, you need to find out if we will accept your proposal before you attempt the record. If we like your idea, where appropriate, we'll draw up rules specifically for your attempt in order to set a standard for all subsequent challenges.

Make sure you give us as much relevant information as possible. Once you've filled in the application, you'll be asked to choose a password, which we'll send you with a membership number. This gives you access to our new tracking system, where you can monitor the progress of your claim or ask any questions about your record attempt.

You'll also be asked to print and sign an agreement form, which you must send to us by post or fax immediately. **We're unable to process any proposals until we've received the signed agreement form.**

Guinness World Records' *Nicola Savage (top) times a jelly-bean sorting record attempt at the Southampton Road Show on 30 October 2004. At the same event, Steve Bugdale (UK, above) attempts the world record for the most push-ups in one minute using the back of the hands, under the watchful eye of adjudicator Chris Marais.*

Steve Fosset (USA, middle) receives his GWR certificate for the first solo circumnavigation by an aircraft without refuelling, accompanied by Sir Richard Branson (left) and adjudicator David Hawksett (right).

Keeper of the Records, Stewart Newport, and Sophie Whiting from Guinness World Records attended the world's biggest simultaneous handshake on 11 February 2005 at the Deira City Centre shopping mall, Dubai, UAE.

Please note that all Guinness World Records must be **approved at our UK headquarters in London**. No one else has the authority to distribute rules or approve records on our behalf – despite any claim to the contrary – so please **do not send any correspondence, or requested evidence, to any address other than our London office**. (Note, also, that **we cannot return any evidence**, so please make sure you have taken copies of any valued photographs and video footage before sending us the originals.)

If your record proposal needs urgent consideration, we offer a premium fast-track service. This means a researcher is assigned to your proposal as soon as we've received your signed agreement and we'll respond within three working days after this. Please note that fast track is a chargeable service and does not guarantee a positive response (more information is available on the website).

INVIGILATION

Most people don't have a Guinness World Record representative at their event – they just send in their documentation afterwards for verification. Invigilation is a premium service that we offer for a fee, dependent on whether we have a relevant invigilator available at the time. Please tick the invigilation box on your application if you want further information on this.

The world's **biggest pair of cowboy boots** are 1.38 m (4 ft 6.75 in) tall and 1.19 m (3 ft 11 in) long.

On 17 January 2005, a record 31 arm-linked people stood up simultaneously at an event organized by UK Radio Aid and adjudicated by Della Torra Howes (holding book).

2. WAIT TO HEAR FROM US

Once we've received your agreement form, your application will be reviewed by one of our specialist researchers. If it is accepted as a new category (or an existing one) we'll contact you with the corresponding **rules and regulations** that must be strictly adhered to. If we reject your idea, we'll reply to you detailing why it was not acceptable.

Although we'll reply as soon as we can, please note that it may take up to eight weeks during busy periods.

3. ORGANIZE YOUR ATTEMPT

Once we've sent you the guidelines it is up to you to organize the event. As long as there is no violation of the rules, the attempt can be arranged in any way you choose.

After the attempt, you have to send us a package with all the verification documents. All evidence must be **marked with your claim identification number** (which will have been provided in prior correspondence).

If your claim passes all inspections, including final scrutiny from the Keeper of the Records (and providing a new record has not been set in the interim), you'll be declared a Guinness World Record holder!

Please bear in mind that with over 60,000 claims coming in

PHOTOGRAPHING YOUR RECORD

PHOTOGRAPHY TIPS

1. **Avoid 'camera shake'** – try to keep the camera as still as possible. If you have a tripod, use it.
2. **Keep the sun behind you.** If you're outside, avoid shooting into bright light – position yourself so that the sun is behind you. (On the other hand, make sure your subject isn't squinting because the light is too strong!)
3. Keep it simple. Whatever you're shooting, don't clutter up the shot with stuff we don't need to see. Shooting against a white background often helps.
4. **Focus on what matters.** If you're photographing your dog because it's very long, for example, make sure the whole dog fits into the frame. But if you're photographing your dog's long eyelashes, get in close – we don't need to see its entire body. Feel free to send us more than one photo, but make sure that at least one of them shows clearly what's going on.
5. **Capture the action.** If you're shooting a mass participation event, make sure the people in the shot are actually doing the record. We don't want to see everyone after the event – we want action! (For example, if it's a mass pillow fight, we want to see lots of people hitting one another with pillows!)

every year, it can take anything between two weeks and three months to process a claim. Please be patient – we will get back to you as soon as we can.

4. RECEIVE YOUR CERTIFICATE

All Guinness World Record holders receive a certificate to commemorate their achievement. However, we can't guarantee that any specific record will appear in our book – but your certificate remains the proof that you are the world record holder.

6. **Show a sense of scale.** If you've made something that is very small (or very large), photograph it next to something of recognizable size to show the scale (see the big boots pictured above together with regular-size boots).

A person is often the best thing for reference, so ask a friend to photograph you next to what you've built. If the subject is really tiny, a coin is a great clue to its size. You could even place a ruler in the shot.
7. **Get the whole picture.** Make sure you get the whole record object in shot. If it's a 'Largest' record, get both the top and bottom of the object in the frame.
8. **Use your flash.** Most cameras have an automatic flash setting, but to make sure, don't trust the camera – switch the flash on – even if you (or the camera) think there's enough light! If your camera has red-eye reduction, use it too.

PRINT PHOTOGRAPHY

Please send prints from the lab. Please DO NOT send laser or bubble jet prints or any photocopies.

DIGITAL PHOTOGRAPHY

Always use the highest quality setting. Often images are taken at the low setting and the resolution (dpi) is not high enough to print. Our minimum print size is 15 x 10 cm at 300 dpi. Please use this as a standard.

*Susan Morrison presents Blair Morgan (Canada) with his certificate at the Winter X Games in January 2005 for the **most Winter X Games Snocross medals**, with seven in total.*

★ LONGEST LINE OF FOOTPRINTS →

A single, unbroken line of 10,932 footprints from children all over the world was created by readers of *National Geographic Kids* magazine and unveiled at the National Geographic Society in Washington DC, USA, on 9 November 2004. Placed together, the prints measured 3,038.75 m (9,969 ft 8 in). They were created from various materials – including paint, glitter, seashells, dried rice, mud and tar – and were submitted from countries as far afield as Mongolia and Australia.

★ LONGEST SCHOOL ATTENDANCE WITHOUT ABSENCES FOR A FAMILY

Sharon (b. 14 May 1967), Neil (b. 28 September 1968), Honor (b. 18 October 1969), Howard (b. 16 September 1972), Olivia (b. 26 March 1977), Naomi (b. 17 June 1981) and Claire Stewart (b. 14 January 1983) of Markethill, Armagh, UK, completed their education from the ages of four to 16 without being absent from their schools – Markethill County Primary and High School – for a single day.

★ LARGEST CLASS WITH PERFECT ATTENDANCE

In 1984–85, 23 pupils in the class of Melanie Murray at David Barkley Elementary School, San Antonio, Texas, USA, were never once absent from class.

★ FASTEST TIME TO PUSH A SOAPBOX CART 1,000 KM

In September 2001, 30 pupils from the Laeveld Primary School in Nelspruit, South Africa, pushed an unpowered soapbox cart a distance of 1,000 km (621 miles) in 62 hr 43 min on the first leg of their 2,061-km (1,280-mile) journey between Komatipoort and Cape Town, South Africa. The attempt was part of an event called the NICRO Race Against Crime and Time.

★ LARGEST SINGLE-VENUE EGG-AND-SPOON RACE

A total of 859 students from Raynes Park High School, London, UK, took part in an egg-and-spoon race on 24 October 2003.

★ LONGEST BALLOON CHAIN

OMR Heerbrugg School in Switzerland created a chain of 30,000 balloons measuring a total of 2,007.55 m (6,586 ft 5.4 in) on 19 September 2003.

← ★ YOUNGEST TV PRESENTER

Luis Tanner (Australia, b. 9 May 1998) currently hosts his own TV show, *Cooking for Kids with Luis* (Nickelodeon). The first episode in this weekly show was aired on 25 October 2004 when Luis was just 6 years 168 days old.

★ LARGEST BOTTLE-CAP MOSAIC

On 23 October 2003, students from Akiba Junior High School in Yokohama, Japan, created a mosaic spelling out the words 'Love & Peace' using a record 150,480 bottle caps.

★ FASTEST MILE OF PENNIES

A mile of 79,200 pennies worth £792 ($1,224) was laid in 2 hr 42 min 29 sec by members of The Willows School in Stratford-upon-Avon, Warwickshire, UK, on 19 October 2002.

★ LONGEST DRINKING-STRAW CHAIN

A chain of drinking straws measuring 6,223.33 m (20,417 ft 8.8 in) and consisting of 41,996 straws was made on campus by 16 students from the Hayground School, Bridgehampton, New York, USA, on 11 June 2004.

★ LONGEST CAN CHAIN

A chain of aluminium drinking cans measuring 7.69 km (4.77 miles) long and using 66,129 cans tied together with string was created by Hillcrest Primary School in Kloof, KwaZulu-Natal, South Africa, on 29 November 2003.

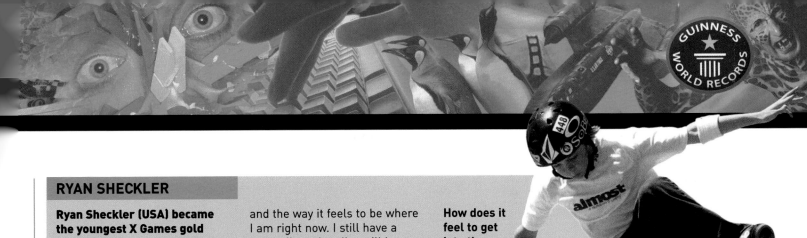

RYAN SHECKLER

Ryan Sheckler (USA) became the youngest X Games gold medallist after securing first place in the Skateboard Park event at the age of 13.

How old were you when you started skating?
At 18 months old, I picked up my dad's board and started pushing around on my knees. By the age of four, I was trying to ollie off furniture around the house!

How does it feel to have won gold at such a young age?
Oh yeah, I love skateboarding

and the way it feels to be where I am right now. I still have a great vibe going. I'm still hungry for it and I'm still really, really excited to skate.

You must get a lot of respect being able to compete against these older skaters.
I'm accepted with these guys, and I'm doing what they're doing. I guess they recognize that and give me credit for it.

What's your next goal?
Keep on skating, come back next year and win X Games again, and have fun with all these guys!

How does it feel to get into the *Guinness World Records* book?
It's crazy! When I was in fifth grade, we'd always go to the library and look through the book and check out all the people in there. I thought how cool it would be if I could get in there... I'm finally there, so I'm psyched.

★ **LARGEST SONG AND DANCE ROUTINE (MULTIPLE VENUE)**
Organized by the North London Performing Arts Centre, a total of 7,596 children from across north London, UK, danced and sang to the song 'To the Show' for five minutes on 22 March 2002.

★ **LONGEST LINE OF DANCERS**
Other than a conga, the longest continuous single line of dancers comprised 331 children at Seathorne Primary School, Skegness, Lincolnshire, UK, on 9 July 2004. The children danced for six minutes to the Steps song '5, 6, 7, 8' in a line that measured 145 m (475 ft) long.

★ **LARGEST MACARENA DANCE**
A total of 1,712 pupils of St Bede's School, Redhill, Surrey, UK, danced the Macarena for at

least five minutes on 9 March 2004. The event was organized by the 6th form for rag week.

★ **LARGEST TWIST DANCE**
On 30 April 2004, a total of 1,691 staff and pupils from St Aidan's Church of England High School and St John Fisher Catholic High School in North Yorkshire, UK, danced for five minutes to Chubby Checker's 'The Twist'.

★ **MOST LEAPFROG JUMPS IN ONE MINUTE**
On 29 September 2004, schoolboys Marius Martinsen Benterud and Christel Ek Blanck (both Norway) achieved 59 leapfrog jumps in one minute at the Jetix Challenge in Ski, Norway.

★ **MOST PEOPLE BRUSHING TEETH SIMULTANEOUSLY**
A total of 31,424 pupils at 261 schools in Hessen, Germany, brushed their teeth at the same time for at least 60 seconds – after being given the start signal via the radio station HR1 – on 21 May 2003.

MOST CONSECUTIVE FOOTBALL PASSES
Members of the McDonald's Youth Football Scheme based in Tsing Yi, Hong Kong, China, achieved a record 557 consecutive football passes on 4 May 2002. Around 1,250 children took part in the event.

→ **WANT TO BE A RECORD BREAKER? FIND OUT HOW ON P.10**

★ YOUNGEST → COMPOSER OF A MUSICAL

Adám Lörincz (Hungary, b. 1 June 1988) was 14 years 76 days old when his 92-minute musical, *Star of the King*, was performed on 16 August 2002 in Szekesfehervar, Hungary. The musical is a tribute to singer Elvis Presley and features 23 performers. It has been performed at numerous locations throughout Hungary.

→ | CONTENTS

LARGEST FEET
ON A LIVING PERSON
Excluding cases of elephantiasis, the biggest known feet belong to actor Matthew McGrory (USA), who wears size 29½ shoes (UK size 29, European size 63). At 44.45 cm (17.5 in), his right foot is 1.27 cm (0.5 in) longer than his left. The star of Tim Burton's *Big Fish* (USA, 2003), Matthew stands 2.29 m (7 ft 6 in) tall and pays up to $22,745 (£11,800) for a pair of shoes.

TALLEST
WOMAN LIVING

Sandy Allen (USA) was last found to measure 2.317 m (7 ft 7.25 in). She currently weighs 142 kg (314 lb; 22 st 5 lb) and wears size 22 shoes (UK size 20½, European size 55). She gets her trainers second-hand from the 2-m 23.5-cm-tall (7-ft 4-in) Indiana Pacers basketball star Rick 'The Dunking Dutchman' Smits.

★TRIPLETS – LIGHTEST → BIRTHS

Peyton (585 g; 1 lb 4.6 oz), Jackson (420 g; 14.8 oz) and Blake (380g; 13.4 oz) Coffey (all USA) became the **lightest triplets** to survive when born in Charlottesville, Virginia, USA, on 30 November 1998.

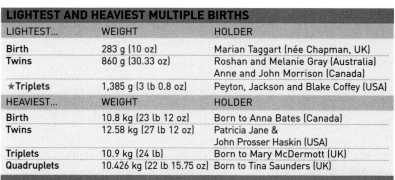

LIGHTEST AND HEAVIEST MULTIPLE BIRTHS		
LIGHTEST...	WEIGHT	HOLDER
Birth	283 g (10 oz)	Marian Taggart (née Chapman, UK)
Twins	860 g (30.33 oz)	Roshan and Melanie Gray (Australia) Anne and John Morrison (Canada)
★Triplets	1,385 g (3 lb 0.8 oz)	Peyton, Jackson and Blake Coffey (USA)
HEAVIEST...	WEIGHT	HOLDER
Birth	10.8 kg (23 lb 12 oz)	Born to Anna Bates (Canada)
Twins	12.58 kg (27 lb 12 oz)	Patricia Jane & John Prosser Haskin (USA)
Triplets	10.9 kg (24 lb)	Born to Mary McDermott (UK)
Quadruplets	10.426 kg (22 lb 15.75 oz)	Born to Tina Saunders (UK)

TALLEST...

MAN LIVING
After seven measurements taken over 22–23 April 1999 at Tunis, Radhouane Charbib's (Tunisia) height was determined at 2.35 m (7 ft 8.9 in).

MAN
The **tallest man** for whom there is irrefutable evidence is Robert Pershing Wadlow (USA, 1918–40), who, when last measured on 27 June 1940, was 2.72 m (8 ft 11.1 in) tall. His size was the result of an overactive pituitary gland, source of the growth hormone somatotrophin.

WOMAN
Zeng Jinlian (China, b. 26 June 1964) of Bright Moon Commune, Hunan Province, China, measured 2.48 m (8 ft 1.75 in) when she died on 13 February 1982. This figure represented her height with assumed normal spinal curvature because she suffered from severe scoliosis (curvature of the spine) and could not stand up straight.

FEMALE TWINS LIVING
Ann and Claire Recht (USA) were measured both horizontally and vertically three times on 19 June 2003 in Oregon, USA, and found to have an average overall height of 1.98 m (6 ft 6 in) and 1.97 m (6 ft 5.9 in) respectively.

MALE TWINS LIVING
Michael and James Lanier (USA) of Troy, Michigan, USA, both stand 2.23 m (7 ft 3.9 in). Their sister Jennifer is 1.57 m (5 ft 2 in) tall.

SHORTEST...

MAN LIVING
Younis Edwan (Jordan) is believed to be 65 cm (25.5 in) tall (he has not been officially measured by GWR). The **shortest man** ever was Gul Mohammed (India, 1957–97), who was examined at Ram Manohar Hospital, New Delhi, India, on 19 July 1990 and found to be just 57 cm (22.5 in) tall.

WOMAN
Pauline Musters was born at Ossendrecht, the Netherlands, on 26 February 1876 and measured 30 cm (12 in) at birth. She died of pneumonia with meningitis on 1 March 1895 in New York, USA, at the age of 19. A post-mortem examination showed 'Princess Pauline', as she was known, to be exactly 61 cm (24 in).

LARGEST →
CHEST MEASUREMENT

In February 1958, shortly before his death at the age of 32, Robert Earl Hughes (USA) weighed 484 kg (1,067 lb; 76 st 3 lb) and had a chest measurement of 3.15 m (10 ft 4 in). At the age of six, he weighed 92 kg (203 lb; 14 st 6.7 lb), and by the age of 10 he weighed 171 kg (378 lb; 26 st 13 lb); at age 25, he reached 406 kg (896 lb; 63 st 13 lb).

TWINS

Matyus and Béla Matina of Budapest, Hungary, who later became naturalized US citizens, both measured 76 cm (30 in). The **shortest living twins** are also the **shortest identical male twins**; find out how they compare on p.22.

IDENTICAL FEMALE TWINS LIVING

Dorene Williams and Darlene McGregor (both USA) each stand 124.4 cm (4 ft 1 in).

★ BABY

Nisa Juarez (USA) was born on 20 July 2002 and measured just 24 cm (9.44 in) long at the Children's Hospital and Clinic in Minnesota, USA. She was born 108 days premature, weighed only 320 g (11.3 oz) and was discharged from hospital on 6 December 2002.

The **longest baby** was delivered by Anna Bates (née Swan, Canada, 1846–88) at her home in Seville, Ohio, USA, on 19 January 1879. At 76 cm (30 in), the baby was born taller than Gul Mohammed (India), the world's **shortest ever man**.

HEAVIEST...

MAN

In March 1978, Jon Brower Minnoch (USA) was admitted to University Hospital, Seattle, USA, where consultant endocrinologist Dr Robert Schwartz calculated that Minnoch must have weighed over 635 kg (1,400 lb; 100 st), much of which was water accumulation owing to congestive heart failure.

Minnoch's wife Jeanette (USA) weighed just 50 kg (110.2 lb; 7 st 12 lb), making theirs the **greatest weight differential for a married couple** at around 585 kg (1,289.7 lb; 92 st 1.7 lb).

WOMAN

Rosalie Bradford (USA) peaked at 544 kg (1,200 lb; 85 st) in January 1987. After a health scare, she reduced her daily intake to 1,200 calories and began to exercise by clapping her hands. Five years later, she had lost the equivalent weight of seven people and claimed another record: the **greatest weight lost by a female**.

TWINS

In November 1978, Billy Leon and Benny Loyd McCrary, alias McGuire, (both USA) weighed 337 kg (743 lb; 53 st 1 lb) and 328 kg (723 lb; 51 st 9 lb) respectively.

← SHORTEST
WOMAN LIVING

Madge Bester (South Africa) is only 65 cm (25.5 in) tall. She suffers from *Osteogenesis imperfecta* (brittle bones and other deformities of the skeleton) and is confined to a wheelchair. Her mother Winnie is not much taller, measuring 70 cm (27.5 in), and is also confined to a wheelchair.

ARE YOU THE WORLD'S HEAVIEST PERSON?

Although we are aware of living people who are in excess of 508 kg (1,120 lb; 80 st), we have been unable to fully authenticate the record for **heaviest person living** – mostly owing to claimants' unwillingness to be weighed under controlled conditions.

While we do not encourage over-eating, if you wish to put yourself forward for this category we ask that you fulfil these two simple requirements:

1. **Medical notes** of the measurements made by suitably qualified individuals must be submitted along with a statement from a qualified medical doctor.

2. A **copy of the birth certificate** must be submitted with the record claim.

MEDICAL MARVELS

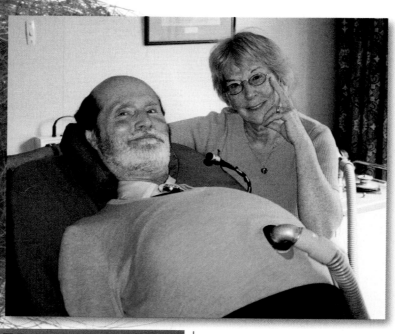

LONGEST SURVIVING
← IRON-LUNG PATIENT

John Prestwich (UK) has been paralysed since being struck by polio on his 17th birthday. Since 24 November 1955, he has been entirely dependent on a negative-pressure respirator ('iron lung') to breathe. An iron lung is an air-tight shell that alters the pressure in the chest cavity, forcing the lungs to inflate and allowing patients with no control of their breathing muscles to breathe.

↑ LARGEST OBJECT REMOVED FROM A STOMACH

A hairball weighing 2.53 kg (5 lb 3 oz) was removed from the gut of a 20-year-old female compulsive swallower in the South Devon and East Cornwall Hospital, UK, on 30 March 1895.

TRANSPLANTS

★ LONGEST LIVED LUNG TRANSPLANT SURVIVOR

On 15 September 1987, Wolfgang Muller (Canada) underwent a single lung transplant at Toronto General Hospital in Ontario, Canada. On 19 July 2004, he became the longest surviving lung transplant recipient at 16 years 307 days.

★ LONGEST LIVED HEART TRANSPLANT SURVIVAL

Derrick Morris (UK) underwent a heart transplant operation on 23 February 1980 at Harefield Hospital in Greater London, UK. The operation gave him a heart that had belonged to a 26-year-old woman.

★ LONGEST SURVIVING HEART-LUNG-LIVER TRANSPLANT PATIENT

Mark Dolby (UK) received a triple transplant (heart-lung-liver) on 21 August 1987 at Harefield Hospital in Greater London, UK. On 4 June 2004, 16 years 288 days later, he was confirmed as the longest-lived survivor of a triple operation.

★ OLDEST KIDNEY TRANSPLANT RECIPIENT

Carroll Basham (USA) had a kidney transplant operation at the age of 77 years 185 days on 2 October 2002, at the Methodist Specialty and Transplant Hospital, San Antonio, Texas, USA. His stepdaughter, Nancy Hildenburg, donated the kidney.

★ FIRST HEART-LUNG TRANSPLANT

After two years of experiments, Dr Bruce Reitz (USA) performed the first successful combined heart-lung transplant at Stanford Medical Center in Stanford, California, USA, in 1981.

LEAST BLOOD TRANSFUSED DURING A TRANSPLANT

In June 1996, a transplant team at St James University Hospital, Leeds, UK, performed a liver transplant on 47-year-old Linda Pearson (UK) without any blood being transfused. Such an operation usually requires up to 3.5 litres (6 pints) of blood, but as a Jehovah's Witness, Pearson is unable to accept blood that is not her own.

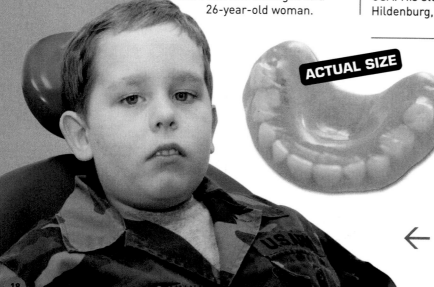

ACTUAL SIZE

★ YOUNGEST PERSON
TO WEAR DENTURES

Alexander Stone (USA) became the youngest recipient of a full set of dentures on 7 June 2001 at the age of 4 years 301 days. Alexander suffers from an hereditary condition called dentinogenesis imperfecta, which weakens and discolours the teeth, removing the pulp. He had his dentures fitted by family dentist Dr Joseph E Morton.

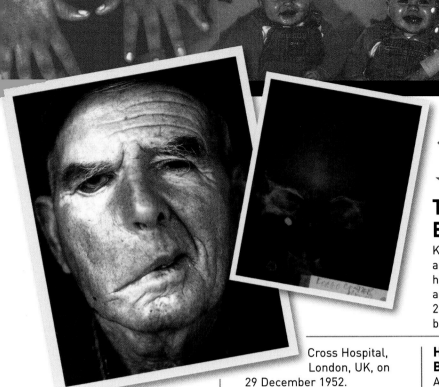

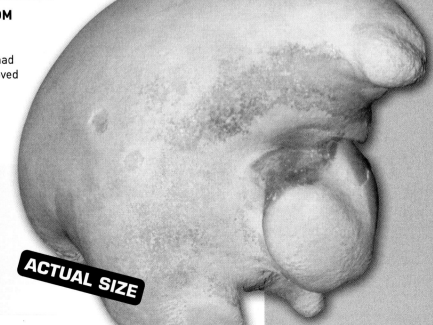

★LONGEST TIME WITH A BULLET IN HEAD

Kolyo Tanev Kolev (Bulgaria) accidentally shot himself behind his right ear with a pistol in 1942, aged 17. X-rays taken on 5 July 2003 show the bullet lodged at the base of the skull, 61 years later.

RECIPIENT OF MOST BLOOD

The average human body contains around 5.5 litres (10 pints) of blood. But while undergoing open-heart surgery at the Michael Reese Hospital in Chicago, Illinois, USA, in December 1970, Warren C Jyrich (USA), a 50-year-old haemophiliac, required 2,400 donor units of blood – equivalent to 1,080 litres (237 gal; 285 US gal) or nearly 15 full bath tubs of blood!

OPERATIONS

★LONGEST SURVIVING TRIPLE-HEART-BYPASS PATIENT

Richard Smith (UK) underwent a triple heart bypass operation on 8 February 1978 at Papworth Hospital, Cambridge, UK, becoming the longest survivor of such a procedure on 12 May 2004, 26 years 93 days later.

★LONGEST SURVIVING OPEN-HEART-SURGERY PATIENT

Sadie Purdy (UK), who was born in 1924 with a hole in her heart, had open-heart surgery on 4 December 1941, aged 17. The six-hour operation, performed at St Bartholomew's Hospital, London, UK, by Oswald Tubbs, was still experimental, but has now extended her life by 63 years.

LARGEST GALLSTONE

A gallstone weighing 6.29 kg (13 lb 14 oz) was removed from an 80-year-old woman by Humphrey Arthure at Charing Cross Hospital, London, UK, on 29 December 1952.

★ LARGEST APPENDIX

The appendix removed from a 55-year-old man at the Pakistan Institute of Medical Sciences, Islamabad, Pakistan, on 11 June 2003, measured 23.5 cm (9.2 in) in length – wider than this page!

★LARGEST TUMOUR AT BIRTH

A 1.2-kg (2-lb 9-oz) benign cystic hygroma was removed from the neck of a baby boy by a team led by Palin Khundongbam (India) at Shija Hospitals and Research Institute, Imphal, Manipur, India, on 17 March 2003. The tumour represented 40% of the child's body weight.

MISCELLANEOUS

★YOUNGEST WISDOM TOOTH EXTRACTION

Matthew Adams (USA, b. 19 November 1992) had two wisdom teeth removed at Midland Oral and Maxillofacial Surgery, Michigan, USA, on 24 October 2002, aged just 9 years 339 days.

HIGHEST BLOOD SUGAR LEVEL

Alexa Painter (USA) survived a blood sugar level 20.7 times above average at 139 mmol/L (2,495 mg/dl) when treated for severe diabetic ketoacidosis at the Community Hospital of Roanoke, Virginia, USA, on 30 December 1991. Normal blood sugar is 4.4–6.6 mmol/litre (80–120 mg/dl).

MOST BLOOD DONATED

Maurice Creswick (South Africa) donated his 336th unit of blood on 9 July 2003, the equivalent of 188.9 litres (41.5 gal; 49 US gal).

Having given blood since his 18th birthday in 1944 – 59 consecutive years to 2003 – he also holds the record for ★ **most blood donated over consecutive years**.

★LARGEST → KIDNEY STONE

Peter Baulman (Australia) had a kidney stone weighing 356 g (12.5 oz) and measuring 11.86 cm (4.66 in) at its widest point removed from his right kidney in December 2003 at The Gold Coast Hospital, Southport, Queensland, Australia.

ACTUAL SIZE

GOLDEN OLDIES

← MALE STRIPPER

Bernie Barker (USA, b. 31 July 1940) began his career as a male stripper in 2000 – at the age of 60 – as a way to get in shape while recovering from prostate cancer. Since leaving his previous job of selling real estate, the 'Silver Tom Selleck' has won more than 40 stripping contests and is a regular performer at clubs in Las Vegas, Nevada, USA.

260 days until Elizabeth's death on 19 January 1891. At this time, Elizabeth was aged 105 years 2 days and Thomas was 104 years 260 days, a total of 209 years 262 days. (Meet the **oldest living married couple** on p.123.)

★ UNSUPPORTED TREKKER TO THE SOUTH POLE
Simon Murray (UK, b. 25 March 1940) completed a trek to the South Pole at the age of 63 years 309 days. He left the Antarctic coastline near Hercules Inlet on 2 December 2003 and arrived at the Pole with his trekking partner, Pen Hadow (UK), on 28 January 2004. The trek covered a distance of about 1,100 km (683 miles).

★ HONORARY DEGREE RECIPIENT
Bridget Dirrane (Ireland, b. 16 November 1894) received an honorary degree from the National University of Ireland, Galway, on 18 May 1998, aged 103 years 183 days. The award followed publication of a book that explored her perceptions of life over the span of a century.

ACTRESS
Jeanne Louise Calment (France, 1875–1997) portrayed herself at the age of 114 in the film *Vincent and Me* (Canada, 1990) – a fantasy about a girl who travels through time to meet Dutch painter Vincent van Gogh. Calment, the **oldest person ever**, whose age of 122 years 164 days has been fully authenticated, is thought to have been the last living person to have known van Gogh.

★ REIGNING MONARCH
Taufa'ahau Tupou IV (b. 4 July 1918) became the king of Tonga when his mother, Queen Salote Tupou III, died in 1965, and has reigned ever since.

He is also the world's **heaviest monarch**. In September 1976, he weighed 209.5 kg (462 lb). By 1985 he was reported to have slimmed down to 139.7 kg (307 lb), in early 1993 he was 127.0 kg (279 lb) and by 1998 he had lost more weight due to a fitness programme.

★ ROYAL
Princess Alice, Duchess of Gloucester (UK, b. Lady Alice Christabel Montagu Douglas Scott, 1901–2004) became the oldest known royal ever when she reached the age of 101 years and 69 days on 20 September 2003. She died on 29 October 2004.

★ MARRIED COUPLE
Thomas Morgan (UK, b. 4 May 1786) married Elizabeth (UK, b. 17 January 1786) at Caerleon, Wales, UK, on 4 May 1809. They remained married for 81 years

OLDEST...

★ WOMAN TO FLY IN ZERO GRAVITY
On 22 July 2004, Dorothy Simpson (USA, b. 27 November 1924) took part in a zero-gravity flight on an Ilyushin IL-76, aged 79 years and 237 days. The flight was organized by Space Adventures (USA).

← ★ BRIDESMAID

Flossie Bennett (UK, b. 9 August 1902, pictured far left) was Matron of Honour at the wedding of Leonard and Edna Petchey (both UK) on 6 February 1999 at St Peter's Church, Holton, Suffolk, UK, at the age of 97 years 181 days. The **oldest recorded bride** is Minnie Munro (Australia), aged 102, who married Dudley Reid (Australia), aged 83, at Point Clare, Australia, on 31 May 1991.

★ REGULAR NEWSPAPER COLUMNIST

Simon Blumenfeld (UK, b. 25 November 1907), aka Sidney Vauncez, has written a column for the performing arts and entertainment trade paper *The Stage* since June 1994.

★ DOMINOES PLAYER

Alf Hill (UK, b. 31 August 1908) became the oldest competitive dominoes player at the age of 92 in 2000. He plays for the Jolly Carter pub team and has been a member of the Lowton and District Darts and Dominoes League for over 25 years.

BASE JUMPER

James Talbot Guyer (USA, b. 16 June 1928) parachuted off the 148-m-high (486-ft) Perrine Bridge near Twin Falls, Idaho, USA, on 2 August 2002 aged 74 years 47 days.

★ OPERA SINGER

Luo Pinchao (China, b. 19 June 1912) began his singing career in 1930 and still regularly performs Cantonese opera. He celebrated his 93rd birthday by performing at the Guandong Cantonese Opera Grand Artistic Theatre, Guangzhou, China, on 20 June 2004.

★ NUN

Sister Julia (France, b. Augustine Teissier) was born on 2 January 1869 in Florensac, France, and died aged 112 years 66 days on 9 March 1981 at Nîmes, France.

★ BALLERINA

Charin Yuthasastrkosol (USA, b. Thailand, 30 December 1930) began ballet lessons at the age of 47 and performed regularly through her senior years. Her most recent performance was for Sakthip Krairikish, Thailand's ambassador to the USA, at New Mexico, USA, on 21 July 2002 at the age of 71 years 203 days.

★ MOUNTAIN CLIMBERS

Carl F Haupt (USA, b. 21 April 1926) reached the summit of Mount Kilimanjaro, Tanzania, on 30 August 2004, aged 78 years 131 days. The oldest person to climb Mount Everest is Yuichiro Miura (Japan, b. 12 October 1932), who reached the summit aged 70 years 222 days on 22 May 2003.

★ LICENSED DRIVERS

Fred Hale Sr (USA, 1890–2004) was issued with a driving licence in February 1995, and drove until it expired on his 108th birthday in 1998. He became

the **oldest living man** in the world and died aged 113 years 354 days on 19 November 2004.

Layne Hall (USA, b. 24/25 December 1884 or 15 March 1880) was issued with a licence on 15 June 1989 when he was either 104 (according to his death certificate) or 109 (according to his driving licence). It was valid until his birthday in 1993, but he died on 20 November 1990.

Maude Tull (USA), the **oldest female driver**, who took to driving aged 91 after her husband died, had her licence renewed on 5 February 1976 aged 104.

★ OLDEST ↑ PERFORMING CLOWN

Andrew Beyer (USA, b. 4 March 1918) has been performing as Bumbo the Clown since 1952 and was recognized as the oldest clown still working at the age of 86 years 250 days on 9 November 2004. Many clowns have lived and performed to a great age. Grock (Germany, 1880–1959) and Otto Griebling (Germany, 1896–1972) worked until the age of 74. Lou Jacobs (Germany, 1903–92) carried on until 82, and Charlie Rivel (Spain, 1896–1983) retired at the age of 85.

CHORUS LINE DANCER ↗

The oldest 'showgirl' who is still regularly performing in a chorus line is Beverly Allen (USA, b. 4 November 1917) of Santa Maria, California, USA. A member of The Fabulous Palm Springs Follies, her jitterbug routine – in which her partner lifts her over his head to spin her 'head-over-heels' – has become an audience favourite.

SHORTEST → LIVING TWINS

John and Greg Rice (USA) are identical twins, born on 3 December 1951. They both measure 86.3 cm (2 ft 10 in) in height.

The **tallest living twins** are Michael and James Lanier (both USA), who stand 2.235 m (7 ft 3.9 in) tall.

RECORD-BREAKING MOTHERS

NAME	RECORD
Maddalena Granata (Italy, 1839–1886)	**Most sets of triplets** Gave birth to 15 sets of triplets.
Mrs F Vassilyev (Russia, 1707–c.1782)	**Most prolific mother ever** In 27 confinements, gave birth to 69 children (16 pairs of twins, 7 sets of triplets and 4 sets of quadruplets). This means that she also holds the record for the **most sets of quadruplets** and the **most sets of twins** born to one mother.
Merryl Thelma Fudel (née Coward, Australia) (b. 1942)	**Oldest mother to have quadruplets** Gave birth to three girls and one boy on 18 April 1998 at the age of 55 years and 286 days.

MOST ⇘ SIBLINGS TO COMPLETE A MARATHON

The 11 Flaherty siblings – Terence, Kathleen, Dennis, Michael, David, Kevin, Brian, Margaret, Patricia, Gerard and Vincent (all UK) – completed the London Marathon on 18 April 2004.

SIBLINGS

★ MOST SIBLINGS TO REACH PENSION AGE

Seven sons and five daughters were born to John Zacher Sr (Canada, 1877–1968) and his wife Elizabeth (Canada, 1886–1981) between 1907 and 1929, all of whom were claiming a state pension in 1999. Their ages ranged from 70 to 92 years.

All 12 daughters born to Albert Scott (UK, 1889–1977) and his wife Edith (UK, née Chittenden, 1889–1978) between 1910 and 1931 were claiming a state pension in November 2002. Their ages ranged from 71 to 92 years.

★ MOST ALBINO SIBLINGS

Of the eight children born to George and Minnie Sesler (USA), the four eldest of their five sons were all born with the rare genetic condition albinism. Identical twins John and George, Kermit and Kenneth were all born with translucent skin, pinkish-blue eyes and white hair.

All four children of Mario and Angie Gaulin – Sarah, Christopher, Joshua and Brendan (all Canada) – were born with the rare genetic condition oculocutaneous albinism. Their father also has the condition and their mother carries the gene.

★ LONGEST SEPARATION OF SIBLINGS

William James Pring (UK) was reunited with his sister Elsie May Ashford (UK, née Pring) on 20 November 1988 through the agency of the Salvation Army. They were reunited in London, UK, by Major Colin Fairclough exactly 81 years after their separation.

★ MOST SIBLINGS TO SERVE IN WORLD WAR II

The nine brothers Albert, Jim, Harry, Arthur, Bill, Tom, Dick, Sid and Wally Windsor (all UK) all served in World War II.

This record is shared with the Lewtas brothers – Edward, Robert, William, Charles, George, Harry, Matthew, Thomas and Christopher (all UK) – who served in various divisions of the forces from 1939 to 1945.

★ MOST SETS OF TWINS
BORN ON THE SAME DAY

There are only two verified examples of a mother producing two sets of twins with coincident birthdays. The first is that of Laura Shelley (USA), who gave birth to Melissa Nicole and Mark Fredrick Julian Jr on 25 March 1990 and Kayla May and Jonathan Price Moore on the same date in 2003 (right, top). The second is that of Caroline Cargado (USA), who gave birth to Keilani Marie and Kahleah Mae on 30 May 1996 and Mikayla Anee and Malia Abigail on the same date in 2003 (right, below). →

→ HOW OLD WAS THE WORLD'S OLDEST BRIDE? FIND OUT ON P.21

FAMILY TREES

LONGEST FAMILY TREE

The lineage of K'ung Ch'iu or Confucius (China, 551–479 BC) can be traced back further than that of any other family. His great-great-great-great grandfather Kung Chia is known from the 8th century BC. Kung Chia has 86 lineal descendants.

MOST DESCENDANTS

In polygamous countries, the number of a person's descendants can be incalculable. At the time of his death on 15 October 1992, the monogamous Samuel S Mast (USA), then aged 96, had 824 living descendants: 11 children, 97 grandchildren, 634 great-grandchildren and 82 great-great-grandchildren.

FURTHEST TRACED DESCENDANT BY DNA

Adrian Targett (UK) is a direct descendant, on his mother's side, of Cheddar Man, a 9,000-year-old skeleton, one of the UK's oldest complete skeletons. This link stretches back 300 generations.

★ MOST GENERATIONS ALIVE AT ONCE

The greatest number of generations from a single family to be alive at the same time is seven. The **youngest great-great-great-great-grandmother** is Augusta Bunge (USA) aged 109 years 97 days, followed by her daughter aged 89, her granddaughter aged 70, her great-granddaughter aged 52, her great-great granddaughter aged 33 and her great-great-great granddaughter aged 15 on the birth of her great-great-great-great grandson on 21 January 1989.

ADOPTION

★ OLDEST ADOPTIVE PARENT

Frances Ensor Benedict (USA, b. 11 May 1918) was aged 83 years 329 days when she officially adopted Jo Anne Benedict Walker (USA) on 5 April 2002 in Putnam County, Tennessee, USA.

★ OLDEST ADOPTION

Jo Anne Benedict Walker (USA) was 65 years 224 days when she was officially adopted by Frances Ensor Benedict (USA) on 5 April 2002 in Putnam County, Tennessee, USA.

★ MOST CHILDREN TO SURVIVE FROM A SINGLE BIRTH →

Bobbie McCaughey (USA) gave birth to septuplets on 19 November 1997 at the Blank Children's Hospital, Des Moines, Iowa, USA, via Caesarean section. Named Kenneth, Nathaniel, Brandon, Joel, Kelsey, Natalie and Alexis, they weighed between 1,048 g and 1,474.3 g (2 lb 5 oz and 3 lb 4 oz).

On 14 January 1998, four boys and three girls were born prematurely to Hasna Mohammed Humair (Saudi Arabia) at the Abha Obstetric Hospital, Aseer. The smallest baby weighed just under 907 g (2 lb).

BODY PARTS

STRETCHIEST → SKIN

Garry Turner (UK) can stretch his skin to a length of 15.8 cm (6.25 in) owing to a medical condition called Elhers-Danlos Syndrome, a disorder of the connective tissues affecting the skin, ligaments and internal organs. It also accounts for his success in another Guinness World Record category – ★ **most clothespegs clipped on a face** – as Garry can attach 159 wooden pegs to the skin of his face.

LARGEST...

BREASTS

Annie Hawkins-Turner (US) has an under-breast measurement of 109.22 cm (43 in) and an around-chest-over-nipple measurement of 177.8 cm (70 in). She currently wears a US size 52I bra, although needs a 48V bra, which is not manufactured.

FEET

Robert Wadlow (USA), the **tallest man ever**, wore US size 37AA shoes (UK size 36), equivalent to 47 cm (18.5 in) long. For the **largest feet on a living person**, see p.14.

★ GAPE

J J Bittner (USA) is able to open his mouth to a width of 8.4 cm (3.4 in). The gape is measured from the incisal edge of his maxillary central incisors to the incisal edge of his mandibular central incisors (that is, from the tips of his incisor teeth).

RECORD-BREAKING BODY PARTS

Heaviest brain

The brain of a 30-year-old US male was reported to weigh 2.3 kg (5 lb 1.1 oz) by Dr George T Mandybur (USA) of the University of Cincinnati, Ohio, USA, in December 1992. A normal brain weighs 1.3–1.4 kg (2.8–3 lb).

★ Longest eyebrow hair (7.81 cm; 3.078 in)

A single hair growing on the left eyebrow of Franklin Ames (USA) was measured on 26 February 2004 to have reached a length of 7.81 cm (3.078 in) long.

Furthest eyeball popper (11 mm; 0.43 in)

Kim Goodman (USA) can pop her eyeballs to a protrusion of 11 mm (0.43 in) beyond her eye sockets.

★ Longest eyelash (4 cm; 1.57 in)

Mark Gordon (USA) has a white eyelash on his left eyelid which, when measured on 4 June 2004 in Batavia, Ohio, USA, was found to be 4 cm (1.57 in) long.

Longest ear hair (13.2 cm; 5.19 in)

Radhakant Bajpai (India) has hair sprouting from the centre of his outer ears (middle of the pinna) that measures 13.2 cm (5.19 in) at its longest point.

Longest nose on a living person (8.8 cm; 3.46 in)

Mehmet Ozyurek (Turkey) has a nose which was 8.8 cm (3.46 in) long from the bridge to the tip when measured in his hometown of Artvin on 31 January 2001.

LONGEST...

BEARD

Shamsher Singh's (India) beard measured 1.83 m (6 ft) from the end of his chin to the tip of the beard, as of 18 August 1997. The **longest beard on a female** belongs to Vivian Wheeler (USA) and last measured 27.9 cm (11 in) from the follicle to the tip of the hair.

★ STRETCHED EARLOBES

Monte Pierce (USA) can stretch his earlobes to a length of 12.7 cm (5 in) for his left lobe and 11.43 cm (4.5 in) for his right. For the **longest earlobes**, see the tribes of south-east Asia on p.52.

HANDS

Robert Wadlow's (USA) hands were 32.3 cm (12.75 in) from wrist to tip of middle finger.

★ TOOTH

A tooth extracted from Mark Henry (Canada) in January 2005 measured 1.2 cm (0.47 in) wide.

WAIST

Walter Hudson (USA) had a waistline that measured 302 cm (119 in) at his peak weight of 545 kg (1,197 lb; 85 st 7 lb).

★ HAIR

The world's longest documented hair belongs to Xie Qiuping (China), and measured 5.627 m (18 ft 5.54 in) on 8 May 2004. She has been growing her hair since 1973, when she was 13.

★ MILK TOOTH

Daniel Valdes (USA) had three milk teeth removed on 9 April 2004 in Westlake, Ohio, USA, the longest of which measured 1.69 cm (0.66 in) long, having a crown length of 0.5 cm (0.19 in).

ACTUAL SIZE

Longest nose (19 cm; 7.5 in)
There are historical accounts that Thomas Wedders, who lived in England during the 1770s and was a member of a travelling circus, had a nose measuring 19 cm (7.5 in) long.

Longest tongue (9.4 cm; 3.7 in)
Stephen Taylor (UK) has a tongue that measures 9.4 cm (3.7 in) from the tip to the centre of his closed top lip. It was measured at Westwood Medical Centre, Coventry, Warwickshire, UK, on 29 May 2002.

Longest toe (12.7 cm; 5 in)
Excluding cases of elephantiasis, the longest toes are 12.7 cm (5 in) long and belong to Matthew McGrory (USA), who also holds records for the **largest feet for a living person.**

★ **Longest nipple hair (8.89 cm; 3.5 in)** Christopher Tyler Ing (Canada)

★ **Longest arm hair (9.7 cm; 3.18 in)** David Hruska (USA)

Leg hair (12.4 cm; 4.88 in) Tim Stinton (Australia)

★ MOST FINGERS AND TOES ON A LIVING PERSON

Brothers Tribhuwan and Triloki Yadav (both India) have the condition polydactylism, whereby each of their hands has five fingers and a thumb, and each foot has six toes.

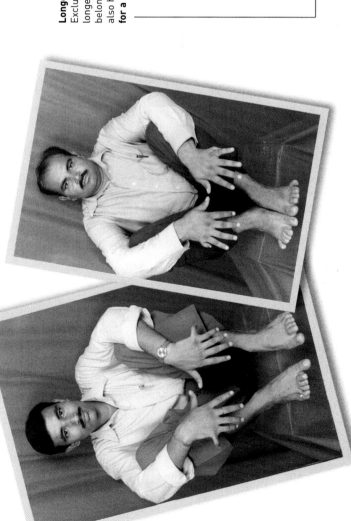

→ HUMAN ACHIEVEMENTS

→ | **CONTENTS**

STRANGEST DIET

Michel Lotito (France) is known as Monsieur Mangetout ('Mr Eat Everything') because he has been eating metal and glass since 1959 (see interview, p.45). Since 1966, he has consumed 18 bicycles, 15 supermarket trolleys, 7 TV sets, 6 chandeliers, 2 beds, a pair of skis, a computer and a Cessna light aircraft. He is also said to have provided the only example in history of a coffin ending up *inside* a man.

By October 1997, Monsieur Mangetout had eaten nearly 9 tonnes (19,840 lb) of metal. Despite this 'iron' constitution, he claims that bananas and hard-boiled eggs make him sick.

EPIC JOURNEYS

← LONGEST JOURNEY
BY WHEELCHAIR

Rick Hansen (Canada), who was paralysed from the waist down in 1973 as a result of a car accident, wheeled his wheelchair 40,075 km (24,901 miles) through four continents and 34 countries. He started his journey from Vancouver, British Columbia, Canada, on 21 March 1985 and arrived back there on 22 May 1987.

★ FARTHEST DISTANCE ON A SNOWMOBILE ON WATER

Tory Allan (Canada) travelled 25.26 km (15.7 miles) on Last Mountain Lake, Saskatchewan, Canada, non-stop on a standard snowmobile on 3 September 2004.

★ LONGEST JOURNEY BY TRACTOR

Vasiliy Hazkevich (Russia) covered 5,512 km (3,425 miles) on an unmodified agricultural tractor from 12 June to 5 July 2004, starting and finishing in Novosibirsk, Russia.

LONGEST JOURNEY BY SKATEBOARD

In July 1976 and again in July 1984, Jack Smith (USA) skateboarded just under 4,830 km (3,000 miles) between Lebanon, Oregon, and Williamsburg, Virginia, USA.

★ LONGEST COASTAL JOURNEY BY AQUABIKE

Paul Fua, Lynden Parmenter and Randall Jones (all Australia) circumnavigated Australia – a total of 16,478 km (10,239 miles) – in 106 days, from 20 August 2000 on personal water crafts (PWCs).

↑ LONGEST LIFEBOAT JOURNEY

After his ship, the *Endurance*, stuck fast in Antarctic sea ice, Sir Ernest Shackleton (UK) and his crew of 28 set course for Elephant Island, around 160 km (100 miles) to the north, in three lifeboats. With five of his men, he then set off in their largest lifeboat for a whaling station in South Georgia – 1,300 km (800 miles) away – reaching the island after 17 days, on 19 May 1916. Ten days later, they reached the whaling station on foot. All the men on Elephant Island were later rescued.

FARTHEST

→ WHEN WAS THE FIRST CIRCUMNAVIGATION OF THE WORLD? FIND OUT ON P.32

★ LONGEST DRIVEN JOURNEY

Since 16 October 1984, Emil and Liliana Schmid (Switzerland) have covered over 587,000 km (364,745 miles) in their Toyota Land Cruiser, crossing more than 150 countries and territories.

★ LONGEST JOURNEY PUSHING A WHEELBARROW

Bob Hanley (Australia) started pushing his wheelbarrow around Australia on 24 April 1975 and finished on 6 May 1978 – some 14,500 km (9,000 miles) later. He started and finished in Sydney, via Townsville, Alice Springs, Perth, Adelaide and Melbourne.

Note: Because of road safety reasons, Guinness World Records no longer monitors claims for point-to-point driving on public roads.

FASTEST ATLANTIC CROSSINGS

MEANS OF TRAVEL	NAME OF CRAFT	HOLDER	ROUTE	DATE	TIME
Aquabike/PWC	–	Alavaro de Marichalar (Spain)	Canary Islands – Antigua	04–21/05/2002	17 days 1 hr 11 min
Powerboat	*Destriero*	Cesare Fiorio (Italy)	New York (USA) – Cornwall (UK)	06–09/08/1992	2 days 10 hr 32 min
Aircraft	SR-71 *Blackbird*	Maj. J Sullivan & N Widdifield (both USA)	New York (USA) – London (UK)	01/09/1973	1 hr 54 min 56 sec
Commercial aircraft	BA Concorde	Leslie Scott (UK)	JFK (New York) – Heathrow (London)	07/02/1996	2 hr 52 min 59 sec
Yacht	*PlayStation*	Steve Fossett (USA)	New York (USA) – Cornwall (UK)	10/10/2001	4 days 17 hr 28 min
Monohull yacht	*Mari-Cha IV*	Robert Miller (UK)	New York (USA) – Cornwall (UK)	02–09/10/2003	6 days 17 hr 52 min
Windsurfer	–	Sergio Ferrero (Italy)	Canary Islands – Barbados	06–30/06/1982	24 days
'Walking' (on floats)	–	Remy Bricka (France)	Canary Islands – Trinidad	02/04–31/05/1988	59 days

★ NEW RECORD   ★ UPDATED RECORD

★ FASTEST CROSSING OF THE ENGLISH CHANNEL BY AMPHIBIOUS VEHICLE

Sir Richard Branson (UK) 'drove' a street-legal Gibbs Aquada between Dover, UK, and Calais, France, in 1 hr 40 min 6 sec on 14 June 2004.

★ LONGEST JOURNEY BY HAND-CRANKED CYCLE

David Abrutat (UK) completed a journey of 5,421.34 km (3,368.67 miles) around the coastline of the UK on a hand-cranked cycle between 10 May and 5 August 2002, starting and finishing at Tower Bridge, London. A former Royal Air Force serviceman, he was partially paralysed in a car accident in 2000.

LONGEST CYCLE JOURNEY BY AN INDIVIDUAL

Itinerant lecturer Walter Stolle (Germany) amassed a mileage of over 646,960 km (402,000 miles) in a cycle tour from 24 January 1959 to 12 December 1976. He visited 159 countries, starting from Romford, Essex, UK.

FASTEST...

CIRCUMNAVIGATION BY CAR

The record for the first and fastest man and woman to have circumnavigated the earth by car covering six continents under the rules applicable in 1989 and 1991, embracing more than an equator's length of driving (40,075 km or 24,901 road miles), is held by Saloo Choudhury and his wife Neena Choudhury (both India). The journey took 69 days 19 hr 5 min from 9 September to 17 November 1989. The couple drove a 1989 Hindustan 'Contessa Classic' starting and finishing in Delhi, India.

★ JOURNEY ON FOOT ACROSS AUSTRALIA

David Parker (UK) walked across the Australian continental mainland from Cottesloe Beach, Perth, Western Australia, to Bondi Beach, Sydney, New South Wales, in 69 days 11 hr 28 min from 1 July to 8 September 1998.

★ UNICYCLE RIDE ACROSS AUSTRALIA

Between 30 June and 20 August 1985, Hanspeter Beck (Australia) unicycled a total of 6,237.96 km (3,876.1 miles) from Port Hedland, Western Australia, to Melbourne, Victoria, in 51 days 23 hr 25 min.

★ UNDERWATER ENGLISH CHANNEL SWIM

On 28 July 1962, Simon Paterson (UK) swam underwater from France to England with an air hose attached to his pilot boat. He covered the distance – in excess of 35 km (22 miles) – in 14 hr 50 min.

JOURNEY ON FOOT VIA THE PAN-AMERICAN HIGHWAY

Between 26 January 1977 and 18 September 1983 – a total of 2,426 days – George Meegan (UK) walked 30,431 km (19,019 miles) in a journey that took him from the southernmost point of South America, at Ushuaia, Argentina, to the northernmost point of North America, at Prudhoe Bay in Alaska, USA.

★ CAPE-TO-CAIRO BICYCLE JOURNEY

Chris Evans, David Genders, Michael Kennedy (all UK), Paul Reynaert (Belgium), Jeremy Wex, Steve Topsham, Scotty Robinson, Andrew Griffin (all Canada) and Sascha Hartl (Austria) cycled from Cairo, Egypt, to Cape Town, South Africa, in 119 days 1 hr 32 min from 18 January to 17 May 2003 during the inaugural Tour d'Afrique. The race covered 10,957 km (6,808 miles).

★ DRIVING
TO THE HIGHEST ALTITUDE

A standard Volkswagen Toureg SUV was driven to an altitude of 6,081 m (19,950 ft) by Rainer Zietlow and Ronald Bormann (both Germany) on the slopes of the volcano Ojos del Salado on the Chile-Argentina border on 29 January 2005. The height they reached is higher than Everest base camp (around 5,500 m, or 18,045 ft) and Mt Kilimanjaro, the tallest peak in Africa at 5,895 m (19,340 ft).

MOUNTAIN OF MOUNTAINS

With steeper and more technical climbing routes and more extreme weather, K2 is generally regarded as being a far tougher challenge than Everest. While over 1,200 people have climbed Everest, only around 200 have conquered K2. No wonder climbing legend Reinhold Messner dubbed it the 'Mountain of Mountains'.

EVEREST & K2

FASTEST ASCENT OF MOUNT EVEREST BY THE NORTH SIDE

Hans Kammerlander (Italy) completed the climb from base camp to the summit in 16 hr 45 min on 23–24 May 1996.

★ FASTEST ASCENT OF MOUNT EVEREST BY THE SOUTH SIDE

Pemba Dorje Sherpa (Nepal) climbed from base camp to summit in a time of 8 hr 10 min on 21 May 2004, the **fastest ever ascent** of the world's tallest mountain.

MOST CONQUESTS OF MOUNT EVEREST

Apa Sherpa (Nepal) reached the summit for the 14th time on 17 May 2004.

FIRST SOLO CLIMB OF MOUNT EVEREST

Reinhold Messner (Italy) reached the summit of Everest on 20 August 1980. The solo climb, without bottled oxygen, took him three days from his base camp at 6,500 m (21,325 ft).

★ MOST SIBLINGS TO HAVE CLIMBED MOUNT EVEREST

By March 2003, Nepalese brothers Nima Gombu Sherpa and Mingma Tsiri Sherpa had each reached the summit eight times. Their siblings Ang Tsering Sherpa and Nima Temba Sherpa (both Nepal) had each made one ascent by the same date.

★ FIRST ASCENT OF K2

Achille Compagnoni and Lino Lacedelli (both Italy) scaled the world's second highest mountain at 8,611 m (28,251 ft) on 31 July 1954. Both men were members of an Italian expedition led by Ardito Desio (Italy). K2 is situated in the Karakoram range on the Pakistan–China border.

NORTH POLE & ARCTIC

★ FASTEST SKI JOURNEY TO THE NORTH POLE BY A WOMAN

Catherine Hartley and Fiona Thornewill (both UK) skied to the North Pole (with support in the form of re-supplies along the way) in 55 days from 11 March to 5 May 2001, after having set out from Ward-Hunt Island, Northwest Territories, Canada.

FIRST SOLO EXPEDITION TO THE NORTH POLE

Naomi Uemura (Japan) became the first person to reach the North Pole in a solo trek across the Arctic sea ice on 1 May 1978. He travelled 725 km (450 miles), setting out on 7 March from Cape Edward, Ellesmere Island, northern Canada.

★ FASTEST SOLO UNSUPPORTED TREK TO THE NORTH POLE

Børge Ousland (Norway) skied his way to the North Pole from the Severnaya Zemlya archipelago in the Russian Federation without any external assistance in 52 days from 2 March to 23 April 1994. He was also the **first person to make a solo and unsupported journey to the North Pole from land**. He did not use any form of motorized transport or parafoil kites.

★ FASTEST UNSUPPORTED CROSSING OF THE ARCTIC

Torry Larsen and Rune Gjeldnes (both Norway) crossed the Arctic Ocean via the North Pole in 109 days without assistance. They set out from the Siberian Severnaya Zemlya archipelago, Russian Federation, on 15 February 2000 and arrived at Ellesmere Island, Northwest Territories, Canada, on 3 June 2000.

← ★ K2: FIRST ASCENT
BY A WOMAN

Wanda Rutkiewicz (Poland) reached the summit of K2, the world's second highest mountain, on 23 June 1986, becoming the first woman to climb the 8,611-m-high (28,251-ft) peak.

← ★YOUNGEST
PERSON TO TREK TO THE SOUTH POLE

Sarah Ann McNair-Landry (USA/Canada, far left) was 18 when she arrived at the Pole on 11 January 2005 without the use of dogs or motorized vehicles. She made the 1,100-km (683-mile) kite-assisted trip as part of an unsupported expedition led by her mother Matty McNair (right), a polar trekking guide. The expedition also included her brother Eric (middle), who was 20.

★FASTEST OVERLAND JOURNEY TO THE SOUTH POLE

Adventurer Shinji Kazama (Japan) travelled to the South Pole from the Patriot Hills on the Antarctic coastline on a specially modified Yamaha motorcycle in 24 days from 10 December 1991 to 3 January 1992. He was supported by a snowmobile that carried emergency supplies and offered occasional assistance over rough terrain.

→ WHAT IS THE FARTHEST DISTANCE TRAVELLED ON ANOTHER WORLD? FIND OUT ON P.104

★FASTEST UNSUPPORTED NORTH POLE TREK BY A WOMAN

Tina Sjögren and her husband Thomas Sjögren (both Sweden) made the journey in 68 days from 22 March to 29 May 2002. They set off from Ward-Hunt Island in Canada's Northwest Territories and received no external support.

SOUTH POLE & ANTARCTICA

FASTEST SOLO CROSSING OF ANTARCTICA

Børge Ousland (Norway) completed the 2,690-km (1,671-mile) trek on 18 January 1997, 64 days after setting out on 15 November 1996. He dragged his 185-kg (408-lb) supply sled from Berkner Island in the Weddell Sea to Scott Base in McMurdo Sound.

★YOUNGEST ANTARCTIC SOLO TREKKER

Ola Skinnarmo (Sweden) arrived unaided at the Scott Base in Antarctica on 20 December 1998, aged 26, after a 47-day, 1,200-km (746-mile) trek on skis across the frozen continent. He pulled a sled that weighed about 120 kg (264 lb) laden, yet still finished 10 days earlier than expected.

★FASTEST UNSUPPORTED JOURNEY TO THE SOUTH POLE

Børge Ousland (Norway) travelled to the South Pole on skis, with assistance from a parafoil kite, in 34 days from 15 November to 19 December 1996. The journey was solo and unsupported, meaning that he received no outside assistance.

FASTEST → SOLO UNSUPPORTED SOUTH POLE TREK

Fiona Thornewill (UK) walked and skied her way to the South Pole from Hercules Inlet at the edge of the Antarctic continent in 41 days 8 hr 14 min from 30 November 2003 to 10 January 2004. She started pulling a 130-kg (285-lb) supply sled – which weighed 45 kg (9 lb) by the time she reached the Pole – and averaged 27.3 km (17 miles) a day.

CIRCUMNAVIGATION

★ FASTEST UNPOWERED ROUND-THE-WORLD TRIP ALONG THE EQUATOR

Mike Horn (South Africa) circumnavigated the Earth along the equator by bicycle, dug-out canoe, sailing trimaran and on foot in 513 days between 2 June 1999 and 27 October 2000. His journey started and finished near Libreville in the west African state of Gabon and proceeded in six legs that included sailing across the Atlantic, Pacific and Indian Oceans, and crossing the Amazon and central Africa.

OLDEST ROUND-THE-WORLD YACHT RACE

The quadrennial Volvo Ocean Race is the oldest regular round-the-world sailing race. It was first held in 1973 when it was called the Whitbread Round the World race, and was known by that name until the 2001/02 event. The next Volvo Ocean Race begins in November 2005 at Vigo, Spain, ending at Goteborg, Sweden, in June 2006.

FASTEST SOLO-SAILING CIRCUMNAVIGATION →

Ellen MacArthur (UK) sailed solo and non-stop around the world in 71 days 14 hr 13 min 33 sec between 28 November 2004 and 7 February 2005 in the trimaran *B&Q*. She started off from Ushant, France, rounded the Cape of Good Hope (South Africa), sailed south of Australia, and rounded Cape Horn (Argentina) before heading back up the Atlantic to Ushant.

BY BOAT

★ FASTEST ROUND-THE-WORLD TRIP BY A CREWED SAILING VESSEL

A crew of 14, captained by Bruno Peyron (France), sailed around the world in 50 days 16 hr 20 min 4 sec in the maxi catamaran *Orange II* from 24 January to 16 March 2005. The journey started and finished off the coast of Ushant, France.

FIRST CIRCUMNAVIGATION OF THE WORLD

This record was first accomplished on 9 September 1522 when the Spanish vessel *Vittoria*, under the command of the Spanish navigator Juan Sebastian de Elcano, reached Seville in Spain. The ship had set out along with four others as part of an expedition led by the Portuguese explorer Ferdinand Magellan in 1519 and had rounded Cape Horn, crossed the Pacific via the Philippines, and returned to Europe after sailing around the Cape of Good Hope. *Vittoria* was the only ship to survive the voyage.

★ LONGEST SERIES OF SAILING CIRCUMNAVIGATIONS

Jon Sanders (Australia) completed a series of three non-stop single-handed circumnavigations in the 13.9-m (45-ft) sloop *Parry Endeavour* in 657 days from 25 May 1986 to 13 March 1988. Starting and finishing in Fremantle, Western Australia, he made one circumnavigation westabout and two eastabout.

SR·1989

SR·1989

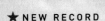
★ NEW RECORD   ☆ UPDATED RECORD

LONGEST SOLO NON-STOP YACHTING RACE

The Vendée Globe Challenge starts and finishes at Les Sables d'Olonne, France. The distance currently sailed without stopping is 22,500 nautical miles (41,652 km; 25,881 miles). The race is for boats 15–18 m (50–60 ft) in size, sailed single-handed.

BY AIR

★ FIRST SOLO ROUND-THE-WORLD BALLOON TRIP

Steve Fossett (USA) circumnavigated the globe in *Bud Light Spirit of Freedom*, a 42.6-m-tall (140-ft) mixed-gas balloon, from 19 June to 2 July 2002. He took off from Northam, Western Australia, and landed at Eromanga, Queensland, Australia, after covering 33,195 km (20,626 miles).

★ MOST FLIGHTS AROUND THE WORLD

Cosmonaut Sergei Avdeyev (Russia) has completed 11,968 orbits of the Earth during his career. He also holds the record for **most time spent in space** (see page 109).

★ FASTEST AERIAL CIRCUMNAVIGATION BY A PROPELLER-DRIVEN AIRCRAFT

Joe Harnish and David Webster (both USA) piloted a Gulfstream Commander 695A twin turboprop around the world at an average speed of 490.51 km/h

STEVE FOSSETT

Steve Fossett (USA, pictured left) is the first person to fly around the world non-stop without refuelling. He started and finished at Salina, Kansas, USA, taking 67 hr 1 min, from 1 to 3 March 2005. The *Virgin Atlantic GlobalFlyer* (below) was built by Scaled Composites (USA). It was powered by a single turbofan jet engine and carried nearly 5 tonnes (11,000 lb) of fuel.

What was the first world record you broke?
It was sailing around the coast of Ireland in September 1993 – the previous record was 72 hours and I did it in 45!

What do you do to prepare yourself for these high-endurance record attempts?
I do a lot of running and try to get some exercise every day. Sometimes I need acclimatization to altitude. For *GlobalFlyer* I went on a low-residue diet before the flight.

What's your next challenge?
To fly a glider into the stratosphere – I'll have to wear a spacesuit and once again I'm cooperating with Nasa. The current altitude record for gliders is 15,000 m (49,000 ft).

(304.8 mph) from 21 to 24 March 1983, starting and finishing at Eckhart, California, USA.

★ FASTEST AERIAL CIRCUMNAVIGATION VIA BOTH POLES

A Boeing 747 SP piloted by Captain Walter H Mullikin (USA) achieved this record in 54 hr 7 min 12 sec (including refuelling stops) between 28 and 31 October 1977. The journey started and finished in San Francisco, USA.

Who are your heroes?
The great polar explorers. My favourite is Shackleton – and also Nansen, who carried out the first crossing of Greenland and never lost a man.

When has your life been in most danger?
In August 1998, my balloon was ruptured by a thunderstorm at an altitude of 8,800 m (29,000 ft). I plummeted into the Coral Sea and was just barely able to slow the balloon down enough to survive.

What record are you most proud of?
The first solo balloon flight around the world. I worked on it for eight years and six attempts. It was something I was uniquely qualified to do – the combination of the hardship of flying solo and the knowledge of ballooning.

★ FASTEST CIRCUMNAVIGATION BY SCHEDULED FLIGHTS, VISITING SIX CONTINENTS

Michael Quandt (Germany), travel editor of the newspaper *Bild am Sonntag*, flew around the world via six continents on scheduled flights in a time of 66 hr 31 min from 6 to 8 July 2004. The journey started and finished in Singapore and covered Sydney (Australia), Los Angeles (USA), Houston (USA), Caracas (Venezuela), London (UK), Cairo (Egypt) and Kuala Lumpur (Malaysia).

STRENGTH & STAMINA

★ HEAVIEST WEIGHT
LIFTED WITH TONGUE

Thomas Blackthorne (UK) lifted 11.025 kg (24 lb 3 oz) on the set of *Guinness World Records: 50 Years, 50 Records* at the London Television Studios, UK, on 11 September 2004.

★ GREATEST HEIGHT ATTAINED ON A CLIMBING MACHINE IN ONE HOUR

Neil Rhodes (UK) climbed 2,238.75 m (7,345 ft) while carrying an 18-kg (40-lb) pack at Cannon's Health Club, Yeovil, Somerset, UK, on 2 November 2004.

★ HIGHEST BEER KEG TOSS (FEMALE)

Heini Koivuniemi (Finland) threw a 12.3-kg (27.1-lb) beer keg over a bar at a height of 3.46 m (11 ft 4.2 in) on 9 August 2001.

Juha Rasanen (Finland) threw a 12.3-kg (27.1-lb) beer keg over a bar at a height of 6.93 m (22.73 ft) on 21 September 2001, the **highest beer keg toss by a man**.

★ HEAVIEST WEIGHT LIFTED WITH EAR

Zafar Gill (Pakistan) lifted gym weights of 51.7 kg (113 lb 15 oz) by using a clamp attached to his right ear and held it for seven seconds on 26 May 2004 at Lahore, Pakistan.

★ LONGEST CRUCIFIX HOLD (10 KG)

Yannick Ollivier (France) held a 10-kg (22-lb) dumbbell in each of his hands at arm's length and at a 90° angle to his body for 1 min 18 sec on the set of *L'Été De Tous Les Records* in Bénodet, France, on 3 August 2004.

MOST BENCH PRESSES – OWN BODY WEIGHT

Michael Williams (UK) achieved 1,438 repetitions of lifting his body weight of 67 kg (147.7 lb) in one hour by bench presses at Don Styler's Gymnasium, Gosport, UK, on 17 April 1989.

★ FASTEST TIME TO RUN 100 MILES ON A TREADMILL

Arulanantham Suresh Joachim (Sri Lanka) ran 100 miles (161 km) on a treadmill in a time of 13 hr 42 min 33 sec at Square One, Mississauga, Ontario, Canada, on 28 November 2004.

★ GREATEST HEIGHT CLIMBED ON A 5-M ROPE IN ONE MINUTE

Using just his hands and from a seated position, Stéphane Bock (France) climbed a 5-m (16-ft 4.8-in) rope to a height of 15.44 m (50 ft) on 27 July 2004.

MOST TYRES LIFTED

Gary Windebank (UK) managed a free-standing 'lift' of 96 tyres weighing 653 kg (1,440 lb) in February 1984. The tyres used were Michelin XZX 155 x 13.

PUSH-UPS TABLE

EVENT	TIME	RECORD	NAME	NATIONALITY	DATE
One finger	consecutive	124	Paul Lynch	UK	21 April 1992
One arm	one minute	120	Yvan de Weber	Switzerland	23 October 2001
★One arm	one hour	1,777	Doug Pruden	Canada	22 October 2004
One arm, back of hand	one hour	441	Bruce Swatton	UK	12 May 2003
★Two arms, back of hand	one minute	95	Steve Bugdale	UK	13 November 2004
★Two hands	one minute	138	Roy Berger	Canada	28 February 2004
Two hands	one hour	3,416	Roy Berger	Canada	30 August 1998
★Vertical	one minute	37	Murad Gadaborchev	Russia	20 July 2004

★ FASTEST IRON-BAR-BEND INTO SUITCASE

The fastest time to bend an iron bar 6 m (19.6 ft) long and with a diameter of 12 mm (0.47 in), and then fit it into a suitcase with dimensions 50 x 70 x 20 cm (19.6 x 27.5 x 7.87 in), is 29 seconds by Les Davis (USA) at Dothan, Alabama, USA, on 17 July 2004. He bent the bar a total of 11 times.

★ MOST CHIN-UPS IN ONE HOUR

Stéphane Gras (France) performed 445 chin-ups in an hour in Artix, France, on 26 April 2004.

★ MOST CONSECUTIVE CHIN-UPS

Lee Chin-Yong (Korea) performed a total of 612 consecutive chin-ups at Jongmyo Park, Seoul, South Korea, on 29 December 1994.

MOST BRICKS LIFTED SIDE BY SIDE

Russell Bradley (UK) lifted 31 bricks – which were laid side by side – off a table, raised them to chest height and held them there for two seconds on 14 June 1992.

★ FASTEST TIME
TO RUN UP THE EMPIRE STATE BUILDING

At the 26th Annual Empire State Building Run-Up, New York City, USA, on 4 February 2003, Paul Crake (Australia, pictured) ran up the 1,576 steps in 9 min 33 sec.

The **fastest woman** to achieve the feat is Belinda Soszyn (Australia), with a time of 12 min 19 sec in 1996.

MOST CAR LIFTS IN ONE HOUR

The greatest number of times the rear of a car has been lifted clear of the ground (i.e. so that the rear wheels do not touch the ground) in one hour is 580 by Mark Anglesea (UK) at The Hind, South Yorkshire, UK, on 3 October 1998. The car was a Mini Metro weighing 810 kg (1,785 lb).

★ FULL-BODY ICE-CONTACT ENDURANCE

Wim Hof (Netherlands) endured contact with ice for 1 hr 8 min on the set of *Guinness World Records: 50 Years, 50 Records* at the London Television Studios, UK, on 11 September 2004. Wim uses meditation and yoga to overcome the dangers inherent in these activities.

★ MOST TELEPHONE DIRECTORIES TORN IN THREE MINUTES

Edward Charon (USA) ripped 39 telephone directories from top to bottom, each with 1,004 numbered pages, in three minutes at Roseburg, Oregon, USA, on 14 August 2004.

GREATEST LABOURER

There are two contenders for this title. Miner Alexei Stakhanov (Ukraine) claimed to have hewn 92.5 tonnes (227,075 lb) of coal in a six-hour shift in August 1935. Steel worker Henry Noll (USA) lifted and loaded 40.8 tonnes (100,751 lb) of pig iron on to railway trucks every day for weeks at a time in the winter of 1899.

HEAVIEST AIRCRAFT ← PULLED

David Huxley (Australia) pulled a Boeing 747-400 weighing 187 tonnes (412,260 lb) a distance of 91 m (298 ft 6 in) in 1 min 27.7 sec on 15 October 1997 at Sydney, Australia.

Huxley pulled his first aircraft, a Boeing 737 weighing 37 tonnes (81,570 lb), in 1991. He progressed to pulling a 105-tonne (231,485-lb) Concorde 143 m (469 ft) and eventually to the 747 at the age of 39.

LONGEST KISS

Louisa Almedovar and Rich Langley (both USA) kissed continuously for 30 hr 59 min 27 sec at the television studios of *Ricki Lake*, New York City, USA, on 5 December 2001. The couple remained standing, without rest breaks, throughout the attempt.

→ HOW MANY PHONE DIRECTORIES WERE TORN FROM TOP TO BOTTOM IN 3 MINUTES? FIND OUT ON P.35

★ AIR HOCKEY

Jaron Carson and Jordan Ouanounou (both Canada) played an air-hockey marathon continuously for 20 hours at Dave & Busters, Toronto, Ontario, Canada, on 26–27 August 2003.

BLACKJACK DEALING

The longest time spent dealing blackjack is 51 hr 33 min by Stephen De Raffaele (Malta) between 24 and 27 August 2001 at the Oracle Casino, Qawra, Malta.

CARD PLAYING

Gareth Birdsall, Sonia Zakrzewski, Gad Chadha, Finn Clark, Sebastian Kristensen, Simon MacBeth, Tim West-Meads and David Gold played a continuous game of bridge for 72 hr 9 min at St John's Wood Bridge Club, London, UK, from 31 October to 3 November 2003. A total of 1,012 hands of bridge were played.

★ CPR

Two teams of two people – consisting of Ray Edensor and Emma Parker and Paul Gauntlett and Mark Brookes (all UK) from the Staffordshire Ambulance Service – completed a CPR (cardiopulmonary resuscitation – 15 compressions alternating with two breaths) marathon of 151 hours at Asda Superstore, Stafford, UK, from 19 to 25 January 2004.

HULA HOOPING

Kym Coberly (USA) hula-hooped for 72 hours in Denton, Texas, USA, from 17 to 20 October 1984.

IRONING

Eufemia Stadler (Switzerland) completed 40 hours of ironing. She continuously ironed 228 shirts while standing at an ironing board from 16 to 18 September 1999.

LECTURING

Errol E T Muzawazi (Zimbabwe) talked on the subject of democracy for 62 hr 30 min, from 12 to 15 December 2003, at a student residence of Politechnika Wroclawska, Wroclaw, Poland.

MAH-JONG

Chris Pittenger, Betty Vance, Doris Natale, Mary Ann Blansett, Rosemarie Cannon, Judy Burt, Ann Wells and Doris MacKenzie (all USA) played two games of mah-jong simultaneously for 25 hours, in two groups of four people. The attempt took place at Sun City Hilton Head, Bluffton, South Carolina, USA, from 28 February to 1 March 2003.

★ MOVIE WATCHING

Timothy Weber (Germany) watched 32 films for 70 hr 1 min at an event organized by CinemaxX Würzburg, Würzburg, Germany, from 16 to 19 December 2003. The attempt ended 49 minutes into the 33rd film, *Finding Nemo* (USA, 2003).

LONGEST DANCE PARTY →

The Heart Health Hop – a dance party marathon organized by St Joseph Aspirin and Rowland Communications Worldwide and held at the Rock and Roll Hall of Fame and Museum, Cleveland, Ohio, USA – began on 29 July 2003 at 5.10 a.m. with 42 dancers, 41 of whom completed the marathon after 52 hr 3 min on 31 July 2003.

→ HOW LONG WAS THE LONGEST KARAOKE SESSION? FIND OUT ON P.172

TOP SIX LONGEST MARATHONS

EVENT	HOURS	RECORD HOLDER(S)	DATE
Trampoline	1,248	Team of 6 (USA)	24 June to 15 August 1974
Swimming	240	Team of 6 (USA)	14 to 24 August 1979
★ Ice hockey	203	Sudbury Angels (Canada)	3 to 11 April 2004
Rollercoaster	192	Richard Rodriguez (USA)	20 to 28 August 2003
★ Snowboarding	180 hr 34 min	Berhard Mair (Austria)	9 to 16 January 2004
Skiing	168	Christian Flühr (Germany)	8 to 15 March 2003

★ POKER PLAYING (INDIVIDUAL)

Larry Olmsted (USA) played poker non-stop for 72 hr 2 min at Foxwoods Resort & Casino, Manshantucket, Connecticut, USA, from 10 to 13 June 2004.

★ PUNCH-BAG HITTING

Ron Sarchian (USA) hit a punch-bag continuously (i.e. striking once every two seconds) for 36 hr 3 min at Premier Fitness, Encino, California, USA, between 15 and 17 June 2004.

QUIZ QUESTIONS

Quiz master Gavin Dare (UK) asked a total of 3,668 general knowledge questions continuously at The Goff's Oak Public House, Hertfordshire, UK, for 32 hr 15 min on 25–26 October 2003.

★ READING ALOUD (INDIVIDUAL)

Adrian Hilton (UK) recited the complete works of Shakespeare in a 'Bardathon' lasting 110 hr 46 min at the Shakespeare Festival, South Bank, London, UK, and Gold Hill Baptist Church, Chalfont St Peter, Buckinghamshire, UK, between 16 and 21 July 1987.

★ READING ALOUD (TEAM)

A team comprising Amy White, Kristy Wright, Brian Jones, Michael Dahl, Jeanette Dean and Georgina Konstana (all Australia) read aloud for 81 hr 15 min at the Sutherland Library, Sydney, Australia, between 24 and 27 May 2004. The record was held to celebrate Australian Library week, and raised money for various youth charities.

RING-BOARD

Joe Norman, Robert Norman, Paul Harkes, Faye Savill, Marion Daly, Betty Murphy, Hazel Gannon and Dennis Curtis (all UK) played ring-board for 24 hours at Silver Hall Social Club, Rainham, Essex, UK, on 12–13 July 2003.

★ ROPE SKIPPING (INDIVIDUAL)

Jed Goodfellow (Australia) skipped a rope for 27 hours at Oasis Shopping Mall, Broadbeach, Queensland, Australia, on 5–6 December 2003.

★ SQUARE DANCE CALLING

Dale F Muehlmeier (USA) called for 28 hours for the American Cancer Society at a Wal-Mart car park, Norfolk, Nebraska, USA, on 26–27 May 2000.

★ TABLE FOOTBALL

Andre Raison, Ghislain De Broyer, Rudy Mortier and Daniel Vanbellinghen (all Belgium) played table football for 24 hr 1 min at the Young Band Brass Pub in Lembeek, Belgium, on 19–20 October 2002.

★ STEEL TOBOGGAN RIDING

Michael Kinzel (Germany) rode the steel summer toboggan at Panorama Park in Kirchhundem, Germany, for 56 hours between 4 and 6 May 2002. A summer toboggan is a combination of a bob-sled and a toboggan.

TRADING CARD GAME PLAYING

William Stone, Bryan Erwin and Christopher Groetzinger (all USA) played *The Lord of the Rings* trading card game for 128 hours from 27 December 2002 to 1 January 2003 at The Courtyard, Colorado Springs, Colorado, USA.

★ TV WATCHING

Terrye Jackson (USA) watched NBC's Olympic coverage at Pat O'Brien's bar, Orlando, Florida, USA, for 50 hr 7 min from 15 August to 17 August 2004.

GREATEST DISTANCE
TRAVELLED ON A POGO STICK

Ashrita Furman (USA) jumped 37.18 km (23.11 miles) on a pogo stick in 12 hr 27 min on 22 June 1997 at Queensborough Community College Track, New York, USA. He also holds the record for the ★ **most pogo-stick jumps in 1 minute** (156), the **fastest mile on a pogo stick** (12 min 15 sec) and the **fastest time to travel up the CN Tower on a pogo stick** (57 min 51 sec).

The record for the **most consecutive jumps on a pogo stick** is held by Gary Stewart (USA), who completed 177,737 jumps at Huntington Beach, California, USA, on 25–26 May 1990.

MASS PARTICIPATION

⭐ HUMAN RAINBOW

The Polytechnic University of the Philippines (PUP) organized a human rainbow consisting of 30,365 participants at the Qurino Grandstand, Rizal Park, Manila, Philippines, on 18 September 2004.

←

human centipede at Tsuruma Track and Field Stadium, Nagoya, Japan, on 13 June 2001.

The ankles of all participants were firmly tied to the ankles of those people next to them; the centipede successfully moved 30 m (98 ft) without any mishaps.

HUMAN DOMINO LINE

On 30 September 2000, 9,234 students aged 18–21 from the NYAA-Poly Connects project formed a human domino chain stretching 4.2 km (2.6 miles) across Siloso Beach, Sentosa Island, Singapore. It was arranged by the National Youth Achievement Award (NYAA) Council, in collaboration with the combined polytechnics of Singapore.

HUMAN LOGO

On 24 July 1999, 34,309 people gathered at the National Stadium of Jamor, Lisbon, Portugal, to create the Portuguese logo for Euro 2004. The event was part of the successful Portuguese bid to UEFA to hold football's 2004 European Championships.

→ WHERE DID THE LARGEST BREAKFAST IN THE WORLD TAKE PLACE? FIND OUT ON P.128

⭐ COFFEE MORNING

Macmillan Cancer Relief (UK) broke their own record set the previous year for the largest coffee morning with 576,157 people attending over 26,000 meetings simultaneously, across the UK, on 26 September 2003.

LARGEST...

⭐ CEILIDH

The Great Glengoyne Ceilidh was held on 17 June 1997 at various venues throughout Scotland simultaneously, catering for 6,568 people.

⭐ CHEERLEADING CHEER

A total of 435 cheerleaders from The Cheerful Dance Company performed a cheer in full uniform on the field of Bedworth United Football Club, Bedworth, Warwickshire, UK, on 4 July 2004.

⭐ CHRISTMAS CRACKER PULLING

On 16 November 2003, 986 people participated in a simultaneous Christmas cracker pull in Culver Square, Colchester, Essex, UK.

⭐ GAME OF LEAPFROG

A group of 1,100 people participated in the largest game of leapfrog at the Virgin Group summer party held in Kidlington, Oxfordshire, UK, on 4 September 2004.

GROUP HUG

On 23 April 2004, a crowd of 5,117 students, staff and friends from St Matthew Catholic High School hugged each other for at least 10 seconds in Orleans, Ontario, Canada. The hug was in support of The Force, a local cancer charity.

HUMAN CENTIPEDE

A total of 2,026 people – comprising Nagoya Otani High School students and their parents and teachers – created the world's largest

⭐ MOST PEOPLE WEARING BALLOON HATS →

At an event organized by Sentosa Leisure Management (Singapore), 1,039 participants designed, made and wore hats constructed from balloons at the Sentosa Balloon Hats Festival held at Palawan Beach, Sentosa, Singapore, on 13 March 2004.

HUMAN NATIONAL FLAG

The world's largest human national flag comprised 10,371 spectators. They formed the shape and colours of the German flag in the south grandstand at the Scotland v Germany European Championships qualifying football match in Westfalenstadion, Dortmund, Germany, on 10 September 2003.

MARCHING BAND

A total of 11,157 people in 317 bands, including a flag team of 1,092, marched at the Japan International Exposition Memorial Grand in Osaka, Japan, on 11 May 1997, to celebrate the 60th anniversary of the Music for Wind Instruments League in Kansai.

★ MARTIAL ARTS DISPLAY

On 10 April 2004, a group of 30,648 people performed wushu shadow-boxing for 16 min 40 sec at the opening ceremony of the 22nd Luoyang Peony Festival in Henan Province, China.

★ PILLOW FIGHT

The largest pillow fight involved 2,773 participants and took place in Dodgeville, Wisconsin, USA, on 29 September 2004.

★ RING-A-RING-O' ROSES RHYME

A group of 1,953 schoolchildren joined hands for the largest ring-a-ring-o' roses at The People's Park, Waterford, Ireland, on 20 April 2004.

The song was repeated for a total of six and a half minutes, with all of the participants falling down and getting up again in unison.

★ SCOTTISH REEL

A Scottish country dance involving a group of 1,254 pupils from Ellon Academy, Ellon, Aberdeenshire, UK, took place on 21 September 2004.

★ ROPE SKIP

On 25 May 2004, a group of 2,350 schoolchildren skipped rope simultaneously at Redlands Sports Ground, Weymouth, Dorset, UK.

SNOWBALL FIGHT

A snowball fight involving a group of 2,473 participants (in two teams, divided 1,162 against 1,311) took place at Triel in the ski resort of Obersaxen-Mundaun at Graubunden, Switzerland, on 18 January 2003.

★ TEETH BRUSHING

A total of 10,240 students brushed their teeth simultaneously for at least 60 seconds at Ai Guo Road, Luohu District, Shenshen City, China, on 20 September 2003.

The event was organized by the Health Bureau of Luohu District, the Education Bureau of Luohu District and the Chamber of Commerce of Luohu District and sponsored by Colgate–Palmolive (Guangzhou) Co. Ltd.

★ TYRE ROLL

In an event sponsored by Michelin, a total of 138 employees of the Nationwide Building Society MAA division simultaneously rolled car tyres over a distance of 100 m (328 ft) at their head office in Swindon, UK, on 2 July 2004.

WALK

The New Paper Big Walk 2000 involved 77,500 participants, starting from the National Stadium, Singapore, on 21 May 2000. It was organized by The Singapore Press Holdings, The Singapore Amateur Athletic Association and The Singapore Sports Council.

★ WATER BALLOON FIGHT

A balloon fight involving 993 participants, who threw 8,000 balloons altogether, took place at the Peace River Bible Institute, Sexsmith, Alberta, Canada, on 1 October 2004.

★ WHOOPEE CUSHION SIT

The Quad City Mallards, a member of the United Hockey League, achieved a simultaneous whoopee cushion sit involving 3,614 participants at Moline, Illinois, USA, on 19 March 2004.

MOST EGGS BALANCED

Students from the Brigham Young University, Utah, USA, balanced 1,290 eggs in 6 hr 30 min at the Wilkinson Student Centre, Provo, Utah, USA, on 15 March 2003.

MOST → SURFERS

A group of 38 surfers rode the same wave simultaneously at Manly Beach, Sydney, New South Wales, Australia, on 1 December 2002.

MASS PARTICIPATION

LARGEST SIMULTANEOUS JUMP

At 11:00 a.m. on 7 September 2001, 559,493 people began jumping up and down for one minute to mark the launch of Science Year in the UK. There were actually 569,069 participants – the extra numbers represent disabled pupils who contributed to the seismic activity by dropping objects on to the ground.

31-LEGGED RACE OVER 50 M
Students from the Sugikami Elementary school in Kumamoto Prefecture, Japan, ran a 31-legged race covering a total of 50 m (164 ft) in 8.94 seconds at Yokohama Arena, Japan, on 23 November 2002.

★ FLYING DISC RELAY
A team of five threw and caught a flying disc up and down a 20-m (65-ft 7-in) course in 16 seconds on 4 August 2004. The record was set by Emmanuelle Tartoue, Yoann Greau, Michel Affile, Vincent Levievse and Amaury Guerin (all France) on the set of *L'Été De Tous Les Records*, Bénodet, France.

★ MONKEY-BAR RELAY
Jean-Philippe Causse, Nicolas Bec and Guillem Briancon (all France) completed a monkey-bar relay in 1 min 23 sec on the set of *L'Été De Tous Les Records*, St-Pierre-la-Mer, France, on 8 September 2003.

FASTEST...

★ BANDAGE RELAY
A total of 114 arm slings were applied in one hour by a St John Ambulance relay team made up of Tony Lazell, Neil Fitch, Dawn Kemp, John Mowles, Rob Perris, Sheila Scott and Bert Wilkins (all UK), working in pairs at the Felixstowe Leisure Centre, Suffolk, UK, on 27 June 2004.

TIME TO BUILD A BRIDGE
A team of British soldiers from 35 Engineer Regiment based at Hameln, Germany, successfully constructed a bridge across a gap 8 m (26 ft 3 in) wide using a five-bay single-storey MGB (medium girder bridge) in a record time of 8 min 19 sec at Hohne, Germany, on 12 November 1998.

COAL-SHOVELLING
The record time for filling a 508-kg (1,120-lb) hopper with coal using only a banjo shovel by a team of two is 15.01 seconds. Brian McArdle and Rodney Spark (both Australia) achieved their feat at the Fingal Valley Festival in Fingal, Tasmania, Australia, on 5 March 1994.

LARGEST TEA PARTY

A simultaneous tea party that featured 11,760 participants was held as part of the Largest Tea and Buns event organized by Emergency Role of Sheltered Housing (ERoSH) at various locations across the UK on 11 June 2004.

LARGEST AEROBICS CLASS →

In total, 48,188 participants took part in an aerobics class at the Quirino Grandstand, Luneta Park, Manila, Philippines (pictured), on 16 February 2003.

The ★ **largest ever simultaneous aerobics display (multiple venues)** occurred on 27 September 2003, and involved 4,845,098 people throughout Kazakhstan.

← MOST PEOPLE TO WEAR A GROUCHO MARX DISGUISE AT SAME TIME

The greatest number of people to wear Groucho Marx-style glasses, nose and moustache simultaneously at one location is 937 students and staff from East Lansing High School, Michigan, USA, on 23 May 2003.

MOST...

★ SKIERS TOWED BEHIND AN AQUABIKE

A single Yamaha GP1300R WaveRunner towed 10 members of the H2O Entertainment water-ski team in Cockle Bay, Sydney, Australia, on 4 September 2004.

★ FACES PAINTED IN AN HOUR (TEAM)

A team of five teachers from Szczecin Primary School Number 1, Szczecin, Poland, painted the faces of 351 different people, using a minimum of three colours per face, in a single hour on 2 October 2004.

PEOPLE SKIPPING ON THE SAME ROPE SIMULTANEOUSLY

A team at the International Rope Skipping Competition, Greeley, Colorado, USA, achieved a total of 220 people skipping on the same rope simultaneously on 28 June 1990.

MISCELLANEOUS

GREATEST DISTANCE TO PUSH A BATH IN 24 HOURS

On 11–12 March 1995, a team of 25 from Tea Tree Gully Baptist Church, Westfield Shopping Town Tea Tree Plaza, Australia, pushed a bath and its passenger 513.32 km (318.96 miles).

★ GREATEST DISTANCE TRAVELLED ON A WATER SLIDE IN 24 HOURS (TEAM)

A team of 10 lifeguards covered a total distance of 696.81 km (432.97 miles) on a water slide at the Pfaffenhofen public swimming pool, Germany, on 12 July 2003.

GREATEST COAL-CARRYING DISTANCE

A team of eight men carried a hundredweight (51-kg; 112-lb) bag of coal for 128.7 km (80 miles) in 11 hr 28 min 33 sec, in West Yorkshire, UK, on 20 May 2000.

★ LONGEST PAPERCLIP CHAIN (TEAM)

On 26–27 March 2004, students from Eisenhower Junior High School, Taylorsville, Utah, USA, made a 35.63-km-long (22.14-mile) paperclip chain.

LONGEST WHEELCHAIR PUSH IN 24 HOURS

A team of 75 volunteers pushed a wheelchair for 386 km (240 miles) in 24 hours, in Cumbria, UK, on 8–9 September 2000.

MOST DISHES → WASHED

After a 3.75-tonne (8,265-lb) serving of pasta bolognese, a team of 150 people from Vester Hæsinge Idrætsforening, Brobyværk Idrætsforening and Sandholt-Lyndelse Forsamlingshus (Denmark) cleaned 23,892 dishes using 1 litre (0.22 gal; 0.26 US gal) of washing-up liquid at the Langelandsfestivalen in Rudkøbing, Denmark, on 28 July 2004.

MOST STRAWS
STUFFED IN THE MOUTH

Marco Hort (Switzerland) stuffed 258 drinking straws in his mouth and held them there for 10 seconds on 22 April 2005 at Belp, Bern, Switzerland.

LOUDEST...

★ FINGER SNAP

Bob Hatch (USA) snapped his fingers with a decibel meter reading of 108 dBA on 17 May 2000. This is equivalent to the volume of a lawnmower heard from 1 m (3 ft) away.

SCREAM

Classroom assistant Jill Drake (UK) had a scream that reached 129 dBA when measured at the Halloween festivities held in the Millennium Dome, London, UK, in October 2000. Jill believes she developed her vocal skills from working in a classroom!

SHOUT

On 16 April 1994, Annalisa Wray (UK) shouted at 121.7 dBA at the Citybus Challenge in Belfast, Antrim, UK. The word shouted was 'quiet'.

★ TONGUE CLICK

Kunal Jain (Canada) generated a decibel reading of 114.2 by clicking his tongue at Richmond Hill, Ontario, Canada, on 6 August 2003.

★ WHISTLE

Marco Ferrera (USA) achieved a whistle measuring 125 dBA at 2.5 m (8 ft 2 in) away at Schtung Music Studios, Santa Monica, California, USA, on 5 March 2004.

SNORE

Although snoring is technically not a talent, Kåre Walkert (Sweden), who suffers from the breathing disorder apnea, recorded peak snoring levels of 93 dBA on 24 May 1993.

★ CLAP

Standing 2.5 m (8 ft 2 in) from a noise level meter, Martha Gibson (UK) produced a 73-dBA hand clap at Harrogate, North Yorkshire, UK, on 9 March 2005.

MOST GLASSES
BALANCED
ON THE CHIN

After breaking hundreds of glasses during his practise attempts, Ashrita Furman (USA) finally balanced 75 pint (20-oz) beer glasses on his chin for 10.6 seconds in his backyard in Jamaica, New York, USA, on 26 April 2001.

MOST...

★ CLOTHES PEGS CLIPPED ON A FACE

Garry Turner (UK) clipped 159 ordinary wooden clothes pegs on his face during the *Guinness World Records 2005 Roadshow*, held in Manchester, UK, on 27 November 2004.

★ BRAS UNHOOKED IN A MINUTE

Chris Nicholson (UK) unhooked 20 bras in one minute using one hand on the set of *Guinness World Records: A Few Records More* (UK) in London, UK, on 11 September 2004.

★ BEER MATS FLIPPED

Mat Hand (UK) flipped and caught a pile of 112 beer mats on 9 May 2001 at the Waterstone's book store in Nottingham, UK. It took him over four hours and 129 attempts to break the record.

★ BULLWHIP CRACKS

Robert Dante (USA) cracked a bullwhip 214 times in a minute at the Third Annual Spirit of the West Festival in Sioux Falls, South Dakota on 19 September 2004.

LONGEST...

★ BEER BOTTLE CAP THROW

Paul van der Merwe (South Africa) threw a beer bottle cap a distance of 69.9 m (229 ft 3 in) at the Lime Acres Airfield, Northern Cape, South Africa, on 15 May 1999.

★ THROWN RIFLE EXCHANGE

Constantine Wilson and Clarence Robbins (both USA) exchanged their rifles at a distance of 5.48 m (18 ft) apart – with both rifles completing 1.5 revolutions in the air before being caught – at George Mason University, Fairfax, Virginia, USA, on 23 April 2004.

★ COIN SPINNING DURATION

Scott Day (UK) spun a coin that took a total of 19.37 seconds to come to a complete rest. The attempt was made at Earls Court in London, UK, on 9 July 2003 as part of the BBC's *Tomorrow's World Roadshow*.

FASTEST...

★ TIME TO THREAD 20 NEEDLES ON A SINGLE THREAD IN THE MOUTH

Meng Xu (China) threaded 20 needles on to a thread in the mouth using just his tongue in 6 min 45 sec at the China Millennium Monument, Beijing, China, on 10 December 2003.

★ WINDOW CLEANERS

Terry 'Turbo' Burrows (UK) cleaned three standard 1,143 x 1,143-mm (45 x 45-in) office windows set in a frame with a 300-mm-long (11.75-in) squeegee and 9 litres (2.4 gal; 2.4 US gal) of water in 9.24 sec at the National Exhibition Centre, Birmingham, UK, on 2 March 2005.

The ★ **fastest female window cleaner** is Janet Palfreyman (UK), who cleaned the same standard office windows, with the same regulation equipment, in 25.99 seconds at Hinkley, Leicestershire, UK, on 24 April 2004.

Competition window cleaning is highly regulated, and strict rules mean that time penalties are deducted for any water marks left on the glass.

GRAHAM HICKS

Despite being deaf and blind, Graham 'G-Force' Hicks (UK) holds the outright quadbike speed record and has also set aquabike (PWC) speed records. He achieves his records with the help of pillion riders who ride behind him and tell him where to steer using a touch system.

What caused your deafblindness?
My optic nerves were severely damaged at birth leaving me with only a very small amount of residual vision. My deafness was progressive from age seven and is believed to have been caused by a childhood illness – probably measles.

Why did you settle on motorized challenges as a way of setting records?
I have always had a great interest and fascination in motorcycles and the sea. I fixed and rode battered old motorbikes in my late teens. Quadbiking and jetskiing are my top two passions!

What inspires you to attempt these records?
I'm very committed to proving that, with the right attitude and support, deafblindness is no barrier to extreme sports. All my challenges are under the auspices of the charity Deafblind UK.

What do your family and friends think about your rather risky pastime?
I think most have got used to the fact I'm a bit mad. My niece once said to me 'it's better to die on your feet than live on your knees'.

What other challenges do you face?
My greatest challenge has nothing to do with my disability directly – it's all about prejudice from others and the barriers that result.

What do you do in your free time?
DIY, such as carpentry, plumbing and mains wiring. I also enjoy socializing and reading.

TALKER

Sean Shannon (Canada) recited Hamlet's soliloquy 'To be or not to be' (260 words) in a time of 23.8 seconds (655 words/minute) at Edinburgh on 30 August 1995.

★ BALLOON DOG MADE BEHIND THE BACK

With his arms behind his back, Craig 'Blink' Keith (UK) made a balloon poodle in just 9.26 seconds on 25 May 2004.

★ LOUDEST BURP

Paul Hunn (UK) produced a burp with a decibel meter reading of 104.9 dBA at the offices of Guinness World Records, London, UK, on 20 July 2004 – louder than a pile driver heard from a distance of 30 m (100 ft). The burp was measured from a distance of 2.5 m (8 ft 2 in) and 1 m (3 ft 3 in) high, on a certified and calibrated class 1 precision measuring noise level meter.

ECCENTRIC BEHAVIOUR

★ LONGEST GUM-WRAPPER CHAIN

March 2005 marked the 40th anniversary of the beginning of Gary Duschl's (USA) record-breaking gum-wrapper chain. Since 11 March 1965, Gary has been linking together chewing-gum wrappers to create a chain that currently measures 14,037 m (46,053 ft) – longer than 125 American football fields. Gary has the chain professionally measured each year, and at the last count it comprised 1,076,656 wrappers and weighed 286 kg (633 lb), representing $53,833 of gum!

FASTEST TIME TO TYPE FROM 1 TO 1 MILLION

Les Stewart (Australia) typed the numbers one to one million in words, manually, from 1982 to December 1998. His aim to become a 'millionaire' cost him seven typewriters, 1,000 ink ribbons and 19,900 sheets of paper. Les, left partially paralysed after a tour of duty in Vietnam, typed with just one finger.

GREATEST DISTANCE WALKED BACKWARDS

The greatest ever exponent of reverse pedestrianism was Plennie L Wingo (USA, b. 24 January 1895), who completed his 12,875-km (8,000-mile) trans-continental walk from Santa Monica, California, USA, to Istanbul, Turkey, from 15 April 1931 to 24 October 1932.

LONGEST DURATION TO STAND MOTIONLESS

Om Prakash Singh (India) stood motionless for 20 hr 10 min 6 sec at Allahabad, India, on 13–14 August 1997.

LONGEST DURATION BALANCING ON ONE FOOT

Arulanantham Suresh Joachim (Sri Lanka) balanced on one foot for 76 hr 40 min from 22 to 25 May 1997. Under the rules, the disengaged foot cannot be rested on the standing foot and no object can be used for support or balance.

LONGEST DISTANCE WALKING ON HANDS

In 1900, Johann Hurlinger (Austria) walked on his hands for 1,400 km (870 miles). He walked from Vienna, Austria, to Paris, France, in 55 daily 10-hour stints at an average speed of 2.54 km/h (1.58 mph).

HEAVIEST VEHICLE PULLED BY HAIR

On 1 May 1999 at Bruntingthorpe Proving Ground, Leicestershire, UK, Letchemanah Ramasamy (Malaysia) pulled a long version Routemaster double-decker bus weighing 7,874 kg (17,359 lb) for a total distance of 30 m (98 ft) using only his hair.

LONGEST BANZAI SKYDIVE

Yasuhiro Kubo (Japan) jumped from a plane at an altitude of

← FASTEST FURNITURE

Edd China (pictured) and David Davenport (both UK) design and build the world's fastest furniture, including bathroom suites and four-poster beds. The fastest to date is the 'Casual Lofa', a motorized sofa with a top speed of 140 km/h (87 mph). Powered by a Mini 1300-cc (79-cu-in) engine, it is licensed for use on UK roads and has covered 10,008.5 km (6,219 miles) since it was built.

3,000 m (9,842 ft) without a parachute and in 50 seconds hooked on to a parachute that was thrown out prior to his jump on 2 September 2000 in Davis, California, USA.

LONGEST LAWNMOWER RIDE

Gary Hatter (USA) drove 23,487.5 km (14,594.5 miles) in 260 consecutive days on a lawnmower. Hatter started his drive in Portland, Maine, USA, on 31 May 2000 and passed through all 48 contiguous US states, as well as Canada and Mexico, before arriving in Daytona Beach, Florida, on 14 February 2001.

★ MOST COUNTRIES VISITED BEFORE RETURNING TO COUNTRY OF DEPARTURE

Mariea Crasmaru left her home in Bucharest, Romania, on 18 March 1997 and visited 102 countries and seven continents, creating a passport of 154 pages. Travelling 300,000 km (186,411 miles), she reached as far north as Murmansk in Russia (69°N), and as far south as the Marambio Research Base in Antarctica (64°S), but had to sell her home half way through her trip for funding. Along the way, she learnt six languages and received eight marriage proposals!

MOST SCORPIONS EATEN

Rene Alvarenga (El Salvador) has eaten an estimated 35,000 live scorpions. He catches them with his bare hands and eats them at a rate of 20–30 a day.

MONSIEUR MANGETOUT

Michel Lotito of Grenoble, France, known as Monsieur Mangetout, has been eating metal and glass since 1959.

Why did you start?
I started to practise sophrology [literally 'the science or study of the tranquil mind', a combination of self-hypnosis and other relaxation techniques that can assist pain control] when I was eight. At the age of 16, I accidentally broke a glass while drinking, and I had a piece in my mouth. I knew other people had eaten glass in the past and decided that I could do it as well. Then I moved on to razor blades, plates and small pieces of metal such as nuts and bolts.

Did you eat bigger things too?
Yes, people started to ask me if I wanted to eat something bigger and so I said, 'OK, I think I can eat a bicycle.' It was a great success – they called me for TV shows in South America and Canada.

Does this mean you can actually digest metal?
My teeth are incredibly strong – their strength has been measured at eight tonnes per cm². But I also secrete strong juices that cause razor blades to begin to melt in my mouth; my gastric juices are so powerful that, during an endoscopy, doctors observed juices attacking objects with a corrosive foam that ate the metal.

Did you receive medical guidance during attempts?
Yes, I would always ask for a doctor's assistance. They would give me all sorts of advice, such as to eat artichokes or paraffin oils together with metal to make things easier, but I soon realized that I was better off simply drinking several litres of water.

LONGEST TIME POLE-SITTING

The monk St Simeon the Stylite (c. AD 386–459) spent around 39 years on a stone pillar on the Hill of Wonders, near Aleppo, Syria. His motivation was self-persecution for people's sins and to be closer to God. He only came down on one occasion – so that the pole could be extended from 12 to 18 m (39 to 59 ft).

★ LONGEST TIME SPENT IN AN ATTIC

Stephan Kovaltchuk spent 57 years in his attic in Montchintsi, Ukraine, before emerging at the age of 75 in 1999 because his sister, who had looked after him, had died. He originally went into hiding from Nazis who had occupied Ukraine in 1942, but remained in isolation to avoid the draft by the Red Army after Russia's victory over Germany.

LONGEST FRENCH KNITTING

Edward Peter Hannaford (UK) has produced a piece of French knitting 18.7 km (11.62 miles) long since he began working on it in April 1989.

MOST SPLITS TO A SINGLE HUMAN HAIR

The greatest reported achievement in hair splitting has been that of Alfred West (UK), who succeeded in splitting a human hair 17 times, into 18 parts, on eight occasions.

Alfred learned how to set a razor during World War I when he worked on wooden component parts for aircraft. Later, he took his talents to unprecedented heights, creating elaborate works of art – including models of a boa constrictor, a monarch's crown and Epping Forest – out of split hairs.

SHARING A BATHTUB WITH THE MOST RATTLESNAKES

Jackie Bibby (pictured) and Rosie Reynolds-McCasland (both USA) jointly hold the record of having sat in two separate tubs each with 75 live Western Diamondback rattlesnakes on the set of *Guinness World Records: Primetime* on 24 September 1999 in Los Angeles, USA.

GAMES & PASTIMES

← HULA HOOPS:
MOST HOOPED SIMULTANEOUSLY

Alesya Goulevich (Belarus) was able to hula hoop with 99 hoops at the Big Apple Circus Big Top, Bayside Expo Center, Boston, Massachusetts, USA, on 26 April 2004. As per the guidelines, Goulevich sustained three full revolutions of the standard hula hoops between her shoulders and her hips.

CHESS: MOST MOVES IN A GAME

Chess masters Goran Arsovic and Ivan Nikolic (both Yugoslavia, now Serbia and Montenegro) played a game with 269 moves on 17 February 1989. The drawn game was played in Belgrade, Yugoslavia (now Serbia and Montenegro), and took 20 hr 15 min.

★ CASINOS: MOST PLAYED IN 24 HOURS

On 29–30 March 2004, brothers Martin and David Lawrance Hallgarth (both UK) visited 55 casinos in 24 hours in Las Vegas, Nevada, USA.

CHESS: LONGEST CORRESPONDENCE GAME

Dr Reinhart Straszacker and Dr Hendrik Roelof van Huyssteen (both South Africa) played their first game of correspondence chess in 1946. After 112 matches – and with both men having won half the games each – their record play of over 53 years ended with the death of Straszacker on 13 October 1999.

★ CHESS: MOST GAMES SIMULTANEOUSLY

International Chess Master Andrew Martin (UK) played against 321 different opponents at Wellington College, Berkshire, UK, on 21 February 2004. Martin won 294 games, drew 26 and lost only one. The attempt took 16 hr 51 min.

CHESS: HIGHEST RATINGS

The highest rating in chess by a male player is 2,851, achieved by Garry Kasparov (Russia) in January 2000. The **highest rating for a woman** is 2,675, achieved by Judit Polgar (Hungary) in 1996.

★ CONKERS: MOST SIMULTANEOUS MATCHES

On 14 October 2004, 143 conkers matches (286 players) were played simultaneously at the inaugural competition for the Croft City Conker Cup in London, UK.

★ CUP STACKING: FASTEST CYCLE FORMATION

Emily Fox (USA) was able to stack plastic cups in the cycle formation (a sequence of stacks combining a 3-6-3 stack, a 6-6 stack and a 1-10-1 stack, concluding with cups in a 3-6-3 tower) in a time of 7.43 seconds at Rocky Mountain Cup Stacking Championships, Colorado, USA, on 6 April 2002.

DOMINOES: MOST STACKED ON A SINGLE PIECE

Matthias Aisch (Germany) stacked 726 dominoes on a single, vertically standing supporting domino on 28 December 2003. The stack remained standing for an hour.

DOMINOES: MOST TOPPLED SINGLE-HANDEDLY

Ma Li Hua (China) single-handedly set up and toppled 303,621 dominoes at Singapore Expo Hall, Singapore, on 18 August 2003. Ma Li Hua spent an average of 10 hours daily from 7 July to 17 August setting up the dominoes. The event was organized by LG Electronics, Inc.

★ EGG & SPOON RACE: LARGEST (MULTIPLE VENUES)

The largest simultaneous egg and spoon race involved 1,277 participants racing at various venues around Herefordshire, UK, in an event organized by Ready Steady Win (UK) on 30 March 2004.

FOOTBAG WORLD RECORDS

A footbag (or hackey sack) is a small bag filled with plastic pellets that is kept aloft for as long as possible using the feet...

Consecutive kicks (men's singles)	63,326	Ted Martin (USA) 8 hr 50 min 42 sec	14 June 1997
Consecutive kicks (women's singles)	24,713	Constance Constable (USA) 4 hr 9 min 27 sec	18 April 1998
Consecutive kicks (doubles)	132,011	Gary Lautt, Tricia George (USA)	21 March 1998
Most kicks in 5 minutes	1,019	Andy Linder (USA)	7 June 1996
Consecutive kicks with two footbags	68	Juha-Matti Rytilahti (Finland)	30 September 2001
Most participants	964	Cornerstone Festival, Illinois, USA	6 July 2001

← JIGSAW PUZZLE:
LARGEST (NON-COMMERCIAL)

The world's largest jigsaw puzzle measured 5,428.8 m² (58,435.1 ft²) and consisted of 21,600 pieces. Devised by Great East Asia Surveyors & Consultants Co. Ltd, it was assembled by 777 people at the former Kai Tak airport, Hong Kong, China, on 3 November 2002.

JIGSAW PUZZLE: MOST PIECES

A puzzle with 212,323 pieces, measuring 10.8 x 11.68 m (35 ft 5 in x 38 ft 3 in), was completed by the Yew Tee CC Youth Executive Committee, Singapore History Museum and members of the public during an event for the Youth Discovery Challenge 2002 in Singapore on 29 June 2002.

LEGO: LARGEST FLAG

A Lego flag measuring 7.72 m x 10.4 m (25 ft 4 in x 34 ft 1.5 in) was made at the Franklin Institute Science Museum on 22 August 2001 to celebrate the hosting of the X Games in Philadelphia, Pennsylvania, USA.

LEGO: LONGEST STRUCTURE

Over 20,000 children built a Lego structure in the shape of a millipede measuring 1,398 m (4,586.6 ft) in Montréal, Quebec, Canada, on 15 August 2004 in an event organized by Lego Canada.

GO: MOST GAMES SIMULTANEOUSLY

In total, 1,000 players played 500 games of Go simultaneously at Take-machi-dohri and Chuo-cho Shopping Streets, Oita, Japan, on 6 June 1999.

HOT WHEELS: LONGEST TRACK

The longest Hot Wheels track measured 502.92 m (1,650 ft) and consisted of 2,100 pieces of track. The attempt, organized by Mattel Canada, Inc., for Big Brothers Big Sisters of Canada, was completed on 7 July 2002 at Thunder Alley, Toronto, Ontario, Canada.

★ HULA HOOP: FASTEST MILE

Ashrita Furman (USA) walked a mile while continuously hula hooping in 14 min 25 sec at Moskvoretskaya, Naberezhnaya, Moscow, Russia, on 31 May 2004.

★ HULA HOOP: LARGEST SPUN

On 1 January 2004, Nozomi Tsuji and Ai Kago (both Japan) hula hooped with a 4.08-m-wide (13-ft 4.6-in) hoop for 30 seconds each at the Nippon Television Network studios in Tokyo, Japan.

JENGA: FASTEST 30 LEVELS

The fastest time to build a stable tower of Jenga bricks 30 levels high – and within the official rules of the game – is 11 min 55 sec by Sabrina Ibrahim, John Chua and Alex Agboola (all UK) on the *Big Toe Radio Show*, London, UK, on 28 January 2003.

★ DOMINOES:
MOST TOPPLED BY A GROUP →

The greatest number of dominoes set up and toppled by a team is 3,992,397 during Domino Day 2004 in Leeuwarden, the Netherlands, on 12 November 2004. A team of 81 from the Netherlands, Germany, France, Spain, Poland, Estonia, Lithuania, Hungary, Czech Republic, Sweden, Austria and Slovakia created 46 themed but connected projects covering an area of 85 x 90 m (278 x 295 ft).

GAMES & PASTIMES

★ PARACHUTE: MOST GAMES SIMULTANEOUSLY

On 17 January 2004, the Chinese YMCA at Wu Kwai Shai Youth Village, Hong Kong, China, organized a record 21 simultaneous games of parachute with 510 participants. Players had to complete four different disciplines with the parachutes, including raising it from the ground and lowering it until taut four consecutive times, and controlling a ball around the parachute in both a clockwise and anticlockwise circle.

★ LOTTERY: LARGEST INDIVIDUAL WIN

Andrew 'Jack' Whittaker Jr (USA) won $314.9 million (then £197.4 million) in the Powerball jackpot on 24 December 2002. He decided to take just over half the prize as a lump sum – $170 million (then £106 million) before taxes – instead of the full prize in 30 annual installments.

★ LEGO: TALLEST STRUCTURE

A Lego tower constructed at Legoland in Carlsbad, California, USA, reached a height of 28.19 m (92 ft 6 in) on 21 February 2005.

★ MINIATURE GOLF: MOST HOLES IN 24 HOURS

Matt Majikas (USA) played 3,035 holes of miniature golf in 24 hours at Mulligan's Miniature Golf, Sterling, Massachusetts, USA, on 26–27 May 2004. The 18-hole course was 334 m (1,097 ft) long, and Matt played the whole course nearly 169 times in 24 hours – a total distance of more than 54 km (33 miles).

MONOPOLY: LARGEST PERMANENT GAME

A granite Monopoly board measuring 9.44 x 9.44 m (31 x 31 ft) was opened to the public on 26 July 2002 in San Jose, California, USA. The tokens, dice, houses and hotels are all in proportion.

PIGGY BACK RACE: FASTEST 100 M

The record for the fastest piggy back race over 100 m is 19.6 seconds, set by Andrew Gadd carrying Lance Owide (both UK) at Kings Langley, Hertfordshire, UK, on 31 August 2003.

PLAYING CARDS: HOUSE OF CARDS WITH MOST STOREYS

On 6 November 1999, Bryan Berg (USA) built a free-standing house of playing cards that stood 131 storeys high and 7.71 m (25 ft 3.6 in) tall. Made from 91,800 standard cards, it was built in the lobby of the casino at Potsdamer Platz, Berlin, Germany, and filmed for the *Guinness – die Show der Rekorde* TV show.

★ POGO STICK: MOST ROPE SKIPS IN ONE MINUTE

Ashrita Furman (USA) made 156 jumps over a skipping rope on a pogo stick in one minute at Yellowstone National Park, Wyoming, USA, on 25 September 2004. He also holds the record for the **fastest mile on a pogo stick**: he took 12 min 16 sec to travel a mile at Iffley Field, Oxford, UK, on 24 July 2001.

★ RUBIK'S CUBE: FASTEST SOLVE

Shotaro Makisumi (Japan) solved a Rubik's cube puzzle in 12.11 seconds at the Caltech Fall tournament, Pasadena, California, USA, on 16 October 2004.

At the same event, Shotaro also set the record for the **★ fastest average time to solve a Rubik's cube in competition**, which he achieved in a time of 14.52 seconds.

Finally, Shotaro is also the holder of the record for the **★ fastest time to solve a Rubik's cube blindfolded**. He achieved this feat in a time of 3 min 10.54 sec at the same event in Pasadena, California, USA, on 16 October 2004.

Shotaro currently holds all the Guinness World Records for manipulation of a Rubik's cube.

SACK RACE: MOST COMPETITORS

A total of 2,095 competitors took part in a sack race involving pupils from Agnieton College and primary school pupils from Zwolle, Wezep and Hattem on 11 October 2002 in Zwolle, the Netherlands.

★ SKIPPING ROPE: MOST IN ONE MINUTE

S Namasivayam (India) achieved 234 skips at Indira Gandhi Stadium, Pondicherry, India, on 3 July 2004.

TIDDLYWINKS: FASTEST POTTING OF 10,000

Allen R Astles (UK) potted 10,000 winks in 3 hr 51 min 46 sec at Aberystwyth, Ceredigion, UK, in February 1966.

Tiddlywinks is a child's game (but often played by adults in competition) that involves flipping a wink – a small plastic counter – into a pot by pressing down on to its edge with a larger counter known as a squidger.

TIDDLYWINKS: FASTEST MILE

Edward Wynn and James Cullingham (both UK) achieved the fastest tiddlywink mile – i.e., they covered the whole distance by means of flipping wink shots – in 52 min 10 sec in Stradbroke, Suffolk, UK, on 31 August 2002.

PLAYING CARDS: FASTEST DECK RE-ARRANGEMENT

Kunihiko Terada (Japan) arranged a shuffled deck of cards in order (ace through ten, jack, queen, king for diamonds, clubs, hearts and spades) in his hands in 40.36 seconds at the Hard Rock Café, Tokyo, Japan, on 25 January 2004.

TIDDLYWINKS: FARTHEST DISTANCE TRAVELLED IN 24 HOURS

Advancing only by means of flipping wink shots, Sean Booth and Barry Green (both UK) travelled from Bacup to Rawtenstall, Lancashire, UK, on 22 November 2003 – a distance of 3.9 km (2.4 miles).

TUNNEL BALL: MOST PLAYERS

A total of 60 pupils from St Columba's School, Wilston, Queensland, Australia, took part in a single game of tunnel ball on 27 November 2002.

TWISTER: LARGEST BOARD

In February 1998, a single Twister sheet measuring 18.28 x 6 m (60 x 20 ft) was manufactured by Vision International of Salt Lake City, Utah, USA.

WHEELBARROW RACE: FASTEST 100 M

On 31 August 2003, Andrew Gadd (pushing the wheelbarrow) and Freddie Gadd (riding) covered 100 m in 18.1 seconds, at Framptons, Kings Langley, UK.

YO-YO: LARGEST

A yo-yo measuring 3.17 m (10 ft 4 in) in diameter and weighing 407 kg (897 lb) was devised by J N Nichols (Vimto) Ltd and made by engineering students at Stockport College, UK. On 1 August 1993, in Manchester, UK, it was launched by crane from a height of 57.5 m (188 ft 7 in) and yo-yo-ed about four times.

★ YO-YO: MOST TRICKS IN ONE MINUTE

Hans Van Dan Helzen (USA) completed 51 yo-yo tricks in one minute on the set of *Blue Peter*, London, UK, on 17 May 2004.

RUSSIAN NESTING DOLLS: LARGEST SET

Youlia Bereznitskaia (Russia) has hand-painted a 51-piece set of nesting dolls (matrioshkas). The largest is 54 cm (1 ft 9.25 in) high and the smallest is 0.31 cm (0.12 in) high. The set was completed on 25 April 2003.

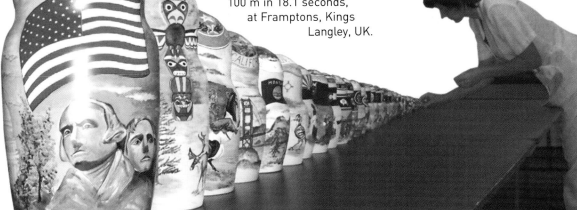

FANTASTIC FOODS

MOST EXPENSIVE
← COFFEE

Only 500 lb (227 kg) of Kopi Luwak coffee is available every year, and it sells for £215 ($300) per pound (0.45 kg). The price reflects the manner in which it is processed: the beans are collected from the excrement of the Sumatran civet cat (*Paradoxurus*), which lives in the mountain ranges of Irian Jaya, Indonesia. The civet climbs into the coffee trees and eats the ripest coffee cherries it can find. Eventually these are digested and reappear in the animal's excrement, after which they are gathered by locals and sold as coffee.

★ MOST EXPENSIVE OMELETTE

The most expensive omelette commercially available is the Zillion Dollar Lobster Frittata, which costs $1,000 (£528.90) and is featured on the menu at Norma's restaurant, Le Parker Meridien Hotel, New York City, USA.

LARGEST...

★ BLACK FOREST GATEAU
Spanhacke's (Germany) created a 7-m-wide (23-ft) giant gateau weighing 2.5 tonnes (5,511 lb) and displayed it at the Vielstedter Bauernhaus restaurant in Hude, Germany, on 17 August 2003.

CANDY
A butterscotch candy made by Nidar (Norway) in August 1997 weighed 1.6 tonnes (3,527 lb).

The ★ **longest candy** is a 1-tonne (2,204-lb) strawberry-sour belt made by Candy Castle (Netherlands) that stretched 2,004 m (6,574 ft) when unrolled in 's-Heerenberg, the Netherlands, on 28 August 2004.

★ CHOCOLATE
In February 2004, The Hard Rock Café in Madrid, Spain, exhibited a single heart-shaped chocolate weighing 6.816 tonnes (15,026 lb). It measured 5 m (16 ft) wide and 4 m (13 ft) high, and was created by www.match.com with Marco de Comunicación (Spain).

★ MUG OF COFFEE
A mug with 3,002 litres (660.5 gal; 793.04 US gal) of latte was created by Nestlé and unveiled in New York City, USA, on 13 May 2004. The mug was 1.69 m (5 ft 7 in) tall, had a diameter of 1.41 m (4 ft 8 in) and required 20 kg (45 lb) of coffee.

★ FUDGE
NorthwestFudgeFactory.com (Canada) made a 1.235-tonne (3,010-lb) slab of maple and chocolate fudge for the FedNor Pavilion Royal Winter Fair, Toronto, Canada, on 5 November 2004. The fudge measured 4.87 x 2.43 m (16 x 8 ft) and was 10.16 cm (4 in) high.

★ HOT CROSS BUN
Manna European Bakery & Deli (Canada) baked a hot cross bun weighing 52.08 kg (114 lb 13.5 oz) on 16 April 2004 in aid of the Canadian Cancer Society.

★ ICE-CREAM CAKE
Carvel (USA) made a giant ice-cream cake weighing 5.48 tonnes (12,096 lb) and displayed it on 25 May 2004 at Union Square Park, New York City, USA, to celebrate the company's 70th birthday.

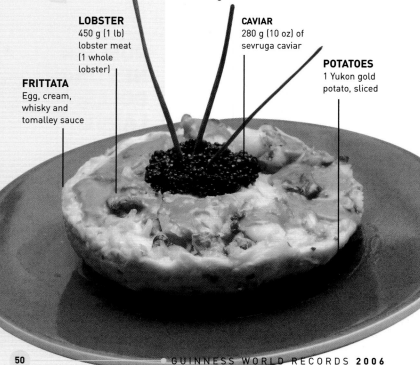

LOBSTER
450 g (1 lb) lobster meat (1 whole lobster)

FRITTATA
Egg, cream, whisky and tomalley sauce

CAVIAR
280 g (10 oz) of sevruga caviar

POTATOES
1 Yukon gold potato, sliced

MOST EXPENSIVE FOOD & DRINK

If money is no object, why not indulge yourself with the world's most costly food and drink?

Item	Place / Description	Price
★ Hamburger*	Bistro Moderne, New York City, USA *db Double Truffle*	$120 (£64.70)
Cocktail*	Hemingway Bar, Paris Ritz, France *Ritz Side Car*	€400 (£277.25; $528.52)
Fruit	Helpston Garden Centre, Cambridge, UK. *A single grape*	£700 ($1,040)
Wine (bottle)*	*Chateau d'Yquem Sauternes, 1787*	$60,000 (£31,402)
Wine (bottle)	Christie's, London, UK *Château Lafite claret, 1787*	£105,000 ($156,030)
Wine (glass)	Pickwick's Pub, Beaune, France *Beaujolais Nouveau, 1993*	FF8,600 (£982; $1,601.34)
Spirit (bottle)	Fortnum & Mason, London, UK *60-year-old Macallan whisky*	£11,000 ($15,662.7)
Chocolate bar	Christie's, London, UK *A bar of Cadbury's chocolate from Captain Robert Scott's (UK) 1901 Antarctic expedition*	£470 ($687)
★ Truffle	Alba, Italy *1.08-kg (2.4-lb) white truffle, 2004*	$41,000 (£22,000)
Wedding cake (piece)	Sotheby's, New York City, USA *The Duke & Duchess of Windsor's (UK) wedding cake, 1937*	$29,900 (£18,163)

*Commercially available

⭐ LONGEST HOT DOG

Students from the University of Pretoria, South Africa, made a hot dog measuring 10.5 m (34 ft 5.25 in), smashing the previous record of 6.9 m (22 ft 8 in) set in August 2002. The single, unbroken sausage – nearly 60 times the length of a regular hot dog – was displayed at the Sonop Hostel in Pretoria, South Africa, on 18 October 2003. To cook their record-breaking wiener, the students had to design and build their own charcoal oven and *braai* (barbecue).

2003 10 18

⭐ JAWBREAKER
Nick Calderaro (Canada), an employee of Oak Leaf Confection (Canada), made a jawbreaker candy with a circumference of 94.6 cm (37.25 in). It weighed 12.6 kg (27.8 lb) and took 476 hours to make between 7 January and 29 May 2003.

⭐ PASTA
A bowl holding 3,336 kg (7,355 lb) of pasta was made for *The Keeler Show* (USA) in conjunction with Tony's Pizzeria at the Sangerton Square Mall, Hartford, New York, USA, on 14 February 2004. The TV show sponsored a contest in which one 'lucky couple' was married inside the giant bowl of macaroni.

⭐ POTATO CRISPS (BAG)
On 11 March 2004, Seabrook Potato Crisps of Bradford, West Yorkshire, UK, unveiled a giant packet containing 51.35 kg (113 lb 3 oz) of salted crinkle-cut crisps. The bag measured 1.79 m (5.87 ft) high, 1.21 m (3.96 ft) wide and 0.62 m (2.03 ft) deep – and held over 275,000 calories-worth of crisp!

⭐ PRETZEL
A 272-kg (599-lb) pretzel was made by Die Wethje GmbH Kunstostofftechnik (Germany) on 30 January 2004 and exhibited in Hengersberg, Germany.

⭐ SANDWICH
A ham, cheese and mayonnaise sandwich weighing 2.403 tonnes (5,297 lb) was made by Grupo Bimbo (Mexico) in conjunction with McCormick, Fud, Chalet and Pétalo Jumbo in the Zócalo, Mexico City, Mexico, on 24 April 2004. The filling comprised 445 kg (981 lb) of ham, 367 kg (809 lb) of cheese, 67 kg (147 lb) of mayo and 37 kg (81 lb) of lettuce.

⭐ STIR-FRY
TV chef Nancy Lam (Singapore) stir-fried a 700-kg (1,543-lb) dish of cabbage, carrots, baby corn, pak choi and bean sprouts on 23 January 2004 in Leicester Square, London, UK, in aid of the National Children's Home charity.

⭐ MOST EXPENSIVE
ICE-CREAM SUNDAE

The Serendipity Golden Opulence Sundae – introduced to the menu of the Serendipity 3 restaurant, New York City, USA, in September 2004 to celebrate the restaurant's 50th anniversary – cost $1,000 (£528.90).

GILDED FLOWERS
Candied flowers covered in edible gold leaf

CAVIAR
Grande Passion caviar with Armagnac and the juice of blood oranges and passion fruit

ICE-CREAM
Five scoops of Tahitian vanilla-bean ice-cream covered in 23-carat edible gold leaf

EXOTIC CANDIED FRUITS
Pineapple, figs, star fruit and prickly pear

GOLD DRAGETS
12 almonds with gold leaf

CHOCOLATE
'Amedei Porceleana' and 'Chuao' chocolate, chunked, flaked and melted

GOLD SPOON
Eat with a spoon of 18-carat gold and mother-of-pearl inlay

CRYSTAL
Served in a Baccarat Harcourt crystal goblet

BODY MODIFICATION

GUINNESS WORLD RECORDS

LONGEST NECKS

The maximum known extension of a human neck is 40 cm (15.75 in) and was created by the successive fitting of copper coils, as practised by the women of the Padaung or Kareni tribe of Myanmar as a sign of beauty. Their necks eventually become so long and weak that they cannot support their heads without the coils. In some tribes the coils are removed to punish women who have committed adultery.

★ MOST PLASTIC SURGERY

Cindy Jackson (USA) has spent $99,600 (£53,148) on 47 cosmetic operations since 1988. These include three full facelifts; two eye lifts; liposuction; two nose operations; thigh, knee, waist, abdomen and jaw-line surgery; lip and cheek implants, chemical peels, chin bone reduction and semi-permanent make-up.

★ MOST POPULAR COSMETIC OPERATIONS

According to a survey of 46 countries, the ★ **most popular** *non-surgical aesthetic* **procedure** performed in 2003 was Botox injections, representing 14.73% of all aesthetic plastic surgeries performed. The ★ **most popular** *surgical aesthetic procedure* was blepharoplasty (eyelid reshaping), at 10.89%.

MOST BODY PIERCINGS IN ONE SESSION

Kam Ma (UK) received a total of 600 new piercings to his body without the aid of an anaesthetic. All piercings were executed by Charlie Wilson (UK) in one continuous session from 9.15 a.m. to 5.47 p.m. at Sunderland Body Art, Tyne and Wear, UK, on 26 May 2002.

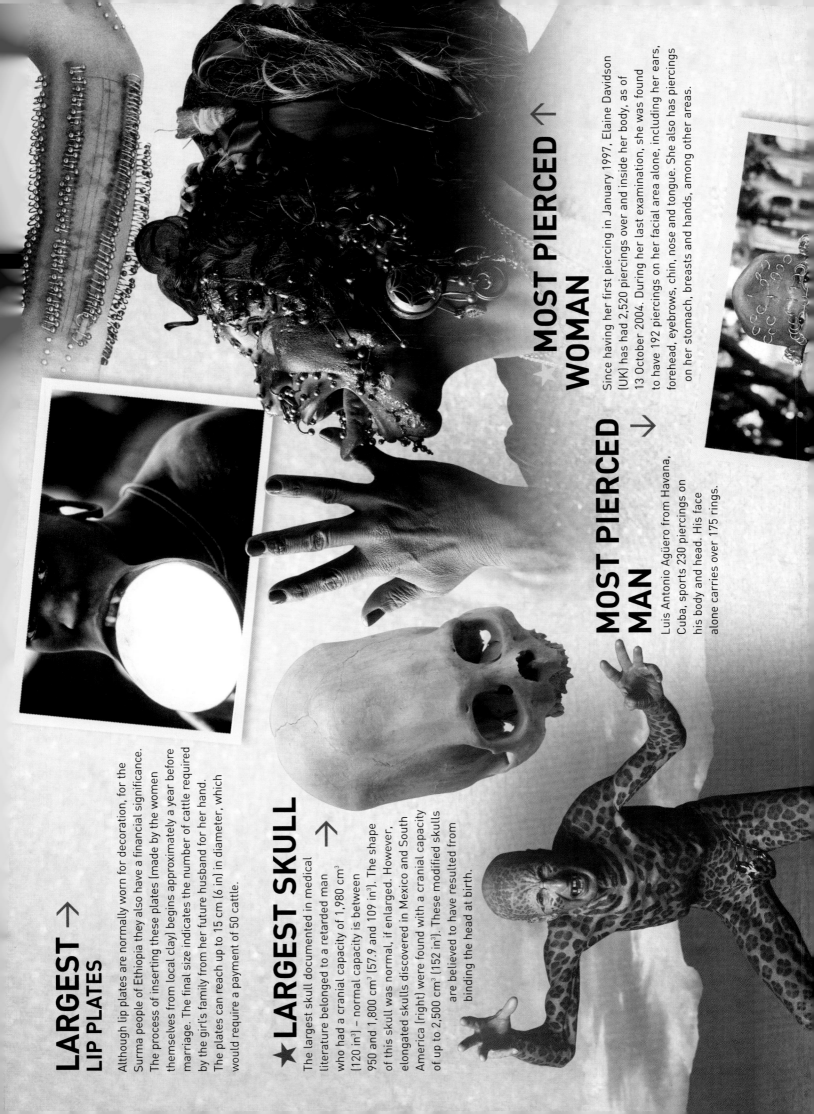

LARGEST → LIP PLATES

Although lip plates are normally worn for decoration, for the Surma people of Ethiopia they also have a financial significance. The process of inserting these plates (made by the women themselves from local clay) begins approximately a year before marriage. The final size indicates the number of cattle required by the girl's family from her future husband for her hand. The plates can reach up to 15 cm (6 in) in diameter, which would require a payment of 50 cattle.

★ LARGEST SKULL

The largest skull documented in medical literature belonged to a retarded man who had a cranial capacity of 1,980 cm³ (120 in³) – normal capacity is between 950 and 1,800 cm³ (57.9 and 109 in³). The shape of this skull was normal, if enlarged. However, elongated skulls discovered in Mexico and South America (right) were found with a cranial capacity of up to 2,500 cm³ (152 in³). These modified skulls are believed to have resulted from binding the head at birth.

MOST PIERCED ↑ WOMAN

Since having her first piercing in January 1997, Elaine Davidson (UK) has had 2,520 piercings over and inside her body, as of 13 October 2004. During her last examination, she was found to have 192 piercings on her facial area alone, including her ears, forehead, eyebrows, chin, nose and tongue. She also has piercings on her stomach, breasts and hands, among other areas.

MOST PIERCED MAN

↓

Luis Antonio Agüero from Havana, Cuba, sports 230 piercings on his body and head. His face alone carries over 175 rings.

ACTUAL SIZE

LARGEST MOTH

The world's largest moth, in terms of overall size, is the atlas moth (*Attacus atlas*), which is native to south-east Asia. Its wing-span alone is 30 cm (12 in), and it is often mistaken for a bird. Atlas moths have no mouth, and consequently live only for about four days, relying on their fatty deposits.

HEAVIEST INSECTS

The heaviest insects are the goliath beetles (family Scarabaeidae) of equatorial Africa. The largest are *Goliathus regius*, *G. meleagris*, *G. goliathus* (*G. giganteus*) and *G. druryi*, and in measurements of one series of males (females are smaller) the lengths from the tips of the small frontal horns to the end of the abdomen were up to 11 cm (4.33 in), with weights of 70–100 g (2.5–3.5 oz).

GREEDIEST ANIMAL

The larva of the polyphemus moth (*Antheraea polyphemus*) of North America eats an amount equal to 86,000 times its own birth weight in its first 56 days. In human terms, this would be the same as a 3.2-kg (7-lb) baby taking on a staggering 273 tonnes (602,000 lb) of nourishment!

MOST TATTOOED MAN

Tom Leppard (UK, pictured) and Lucky Rich (Australia) have both had 99.9% of their bodies covered with tattoos. Tom has a leopard skin design, with all the skin between the dark spots tattooed saffron yellow. Lucky Rich has had his existing tattoos blacked over with a white design tattooed on top.

★ MOST GENDER REASSIGNMENT SURGERY

Fulvia Celica Siguas Sandoval (Peru) has had 64 surgical operations since December 1979 to complete gender reassignment (sex change). Of these, over 25 have been to her face and neck, with other alterations including ear reductions, arm liposuction and transformations to her legs. Fulvia, a TV clairvoyant, hit the headlines in 1998 when she registered as a candidate in the mayoral elections in Lima, Peru.

★ LONGEST EARLOBES

The practice of ear elongation, thought to have been used since the Neolithic period (around 8000–6000 BC), can still be found today carried out by tribes of south and south-east Asia. Traditionally associated with either a long life, beauty or cultural identity, stretched lobes are attained by inserting earplugs or heavy rings into the lower ear – in some cases reaching a weight of 0.5 kg (1 lb) per ear. Commonly seen on Hindu and Buddhist statues, elongated earlobes are said to represent extraordinary wisdom and spiritual advancement.

← LARGEST SPIDER

The world's largest known spider is a male goliath bird-eating spider (*Theraphosa blondi*) collected by members of the Pablo San Martin Expedition at Rio Cavro, Venezuela, in April 1965. It had a record leg-span of 28 cm (11 in) – sufficient to cover a dinner plate. This species is found in the coastal rainforests of Suriname, Guyana and French Guiana, but isolated specimens have also been reported from Venezuela and Brazil.

ACTUAL SIZE

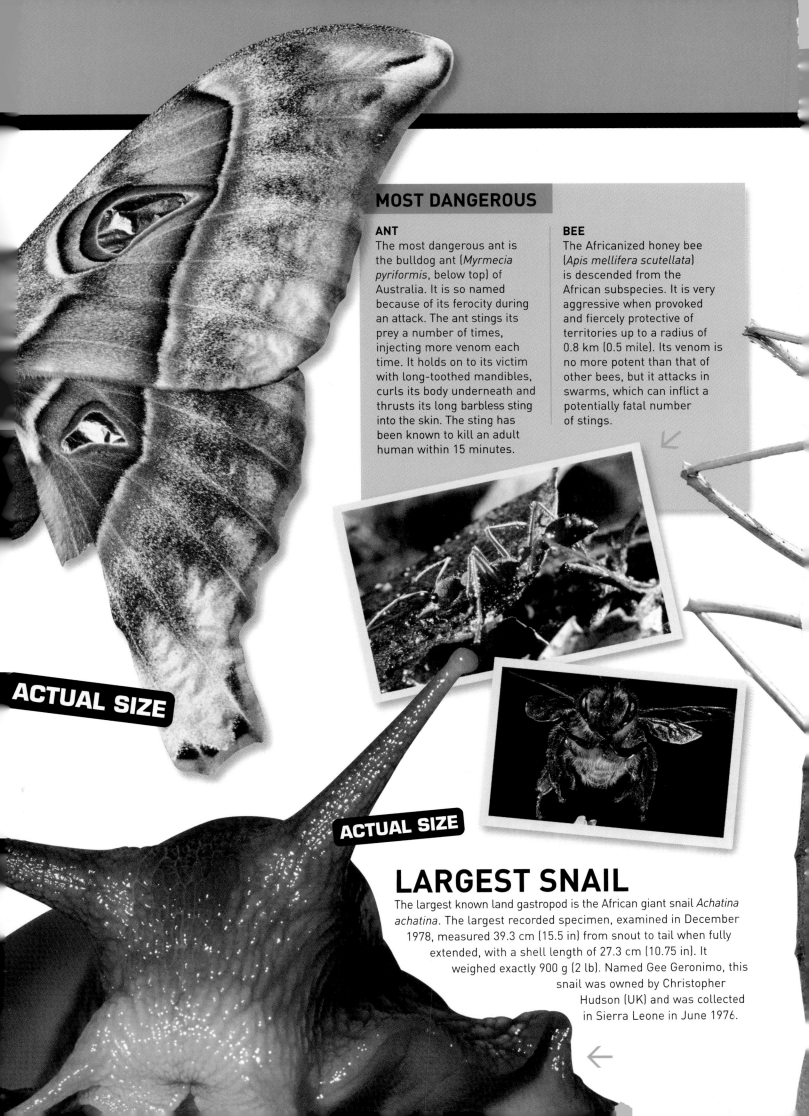

MOST DANGEROUS

ANT
The most dangerous ant is the bulldog ant (*Myrmecia pyriformis*, below top) of Australia. It is so named because of its ferocity during an attack. The ant stings its prey a number of times, injecting more venom each time. It holds on to its victim with long-toothed mandibles, curls its body underneath and thrusts its long barbless sting into the skin. The sting has been known to kill an adult human within 15 minutes.

BEE
The Africanized honey bee (*Apis mellifera scutellata*) is descended from the African subspecies. It is very aggressive when provoked and fiercely protective of territories up to a radius of 0.8 km (0.5 mile). Its venom is no more potent than that of other bees, but it attacks in swarms, which can inflict a potentially fatal number of stings.

ACTUAL SIZE

ACTUAL SIZE

LARGEST SNAIL
The largest known land gastropod is the African giant snail *Achatina achatina*. The largest recorded specimen, examined in December 1978, measured 39.3 cm (15.5 in) from snout to tail when fully extended, with a shell length of 27.3 cm (10.75 in). It weighed exactly 900 g (2 lb). Named Gee Geronimo, this snail was owned by Christopher Hudson (UK) and was collected in Sierra Leone in June 1976.

★ LARGEST LITTER OF PUPPIES

On 29 November 2004, 24 puppies were born to Tia, a Neopolitan mastiff owned by Damian Ward (UK) and Anne Kellegher (Ireland) of Manea, Cambridgeshire, UK.

SMALLEST LIVING CAT

This year, we received two claims for the world's smallest cat. The first came from the owners of Mr Peebles (pictured), who measures 15.5 cm (6.1 in) high and 49 cm (19.2 in) long. But then we heard about Itse Bitse who belongs to Mayo and Dea Whitton (both USA) – even smaller at 9.52 cm (3.75 in) high and 38.1 cm (15 in) long from nose tip to tail tip.

PET LONGEVITY

ANIMAL	NAME	RECORD AGE	AVE. AGE	OWNER	DIED
Cat	Creme Puff	37 years 6 months	10–15 years	J Perry (USA)	*alive*
Chinchilla	Bouncer	27 years	10–14 years	J Bowen (UK)	*alive*
Dog	Bluey	29 years 5 months	12–15 years	L Hall (Australia)	1939
Goldfish	Tish	43 years	20+ years	H & G Hand (UK)	1999
Guinea pig	Snowball	14 years 10.5 months	4–8 years	M A Wall (UK)	1979
Hamster	*Unnamed*	4 years 6 months	2–2.5 years	K Smeaton (UK)	*unknown*
Horse	Old Billy	62 years	25–30 years	E Robinson (UK)	1822
Mouse	Fritzy	7 years 7 months	1.5–2 years	B Beard (UK)	1985
Pony	Sancho	54 years	30 years	E Saunders (UK)	2003
Rabbit	Flopsy	18 years 10.75 months	5–10 years	L B Walker (Australia)	1982
Rat	Rodney	7 years 4 months	2–2.5 years	R Mitchell (USA)	1990

★ LONGEST DOG TUNNEL

The record for the longest human tunnel through which a dog has run involved 222 people and four dogs in an event organized by the North Northumberland Dog Training Club at The Alnwick Castle Tournament in Northumberland, UK, on 25 July 2004.

The word 'insect' – which comes from the Greek for 'to cut up' – was originally used to describe small animals that appeared to be divided or cut up into two or three parts. Members of this family usually have six legs and three body parts, and include flies, butterflies and bees. Of course, slugs and snails aren't insects, they're molluscs, and spiders are arachnids.

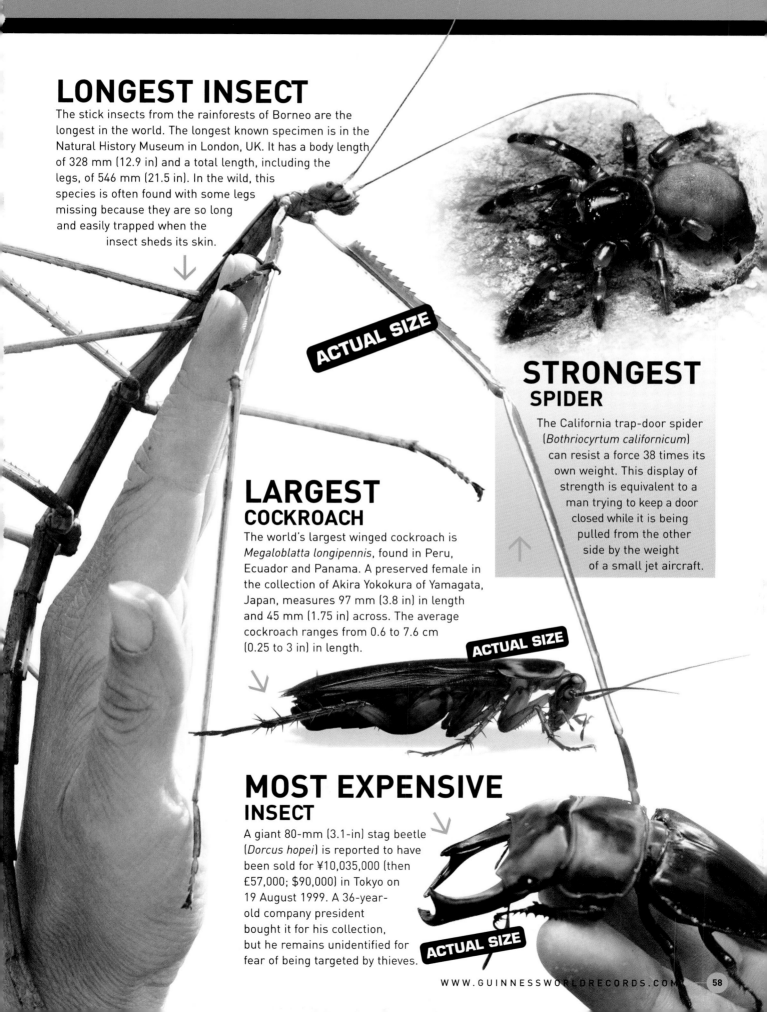

LONGEST INSECT

The stick insects from the rainforests of Borneo are the longest in the world. The longest known specimen is in the Natural History Museum in London, UK. It has a body length of 328 mm (12.9 in) and a total length, including the legs, of 546 mm (21.5 in). In the wild, this species is often found with some legs missing because they are so long and easily trapped when the insect sheds its skin.

ACTUAL SIZE

STRONGEST
SPIDER

The California trap-door spider (*Bothriocyrtum californicum*) can resist a force 38 times its own weight. This display of strength is equivalent to a man trying to keep a door closed while it is being pulled from the other side by the weight of a small jet aircraft.

LARGEST
COCKROACH

The world's largest winged cockroach is *Megaloblatta longipennis*, found in Peru, Ecuador and Panama. A preserved female in the collection of Akira Yokokura of Yamagata, Japan, measures 97 mm (3.8 in) in length and 45 mm (1.75 in) across. The average cockroach ranges from 0.6 to 7.6 cm (0.25 to 3 in) in length.

ACTUAL SIZE

MOST EXPENSIVE
INSECT

A giant 80-mm (3.1-in) stag beetle (*Dorcus hopei*) is reported to have been sold for ¥10,035,000 (then £57,000; $90,000) in Tokyo on 19 August 1999. A 36-year-old company president bought it for his collection, but he remains unidentified for fear of being targeted by thieves.

ACTUAL SIZE

PLEASE NOTE: WE DO **NOT** ACCEPT CLAIMS FOR 'HEAVIEST PET', SO PLEASE DON'T OVERFEED ANY ANIMAL IN ORDER TO CLAIM A GUINNESS WORLD RECORD

ACTUAL SIZE

HIGHEST JUMP
BY A DOG

The world record for the highest jump cleared by a dog is 167.6 cm (66 in), achieve Cinderella May A Holly Grey, a greyhound tr by Lourdes Edlin and Sally Roth and owned Kathleen Conroy and Kate Long (all USA). Th record-breaking leap was made at a dog sh in Gray Summit, Missouri, on 3 October 2003.

⭐ # SMALLEST DOG (LENGTH)

Heaven Sent Brandy, a female chihuahua belonging to Paulette Keller (USA), measured 15.2 cm (6 in) from the nose to the tip of the tail on 31 January 2005.

⭐ # SMALLEST DOG (HEIGHT) ↗

A long-haired chihuahua called Danka Kordak Slovakia – owned by Ing. Igor Kvetko (Slovakia) – measured 13.8 cm (5.4 in) tall and 18.8 cm (7.4 in) long when examined on 30 May 2004.

⭐ # LONGEST ↓
CAT WHISKERS

On 30 July 2004, a whisker belonging to Mingo, a Maine coon cat, was measured at 17.4 cm (6.8 in). Mingo lives with her owner, Marina Merne, in Turku, Finland.

ACTUAL SIZE

MOST VALENTINE
CARDS SENT TO A GUINEA PIG

Sooty, a three-year-old guinea pig from South Wales in the UK, became globally infamous in 2001 for 'romancing' 24 partners in a single evening and fathering 43 guinea piglets. On Valentine's Day that year, Sooty proved that his romantic reputation was still intact when he received over 206 cards from as far away as New Zealand.

★HIGHEST JUMP
BY A PIG

The world record for the highest jump by a pig is 70 cm (27.5 in), achieved by Kotetsu, a pot-bellied pig, on 22 August 2004 at the Mokumoku Tedsukuri Farm in Mie, Japan.

ACTUAL SIZE

★LONGEST
EARS ON A RABBIT

The longest rabbit ears measured 79 cm (31.125 in) – longer than the three pages you are now looking at – in a complete span on 1 November 2003 at the US Rabbit Breeders Association National Show in Wichita, Kansas, USA. The ears belong to an English lop called Nipper's Geronimo, owned by Waymon and Margaret Nipper (both USA).

← TALLEST HORSE

Radar, a Belgian draught horse, measured 19 hands 3.5 in (202 cm; 79.5 in), without shoes, on 27 July 2004 at the North American Belgian Championship in London, Ontario, Canada. Radar is owned by Priefert Manufacturing, Inc., of Mount Pleasant, Texas, USA.

MOST →
TENNIS BALLS
HELD IN THE MOUTH
BY A DOG

Augie, a golden retriever owned by the Miller family of Dallas, Texas, USA, successfully gathered and held a record five regulation-sized tennis balls in his mouth on 6 July 2003.

20 cm
Highest jump by a guinea pig

17.4 cm
Longest cat whiskers

13.8 cm
Smallest living dog

11.7 cm
Longest eyelashes on a dog

9.52 cm
Smallest living cat

7.11 cm
Smallest dog ever

7 cm
Smallest cat ever

4–5 cm
Smallest breed of domestic hamster

0.0 cm

FOOD FEATS

★ MOST BIG MACS CONSUMED →

Donald Gorske (USA) consumed his 20,500th McDonald's Big Mac on 27 March 2005, in his 33rd year of eating Big Macs on a daily basis. Donald is proud to declare that he has eaten Big Macs from all 50 states of the USA, at all 32 National Football League stadiums, all 30 Major League Baseball stadiums and over 30 NASCAR/ Busch racetracks.

PLAYING WITH YOUR FOOD...

★ FASTEST JELLYBEAN SORTING BY STRAW

The fastest time in which 30 Jelly Belly jellybeans have been sorted into five flavours using a drinking straw is 27.78 seconds by Richard Parry (UK) as part of the *Guinness World Records 2005 Roadshow* at the Trafford Centre, Manchester, Lancashire, UK, on 27 November 2004.

★ FARTHEST DISTANCE TO SQUIRT MILK

Ilker Yilmaz (Turkey) squirted milk from his eye across a distance of 2.795 m (9 ft 2 in) at the Armada Hotel, Istanbul, Turkey, on 1 September 2004.

★ FASTEST TIME TO EAT A RAW ONION

Brian Duffield (UK) ate a raw onion in 1 min 32 sec on the set of *The Paul O'Grady Show* at the London Television Centre, UK, on 17 November 2004. The onion weighed 212 g (7.47 oz) after preparation. The minimum weight requirement is 210 g (7.4 oz).

★ MOST BANANAS SNAPPED IN ONE MINUTE

Thomas Schuster (Germany) snapped 72 bananas in a minute at the Ravensburg town fair, Germany, on 6 September 2003.

★ MOST WATERMELONS CRUSHED WITH THE HEAD

Leonardo D'Andrea (Italy) smashed 22 watermelons with his head in one minute on the set of *Guinness World Records: 50 Years, 50 Records*, at London Television Studios, UK, on 11 September 2004.

MOST EGGS CRUSHED WITH THE TOES IN 30 SECONDS

Alan 'Nasty' Nash (UK) crushed 23 eggs with his toes on the set of *Guinness World Records: A Few Records More* in London, UK, on 11 September 2004.

★ MOST ICE-CREAM CONES PREPARED IN ONE MINUTE

Mitch Cohen (USA) prepared 18 ice-cream cones in one minute at Times Square, New York, USA, as part of ABC's *Good Morning America* TV show on 22 July 2004.

★ LARGEST CUSTARD PIE FIGHT

On 11 April 2000, 3,312 custard pies were thrown in three minutes by 20 people at the Millennium Dome in London, UK. Half a tonne (1,100 lb) of custard powder was mixed in with 1,000 litres (220 gal; 264 US gal) of water in six cement mixers to make the pies.

← ★ FASTEST TIME TO PUSH AN ORANGE 1 MILE WITH THE NOSE

Using only his nose, multiple record-holder Ashrita Furman (USA) pushed an orange 1.6 km (1 mile) in a time of 24 min 36 sec at Terminal 4 of JFK Airport, New York, USA, on 12 August 2004. The secret of Ashrita's success was partly owing to his choice of an unripe (green) orange.

WORLD'S FASTEST EATERS

FOOD	MOST EATEN IN 30 SEC	HOLDER
Ice cream	264 g (9.3 oz)	Diego Siu (USA)
★ Worms	200	C Manoharan 'Snake' Manu (India)
IN 1 MIN		
Brussels sprouts	43	Dave Mynard (UK)
Jalapeño chillis	8	Anita Crafford (South Africa)
Sausages (eaten)	8	Stefan Paladin (New Zealand)
★ Sausages (swallowed whole)	8	Cecil Walker (USA)
★ Smarties (with chopsticks)	170	Kathryn Ratcliffe (UK)
Meatballs (with cocktail stick)	27	Nick Marshall (UK)
Cockroaches	36	Ken Edwards (UK)
IN 3 MIN		
Grapes (with teaspoon)	133	Mat Hand (UK)
Hot dogs (inc. bun)	4	Peter Dowdeswell (UK)
Doughnuts (jam)	6	Steve McHugh (UK)
Doughnuts (powdered)	4	Simon Krischer, Jay Weisberger, Adam Fenton, Anthony Albelo (all USA)
★ Oysters	187	Rune Naeri (Norway)
Shrimps	272.1 g (9.6 oz)	William E Silver (USA)
Sweetcorn kernels (with cocktail stick)	236	Ian Richard Purvis (UK)
Grains of rice (with chopsticks)	64	Tae Wah Gooding (South Africa)
Tinned peas (with cocktail stick)	211	Mat Hand (UK)

★ FASTEST TIME TO EAT A 12-INCH PIZZA
Zaphod Xerxes Leigh (UK) ate a regulation-sized 12-inch pizza in 4 min 56 sec at Caffé Mamma Restaurant, Richmond, Surrey, UK, on 16 November 2003. The pizza weighed 0.34 kg (0.76 lb).

★ LONGEST PIZZA DELIVERY
On 17 November 2004, Domino's Pizza UK, in conjunction with Make-A-Wish Foundation UK, hand-delivered a pizza to the set of Australian TV show *Neighbours* in Melbourne, Victoria, Australia, from the Domino's Pizza franchise in Feltham, London, UK, a distance of 16,659 km (10,532 miles) as the crow flies.

★ FASTEST TIME TO EAT THREE CREAM CRACKERS
Ambrose Mendy (UK) ate three crackers in 37.44 seconds at the MTV Studios in Leicester Square, London, UK on 16 November 2004.

FASTEST TURKEY PLUCKER
Vincent Pilkington (Ireland) plucked a turkey in 1 min 30 sec on RTE television in Dublin, Ireland, on 17 November 1980.

...AND DRINK

★ FASTEST MILKSHAKE DRINKER
Dan Orchard (Canada) drank 500 ml (5 fl oz) of milkshake through a straw in 10 seconds as part of Nestlé's 'Grab, Gulp and Go' event at Yonge-Dundas Square, Toronto, Canada, on 18 September 2003.

★ LARGEST SHOT SLAM
A total of 1,044 students from Macquarie University, North Ryde, New South Wales, Australia, slammed spirits on 26 September 2003 to honour the founding of the university.

FASTEST TIME TO DRINK TWO PINTS OF MILK
Peter Dowdeswell (UK) drank 2 pints (1.13 litres) of milk in 3.2 seconds at Dudley Top Rank Club, West Midlands, UK, on 31 May 1975.

FASTEST TOMATO KETCHUP DRINKER
Dustin Phillips (USA) consumed 91% of a standard 396-g (14-oz) glass bottle of Heinz tomato ketchup though a 0.63-cm-wide (0.25-in) drinking straw in just 33 seconds at the studios of *Guinness World Records: Primetime* in Los Angeles, California, USA, on 23 September 1999.

★ TALLEST SUGAR CUBE TOWER
Anita Cash (UK) erected a circular tower of sugar cubes measuring 140.5 cm (55.3 in) high at the offices of *K-Zone Magazine* in Shrewsbury, Shropshire, UK, on 30 September 2003.

Henry's 30th
Caviar
Duck
Chocolate Bombe
Cheese & Wine
Birthday Cake

★ DINING OUT AT THE HIGHEST ALTITUDE
Henry Shelford, Thomas Shelford, Nakul Misra Pathak, Robert Aitken, Robert Sully (all UK), Caio Buzzolini (Australia) and appointed butler Joshua Heming (UK) enjoyed a formal meal at 6,805 m (22,326 ft) on Lhakpa Ri, Tibet, on 3 May 2004. The team carried the tables, chairs and silver cutlery as part of their expedition to celebrate Henry Shelford's 30th birthday.

COLLECTIONS

← TRAFFIC CONES

David Morgan (UK) has put together a collection of 137 traffic cones, each of them different. David – the proprietor of a plastics factory that produces more than 1 million cones each year – owns a cone from approximately two-thirds of all cone types ever made.

COLOURED VINYL RECORDS

Alessandro Benedetti (Italy) has collected 1,180 music records made of coloured vinyl. His collection comprises 866 LPs (792 coloured, 74 with pictures), 291 singles (277 coloured, 14 with pictures) and 23 in unusual shapes.

DO YOU HAVE A RECORD-BREAKING COLLECTION?

1. A record-breaking collection is based on the number of items of a particular kind that are distinguishable in some way (i.e., no two items should be the same).

2. All items should have been accumulated by an individual over a significant period of time.

3. An inventory of all items should be compiled in the presence of two witnesses. The final total should be included in the form of two independent witness statements.

4. Owing to the infinite number of items it is possible to collect, priority will be given to those that reflect proven widespread interest.

For the full details on how to register your record claim, visit www.guinnessworldrecords.com or see p.10.

★ AEROPLANE SICK BAGS

Niek Vermeulen (Netherlands) has accumulated 3,728 airline sickness bags from 802 different airlines since the 1970s. 'Somebody has to do it,' says Niek, who began collecting airsickness bags when he and a friend made a bet to see who could accumulate the most of any one item and make it into the *Guinness World Records* book.

★ AIRLINE TAGS

Raghav Somani (India) has a collection of 637 airline tags from 174 airlines around the world. Raghav started his collection in 1994.

★ BADGES

Daniel Hedges (UK) began collecting badges as a boy scout in 1994, and has since amassed a total of 13,516 different items, including badges donated personally by pop stars Madonna and Janet Jackson.

★ BAR TOWELS

Terry Sanderson (UK) has 1,815 bar towels that he has been collecting from around the world since 1997. Terry estimates that if laid out they would cover an area of 189.6 m² (2,040.8 ft²) – enough to cover at least two badminton courts!

★ BEER BOTTLES

Ron Werner (USA) has amassed a collection of 16,321 beer bottles since 1982. This includes 10,755 bottles that are still unopened.

★ CHEWING GUM PACKETS

Former art and design teacher Steve Fletcher (UK) began collecting chewing gum and bubble gum packets in 1980, following an art assignment with his pupils. Today, his collection numbers 5,100 different packets.

★ CRISP PACKETS

Bernd Sikora (Germany) owns 1,482 crisp packets from 43 countries. He has been collecting since 1993.

★ CROSSES

Since 1938, Ernie Reda (USA) of San Jose, California, has collected 13,014 individual religious crosses. Reda's home and garage also house a collection of more than 4,000 different religious artefacts and books.

CREDIT CARDS →

Walter Cavanagh (USA) has collected 1,497 individual valid credit cards. The cost of acquisition to 'Mr Plastic Fantastic' was nil, but they are worth more than $1.7 million (£912,213) in credit.

'I told my wife that my last request is to be buried with a bag of buttons, a needle, threads and a flashlight... just in case I wake up and have nothing else to do!'

Dalton Stevens, Button King

← BUTTONS

Dalton Stevens (USA) has collected 439,900 buttons with no duplicates. The 'Button King of Bishopville' suffers from chronic insomnia, and to relieve the boredom of many sleepless nights he has resorted to decorating various objects – including a car, an outhouse, a coffin, a hearse and a guitar – with buttons.

★ DICE

Kevin Cook (USA) has a collection of 11,097 dice that he has amassed since 1977. A member of the Dice Maniacs Club (aka the Random Fandom), Kevin began collecting dice from gaming shops after taking up Dungeons & Dragons. Since 1998, about 80% of his dice have been acquired from eBay, the online auction company.

★ DUMMIES (PACIFIERS)

Since 1995, Dr Muhammad Mustansar (Pakistan) of the Children's Hospital and Institute of Child Health in Lahore, Pakistan, has been collecting dummies as part of an educational movement to warn of the possible hazards of their use. The current collection comprises 1,994 dummies of different colours and shapes, each of which has been obtained from individual mothers.

★ ERASERS

Leanna Allison (USA) has accumulated 6,003 non-duplicate erasers since 1998.

★ GOLF CLUBS

Robert Lantsoght (Spain) has a collection of 4,393 individual golf clubs that he has been collecting since 1992.

HOTEL BAGGAGE LABELS

Robert Henin (USA) has collected 2,016 hotel baggage labels from different countries worldwide over the past 40 years.

★ MODEL CARS

Michael Zarnock (USA) has a collection of 3,711 Hot Wheels model cars that he has amassed since 1968, when he was a child. Michael's favourites are the replicas of cars dating from his childhood, including the '56 Ford Panel, the '65 Mustang and the '70 RoadRunner.

★ PASSPORTS

Guy Van Keer (Belgium) owns 8,110 used passports and travel documents presented in lieu of passports. They represent 130 countries and passport-issuing authorities, including many countries that no longer exist. The oldest dates back to 1615.

★ RUBBER DUCKS

Charlotte Lee (USA) has 1,439 different rubber ducks, which she has collected since 1996.

TOP 20 COLLECTIONS

The following list reveals the 20 largest collections from the Guinness World Records archives.

1.	Matchbook covers	Ed Brassard (USA)	3,159,119
2.	Human teeth	Giovanni Battista Orsenigo (Italy)	2,000,744
3.	Books (private)	John Q Benham (USA)	1,500,000
4.	Matchbox labels	Teiichi Yoshizawa (Japan)	743,512
5.	Buttons	Dalton Stevens (USA)	439,900
6.	Beer labels	Jan Solberg (Norway)	424,868
7.	Scratch cards	Darren Haake (Australia)	319,011
8.	Ballpoint pens	Angelika Unverhau (Germany)	285,150
9.	Cigar bands	Alfred Manthe (Germany)	211,104
10.	Train tickets	Frank Helker (Germany)	163,235
11.	Beer coasters	Leo Pisker (Austria)	152,860
12.	Paper and plastic bags	Heinz Schmidt-Bachem (Germany)	150,000
13.	Cigarette packets	Claudio Rebecchi (Italy)	143,027
14.	Bottle caps	Poul Høegh Poulsen (Denmark)	101,733
15.	Beer cans	William B Christensen (USA)	75,000
16.	Golf balls	Ted Hoz (USA)	74,849
17.	Four-leaf clovers	George J Kaminski (USA)	72,928
18.	Cigarette lighters	Francis Van Herle (Belgium)	58,529
19.	Fridge magnets	Louise J Greenfarb (USA)	35,000
20.	Fruit stickers	Antoine Secco (France)	34,500

★**LARGEST UNITED NATIONS**
EMERGENCY APPEAL

On 26 December 2004, a tsunami wave inundated the coastlines of at least 12 countries around the Indian Ocean, resulting in the ★ **highest death toll from a tsunami**, with up to 285,000 confirmed dead. The subsequent emergency appeal launched by the United Nations was the largest ever for a natural distaster – providing $977 million (£514 million) to five million people in southeast Asia, the Seychelles, Sri Lanka and Somalia.

→ | **CONTENTS**

← GREATEST MASS EXTINCTION

About 248 million years ago, at the end of the Permian geological period, a mass extinction wiped out approximately 90% of all marine species and 70% of all higher land animals. Factors that could have contributed to it include: comet or asteroid impact (illustrated), environmental change owing to Earth's shifting continents, and changes in the composition of the oceans.

GREATEST IMPACT

Most astronomers believe that a planet the size of Mars collided with the Earth 4.5 billion years ago. Some of the debris from this cataclysm went into orbit around the Earth and collected together under its own gravity to form the Moon. The effect of this impact would have been devastating to the Earth. The planet's crust would probably have been blasted off into space, leaving behind an Earth whose entire surface was an ocean of molten magma.

OLDEST CONFIRMED IMPACT

On 23 August 2002, a team of US scientists led by Gary Byerly (Louisiana State University) and Donald Lowe (Stanford University) announced their discovery of the impact of an asteroid on Earth 3.47 billion years ago. Geological evidence suggests that the asteroid had a diameter of around 20 km (12 miles), but no crater has been found, as Earth's geological processes have had plenty of time to erase it.

LARGEST METEORITE

A meteorite measuring 2.7 m (9 ft) long by 2.4 m (8 ft) wide, and weighing an estimated 59 tonnes (130,000 lb), was found in 1920 at Hoba West, Namibia.

★ LARGEST LUNAR METEORITE

Around 30 of the meteorites on Earth originated from the Moon. The largest is Dar al Gani 400, with a mass of 1.425 kg (3 lb 2.24 oz). It was discovered in Libya in 1998.

★ LARGEST MARTIAN METEORITE

At 18 kg (40 lb), the Zagami meteorite, which struck Earth on 3 October 1962 in a field near Zagami, Nigeria, is the largest of at least 30 meteorites known to have originated from Mars.

★ LARGEST TEKTITE

A tektite weighing 3.2 kg (7 lb) was discovered in 1932 at Muong Nong, Laos. It is now on display at the Paris Museum, France.

DEFINITIONS

Meteoroid: A tiny speck of dust, often no larger than the full stop at the end of this sentence, in orbit around the Sun.

Meteor: The shooting star caused by a meteoroid vapourizing as it enters Earth's atmosphere at speeds of around 50 km (31 miles) a second.

Meteorite: Often seen entering Earth's atmosphere as a fireball, these are larger iron or rocky chunks from space that survive to hit the ground.

Tektite: Glassy piece of rock formed during the impact of large meteorites and asteroids with the Earth's surface.

→ WHERE'S THE DEADLIEST LAKE ON EARTH? FIND OUT ON P.71

METEORITES & IMPACT CRATERS

LARGEST IMPACT CRATER

The Vredefort crater near Johannesburg, South Africa, has an estimated diameter of 300 km (186 miles) and is the largest of about 150 known impact craters. Formed 2 billion years ago when an asteroid or comet struck Earth, it is large enough to accommodate more than 270,000 tennis courts!

LARGEST ← DESERT

Nearly an eighth of the world's land surface is arid, with a rainfall of less than 25 cm (10 in) a year. The Sahara in north Africa is the largest hot desert in the world. At its greatest length it is 5,150 km (3,200 miles) from east to west, and from north to south it is between 1,280 km and 2,250 km (800–1,400 miles) long. The area covered by the desert is about 9,269,000 km² (3,579,000 miles²).

MOUNTAINS

HIGHEST MOUNTAIN
Mount Everest, in the Himalayas, is 8,848 m (29,028 ft) high, and its peak is the highest point in the world. It was first conquered in 1953 by Sherpa Tenzing Norgay (Nepal) and Sir Edmund Hillary (New Zealand).

TALLEST MOUNTAIN
Mauna Kea (White Mountain) on the island of Hawaii, USA, is the world's tallest mountain. From its submarine base in the Hawaiian Trough to its peak, it has a combined height of 10,205 m (33,480 ft), of which 4,205 m (13,796 ft) is above sea level.

★ LONGEST LINES OF SIGHT
In Alaska, USA, Mount McKinley (6,194 m; 20,320 ft) can be seen from Mount Sanford (4,949 m; 16,237 ft) – a direct distance of 370 km (230 miles).

Owing to the light-bending effects of atmospheric refraction, Vatnajökull (2,119 m; 6,952 ft), Iceland, can sometimes be seen from the Faroe Islands, some 550 km (340 miles) away.

DEEP EARTH

★ DEEPEST CAVE
The world's deepest cave is Krubera (or Voronja) beneath the Arabika Massif in Georgia. In 2004, an expedition of the Ukrainian Speleological Association explored it to a depth of 2,080 m (6,824 ft).

LARGEST CAVE
The Sarawak Chamber, Lubang Nasib Bagus, in the Gunung Mulu National Park, Sarawak, Malaysia, is 700 m (2,300 ft) long and at least 70 m (230 ft) high. Ten 747 jumbo jets, parked end to end, could be accommodated within the cave.

DEEPEST VALLEY
The Yarlung Zangbo valley, Tibet, has an average depth of 5,000 m (16,400 ft), but in 1994 explorers discovered that its deepest point was 5,382 m (17,657 ft) – three times deeper than the Grand Canyon and sufficient to house a stack of almost 10 CN Towers, the world's tallest tower.

DEEPEST NATURAL SHAFT
Vrtiglavica (meaning 'vertigo') in Monte Kanin, Slovenia, is an unbroken vertical shaft 643 m (2,110 ft) deep – enough to accommodate two Eiffel Towers.

LARGEST SINGLE CRYSTAL
Earth's inner core is a sphere of around 2,442 km (1,516 miles) in diameter, with a temperature of 5,000–6,000°C (9,000–11,000°F), and is composed mostly of iron. Many geologists believe that this gigantic ball is a single crystal with a mass of around one hundred million million million tonnes. This assumption is based on differences in the behaviour of seismic waves passing through the core in different directions.

LARGEST LIQUID BODY
Earth's liquid outer core has a width of around 1,221 km (758 miles) and a volume of about 1.719×10^{20} m^3 (60.7×10^{20} ft^3). This represents around 29.3% of Earth's mass and 16% of its volume.

EARLIEST EVIDENCE FOR PLATE TECTONICS
On 8 July 2002, a team of Chinese and US scientists announced their discovery of rocks indicating that plate tectonics were active on Earth some 2.5 billion years ago.

This is approximately 500 million years earlier than previously thought.

LONGEST MOUNTAIN RANGE ON LAND
←
The Andes in South America stretches for 7,600 km (4,700 miles) across seven countries and includes more than 50 peaks of over 6,000 m (20,000 ft) high. For most of its extent, it is around 300 km (200 miles) wide.

LONGEST ↓ NATURAL ARCH

Landscape Arch (below) in Arches National Park, and Kolob Arch in Zion National Park – both in Utah, USA – stand over openings 94.5 m (310 ft) wide. Landscape Arch is the more dramatic, as it spans an open gully and narrows to only 5 m (16 ft) thick.

The **highest natural arch** – Rainbow Bridge in Lake Powell National Monument, Utah – is just 82.3 m (270 ft) long but rises to a height of 88 m (290 ft) – nearly twice the height of the Statue of Liberty.

★ LARGEST SWAMP →

The Pantanal in the states of Mato Grosso and Mato Grosso do Sul in Brazil is the world's largest tract of swamp, covering an area of 109,000 km² (42,000 miles²). The diverse areas of the swamp include rivers and lakes, seasonally flooded grasslands, forests and wetlands. During the wet season, heavy tropical rains cause the Pantanal waters to overflow, flooding an area roughly the size of Cuba. During the region's dry season, the flood waters recede and leave behind a rich landscape of lakes, forests and lagoons.

ICE & GLACIERS

★ LARGEST AREA OF SEA ICE

The Southern Ocean around Antarctica is covered in an area of ice larger than Russia. Between 17 and 20 million km² (6.5 and 7.7 million miles²) of ocean is covered by ice in winter, decreasing to 3–4 million km² (1.1–1.5 million miles²) in summer. By comparison, the Arctic Ocean is covered in winter by 16 million km² (6 million miles²), decreasing in summer to 7–9 million km² (2.7–3.5 million miles²).

FASTEST GLACIER

The Columbia Glacier, between Anchorage and Valdez, in Alaska, USA, was measured in 1999 to be flowing at an average rate of 35 m (115 ft) per day.

LONGEST GLACIER

The Lambert Glacier, discovered by an Australian aircraft crew in Australian Antarctic Territory in 1956–57, is up to 64 km (40 miles) wide. Including its seaward extension (the Amery Ice Shelf), it measures at least 700 km (440 miles) in length – longer than the entire state of Florida. It drains about a fifth of the East Antarctic ice sheet.

★ OLDEST CONTINUOUS ICE CORE

An 'ice core' is a long cylinder of ice extracted from an ice sheet. The farther down the core, the older the ice, so scientists can investigate the history of global climate change by slicing into the core and studying ancient bubbles of air trapped in the ice. The oldest continuous ice core covers 740,000 years of climate history. It measures 3,139 m (10,298 ft) in length and is 10 cm (4 in) in diameter. It was drilled at Dome C, Antarctica, by the European Project for Ice Coring in Antarctica (Epica) and announced on 9 June 2004.

ACTUAL SIZE

LARGEST SUBGLACIAL LAKE

Lake Vostok in Antarctica was discovered in 1994 by analyzing radar imagery of the icy continent. Buried under 4 km (2.5 miles) of ice, it is one of the oldest and most pristine lakes on Earth, having been isolated from the rest of the world for at least 500,000 years. Covering around 14,000 km² (5,400 miles²), it is the 18th largest lake in the world and has a depth of at least 100 m (330 ft).

★ LONGEST ICE CORE

In 1998, an ice core measuring 3,623 m (11,886 ft) in length was drilled from the ice above Lake Vostok. The drilling stopped around 150 m (492 ft) above the surface in order to avoid possible contamination of the lake's pristine environment.

LARGEST PINGO

Pingoes – conical mounds that have a core of ice – form when lakes in permafrost regions drain. As residual water in the ground under the lake freezes, it expands, pushing up a mound of land. Ibyuk Pingo, on the western Arctic coast of Canada, is the largest in the world. It measures around 50 m (160 ft) high and has a 300-m (990-ft) circumference.

LAKES

LARGEST LAKE
The Caspian Sea (in Azerbaijan, Turkmenistan, Iran, Russia and Kazakhstan) is 1,225 km (760 miles) long, with an area of 371,800 km² (143,550 miles²) – large enough to accommodate the entire UK and the island of Cuba. Its maximum depth is 1,025 m (3,360 ft), and the surface is 28.5 m (93 ft) below sea level.

DEEPEST LAKE
Lake Baikal in the southern part of eastern Siberia, Russia, was measured in 1974 by the Soviet Pacific Navy's Hydrographic Service and found to be 1,637 m (5,371 ft) deep, of which 1,181 m (3,875 ft) is below sea level.

LARGEST LAKE WITHIN A LAKE
The largest lake within a lake is Manitou Lake, with an area of 106 km² (41 miles²). It is situated on the world's **largest lake island**, Manitoulin Island (2,766 km²; 1,068 miles²), in the Canadian part of Lake Huron. The lake itself contains a number of islands.

LARGEST FRESHWATER LAKE BY SURFACE AREA
Lake Superior on the USA–Canada border has the greatest area of any freshwater lake. Covering 82,100 km² (31,700 miles²), more than 500,000 people live along its 4,385-km (2,726-mile) shoreline.

LARGEST FRESHWATER LAKE BY VOLUME
Lake Baikal in Siberia, Russia, boasts an estimated volume of 23,000 km³ (5,500 miles³) – one-fifth of the planet's fresh surface water. It is also the **oldest freshwater lake**, having formed 20–25 million years ago.

LARGEST UNDERGROUND LAKE
In 1986, a lake some 66 m (217 ft) underground was discovered in the Drachenhauchloch (Dragon's Breath) cave near Grootfontein, Namibia. It has a surface area of 26,100 m² (280,900 ft²) and is 84 m (276 ft) deep.

SALTIEST LAKE
Don Juan Pond in Wright Valley, Antarctica, contains 671 parts per thousand salt (compared with 35 parts per thousand for the ocean). It is so salty that it remains liquid at temperatures as low as -53°C (-63.4°F).

ISLANDS

HIGHEST ISLANDS
Lake Orba in Tibet stands 5,209 m (17,090 ft) above sea level. It has a surface area of 100 km² (38 miles²) and houses several small islands.

LARGEST ISLAND WITHIN AN ISLAND
Samosir in Lake Toba, Sumatra, Indonesia, has an area of 630 km² (245 m²).

WORLD'S GREATEST RIVERS

RIVER	SOURCE	LENGTH
Nile	Burundi	6,670 km (4,145 miles)
Amazon	Lago Villafro, Peru	6,448 km (4,007 miles)
Yangtze	Kunlun Shan, China	6,300 km (3,915 miles)
Mississippi-Missouri	Montana, USA	6,020 km (3,741 miles)
Yenisey-Angara	Mongolia	5,540 km (3,442 miles)
Hwang He (Yellow River)	Qinghai Province, China	5,464 km (3,395 miles)

← DEADLIEST LAKE

The lake responsible for the most deaths without drowning is Lake Nyos in Cameroon, west Africa, where toxic gases have claimed nearly 2,000 lives in recent decades. On one night in August 1986, up to 1,800 people and countless animals were killed by a large natural release of carbon dioxide gas.

Scientists disagree on the source of Nyos's deadly gas. The lake lies in the crater of an old volcano, suggesting that the gas is volcanic in origin. But the decomposition of organic matter, plus changes in surface temperature, may also be responsible.

LONGEST RIVER ↑

The Nile's main source is Lake Victoria in east-central Africa, and from its farthest stream in Burundi, it extends 6,670 km (4,145 miles) in length – nearly twice the length of the Great Wall of China. The picture above shows the Nile in Egypt.

VOLCANOES

⚡ HIGHEST DEATH TOLL
← FROM A PYROCLASTIC FLOW

On 8 May 1902, Mont Pelee on the island of Martinique in the West Indies erupted, releasing a pyroclastic flow – or *nuée ardente* ('glowing cloud') – of incandescent rock and gas that travelled down the volcano's flank at speeds of up to 160 km/h (100 mph). The pyroclastic flow enveloped the city of St Pierre, killing some 30,000 inhabitants.

also holds the record for the **highest death toll from a volcano**: an estimated 92,000 people were killed following the 1815 eruption.

⚡ LARGEST FLOOD BASALT ERUPTION

The Siberian Traps eruption began 248.3 million years ago and lasted 1 million years. The volume of lava that erupted in this event is estimated at several million km³ – enough to cover the surface of the Earth to a depth of a few metres.

FARTHEST DISTANCE FROM WHICH A VOLCANIC ERUPTION HAS BEEN HEARD

The 1883 eruption of Krakatau (Indonesia) was heard 4,653 km (2,908 miles) away by people on Rodriguez Island. This makes it the **loudest noise heard by humans** in recorded history.
  Krakatau erupted with a force nearly 10,000 times that of the Hiroshima atomic bomb. It caused a tsunami wave 40 m (131 ft) high, which carried a steamship a distance of 2.5 km (1.5 miles).

⚡ NORTHERNMOST VOLCANO

Mount Beerenberg is 2,276 m (7,470 ft) high and is found on the island of Jan Mayen (71°05'N) in the Greenland Sea. It erupted on 20 September 1970, and the island's 39 inhabitants (all men who were working on whaling stations) had to be evacuated.

⚡ SOUTHERNMOST VOLCANO

Mount Erebus, an active volcano standing 3,794 m (12,447 ft) high, is located on Ross Island (77°35'S) in the Southern Ocean.

→ WHERE IS THE LONGEST SUBMARINE MOUNTAIN RANGE? FIND OUT ON P.76

ERUPTIONS

GREATEST ERUPTION VOLUME
The volume of matter discharged in the eruption of Tambora, a volcano on the Indonesian island of Sumbawa, in April 1815, was 150–180 km³ (36–43 miles³) – a volume equivalent to that of 72,000 Great Pyramids. This compares with about 65 km³ (16 miles³) of matter ejected by Santorini (Greece) and 20 km³ (5 miles³) by Krakatau. Tambora

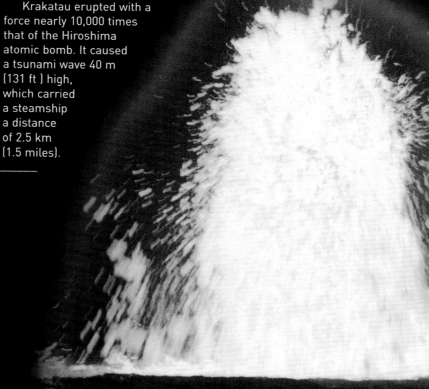

LARGEST ACTIVE VOLCANO →

Mauna Loa in Hawaii has the shape of a broad, gentle dome 120 km (75 miles) long and 50 km (31 miles) wide above sea level. It rises 4,170 m (13,680 ft) and has a total volume of 42,500 km³ (10,200 miles³), of which 84.2% is below sea level. Its caldera (volcano crater), Mokuaweoweo, measures 10.5 km² (4 miles²) and is 150–180 m (500–600 ft) deep. The volcano's last major eruption was in 1984.

✦HIGHEST VOLCANO

Cerro Aconcagua, a snow-clad peak 6,960 m (22,834 ft) high in the Andes of Argentina, is the world's highest volcano, although it is no longer active. The **highest active volcano** is Ojos del Salado (6,887 m; 22,595 ft) on the border between Chile and Argentina.

✦YOUNGEST VOLCANO

Paricutin, 320 km (200 miles) west of Mexico City, Mexico, is a volcanic cone that erupted from a cornfield on 20 February 1943 and was active until 1953. Most of the activity occurred in the first year, when the volcanic cone grew to a height of 336 m (1,100 ft), offering geologists a rare opportunity to witness the birth, evolution and death of a volcano.

LARGEST STEAM RINGS

Mount Etna, in Sicily, is the **tallest and most active volcano in Europe**. A complex physical process is causing it to emit huge steam rings, similar to smoke rings. The steam rings of Mount Etna are approximately 200 m (650 ft) across and can last up to around 10 minutes as they slowly drift upwards to a height of 1,000 m (3,300 ft) above the volcanic vent.

The rings are thought to be due to unusual geometric conditions in the shape of the volcanic vent that produces them.

LAVA

✦FASTEST LAVA FLOW

Nyiragongo, in the Democratic Republic of the Congo (formerly Zaire), erupted on 10 January 1977. Lava burst through the volcano's flank at speeds of up to 60 km/h (40 mph); around 2,000 people died when it hit the city of Goma.

GREATEST MODERN-DAY LANDSLIDE

The landslide on Mount St Helens on 18 May 1980 was the largest witnessed by a survivor. About 2,800 million m³ (96,000 million ft³) of rock slipped off the mountain prior to the eruption – equivalent to a block of earth nearly 1.5 km (0.8 mile) high, wide and long.

✦LONGEST LAVA CAVE

The longest and **deepest lava cave** (an open tube down the inside of a lava flow) is Kazumura Cave on Hawaii, USA. The 59.3-km-long (36.9–mile) cave descends 1,099 m (3,604 ft) down the eastern flank of the Kilauea volcano.

COLDEST ERUPTING LAVA

Common basaltic lavas erupt at 1,100–1,200°C (2,012–2,192°F), but the natrocarbonatite lava of Ol Doinyo Lengai, Tanzania, erupts at just 500–600°C (932–1,112°F).

GREATEST LAVA FLOW DIVERSION

In 1973, the Eldfell volcano on the Icelandic island of Heimaey erupted and vast quantities of molten lava flowed towards the town of Vestmannaeyjar.

One third of the town was destroyed before islanders could defend the remaining area by spraying vast quantities of water on to the approaching lava, forcing it to cool and solidify to form a series of rock dams.

↑

MOST ACTIVE VOLCANO

The world's most active volcano is Kilauea in Hawaii, USA, which has erupted continually since 1983. Lava is being discharged from the volcano at a rate of 5 m³ (176.5 ft³) per second, hence the Hawaiian name 'Kilauea', which means 'spewing' or 'much spreading'.

MORE MAJOR VOLCANIC ERUPTIONS IN HISTORY

VOLCANO	DATE	EFFECT
Mount St Helens (Washington, USA)	1980	Avalanche travelled at a record 402.3 km/h (250 mph); smoke and ash rose 6,000 m (20,000 ft); ash deposited 800 km (440 miles) away
Krakatau (Krakatau, Indonesia)	1883	10,000 times more powerful than Hiroshima bomb; rocks hurled 55 km (34 miles) into air; dust still falling 5,330 km (3,313 miles) away 10 days later
Etna (Sicily, Italy)	1669	Eruption continued for over one month; lava overran western part of city of Catania, 28 km (17 miles) from summit; up to 20,000 people killed
Vesuvius (Bay of Naples, Italy)	AD 79	Towns of Pompeii, Stabiae and Herculaneum buried under cinders and ash, preserving sites until 1748; 35,000 deaths estimated
Santorini (Cyclades, Greece)	1550 BC	Huge explosion – estimated to be four times more powerful than 1883 eruption of Krakatau – almost completely destroyed the island

58°C (136°F)	**Highest recorded temperature** Al'Aziziyah, Sahara Desert, Libya, 13 September 1922
31.4°C (88.5°F)	**Most equable temperature** From 1927 to 1935, Garapan on Saipan Island in the Pacific Ocean, experienced a temperature range of just 11.8°C (21.2°F)
19.6°C (67.3°F)	
14.6°C (58.2°F)	*Average global temperature (2004)*
7°C (45°F)	**Most freakish temperature rise** The temperature rose from -20°C (-4°F) to 7°C (44°F) in 2 min at Spearfish, South Dakota, USA, on 22 January 1943
-20°C (-4°F)	
-49°C (-56°F)	**Greatest temperature variation (1 day)** The temperature dropped 56°C (100°F) from 7°C (44°F) to -49°C (-56°F) at Browning, Montana, USA, on 23–24 January 1916
-68°C (-90°F)	**Coldest inhabited place** Oymyakon, Siberia, Russia
-89.2°C (-128.6°F)	**Lowest recorded temperature** Vostok, Antarctica, 21 July 1983

CLOUDS

HIGHEST CLOUDS
The highest clouds are noctilucent clouds, which are best seen in the lower and higher latitudes. These beautiful, tenuous phenomena form at altitudes of around 80 km (50 miles), above 99.9% of the atmosphere. They can be seen after the Sun has set when, owing to their altitude, they are still lit by the Sun's rays. They are believed to be formed from a mixture of ice crystals and dust from meteors.

HIGHEST CLOUD EXTREME
The highest standard cloud form is cirrus, averaging 9,000 m (29,500 ft), but the rare nacreous or mother-of-pearl formation may reach 24,500 m (80,000 ft). The **lowest standard cloud form** is stratus, which lies below 460 m (1,500 ft).

CLOUDS WITH THE GREATEST VERTICAL RANGE
Cumulonimbus has been observed to reach a height of nearly 20,000 m (65,600 ft) from a base of around ground level – nearly three times the height of Mount Everest – in the tropics.

RAINFALL

GREATEST RAINFALL IN 24 HOURS
A record 1,870 mm (73 in) of rain fell in 24 hours at Cilaos, Reunion, Indian Ocean, on 15–16 March 1952. This is equal to 7,554 tonnes (16,653,700 lb) of rain per acre.

MOST RAINY DAYS
Mount Wai-`ale-`ale (1,569 m; 5,148 ft) in Hawaii has up to 350 rainy days a year – an average rainfall of over 10 m (33 ft).

GREATEST
PRESSURE DROP MEASURED IN A
← TORNADO
On 24 June 2003, severe storms researcher Tim Samaras (USA) placed an instrument probe into the path of an F4 tornado near Manchester, South Dakota, USA, and measured a pressure drop of 100 millibars. The tornado destroyed a 40-km-long (25-mile) stretch of the community of Manchester. The work was co-funded by National Geographic.

The F rating refers to the Fujita tornado intensity scale – an F4 being a tornado clocked at 93–116 m/sec (207–260 mph).

OLDEST FOSSILIZED RAINDROPS
On 15 December 2001, Indian geologist Chirananda De announced his discovery of the fossilized imprints of raindrops in ancient rocks in the lower Vindhyan range, Madhya Pradesh, India. These rocks prove that rain fell on Earth at least 1.6 billion years ago.

★ LARGEST RAINDROPS
Raindrops measuring a minimum of 8.6 mm (0.3 in) across have been detected on two occasions: in September 1995 (in Brazil) and July 1999 (in the Marshall Islands). The raindrops were measured while falling by a laser instrument on board a research aircraft in studies by Peter V Hobbs and Arthur Rango (both USA) of the University of Washington (USA).

HEAVIEST RAINFALL →
By average annual rainfall, the wettest place is Mawsynram in Meghalaya, India, with 11,873 mm (467 in) of rain a year. Most of the rain in Meghalaya – which means 'land of the clouds' – occurs during the monsoon season, between June and September. The highest rainfall in a calendar month is 9,300 mm (366 in) and occurred at Cherrapunji, also in Meghalaya, in July 1861.

SNOW & HAIL

GREATEST SNOWFALL
Between 1971 and 1972, a total of 31,102 mm (1,224 in) of snow fell at Paradise, Mount Rainier, Washington, USA. The **greatest recorded depth of snow** was 11.46 m (37 ft 7 in) at Tamarac, California, USA, in March 1911.

WORST DAMAGE TOLL FROM A SNOWSTORM
A total of 500 people died in a snowstorm that crossed the entire east coast of the USA on 12–13 March 1993. The storm, described by one meteorologist as 'a storm with the heart of a blizzard and the soul of a hurricane', caused $1.2 billion (£825.1 million) worth of damage.

HEAVIEST HAILSTONES
Hailstones weighing up to 1 kg (2.2 lb) were reported to have killed 92 people in the Gopalganj district of Bangladesh on 14 April 1986. The **highest death toll in a hailstorm**, however, occurred on 20 April 1888, when a total of 246 people perished during a storm at Moradabad, Uttar Pradesh, India.

LARGEST PIECE OF FALLEN ICE
On 13 August 1849, a piece of ice 6 m (20 ft) long was reported to have fallen from the sky in Ross-shire, UK. The ice was clear but appeared to be composed of smaller pieces. One explanation is that hailstones were fused together by a bolt of lightning.

★ FASTEST JETSTREAM →
Jetstreams are narrow, fast-flowing currents of air in the upper atmosphere. They average speeds of 400 km/h (250 mph), though the fastest measured to date is 656 km/h (408 mph) above South Uist, Western Isles, UK, at a height of 47,000 m (154,200 ft) on 13 December 1967. Pictured here are clouds being carried by a jetstream at more than 160 km/h (100 mph) over Egypt and the Red Sea.

LIGHTNING

MOST STROKES IN A LIGHTNING FLASH
The majority of lightning flashes consist of several 'strokes' – major pulses of current. It is these pulses that can cause some flashes to appear to flicker. The most detected in a single flash is 26, in a cloud-to-ground flash in New Mexico in 1962, recorded by Marx Brook (USA).

LONGEST LIGHTNING FLASH
At any one time, around 100 lightning bolts a second hit the Earth. Typically, the actual length of these bolts can be around 9 km (5.5 miles). In 1956, meteorologist Myron Ligda (USA) observed and recorded a lightning flash, using radar, that covered a horizontal distance of 149 km (93 miles) inside clouds.

HIGHEST DEATH TOLL FROM A LIGHTNING STRIKE
A total of 81 people on board a Boeing 707 jet airliner died when the plane was struck by lightning near Elkton, Maryland, USA, on 8 December 1963.

MOST LIGHTNING STRIKES SURVIVED
Roy C Sullivan (USA) remains the only man in the world to survive being struck by lightning seven times. The 'human lightning conductor' was first struck in 1942 (losing his big toenail), then again in 1969 (lost eyebrows), 1970 (left shoulder seared), 1972 (hair set on fire), 1973 (regrown hair singed and legs seared), 1976 (ankle hurt) and 1977 (stomach and chest burns). In 1983 he died by his own hand, reportedly rejected in love.

DRIEST PLACE
For the period between 1964 and 2001, the average annual rainfall for the meteorological station in Quillagua in the Atacama Desert, Chile, was just 0.5 mm (0.01 in). This discovery was made during the making of the documentary series *Going to Extremes* by Keo Films in 2001. The oddly shaped salt deposits seen below are located in a former lake bed in the desert.

← LONGEST REEF

The Great Barrier Reef off Queensland, Australia, is around 2,027 km (1,260 miles) in length. It is not actually a single reef but consists of thousands of separate reefs. It is also the **largest marine structure built by living creatures**, as it consists of countless billions of dead and living stony corals (order Madreporaria and Scleractinia).

UNDERWATER

TALLEST MOUNTAIN

Monte Pico in the Azores islands (Portugal) has an altitude of 2,351 m (7,711 ft) above sea level and extends a record 6,098 m (20,000 ft) from the surface to the sea floor – in total 399 m (1,317 ft) shorter than Mt Everest.

LONGEST SUBMARINE MOUNTAIN RANGE

The Mid-Ocean Ridge extends 65,000 km (40,000 miles) from the Arctic Ocean to the Atlantic Ocean, around Africa, Asia and Australia, and under the Pacific Ocean to the west coast of North America. It has a maximum height of 4,200 m (13,800 ft) above its base on the ocean floor.

★ WIDEST CONTINENTAL SHELF

Continental shelves are an extension of coastal plains and are characterized by broadly sloping submerged plains. About 7.4% of the world's ocean surface sits above continental shelves, which have a global average width of 78 km (48 miles). The widest shelf extends 1,210 km (750 miles) off the coast of Siberia, Russia, into the Arctic Ocean.

★ STRONGEST NATURAL WHIRLPOOL

There are several permanent whirlpools in the world, caused by tides, narrow straits and fast-flowing water. The most powerful are Mosskstraumen, near Loften Island, Norway, and Old Sow, off the coast of Maine, USA. Both have experienced currents measuring 28 km/h (17 mph).

HIGHEST TEMPERATURE

The highest temperature recorded in the ocean is 404°C (759°F) for a hydrothermal vent measured by a US research submarine 480 km (300 miles) off the American west coast in 1985.

STRONGEST GLOBAL CURRENT

The Antarctic Circumpolar Current, or West Wind Drift, is the greatest current in the oceans. It moves at around 130 million m³ (4,590 million ft³) of water per second – six to seven times the flow rate of the Gulf Stream.

FASTEST CURRENT

During the monsoon, the Somali current flows at 12.8 km/h (9 mph) in the northern Indian Ocean.

WORLD OCEANS

Pacific Ocean	155,557,000 km²	(60,060,900 miles²)
Atlantic Ocean	76,762,000 km²	(29,638,000 miles²)
Indian Ocean	68,556,000 km²	(26,469,600 miles²)
Southern Ocean	20,327,000 km²	(7,848,300 miles²)
Arctic Ocean	14,056,000 km²	(5,427,050 miles²)

LARGEST OCEAN ↑

The Pacific is the largest ocean in the world. Excluding adjacent seas, it represents 45.9% of the world's oceans and covers 155,557,000 km² (60,060,900 miles²) in area. Its average depth is 3,940 m (12,925 ft).

★ CLEAREST SEA

The Weddell Sea, off Antarctica, has the clearest water of any sea or ocean. On 13 October 1986, scientists from the Alfred Wegener Institute in Bremerhaven, Germany, measured its clarity using a Secchi disc – a piece of black-and-white PVC measuring 30 cm (1 ft) wide (right). The disc is dropped into the water and monitored until it is no longer visible. In the Weddell Sea, the Secchi disc was visible until it reached a depth of 80 m (262 ft) – clarity similar to that of distilled water.

LARGEST ARCHIPELAGO →

The world's largest archipelago is the East Indian or Malay Archipelago crescent that forms Indonesia. It is 5,600 km (3,500 miles) long and contains more than 17,000 islands – including Sipadan Island, pictured – with a combined coastline length of over 80,000 km (50,000 miles).

LARGEST...

GULF

The Gulf of Mexico stretches from Cape Sable in Florida, USA, to Cabo Catoche in Mexico. It has a total area of 1,544,000 km² (596,000 miles²) and a shoreline of 5,000 km (3,100 miles).

BAY

The world's largest bay – in terms of shoreline length – is Hudson Bay, Canada, with a shoreline of 12,268 km (7,623 miles) – similar to the length of the UK coastline – and an area of 1,233,000 km² (476,000 miles²). Measured by area, the Bay of Bengal in the Indian Ocean is larger, at 2,172,000 km² (839,000 miles²).

ATOLL

Kwajalein, part of the Marshall Islands in the Pacific Ocean, is the world's largest atoll. Its coral reef, 283 km (176 miles) long, encloses a 2,850-km² (1,100-mile²) lagoon.

POLYNYA

A polynya is an area of open sea surrounded by sea ice. During the winter months of 1974, 1975 and 1976, a polynya about 1,000 x 350 km (620 x 220 miles) occurred in the Weddell Sea, Antarctica.

★ AREA OF STILL WATER

The still waters of the Sargasso Sea in the north Atlantic Ocean cover about 6.2 million km² (2.4 million miles²). The sea is so calm that sargassum seaweed has been able to grow on it and now covers most of the surface.

TIDES & WAVES

HIGHEST WAVE

The highest officially recorded sea wave – dependent on weather or climate – was calculated as 34 m (112 ft) from trough to crest. It was measured by Lt Frederic Margraff, of the US navy, from the USS *Ramapo* proceeding from Manila, Philippines, to San Diego, California, USA, on the night of 6–7 February 1933, during a 126-km/h (78-mph) hurricane.

★ LARGEST WAVE WAVELENGTH

The longest wavelength (the distance between successive peaks or troughs) of any ocean wave is around 12,000 km (7,500 miles) for the tides caused by the Sun and Moon.

By way of comparison, normal wind-driven ocean waves have a wavelength of around 50–100 m (165–330 ft).

HIGHEST AVERAGE TIDE

The greatest tides occur in the Bay of Fundy, which divides the peninsula of Nova Scotia, Canada, from the US state of Maine and the Canadian province of New Brunswick. Burncoat Head in the Minas Basin, Nova Scotia, has the greatest mean spring range, with 14.5 m (47 ft 6 in).

HIGHEST TIDE EVER

A tide range of 16.6 m (54 ft 6 in) was recorded at springs in Leaf Basin, Quebec, Canada, in 1953.

LARGEST CONTINUOUS CURRENT SYSTEM

The Thermohaline Conveyor is a global system of ocean circulation, driven by differences in seawater density and salinity. It moves cold, salty water from the north Atlantic down to the Southern Ocean, where it travels east and north to the Indian and Pacific Oceans. Here it rises and becomes warm, travelling back westwards where it sinks again in the north Atlantic. The entire cycle can last for 1,000 years.

← LARGEST DELTA

The world's largest delta – a triangular area of clay, silt and sand deposits at the mouth of a river – is the Bengal Delta created by the rivers Brahmaputra and Ganges in Bangladesh and West Bengal, India. It covers a total area of 75,000 km² (30,000 miles²) – nearly twice the size of Switzerland.

HIGHEST TSUNAMI WASH

The highest known tsunami (meaning 'harbour wave') was 524 m (1,719 ft) high and occurred along the fjord-like Lituya Bay in Alaska, USA, on 9 July 1958. The wave was caused by a giant landslip and moved at 160 km/h (100 mph). It would have swamped New York's Empire State Building, which, at 449 m (1,472 ft), was the world's tallest building at the time.

THE DEEP

202 m (663 ft) Deepest sea cave: Dean's Blue Hole, Bahamas

210 m (690 ft) Deepest dive by a flying bird: Thick-billed murre (*Uria lomvia*)

282.6 m (927.1 ft) Deepest freshwater cave dive: Nuno Gomes (South Africa), Boesmansgat Cave, South Africa

307.8 m (1,010 ft) Deepest seawater scuba dive: John Bennett (UK), Escarcia Point, Puerto Galera, Philippines

534 m (1,751 ft) Deepest dive by a bird: Emperor penguin (*Aptenodytes forsteri*)

1,200 m (3,937 ft) Deepest dive by a chelonian: leatherback turtle (*Dermochelys coriacea*)

1,529 m (5,017 ft) Deepest pinniped dive: northern elephant seal (*Mirounga angustirostris*), California, USA

2,000 m (6,500 ft) Deepest dive by a mammal: sperm whale (*Physeter macrocephalus*)

2,400 m (1.5 miles) Deepest live TV broadcast: *Abyss Live* (BBC, UK), mid-Atlantic Ridge

4,500 m (15,000 ft) Deepest commercial recovery: US spacecraft *Liberty Bell 7*, Atlantic Ocean

5,650 m (18,500 ft) Deepest sponges

6,526 m (21,414 ft) Deepest diving submersible: *Shinkai 6500* (Japan)

7,584 m (24,881 ft) Deepest starfish: *Porcellanaster ivanovi*

8,370 m (27,460 ft) Deepest fish: cuskeel (*Abyssobrotula galatheae*)

10,911 m (35,797 ft) Deepest point in the ocean: Challenger Deep

SALVAGE & RECOVERY

DEEPEST AIRCRAFT RECOVERY

A helicopter that crashed into the Pacific Ocean in August 1991 was successfully recovered by the crew of the USS *Salvoron* on 27 February 1992 from a depth of 5,258 m (17,251 ft), allowing the cause of the crash to be studied.

DEEPEST COMMERCIAL RECOVERY

On 20 July 1999, the US spacecraft *Liberty Bell 7* was recovered from the bottom of the Atlantic Ocean, where it had sat since splashdown on 21 July 1961. The spacecraft was in over 4,500 m (15,000 ft) of water before being raised by the ship *Ocean Project*, in a project financed by the Discovery Channel.

DEEPEST UNDERWATER SALVAGE WITH DIVERS

HM cruiser *Edinburgh*, sunk on 2 May 1942 in the Barents Sea off northern Norway, is in 245 m (803 ft) of water. From 7 September to 7 October 1981, 12 divers worked on the wreck in pairs, recovering 460 gold ingots.

DEEPEST SHIPWRECK

On 28 November 1996, Blue Water Recoveries Ltd (UK) discovered the wreck of the SS *Rio Grande*, using side-scanning sonar at the bottom of the South Atlantic Ocean. The find was confirmed by Blue Water on 30 November 1996 using a remotely operated vehicle. The wreck, a World War II German blockade runner, lies at a depth of 5,762 m (18,904 ft).

GREATEST TREASURE RECOVERED FROM A SHIPWRECK

An estimated $2,000 million (£1,500 million) in gold and platinum was retrieved in August 1984 from the Tsarist battleship *Admiral Nakhimov* lying 60 m (200 ft) down off the Japanese island of Tsushima.

Also, the *Nuestra Señora de Atocha*, which sank off the Florida coast in 1622, was salvaged on 20 July 1985. The ship carried 40 tonnes (88,000 lb) of gold and silver and some 31.75 kg (70 lb) of emeralds.

↑ LARGEST EYE-TO-BODY RATIO

Vampyroteuthis infernalis – literally, the 'vampire squid from hell' – resides in tropical waters at depths of over 600 m (1,970 ft). It has a maximum body length of 28 cm (11 in) and eyes with a diameter of 2.5 cm (0.9 in) – a ratio of 1:11, the greatest in the animal kingdom. The human equivalent would be eyes the size of table-tennis bats!

DEEPEST...

MANNED DESCENT

Jacques Piccard (Switzerland) and Donald Walsh (USA) piloted the Swiss-built US navy bathyscaphe *Trieste* to a depth of 10,911 m (35,797 ft) in the 'Challenger Deep' section of the Mariana Trench on 23 January 1960. Challenger Deep is thought to be the **deepest point on Earth** and is situated 400 km (250 miles) south-west of Guam in the Pacific Ocean.

SEAWATER SCUBA DIVE

John Bennett (UK) scuba-dived to a depth of 307.8 m (1,010 ft) on 6 November 2001 off Escarcia Point in the Philippines. It took just over 12 minutes to descend, while the ascent took 9 hr 36 min to allow for decompression. Bennett used 60 air tanks.

MOST HEAT-TOLERANT ORGANISM

Strain 121 is a microbe belonging to the ancient group of bacteria-like organisms called archae. Strain 121 was discovered in superheated water from hydrothermal vents at the bottom of the Pacific Ocean, and can survive temperatures of 121°C (250°F).

DEEPEST DIVING →
SUBMERSIBLE IN SERVICE

Of the submersibles now in service, the Japanese research submarine *Shinkai 6500* is capable of diving the deepest. On 11 August 1989, it reached a depth of 6,526 m (21,414 ft) in the Japan Trench off Sanriku, Japan. The three-person craft is 9.5 m (31 ft 2 in) long, 2.7 m (8 ft 10 in) wide and 3.2 m (10 ft 6 in) high and continues to explore the seabed.

WILDLIFE

DEEPEST PLANT

The greatest depth at which plant life has been found is 269 m (882 ft) for algae found in October 1984 by Mark and Diane Littler (both USA) off San Salvador Island in The Bahamas. These maroon-coloured plants survived, even though 99.9995% of sunlight was filtered out.

DEEPEST FISH

A cuskeel (family Ophidiidae) called *Abyssobrotula galatheae* has been collected from the Puerto Rico Trench at a depth of 8,370 m (27,460 ft).

DEEPEST DIVE BY A MAMMAL

The deepest dive by a mammal was made by a bull sperm whale (*Physeter macrocephalus*) in 1991 off the coast of Dominica in the Caribbean. Scientists from the Woods Hole Oceanographic Institute (USA) recorded the dive to be 2,000 m (6,500 ft) deep, and it lasted a total of 1 hr 13 min.

★ DEEPEST DIVE BY A PINNIPED

In May 1989, scientists testing the diving abilities of northern elephant seals (*Mirounga angustirostris*) off the coast of San Miguel Island, California, USA, documented an adult male that reached a maximum depth of 1,529 m (5,017 ft).

★ LARGEST CREATURE NEVER OBSERVED IN ITS HABITAT

Scientists do not know exactly where in the sea the *Architeuthis dux* ('king of the giant squids') lives, and so have never been able to study it, but specimens have been measured at up to 18 m (59 ft) in length and 900 kg (1,980 lb) in weight.

LONGEST ANIMAL

The siphonophore *Praya dubia* (a variety of jellyfish) is considered to be the longest organism in the world, measuring up to 50 m (160 ft) – the length of an Olympic swimming pool. This blue bioluminescent recluse lives in the mid-water zone that extends down from 300 m (1,000 ft) below the surface. It has large, paired swimming bells at the head, and trailing behind is a long stem of reproductive units called cormidia, and thin tentacles that can deliver a powerful sting.

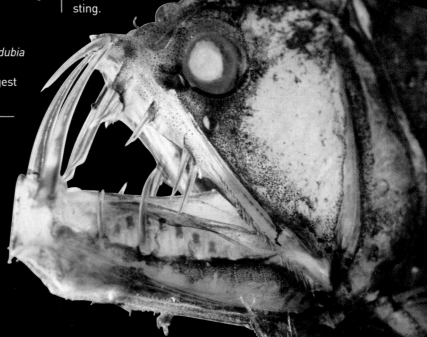

LARGEST TEETH →
RELATIVE TO HEAD SIZE (FISH)

The viperfish (*Chauliodus sloani*) has teeth so large it must open its mouth to make its jaws vertical before it can swallow prey. Its body is approximately 28 cm (11 in) long, its head about 2 cm (0.8 in) and its teeth are just over half this length. The teeth overlap the jaws when the mouth is closed.

The viperfish eats large prey by lowering the internal skeleton of the gills, allowing the prey to pass into the throat without interference. It can impale prey on the teeth by swimming at them with the first vertebra behind the head acting as a shock absorber.

← HIGHEST CRAB DENSITY

An estimated 120 million red crabs (*Gecarcoidea natalis*) live exclusively on the 135-km² (52-mile²) Christmas Island in the Indian Ocean – a density of approximately one crab per square metre for the whole island. Every year (from around November until Christmas, appropriately enough), millions of the crabs swarm out of their forest burrows to mate and spawn at the coast.

MOST ABUNDANT ANIMAL

Copepods are crustaceans and are found almost everywhere that water is available. They include more than 12,000 species and, with krill, form the most important members of zooplankton. Copepods form groups that can reach a trillion individuals. Most are very small – less than 1 mm (0.04 in) long – but some rare oceanic species are over 1 cm (0.4 in) in length. They are also the **only known animal with just one eye**.

★ OLDEST FOSSIL CRUSTACEAN

The discovery of a complete fossilized crustacean measuring less than 0.5 mm (0.019 in) long was announced in July 2001 by geologists Mark Williams, David Siveter (both UK) and Dieter Waloszek (Germany). At 511 million years old, this tiny life-form – found in Shropshire, UK – is the oldest crustacean ever discovered.

FISH

FASTEST FISH

In a series of speed trials carried out at Long Key Fishing Camp, Florida, USA, a cosmopolitan sailfish (*Istiophorus platypterus*) took out 91 m (300 ft) of line in 3 seconds – equivalent to a velocity of 109 km/h (68 mph).

In comparison, the cheetah – the **fastest mammal on land over short distances** – reaches speeds of 100 km/h (62 mph).

LARGEST FISH

The rare plankton-feeding whale shark (*Rhincodon typus*) is found in the warmer areas of the Atlantic, Pacific and Indian oceans. The largest scientifically recorded specimen was 12.65 m (41 ft 6 in) long, measured 7 m (23 ft) round the thickest part of the body and weighed an estimated 15–21 tonnes (33,000–46,200 lb).

LIGHTEST FISH

The Indo-Pacific dwarf goby (*Schindleria praematurus*) weighs only 2 mg (equivalent to 14,184 individuals to an ounce) and is 12–19 mm (0.47–0.74 in) long.

LARGEST PREDATORY FISH

The largest predatory fish is the great white shark (*Carcharodon carcharias*). Adult specimens average 4.3–4.6 m (14–15 ft) in length, and generally weigh 520–770 kg (1,150–1,700 lb). Circumstantial evidence suggests that some terrifying great whites grow longer than 6 m (20 ft).

LONGEST FIN

The largest and most common species of thresher shark (*Alopias vulpinus*) has a huge scythe-shaped caudal (tail) fin that is roughly as long as the body itself. Found worldwide in temperate and tropical seas, the shark can grow to a length of 6 m (20 ft), of which almost 3 m (10 ft) consists of the greatly elongated upper tail fin.

CRUSTACEANS

HEAVIEST MARINE CRUSTACEAN

An American or North Atlantic lobster (*Homarus americanus*) caught off Nova Scotia, Canada, on 11 February 1977, measured 1.06 m (3 ft 6 in) from the end of the tail-fan to the tip of the largest claw and weighed 20.14 kg (44 lb 6 oz). It was later sold to a restaurant owner in New York City, USA.

→ WHAT'S THE GREEDIEST ANIMAL IN THE WORLD? FIND OUT ON P.56

LARGEST MARINE CRUSTACEAN

The largest of all marine crustaceans, as opposed to the heaviest, is the taka-ashi-gani or giant spider crab (*Macrocheira kaempferi*). One known specimen had a claw-span of 3.7 m (12 ft 18 in) and weighed 18.6 kg (41 lb).

LARGEST LAND CRAB

The robber or coconut crab (*Birgus latro*), which lives on islands and atolls in the Indo-Pacific region, weighs up to 4.1 kg (9 lb) and has a leg-span of up to 1 m (39 in). It is almost entirely terrestrial and will drown if submerged.

★ SMALLEST AMPHIBIAN ∨

Eleutherodactylus limbatus of Cuba is 8.5–12 mm (0.33–0.47 in) long from snout to vent when fully grown. The **largest frog** is the goliath (*Conraua goliath*), which measures up to 36.8 cm (14.5 in) from snout to vent.

ACTUAL SIZE

← MOST POISONOUS EDIBLE FISH

Many species of fish are poisonous to eat, but the most poisonous are the puffer fish (*Tetraodon*) of the Red Sea and Indo-Pacific region, which deliver a fatal poison called tetrodotoxin, one of the most powerful nonproteinous poisons.

The fish's ovaries, eggs, blood, skin, liver and intestines contain the poison, and less than 0.1 g (0.004 oz) is enough to kill a human in as little as 20 minutes.

AMPHIBIANS

LARGEST AMPHIBIAN

One specimen of Chinese giant salamander (*Andrias davidianus*) – the largest of all amphibians – collected in Hunan Province, China, measured 1.8 m (5 ft 11 in) long and weighed 65 kg (143 lb). Giant salamanders are also the **longest-living amphibians** and have been known to survive for 55 years.

FARTHEST JUMP BY A FROG

A South African sharp-nosed frog (*Ptychadena oxyrhynchus*) named Santjie achieved a 'triple jump' of 10.3 m (33 ft 5.5 in) – about half the length of a basketball court – at a frog derby held at Petersburg, KwaZulu-Natal, South Africa, on 21 May 1977. Competition jumps are the aggregate length of three consecutive leaps.

MOST COLD-RESISTANT ANIMAL

The wood frog (*Rana sylvatica*) is the only animal that is able to survive after it has been frozen. These frogs live north of the Arctic Circle and survive for weeks in a frozen state. Glucose in their blood acts as a kind of antifreeze that concentrates in the frogs' vital organs, thereby protecting them from damage while the rest of the body freezes solid.

MOLLUSCS

LARGEST MOLLUSC

The body of a giant squid (*Architeuthis dux*) that washed ashore in Thimble Tickle Bay, Newfoundland, Canada, on 2 November 1878 was 6 m (20 ft) long. One of its tentacles measured 10.7 m (35 ft).

LARGEST OYSTER

In 1999, a common oyster (*Ostrea edulis*) from Chesapeake Bay, Virginia, USA, measured 30.5 cm (12 in) long, 14 cm (5.5 in) wide and weighed 3.7 kg (8.1 lb).

LARGEST TOAD →

The cane or marine toad (*Bufo marinus*) of tropical South America and Queensland, Australia (introduced, not native), averages 450 g (1 lb) in weight. The largest known specimen was a male owned by Håkan Forsberg (Sweden). In March 1991, it weighed 2.65 kg (5 lb 13.5 oz) and measured 38 cm (15 in) from snout to vent.

By comparison, the **smallest toad** is Africa's *B. taitanus beiranus*, which is just 24 mm (0.9 in) long.

ACTUAL SIZE

ZOO & FARM ANIMALS

LARGEST HORNS (STEER)

Lurch, an African watusi steer owned by Janice Wolf (USA), has horns with a circumference that measured 95.25 cm (37.5 in) on 6 May 2003.

The ★largest horn circumference on a bull measured 103.5 cm (40.75 in) on 20 September 2004 and belongs to C T Woodie, an Ankole watusi bull owned by Duane and Kolene Gilbert (both USA).

FARMS & CATTLE MARKETS

★LARGEST CATTLE MARKET

Every day, an estimated 12,000–18,000 heads of cattle reach Liniers Market in Buenos Aires, Argentina, to be bought or sold. The cattle market covers a total area of 34 ha (84 acres), has 450 entry/exit pens for the cattle, 2,000 corrals for selling and 40 weighing scales, and employs approximately 4,000 people.

LARGEST FARM EVER

The pioneer farm owned by Laucídio Coelho (Brazil) near Campo Grande, Mato Grosso, Brazil, covered 8,700 km² (3,360 miles²) and supported 250,000 head of cattle at the time of the owner's death in 1975. The smallest US state, Rhode Island, would fit into this area three times.

LARGEST CATTLE BREED

Chianini cattle were brought to the Chiana Valley, Italy, from the Middle East in pre-Roman times. Four types exist, the largest of which is the Val di Chianini, found on the plains and low hills of Arezzo and Siena. Bulls average 1.73 m (5 ft 8 in) at the shoulder and weigh 1,300 kg (2,865 lb), but Chianini oxen have been known to attain heights of 1.9 m (6 ft 2.75 in).

★SMALLEST CATTLE BREED

The average height of the Vechur cattle breed, from the ground to the hump, is 81–91 cm (31–35 in) for the cow and 83–105 cm (32–41 in) for the bull. The cattle are native to Kerala, India.

LARGEST HORN SPREAD FOR DOMESTIC CATTLE

A pair of horns from a Texas longhorn measured a total length of 251 cm (98 in) in July 2002. The horns are owned by Jim Williams (USA) of Midland, Texas, USA. Measured vertically in a straight line from the ground to the base of the horn, one was 128.2 cm (50.5 in) and the other 122.8 cm (48.3 in).

SHELTERS

★LARGEST DOG SHELTER

Ute Langenkamp: Iubiti Maidanezii, a dog rescue shelter near Pitesti, Romania, can comfortably house up to 3,000 dogs over an area of 45,543 m² (490,220 ft²). The German-Romanian project has been involved in the sheltering, treating and re-housing of dogs since May 2001.

★OLDEST KOALA EVER

A koala named Sarah died in 2001 aged 23 years old. Sarah was born in 1978 and lived at the Lone Pine Koala Sanctuary, Queensland, Australia. The average age for a koala is 12 years in the wild and 16 years in captivity.

LARGEST BEAR LITTER

A litter of five brown bears (*Ursus arctos*) were born in captivity at Zoo Kosice, Kosice-Kavecany, Slovakia, on 6 January 2002. There were three males and two females, named Miso, Tapik, Dazzle, Bubu and Cindy. Pictured are three of the cubs being bottle-fed by their carers.

★ LONGEST GIANT PANDA PREGNANCY

Shu Lan, a giant panda (*Ailuropoda melanoleuca*), endured a pregnancy that lasted 200 days before giving birth to a healthy male cub on 21 October 2004 at Chengdu Research Base for Giant Pandas, Sichuan Province, China. The average pregnancy for a panda is 95–160 days.

ANIMAL HYBRIDS

PARENTS	OFFSPRING
Lion + tiger	Liger; tiglon; tigon; tigron; tion
Horse + zebra	Zebrinny; zebroid; zinny; zors
Bison + cow	Beefalo; cattalo
Horse + donkey	Mule; hinny
Lion + leopard	Leopon
Camel + llama	Cama
Cow or bull + yak	Dzo
Dog + wolf	Wolfdog
Whale + dolphin	Wolphin

★ OLDEST KOALA SANCTUARY

The Lone Pine Koala Sanctuary, Brisbane, Queensland, Australia, was established in 1927 by Claude Reid (Australia) and still operates today. As of 9 December 2004, the sanctuary housed 137 koalas – the largest number in captivity.

ZOOS

FIRST ZOO

The earliest known collection of animals was established at modern-day Puzurish, Iraq, by Shulgi, a third-dynasty ruler of Ur from 2097 to 2094 BC.

★ OLDEST ELEPHANT

Lin Wang, an Asian elephant (*Elephas maximus*), died at the age of 86 on 26 February 2003, at Taipei Zoo, Taiwan. Grandpa Lin, as Lin Wang became known, carried supplies through the jungles of Myanmar for the Japanese army during World War II. He was even taken prisoner by the Chinese in 1943.

LARGEST LION EVER

Simba, a black-maned lion, had a shoulder height of 1.11 m (44 in) in July 1970. He lived at Colchester Zoo, Essex, UK (afterwards Knaresborough Zoo, North Yorkshire, UK) until his death on 16 January 1973, aged 14. He weighed 375 kg (826 lb).

★ LARGEST LITTER OF TIGERS BORN IN CAPTIVITY

Six tigers were born to parents Bety and Conde on 18 November 2003 at Buenos Aires Zoo, Argentina. The three male and three female cubs are Bengal white tigers (*Panthera tigris tigris*).

LONGEST TUSK

Excluding prehistoric examples, the longest tusks are a pair from an African elephant, *Loxodonta africana*, obtained in the Democratic Republic of the Congo and kept in the New York Zoological Society in Bronx Park, New York City, USA. The right tusk measures 3.49 m (11 ft 5 in) along the outside curve and the left is 3.35 m (10 ft 11 in).

★ LARGEST CAT HYBRID →

The largest hybrid of the cat family (Felidae) is the liger (no scientific name), which is the offspring of a male lion and a tigress. Ligers typically grow larger than either parent, reaching lengths of 3–3.6 m (10–12 ft). The size and appearance of the liger can vary, depending upon which subspecies of lion or tiger is involved. Although these hybrids could occur in the wild (where lions and tigers inhabit the same territory), such cross-breeding usually happens in zoos or private menageries.

★LARGEST
MARSUPIAL CARNIVORE

Adult male Tasmanian devils (*Sarcophilus harrisii*) typically measure 30 cm (12 in) to the shoulder, 78 cm (30 in) in length and weigh 12 kg (26 lb). Found naturally only in Tasmania, Australia, they use their powerful jaws and long teeth to feed on mammals, birds, reptiles and insects, eating everything – even the bones and fur.

Australia is also home to the **smallest marsupial carnivores**. The long-tailed planigale (*Planigale ingrami*) weighs up to 4.5 g (0.15 oz) and has a body length of 5.5–6.3 cm (2.1–2.4 in); the Pilbara ningaui (*Ninguai timealeyi*) measures 4.6–5.7 cm (1.8–2.2 in) and weighs up to 9.4 g (0.33 oz).

CARNIVORES

LARGEST LAND CARNIVORE

Adult male polar bears (*Ursus maritimus*) weigh up to 600 kg (1,320 lb) and have a nose-to-tail length of 2.4–2.6 m (7 ft 10 in–8 ft 6 in). In 1960, a bear estimated at around 900 kg (1,980 lb) was shot on an ice pack in the Chukchi Sea off Alaska, USA. It measured 3.5 m (11 ft 5 in) from nose to tail over the contours of the body and 1.5 m (4 ft 11 in) around the body.

→ WHICH MAMMAL HAS THE LARGEST BRAIN? FIND OUT ON P.87

★LARGEST HOME RANGE FOR A LAND MAMMAL

The polar bear has the largest home range of any land mammal. Typically, it will tramp over areas of 30,000 km² (11,500 miles²) – the size of Italy – in a single year.

★MOST SENSITIVE NOSE FOR A LAND MAMMAL

Polar bears can detect prey, such as seals, over 30 km (18 miles) away and often under thick ice. One bear was recorded walking in a direct line for 32 km (20 miles) to reach food.

★LARGEST PREY

An adult male polar bear has a stomach capacity of about 68 kg (150 lb) and is known to kill prey as large as walruses weighing 500 kg (1,100 lb) and beluga whales at 600 kg (1,320 lb). Its digestive system is also more adapted for processing meat than plant material, making the polar bear one of the most carnivorous bear species.

LARGEST FELINE CARNIVORE

The male Siberian tiger (*Panthera tigris altaica*) averages 3.15 m (10 ft 4 in) in length from the nose to the tip of the tail, stands 99–107 cm (39–42 in) at the shoulder and weighs about 265 kg (580 lb). Because it can go for days without eating any food, a Siberian tiger can eat about 45 kg (100 lb) of meat at one sitting.

SMALLEST FELINE CARNIVORE

The rusty-spotted cat (*Prionailurus rubiginosus*) of southern India and Sri Lanka has a head-to-body length of 350–480 mm (13.7–18.8 in), a tail of 150–250 mm (5.9–9.8 in) and a weight of 1 kg (2 lb 3 oz) for the female and 1.5 kg (3 lb 5 oz) for the male.

RODENTS

LARGEST MAMMAL GROUP

Living in every continent except Antarctica, rodents account for almost 40% of all mammal species on Earth. Out of around 4,000 mammal species, rodents make up 1,500, followed by bats, with 1,000 species.

LARGEST MAMMAL COLONY

The black-tailed prairie dog (*Cynomys ludovicianus*), a rodent of the family Sciuridae found in the western USA and northern Mexico, builds huge colonies. One single 'town' discovered in 1901 contained 400 million individuals and was estimated to cover 61,400 km² (23,700 miles²), almost the size of Ireland.

←★FASTEST EATER

According to research published in February 2005 by Dr Kenneth Catania at Vanderbilt University, Tennessee, USA, the star-nosed mole (*Condylura cristata*) has an average food 'handling time' – identifying food as edible, capturing it, eating it and moving on to the next piece – of 230 milliseconds, with the fastest time being 120 milliseconds. The star-nosed mole is a semi-aquatic animal that gets its name from its 22-probed nose, which is the **most sensitive mammal touch organ**, five times as sensitive as the human hand.

★ LARGEST RODENT

The capybara or carpincho (*Hydrochoerus hydrochaeris*) of South America has a head and body length of 1–1.3 m (3 ft 3 in–4 ft 3 in) and can weigh up to 79 kg (174 lb), although one cage-fat specimen attained a record weight of 113 kg (249 lb).

SMALLEST RODENT

At least two species vie for this record title. The northern pygmy mouse (*Baiomys taylori*) of Mexico and the USA, and the Baluchistan pygmy jerboa (*Salpingotus michaelis*) of Pakistan both have a head–body length of as little as 3.6 cm (1.4 in) and a tail length of 7.2 cm (2.8 in).

PRIMATES

LARGEST PRIMATE

The male eastern lowland gorilla (*Gorilla gorilla graueri*) found in the eastern Congo has a bipedal (two-footed) standing height of up to 1.75 m (5 ft 9 in) and weighs up to 163 kg (360 lb).

SMALLEST PRIMATE

Excluding tree shrews, which are normally classified separately, the smallest true primate is the pygmy mouse lemur (*Microcebus myoxinus*), which was discovered in the deciduous forests of western Madagascar. It has a head–body length of about 62 mm (2.4 in), a tail length of 136 mm (5.4 in) and an average weight of 30.6 g (1.1 oz).

★ LARGEST TREE-DWELLING MAMMAL

The orang-utan is the largest arboreal mammal. It lives in the canopy of tropical rainforests in Borneo and Sumatra, Malaysia. Sumatran orang-utan (*Pongo abelii*) and Bornean orang-utan (*P. pygmaeus*) males typically weigh 83 kg (183 lb) and measure 1.5 m (5 ft) tall. 'Orang-utan' is Malay for 'man of the forest'.

★ FASTEST PRIMATE

The patas monkey (*Erythrocebus patas*) of western and eastern Africa can reach speeds of 55 km/h (34 mph) over the ground. With their long, slender limbs, patas monkeys are often called 'primate cheetahs'.

BURROWERS & GLIDERS

★ LARGEST BURROWER

The wombat (*Vombatus ursinus*), an Australian bear-like marsupial, can grow up to 1.2 m (4 ft) long and weigh up to 35 kg (77 lb). Its large paws, strong claws and backwards-opening pouch help it dig burrows up to 20 m (65 ft) long and 2 m (6 ft) deep.

★ SMALLEST BURROWER

Savi's pygmy shrew (*Suncus etruscus*) has an average body length of 36–53 mm (1.4–2 in) and a tail 24–29 mm (0.9–1 in) long, enabling it to utilize tunnels and holes dug by large earthworms!

LARGEST MAMMAL ON LAND

The adult male African elephant (*Loxodonta africana*) typically stands 3–3.7 m (9 ft 10 in–12 ft 1 in) at the shoulder and weighs 4–7 tonnes (8,800–15,400 lb). *See below for the largest ever specimen.*

Land mammal extremes

Largest: A bull African elephant shot in 1974 measured 4.16 m (13 ft 7 in) to the shoulder and weighed 12.24 tonnes (26,984 lb)

Tallest: A Masai bull giraffe named George stood at 5.8 m (19 ft) tall when measured in 1959 at Chester Zoo, UK

Smallest: A typical bumblebee bat/Kitti's hog-nosed bat has a body length of 29–33 mm (1.14–1.29 in) and weighs 1.7–2 g (0.05–0.07 oz)

★ Smallest (non-flying): Savi's pygmy shrews measure just 36–53 mm (1.4–2 in) and weigh 1.5–2.6 g (0.05–0.09 oz)

Fastest: In 1965, a 35-kg (77-lb) adult female cheetah was recorded running at 104.4 km/h (64.3 mph) over a measured distance of 201.2 m (660 ft)

FASTEST → MARINE MAMMAL

On 12 October 1958, a bull killer whale (*Orcinus orca*) was timed at 55.5 km/h (34.5 mph) in the north-eastern Pacific. Similar speeds have also been reported for a Dall's porpoise (*Phocoenoides dalli*) in short bursts.

★ LARGEST CLAWS

The anterior claws on the third digit of the giant armadillo (*Priodontes maximus*) typically measure 20 cm (8 in) long. These burrowers, found throughout South America, use their claws – the largest in the animal kingdom – for digging and ripping apart termite mounds. The armadillo is also the ★ **land mammal with the most teeth**, typically having up to 100 in its jaws.

★ LARGEST GLIDING MAMMAL

The giant flying squirrels (genus *Petaurista*) of Asia are able to 'fly' between trees using the skin-membranes on the sides of their bodies, which act as a parachute. Up to 1.1 m (3.6 ft) long, including tail, these squirrels can glide for 400 m (1,310 ft), although the farthest recorded distance covered by one – and the ★ **farthest glide by any mammal** – is 450 m (1,475 ft), or four lengths of an American football field.

★ SMALLEST GLIDING MAMMAL

The feathertail glider (*Acrobates pygmaeus*) of Australia can glide between trees up to 25 m (82 ft) apart – slightly more than the length of a tennis court – despite its tiny body length of just 65–80 mm (2.5–3.1 in).

PINNIPEDS

LARGEST PINNIPED

The largest of the 34 known species of pinniped – the aquatic suborder that includes seals and walruses – is the southern elephant seal (*Mirounga leonina*) of the sub-Antarctic islands. Bulls average 5 m (16 ft 6 in) in length, from the inflated snout to the tips of the outstretched tail flippers, have a maximum girth of 3.7 m (12 ft) and weigh about 2,000–3,500 kg (4,400–7,720 lb).

The **largest accurately measured specimen** was a bull caught in 1913 that measured 6.5 m (21 ft 4 in) and weighed at least 4 tonnes (8,810 lb).

MOST DANGEROUS PINNIPED

The carnivorous leopard seal (*Hydrurga leptonyx*) is the only species with a reputation for apparently unprovoked attacks on humans. There are a number of documented cases of leopard seals suddenly lunging through cracks in the ice to snap at people's feet. Divers have also been attacked by these seals on at least one occasion and there are instances of several people being chased across the ice over distances of up to 100 m (330 ft) by them. Scientists believe that the seals confuse the dark vertical shape of a person with that of an emperor penguin.

SMALLEST PINNIPED

The female Galapagos fur seal (*Arctocephalus galapagoensis*) averages 1.2 m (3 ft 11 in) in length and weighs about 27 kg (60 lb). Males are usually considerably larger, averaging 1.5 m (4 ft 11 in) in length and weighing around 64 kg (141 lb).

OLDEST PINNIPED

The greatest authenticated age for a pinniped was estimated by scientists at the Limnological Institute in Irkutsk, Russia, to be 56 years for the female Baikal seal (*Phoca sibirica*) and 52 years for the male. This estimate was based on cementum layers in the canine teeth.

LARGEST GREY SEAL COLONY

The grey seal (*Halichoerus grypus*) colony on Sable Island off Nova Scotia, Canada, numbers around 100,000 individuals every winter during the breeding season. After 18 days, the newly born pups are left to fend for themselves.

CETACEANS

LARGEST MAMMAL

The blue whale (*Balaenoptera musculus*) is the largest mammal – and the **largest animal** – on Earth. The whale's average length is 24 m (80 ft) and it can weigh up to 160 tonnes (352,000 lb). A huge specimen caught in the Southern Ocean, Antarctica, on 20 March 1947 weighed 190 tonnes

(418,000 lb), making it the **heaviest mammal recorded**. The **longest known mammal** was a female blue whale measuring 33.58 m (110 ft 28 in) that landed in 1909 at Grytviken, South Georgia, in the South Atlantic.

By comparison, the blue whale is 80,000,000 times heavier than the **smallest mammal**! The bumblebee bat or Kitti's hog-nosed bat (*Craseonycteris thonglongyai*) has a head-body length of only 29–33 mm (1.14–1.29 in) and a weight of 1.7–2 g (0.05–0.07 oz). It can be found only in a few select caves on the Kwae Noi river, Kanchanaburi Province, south-west Thailand.

SLOWEST HEARTBEAT IN A MAMMAL

The blue whale is presumed to have the slowest heartbeat of any warm-blooded animal, with four to eight beats per minute (dependent upon whether the whale is diving or not). By comparison, the average adult human heart beats 70 times per minute.

LOUDEST ANIMAL SOUND

Fin whales (*B. physalus*) and blue whales utter low-frequency pulses when 'singing' to each other. These whales reach an amazing 188 dB on the decibel scale, creating the **loudest sounds emitted by any living source**. Using specialist equipment, scientists have detected the whale sounds 850 km (530 miles) away.

LARGEST MAMMAL JAW

A jaw belonging to a sperm whale or cachelot (*Physeter macrocephalus*) and measuring 5 m (16 ft 5 in) long was exhibited in the Natural History Museum in London, UK. The massive lower jaw belonged to a male whale nearly 25.6 m (84 ft) in length. Sperm whales are also the **largest-toothed whales**.

SMALLEST WHALE

The are two contenders for the smallest cetacean: Hector's dolphin (*Cephalorhynchus hectori*) and vaquita (*Phocoena sinus*), both of which can be as small as 1.2 m (3 ft 11 in) long.

DENSEST FUR

The sea otter (*Enhydra lutris*) – found mostly off the coast of Alaska, USA – has the densest fur of any animal, with more than 101,560 hairs per cm² (650,000 hairs per in²). By comparison, humans typically have just 156 hairs per cm² (1,000 hairs per in²).

LARGEST ANIMAL BRAIN

The largest brain of any animal belongs to the sperm whale (*Physeter macrocephalus*) and weighs approximately 9 kg (19 lb 13 oz). In comparison, the weight of a bull African elephant's (*Loxodonta africana*) brain can reach 5.4 kg (11 lb 14 oz) and a human brain is, on average, 1.4 kg (3 lb).

→ HOW MUCH DID THE HEAVIEST EVER HUMAN BRAIN WEIGH? FIND OUT ON P.24

BIRDS

HIGHEST FLYING BIRDS

The highest altitude recorded for a bird is 11,300 m (37,000 ft) for a Ruppell's vulture (*Gyps rueppellii*), which collided with a commercial aircraft over Abidjan, Ivory Coast, on 29 November 1973. The impact damaged one of the aircraft's engines, causing it to shut down, but the plane landed safely without further incident. Sufficient remains of the bird were recovered to allow the US Museum of Natural History to make a positive identification of this high-flier, which is rarely seen above 6,000 m (20,000 ft).

SMALLEST BIRD EGG

Jamaica's vervain hummingbird (*Mellisuga minima*) produces the smallest egg of any bird species (below, seen next to an ostrich egg, the **largest bird egg**). Two known specimens measure less than 10 mm (0.39 in) in length and weigh 365 mg (0.0128 oz) and 375 mg (0.0132 oz).

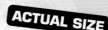
ACTUAL SIZE

SIZE

HEAVIEST BIRD OF PREY

The male Andean condor (*Vultur gryphus*) has an average weight of 9–12 kg (20–27 lb) and a wing-span of 3 m (10 ft). A weight of 14.1 kg (31 lb) has been claimed for a male California condor (*Gymnogyps californianus*), now preserved in the California Academy of Sciences at Los Angeles, USA, but this species is generally much smaller than the Andean condor and rarely exceeds 10.4 kg (23 lb).

SMALLEST BIRD OF PREY

This title is held jointly by the black-legged falconet (*Microhierax fringillarius*) of south-east Asia and the white-fronted or Bornean falconet (*M. latifrons*) of north-western Borneo. Both species have an average length of 14–15 cm (5.5–6 in), including a 5-cm (2-in) tail, and weigh about 35 g (1.25 oz).

HEAVIEST FLYING BIRD

Mute swans (*Cygnus olor*) can reach 18 kg (40 lb), although there is a record from Poland of a cob (male) that weighed 22.5 kg (49 lb 10 oz). It had temporarily lost the power of flight.

LARGEST BIRD

Male north African ostriches (*Struthio camelus camelus*) have been recorded up to 2.75 m (9 ft) tall and weighing 156.5 kg (345 lb). The north African ostrich is a ratite (flightless) subspecies.

LARGEST EAGLE

The Stellar's sea eagle (*Haliaeetus albicilla*) weighs between 5 and 9 kg (11 and 20 lb) with a wing-span of 2.2–2.45 m (7.2–8 ft). It breeds mainly in Russia, but has also been located in Korea and Japan.

SMALLEST FLIGHTLESS BIRD

The Inaccessible Island rail (*Atlantisia rogersi*) of Inaccessible Island, South Atlantic, weighs a mere 40 g (1.04 oz).

LARGEST BIRD EGG

An ostrich egg weighing 2.35 kg (5 lb 2 oz) was laid in June 1997 at Datong Xinda ostrich farm, Datong, Shanxi, China.

LARGEST AVIAN REPRODUCTIVE ORGAN

The penis of the Argentinian lake drake (*Oxyura vittata*) has been measured everted (upside down) and unwound at 42.5 cm (16.7 in).

The base of this retractable penis is covered with spines, yet the tip is soft and brush-like.

ON THE WING

MOST AIRBORNE BIRD

After leaving the nesting grounds as a youngster, the sooty tern (*Sterna fuscata*) remains aloft for three to ten years while maturing, settling on water from time to time before returning to land to breed as an adult.

TALLEST FLYING BIRD

Cranes, which are wading birds, belong to the family Gruidae. The largest can stand to a height of almost 2 m (6 ft 6 in).

GREATEST DISTANCE FLOWN

A common tern (*Sterna hirundo*), banded as a juvenile on 30 June 1996 in central Finland was recaptured alive at Rotamah Island, Victoria, Australia, in January 1997, some 26,000 km (16,250 miles) away. To have reached this destination, it is believed that the bird had to travel 200 km (124 miles) a day.

SMALLEST BIRD

The smallest bird is the bee hummingbird (*Mellisuga helenae*) of Cuba and the Isle of Youth. Males measure 57 mm (2.24 in) in length, half of which is taken up by the bill and tail, and weigh 1.6 g (0.056 oz). Females are slightly larger. The bee hummingbird is believed to have the lowest weight limit of any warm-blooded animal.

ACTUAL SIZE

★ NEW RECORD　　★ UPDATED RECORD

LONGEST MIGRATION

The Arctic tern (*Sterna paradisea*) breeds north of the Arctic Circle, then flies south to the Antarctic during the northern winter and back again – a round trip of about 35,000 km (21,750 miles), more than twice the Earth's diameter.

The terns spend a second summer in the southern hemisphere so they can use the long days to feed.

LONGEST...

FEATHERS

A phoenix fowl (or Yokohama chicken) – a strain of red junglefowl (*Gallus gallus*) – had a tail covert measuring 10.6 m (34 ft 9.5 in) in 1972. It was owned by Masasha Kubota (Japan).

FEATHERS ON A WILD BIRD

When courting, the male crested Argus pheasant (*Rheinhartia ocellata*) displays feathers up to 1.73 m (5 ft 8.4 in) long.

SMALLEST → BIRD NEST

The nest (right) built by the vervain hummingbird (*Mellisuga minima*) is about half the size of a walnut shell, while the deeper but narrower one of the bee hummingbird (*M. helenae*) is thimble-sized.

BILLS

The bill of the Australian pelican (*Pelecanus conspicillatus*) is 34–47 cm (13–18.5 in) long, but the longest beak in relation to overall body length is that of the sword-billed hummingbird (*Ensifera ensifera*). The beak measures 10.2 cm (4 in) – longer than the bird's body if the length of the tail is excluded.

The **shortest bills** belong to the smaller swifts (the Apodidae family), and in particular the glossy swiftlet (*Collocalia esculenta*), whose bill is almost non-existent.

ACTUAL SIZE

OLDEST...

BIRD

An unconfirmed age of 82 years was reported for a male Siberian white crane (*Grus leucogeranus*) named Wolf at the International Crane Foundation, Baraboo, Wisconsin, USA. The **greatest irrefutable age** reported for any bird is over 80 years for a male sulphur-crested cockatoo (*Cacatua galerita*) named Cocky, who died at London Zoo in 1982.

LIVING PIGEON

Former racing pigeon Old Man, owned by George Seagroatt (UK), was born on 16 February 1980.

FASTEST BIRDS

Fastest dive:
Peregrine falcon
(*Falco peregrinus*)
300 km/h (186 mph)

Fastest in level flight:
Ducks and geese (Anatidae)
90–100 km/h (56–62 mph)

Fastest on land:
Ostrich (*Struthio camelus*)
72 km/h (45 mph)

Fastest swimming:
Gentoo penguin
(*Pygoscelis papua*)
27 km/h (17 mph)

Slowest in flight:
American woodcock
(*Scolopax minor*) and
Eurasian woodcock
(*S. rusticola*)
8 km/h (5 mph)

LARGEST WING-SPAN
OF ANY LIVING SPECIES OF BIRD

A male wandering albatross (*Diomedea exulans*) of the southern oceans, caught by members of the Antarctic research ship USNS *Eltanin* in the Tasman Sea on 18 September 1965, had a wing-span of 3.63 m (11 ft 11 in) – the length of a Mini Cooper!

REPTILES

OLDEST LIVING
CHELONIAN

The term 'chelonian' refers to members of the order Testudines (formerly Chelonia), including tortoises and turtles. A female giant Galapagos land tortoise (*Geochelone nigra porteri*) called Harriet, one of three collected by Charles Darwin from the Galapagos Islands in 1835, is, at 175 years, the world's oldest resident.

Born on 15 November 1830, she weighs about 81 kg (180 lb) and currently resides at Australia Zoo, near Brisbane, Australia. *(Find out more about Harriet in the interview with Steve Irwin, below.)*

STEVE IRWIN

World-famous crocodile hunter Steve Irwin has been fascinated by reptiles since he was a boy. He runs a wildlife park in Queensland, Australia, with his wife Terri, and works at Australia Zoo, home to Harriet the giant Galapagos land tortoise.

Harriet holds the Guinness World Record for the oldest living chelonian, but is she also the oldest creature on Earth?
She would definitely be the oldest living animal on Earth. She was hatched in 1830 on the island of Santa Cruz, which is in the Galapagos Islands. Harriet was collected by Sir Charles Darwin in 1835 when she was five years old, then came to Australia, after being in England, with John Wickham in 1842.

How is she?
She's 175 years old and in perfect health!

Does anyone know how long Harriet will live?
Nobody knows. I can't see why she shouldn't live till 200, though.

What's the worst injury an animal has given you?
When we were filming our movie *The Crocodile Hunter* in 2000, a crocodile did a very severe thrash and I had all his weight on my knee – it pulled all the cartilage off both sides of the joint and snapped off pieces of bone inside my knee. I had to have an artificial knee put in.

How would somebody follow in your footsteps?
If you want to become a zoologist you've got to do all the tertiary education, but don't lose your passion or enthusiasm despite the hard work and homework that you have to do. Just follow through. Passion and enthusiasm will get you everywhere you want to go in the world.

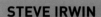
Read the full interview at www.guinnessworldrecords.com/steveirwin

SNAKES

FASTEST ON LAND
The black mamba (*Dendroaspis polylepis*) of tropical Africa can reach speeds of 10–12 mph (16–19 km/h) in short bursts over level ground.

HEAVIEST LIVING
A Burmese python (*Python molurus bivittatus*) called Baby weighed 182.76 kg (403 lb) on 20 November 1998. She is 8.22 m (27 ft) long with a girth of 71.12 cm (28 in). It takes nine people to lift her and she eats four to five chickens every two weeks. Baby lives at the Serpent Safari Park in Gurnee, Illinois, USA, and is owned by Lou Daddano (USA).

★ RAREST
The Antiguan racer (*Alsophis antiguae*) is restricted to Great Bird Island, a 9.9-hectare (24.5-acre) area off the coast of Antigua in the Lesser Antilles. From 1996 to 2001, the number of species aged one year or more fluctuated between 51 and 114, and currently stands at about 80.

HEAVIEST VENOMOUS
The eastern diamondback rattlesnake (*Crotalus adamanteus*) of the south-eastern United States weighs around 5.5–6.8 kg (12–15 lb) and is 1.52–1.83 m (5–6 ft) in length. The heaviest diamondback rattlesnake on record weighed 15 kg (34 lb) and was 2.36 m (7 ft 9 in) long.

LONGEST
The reticulated python (*Python reticulatus*) of south-east Asia, Indonesia and the Philippines regularly exceeds 6.25 m (20 ft 6 in). The record length is 10 m (32 ft 9.5 in) for a specimen shot in Celebes, Indonesia, in 1912.

MOST WIDELY DISTRIBUTED
VENOMOUS SNAKE

The saw-scaled or carpet viper (*Echis carinatus*), which ranges from west Africa to India, bites and kills more people in the world than any other species. The snake has an extremely toxic haemorrhagic poison and is very aggressive when provoked. A haemorrhagic poison is a toxin that causes uncontrollable bleeding.

ACTUAL SIZE

SNAKE WITH THE
LONGEST FANGS →

The longest fangs of any snake are those of the highly venomous gaboon viper (*Bitis gabonica*) of tropical Africa. In a specimen of 1.83 m (6 ft) in length, they measured 50 mm (2 in).

ACTUAL SIZE

OLDEST

The greatest reliable age recorded for a snake is 40 years 3 months 14 days for a male common boa (*Boa constrictor*) named Popeye, who died at Philadelphia Zoo, Pennsylvania, USA, on 15 April 1977.

CROCODILES

★ MOST FATALITIES FROM AN ATTACK

On 19 February 1945, an imperial Japanese army unit guarding a stronghold on the Burmese island of Ramree was outflanked by a British naval force, and forced to cross 16 km (10 miles) of mangrove swamps to rejoin a larger force of Japanese infantry. The swamps were home to many 4.5-m-long (15-ft) saltwater crocodiles (*Crocodylus porosus*). On the morning of 20 February, of the 1,000 Japanese soldiers that entered the swamp, only 20 had survived.

LARGEST

The estuarine or saltwater crocodile (*Crocodylus porosus*), which ranges throughout the tropical regions of Asia and the Pacific, is the world's largest crocodile. The Bhitarkanika Wildlife Sanctuary in India houses four protected estuarine crocodiles measuring more than 6 m (19 ft 8 in) in length, the largest being more than 7 m (23 ft) long. There are several unauthenticated reports of specimens up to 10 m (33 ft) in length.

TORTOISES

★ FASTEST

A tortoise named Charlie covered a 5.48-m (18-ft) course at the National Tortoise Championship at Tickhill, South Yorkshire, UK, in 43.7 seconds at a speed of 0.45 km/h (0.28 mph) on 2 July 1977.

LONELIEST CREATURE

The Abingdon Island giant tortoise (*Geochelone elephantopus abingdoni*) is represented by a single living specimen, an aged male called Lonesome George. Attempts to mate him with his closest relatives on other islands have so far been unsuccessful, and so this particular subspecies of Galapagos giant tortoise is effectively extinct while still alive.

LIZARDS

FASTEST

The highest burst of speed recorded for any reptile on land is 34.9 km/h (21.7 mph) by a *Ctenosaura*, a spiny-tailed iguana from Central America.

LARGEST

The male Komodo dragon (*Varanus komodoensis*), otherwise known as the Komodo monitor or ora, averages 2.25 m (7 ft 5 in) in length and weighs about 59 kg (130 lb). It is found on the Indonesian islands of Komodo, Rintja, Padar and Flores.

LARGEST CROCODILE EVER

Sarchosuchus imperator was a prehistoric species of crocodile that lived around 110 million years ago. Recent fossilized remains found in the Sahara Desert suggest that this creature took around 50–60 years to grow to its full length of around 11–12 m (37–40 ft) and its maximum weight of around 8 tonnes (17,600 lb).

PREHISTORIC LIFE

SMALLEST
DINOSAUR

The chicken-sized *Compsognathus* of southern Germany and south-east France measured 60 cm (2 ft) from the snout to the tip of the tail and weighed about 3 kg (6 lb 8 oz).

DINOSAUR NAMES

Archaeopteryx
– 'ancient wing'

Brachiosaurus brancai
– 'arm lizard'

Compsognathus
– 'pretty jaw'

Dilong paradoxus
– 'dilong', from the
Mandarin Chinese word
for 'emperor' and 'dragon';
'paradoxus', referring to the
creature's unusual features

Diplodocus – 'double-beamed'

Dromornis stirtoni
– 'Stirton's thunder bird', after
palaeontologist Reuben Stirton

Pachycephalosaurus
– 'thick-headed lizard'

Pederpes finneyae – 'Peder' –
Norwegian for Peter (Peter
Aspen, discoverer), 'erpes'
meaning 'crawler' and 'finneyae'
after Sarah Finney, who prepared
the fossil for study

Pikaia gracilens – After Mount
Pika, British Columbia, and
'gracilens', meaning 'slender'

Protarchaeopteryx
– 'primitive, or first, ancient wing'

Protohadros byrdi
– 'Byrd's primitive hadrosaur'
(duck-billed) – or 'first hadrosaur';
discovered by Gary Byrd

Sauroposeidon
– 'earthquake god lizard'

Sinornithosaurus millenii
– 'millennium Chinese
bird-lizard'

Titanis walleri – 'terror bird'

Tyrannosaurus rex
– 'tyrant lizard king'

SIZE

★ TALLEST MOUNTED DINOSAUR SKELETON

A *Brachiosaurus brancai* skeleton from Tanzania was constructed from the remains of several individuals. It measures 22.2 m (72 ft 10 in) long and has a raised head height of 14 m (46 ft).

★ THICKEST DINOSAUR SKULL

Pachycephalosaurus, a dome-headed herbivore that lived during the Late Cretaceous period about 76 to 65 million years ago, had a skull 60 cm (2 ft) long with a bone dome 20 cm (8 in) thick.

LONGEST DINOSAUR

A diplodocid excavated in 1980 from New Mexico, USA, and reconstructed in 1999 at the Wyoming Dinosaur Center, USA, was 41 m (134 ft) long – equivalent to five double-decker buses.

★ DINOSAUR WITH THE LONGEST NECK

Fossils found in Oklahoma, USA, in 1994, indicate that the sauropod *Sauroposeidon* was a herbivore with a neck that could stretch up to 17 m (55 ft). Individual *Sauroposeidon* vertebrae have been found measuring up to 1.2 m (4 ft) long. *Sauroposeidon* lived about 110 million years ago, during the Middle Cretaceous period.

DINOSAUR WITH THE LONGEST TAIL

The diplodocid *Diplodocus* was a long-necked sauropod dinosaur from the Late Jurassic period, 155 to 145 million years ago, with a tail 13–14 m (43–45 ft) long.

★ LARGEST CARNIVORE COPROLITE

In 1995, coprolite (fossilized excrement) from a *Tyrannosaurus rex* was discovered that measured 50 cm (19.6 in) across and weighed around 7 kg (15 lb 6 oz).

OLDEST...

★ DUCK-BILLED DINOSAUR

Fossils of the hadrosaur *Protohadros byrdi*, found near Flower Mound, Texas, USA, in 1994 by Gary Byrd (USA), are thought to date back 95.5 million years.

★ TYRANNOSAUROID

Dilong paradoxus, the oldest known ancestor of *T. rex*, lived between 139 and 128 million years ago. It measured some 1.5 m (5 ft) in length and stood on two legs. There is also evidence that this creature had hair-like protofeathers on its jaw and the tip of its tail.

D. paradoxus was discovered in the famous fossil beds of Liaoning Province, China.

★ KNOWN CHORDATE

Pikaia gracilens is the oldest known chordate (a member of the phylum to which humans and all vertebrates belong). It lived during the Middle Cambrian age, over 500 million years ago. The first *P. gracilens* specimen was found in the Burgess Shale fossil site, British Columbia, Canada.

P. gracilens resembled a contemporary jawless marine invertebrate called the lancet.

★ SMALLEST
DINOSAUR FOOTPRINT

The smallest dinosaur footprint discovered to date measures just 1.78 cm (0.7 in) from the heel to the tip of digit III. It was discovered on the Isle of Skye, Highland, UK, by Dr Neil Clark (UK, pictured) of the Hunterian Museum of the University of Glasgow, UK, and announced in June 2004. The footprint was made during the Middle Jurassic period, around 165 million years ago.

ACTUAL SIZE

★ FIRST
NON-FLYING BIRD

The earliest non-flying bird is the feathered dinosaur *Protarchaeopteryx*. A fossil was found in Liaoning Province, north-eastern China, in 1997. The size of a turkey and similar in appearance to carnivorous therapod dinosaurs, this species had relatively short arms and symmetrical feathers – evidence that it could not fly.

The *Protarchaeopteryx* is believed to be an ancestor of the **first flying bird**, the *Archaeopteryx*, pictured left.

BIRDS

LARGEST PREHISTORIC BIRD

The flightless *Dromornis stirtoni* was a huge emu-like creature that lived in central Australia between 15 million and 25,000 years ago. Fossilized leg bones found near Alice Springs in 1974 indicate that the bird must have stood about 3 m (10 ft) tall and weighed about 500 kg (1,100 lb).

★ MOST COMPLETE FEATHERED DINOSAUR FOSSIL

In April 2001, a complete fossil of *Sinornithosaurus millenii*, a relative of the *Velociraptor*, was discovered by farmers at the Yixian Formation fossil bed, Liaoning Province, China. It is approximately 60 cm (2 ft) long, completely covered in downy fluff and primitive feathers and resembles a large duck with a long tail. This is the first time a complete feathered fossil has been found, and supports the theory that present-day birds evolved from dinosaurs.

LARGEST PREHISTORIC CARNIVOROUS BIRD

The *Titanis walleri* had a total body height of 2.5 m (8 ft 2 in) and its weight probably reached 200 kg (440 lb). It is known to have lived until the Late Pleistocene (Ice Age).

FOOTPRINTS

LONGEST SET OF DINOSAUR FOOTPRINTS

The Cal Orcko quarry near Sucre, Bolivia, contains more than 5,000 individual dinosaur footprints. More than 250 trackways have been identified among these prints, the longest of which measures some 350 m (1,150 ft) in length and was made by a therapod dinosaur around 68 million years ago.

EARLIEST ANIMAL TO WALK ON LAND

Remains of a tetrapod, *Pederpes finneyae*, discovered in 1971 north of Dumbarton, West Dunbartonshire, UK, are around 350 million years old. The legs and one complete foot were identified by Dr Jenny Clack (UK) of the University Museum of Zoology, University of Cambridge, UK, and announced on 4 July 2002.

LARGEST HERBIVORE DINOSAUR →

The largest ever land animals were sauropod dinosaurs, a group of long-necked, long-tailed, four-legged plant-eaters that lumbered around most of the world in the Jurassic and Cretaceous periods, 208–65 million years ago. The largest measured 40 m (131 ft) and weighed up to 100 tonnes (220,400 lb). The picture to the right shows a femur (thigh bone) from one of these creatures.

★ MOST DINOSAUR FOOTPRINTS DISCOVERED IN ONE PLACE

The Bolivian Cal Orcko quarry has a limestone wall 800 m (0.5 miles) long and 260 m (850 ft) high that contains more than 5,000 individual dinosaur footprints. The variety of prints demonstrates that dinosaur species were diverse right up to the point of their extinction, 65 million years ago.

★ LARGEST DINOSAUR EGG COLLECTION

The Heyuan Museum, Guangdong Province, China, held 10,008 individual dinosaur eggs as of November 2004. All come from the Late Cretaceous period (89–65 million years ago).

→ **HOW BIG WAS THE LARGEST CROCODILE EVER? FIND OUT ON P.91**

MICROSCOPIC LIFE

MOST DANGEROUS
← PARASITE

The malarial parasites of the genus *Plasmodium*, carried by mosquitoes of the genus *Anopheles*, have, excluding wars and accidents, probably been responsible for half of all human deaths since the Stone Age. According to 1998 World Health Organization estimates, malaria causes more than 1 million deaths a year and is endemic in a total of 101 countries and territories.

BACTERIA

DEADLIEST NATURAL TOXIN

The anaerobic bacterium of spoiled food, which causes botulism (*Clostridium botulinum*) is so deadly (more so than strychnine, arsenic or even snake venoms) that one pound (450 g) could, in theory, wipe out the human race.

LARGEST BACTERIUM

According to the journal *Science*, the bacterium *Thiomargarita namibiensis* (Sulphur Pearl of Namibia) is about 750 times larger than the typical bacterium – and visible to the naked eye.

★ PATHOGEN WITH THE HIGHEST MORTALITY AND MORBIDITY RATES

One third of the world's population is infected with *Mycobacterium tuberculosis*, the bactericum that causes tuberculosis (TB). Around 8 million people contract TB each year, and 1 million die from it. It is estimated that someone is infected by absorbing TB bacilli (germs) every second.

OLDEST LIVING BACTERIA

In 2000, bacteria trapped in suspended animation inside salt crystals for 250 million years have been revived and cultured by US scientists. Designated *Bacillus 2-9-3*, this species is 10 times older than the previous oldest revived bacteria.

EXTREMOPHILES

ACID RESISTANT

The most acidic conditions in which microbial (or any) life has been discovered to survive is pH 0, equivalent to hydrochloric acid. Several organisms are known to thrive in these conditions – including *Cyanidium caldarium*, which lives in the vents of active volcanoes.

ALKALINE RESISTANT

A bacteria discovered in 2003 near Chicago, Illinois, USA, lives in groundwater contaminated by more than a century's worth of industrial iron slag tipping, where it survives pH levels of up to 12.8. By way of comparison, a pH value of 12.8 is equivalent to caustic soda or floor stripper.

DISEASES

Commonest (non-infectious)	Periodontal disease (e.g. gingivitus)	Affects 60–90% of school children and the majority of adults
Commonest (infectious)	Common cold (family of rhinoviruses)	At least 40 different airborne or direct-contact viruses, almost universal
Most virulent (re-emerging)	Dengue (and dengue haemorrhagic fever)	275,000 cases in tropical Central and South America
Most virulent (viral)	Ebola haemorrhagic fever	Kills 90% of those who contract it; 1,200 deaths since first discovered in 1976
Oldest contagious	Leprosy	Described in ancient Egypt in 1350 BC
Rarest	Smallpox	Zero cases since 1978
Worst flesh-eating	Necrotizing fasciitis	Attacks layer of tissue below the skin and requires surgical removal of tissue

According to the World Health Organization, there are six contenders for the **deadliest disease** record: HIV, tuberculosis, malaria, measles pneumonia and diarrhoeal diseases caused 90% of all deaths from infectious diseases as of 1999. HIV is the ★ **fastest growing disease**.

→ WHERE WOULD YOU FIND THE MOST HEAT-TOLERANT ORGANISMS ON THE PLANET? FIND OUT ON P.78

★ SMALLEST BACTERIA →

The smallest living bacteria, and the smallest organisms discovered to date, are 'nanobes'. Measuring just 20–150 nm (nanometres) across, they were found in sandstone samples 3–5 km (2–3 miles) beneath the ocean floor by Dr Phillippa Uwins (Australia) and colleagues from the University of Queensland, Australia. These organisms are around 10 times smaller than the smallest conventional bacteria.

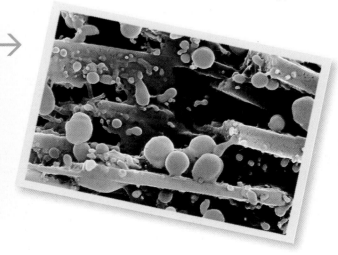

LONGEST →
QUARANTINED ISLAND

Gruinard Island off the west coast of Scotland, UK, was quarantined in 1942 following a release of anthrax to wipe out a flock of sheep. The test was ordered at a time when it was feared that Adolf Hitler may launch chemical or biological attacks on Britain. The quarantine was not lifted until 24 April 1990, a total of 48 years later.

The island was declared safe after a junior defence minister travelled to the 210-ha (520-acre) island to remove the red warning sign.

RADIATION RESISTANT
The bacterium *Deinococcus radiodurans* can withstand atomic radiation of 6.5 million röntgens, or 10,000 times more than the radiation levels that an average human could withstand.

LONGEST SURVIVAL IN SPACE
From 7 April 1984 to 11 January 1990, *E. coli* bacteria cells survived unshielded on board Nasa's Long Duration Exposure Facility satellite in Earth orbit.

In November 1969, hardware samples removed from the US unmanned lunar probe *Surveyor 3* were returned to Earth by the crew of *Apollo 12*. Analysis of the hardware revealed bacterial organisms (*Streptococcus mitis*) – which had contaminated *Surveyor 3* before its launch on 17 April 1967 – had survived over two-and-a-half years in space.

The **highest altitude** at which bacteria has been discovered is 41.14 km (25.5 miles).

VIRUSES

LARGEST VIRUS
The Mimivirus contains 900 genes and has a diameter of 400 nm (0.0000157 in). It was discovered in 1992 in a sample from a water cooling tower in Bradford, UK. The virus was examined by researchers at the National Centre for Scientific Research in Paris, France, who released their results on 27 March 2003 in the journal *Science*. Mimivirus has genetic similarities to the virus family that includes smallpox.

MOST HIV SUFFERERS
In December 2003, South Africa had 5.3 million people infected with HIV (Human Immunodeficiency Virus) – around an eighth of the population. In December 2004, 39.4 million people worldwide had HIV, which can lead on to Acquired Immune Deficiency Syndrome (AIDS).

★ ONLY ANIMAL IMMUNE TO RABIES
The hyena is the only wild animal that is naturally immune to rabies. Researchers studied several hundred hyenas in the Serengeti, Africa, for up to 13 years and discovered that hyenas seem to be able to carry the virus without displaying any of the usual symptoms associated with it, i.e. hyperactivity, paralysis and death.

DEAD OR ALIVE?

Viruses (Latin: 'poison') are considered to exist on the boundary between living and non-living things. They are composed of proteins and nucleic acids contained within a protective protein coat. Much smaller than conventional bacteria, viruses are parasites that invade cells and force the cell to become a factory for more viruses. Eventually the cell bursts, releasing copies of the virus to attack other cells.

Bacteria (Greek: 'rod', after certain bacteria's rod-like shape) are single-celled organisms that can cause disease. Although once considered part of the plant kingdom, they now belong to a kingdom of their own, named 'monera'.

Extremophiles are organisms that thrive in, or require, 'extreme' conditions, such as high temperatures or excessive acidity. They are usually unicellular (one-celled), though not always.

★ LONGEST
FOSSIL RECORD

Stromatolites have the longest fossil record of any life-form on Earth. These cauliflower-shaped, rock-like structures are formed by the activity of cyanobacteria (blue-green algae), and appeared on Earth 3.5 billion years ago, during the Precambrian era. In 1954, a colony of living stromatolites was found in Shark Bay, Australia, with forms similar to these ancient ancestors.

WILD PLANTS

LONGEST SEAWEED →

Pacific giant kelp (*Macrocystis pyrifera*) can reach 60 m (195 ft) long. It grows at a rate of 45 cm (18 in) – the width of this open book – in one day.

SMALLEST FRUIT ↓

The smallest fruit in the world is produced by the **smallest flowering plant**, the floating duckweed, which belongs to the genus *Wolffia*. The fruit of *W. augusta* is only 0.25 mm long (1/100th of an inch) and weighs about 70 micrograms (1/400,000 of an ounce) – smaller than a single grain of table salt.

ACTUAL SIZE

PLANTS

LARGEST SINGLE FLOWER

The mottled orange-brown and white parasite *Rafflesia arnoldii* has the largest of all flowers – up to 91 cm (3 ft) wide and weighing around 11 kg (24 lb). Their petals are 1.9 cm (0.75 in) thick.

★ LARGEST BLOOM

An example of *Amorphophallus titanum* on display at the Botanical Gardens of Bonn University, Germany, was 3.06 m (10 ft) tall on 23 May 2003. The species was discovered in Sumatra, Indonesia, in 1878, and has a very unpleasant smell. The **smelliest flower** is the 'corpse flower'. Its 'rotting-flesh' odour can be detected 0.8 km (0.5 mile) away.

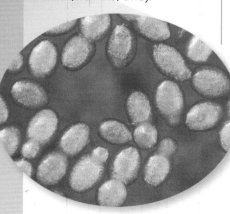

SMALLEST SEED

The seeds of epiphytic orchids (non-parasitic plants growing on others) number 992.25 million seeds per gram (28,129.81 million per ounce) – similar in size to a speck of dust.

LARGEST SEED

The giant fan palm *Lodoicea maldivica*, commonly known as the 'double coconut' or 'coco de mer', is found wild only in the Seychelles. Its single-seeded fruit weighs up to 20 kg (44 lb) – equivalent to the weight of approximately six newborn babies.

MOST MASSIVE PLANT

In December 1992, a network of quaking aspens (*Populus tremuloides*) growing from a single root system in the Wasatch Mountains, Utah, USA, was estimated to cover a total of 43 hectares (106 acres) and weigh 6,000 tonnes (13,227,720 lb). The organism – nicknamed 'Pando' (from the Latin for 'I spread') – looks like a forest of trees, but is, in fact, what the scientists studying it call 'suckers' – plants that have grown from the root system of a single tree.

MOST POISONOUS PLANT

Based on the amount it takes to kill a human, the most poisonous common plant in the world is the castor bean (*Ricinus communis*). According to the *Merck Index: An Encyclopedia of Chemicals, Drugs, and Biologicals* (1997), a dose of 70 micrograms (2 millionths of an ounce) is enough to kill a person weighing 72 kg (160 lb; 11 st 4 lb). The plant's poison is called ricin and is actually a protein found in the seeds of the castor bean. One gram of ricin is approximately 6,000 times more poisonous than cyanide and 12,000 more poisonous than rattlesnake venom.

LARGEST PREY OF ANY CARNIVOROUS PLANT

Carnivorous plants belonging to the Nepenthaceae family (genus *Nepenthes*) – particularly *N. rajah* and *N. rafflesiana* – have been known to eat large frogs, birds and even rats. They do so by using colour, smell and nectar to attract the prey, then trapping and digesting them using enzymes. These species are commonly found in the rainforests of Asia, in particular Borneo, Indonesia and Malaysia.

MOST SELECTIVE CARNIVOROUS PLANT

Nepenthes albomarginata is the most selective of all carnivorous plants, attracting and feeding only on foraging termites called *Hospitalitermes bicolor*. Growing in the rainforests of Malaysia and Indonesia, *N. albomarginata* is also the only plant to offer its own tissue to secure a meal: it grows a ring of edible white hairs (called trichomes) that attracts the termites, which then slip down the 'throat' of the plant to be digested.

MOST DANGEROUS STINGER

New Zealand's tree nettle (*Urtica ferox*) injects toxins into the skin powerful enough to kill dogs and horses. In one case, the plant is known to have killed a man within just five hours of him making contact with it.

RAREST PLANT

Only 46 mandrinettes (*Hibiscus fragilis*) are left – at two locations on Mauritius in the Indian Ocean.

FASTEST GROWING PLANT

Certain species of bamboo grow at up to 91 cm (35 in) a day – a rate of 0.00003 km/h (0.00002 mph). At such a speed, the length of bamboo seen right would have taken just seven hours to grow.

The **fastest growing flowering plant** is the *Hesperoyucca whipplei* of the Liliaceae family, one example of which grew 3.65 m (11 ft 11 in) in 14 days – a rate of about 25.4 cm (10 in) a day. The **slowest flowering plant** is Bolivia's rare *Puya raimondii* (which is also the **largest herb**). The panicle (a cluster of flowers) emerges after about 80–150 years.

TREES

★ LARGEST BURL

Tree burls are abnormal swellings on branches or stems following a disturbance to wood cells in the cambial layer under the bark. The largest ever weighed 20,361 kg (44,888 lb) and measured 18.7 m (61 ft 4 in) around its widest point when it was cut and moved in 1976. It was originally found growing at the base of a 351-year-old Sitka spruce (*Picea sitchensis*) tree in Port McNeill, British Columbia, Canada.

★ THICKEST BARK

The bark of the giant sequoia (*Sequoiadendron giganteum*) growing in the Sierra Nevada mountains of California, USA, varies in thickness between 25 and 121 cm (10 and 48 in).

HIGHEST RING COUNT

'Prometheus', a bristlecone pine (*Pinus longaeva*) felled in 1963 on Mount Wheeler, Nevada, USA, had a record ring count of 4,867. The tree grew in a harsh environment and was possibly closer to 5,200 years old. This makes it the **oldest tree** ever recorded growing on Earth.

EX-TREE-MES

Tallest living: 'Stratosphere Giant', a coast redwood (*Sequoia sempervirens*) in Humboldt Redwoods State Park, California, USA, measures 112.7 m (370 ft).

Tallest ever measured: A *Eucalyptus regnans* at Mount Baw Baw, Victoria, Australia, measured 143 m (470 ft) in 1885.

Largest living: 'General Sherman', a giant sequoia (*Sequoiadendron giganteum*) growing in Sequoia National Park, California, USA, stands 82.6 m (271 ft) tall, has a diameter of 8.2 m (27 ft 2 in) and a circumference of approximately 25.9 m (85 ft) – enough to make more than 5 billion matches.

Rarest: Just 43 adult Wollemi pines (*Wollemia nobilis*) exist in Wollemi National Park, Australia.

Earliest species: The maidenhair (*Ginkgo biloba*) of China appeared about 160 million years ago.

Remotest: A Norwegian spruce (*Picea abies*) on Campbell Island, Antarctica, is more than 222 km (119.8 nautical miles) away from the next nearest tree.

← ★ LARGEST FAMILY OF PLANTS

The largest family of plants is generally acknowledged to be the orchid family (Orchidaceae), with 25,000 species officially listed as of April 2004. The rate at which new orchids are confirmed, however, suggests that there are in excess of 30,000 species in total. Orchids occupy nearly all of the world's habitats except on the continent of Antarctica and underwater.

CULTIVATED PLANTS

★ HEAVIEST CANTALOUPE MELON (MUSKMELON)

Scott and Mardie Robb (both USA) grew a cantaloupe melon that weighed 29.4 kg (64 lb 13 oz) at the Alaska State Fair, Palmer, USA, on 16 August 2004.

FLORAL ARRANGEMENT WITH MOST TYPES OF FLOWERS

A flower arrangement containing 1,010 different types of flowers was created on 21 July 2002 by 34 designers at the Floriade, Vijfhuizen, the Netherlands, in an event organized by The Flower Council of Holland. The arrangement measured 110 m (360 ft) long, 1 m (3.2 ft) high and was built on a stand 3 m (9 ft 9 in) above the ground.

HEAVIEST PARSNIP

The heaviest parsnip was grown by Norman Lee Craven (Canada) and weighed 3.8 kg (8 lb 6 oz) on 4 November 2003 at the Royal Agriculture Winter Fair, Ontario, Canada.

★ LARGEST DISPLAY OF POTATO VARIETIES

A total of 589 varieties of potato were shown on the Three Countries Potatoes display, sponsored by Thompson and Morgan, Furrows (Ford) Motors and the Shropshire Horticultural Society, and held at the Shrewsbury Flower Show on 13–14 August 2004. The potato varieties on show included Adam's Apple, Russian Banana and Voyager.

★ LARGEST FLOWER AUCTION

The world's largest flower auction and flower market is Bloemenveiling Aalsmeer (VBA)

← ★ HEAVIEST TURNIP

The heaviest turnip weighed 17.7 kg (39 lb 3 oz) and was grown by Scott (pictured) and Mardie Robb (both USA), who presented it at the Alaska State Fair, USA, on 1 September 2004.

HEAVIEST FRUIT AND VEGETABLES

FRUIT/VEGETABLE	WEIGHT	NAME	DATE
Apple	1.67 kg (3 lb 11 oz)	Alan Smith (UK)	1997
Avocado	1.99 kg (4 lb 6 oz)	Anthony Llanos (Australia)	1992
Beetroot	23.4 kg (51 lb 9.4 oz)	Ian Neale (UK)	2001
Brussels sprout	8.3 kg (18 lb 3 oz)	Bernard Lavery (UK)	1992
Cabbage	56.24 kg (124 lb)	Bernard Lavery (UK)	1989
Cabbage (Red)	19.05 kg (42 lb)	R Straw (UK)	1925
★ Cantaloupe melon	29.4 kg (64 lb 13 oz)	Scott & Mardie Robb (USA)	2004
Carrot	8.61 kg (18 lb 13 oz)	John Evans (USA)	1998
Cauliflower	24.6 kg (54 lb 3 oz)	Alan Hattersley (UK)	1999
Celery	28.7 kg (63 lb 4.8 oz)	Scott & Mardie Robb (USA)	2003
Cherry	21.69 g (0.76 oz)	Gerardo Maggipinto (Italy)	2003
Courgette	29.25 kg (64 lb 8 oz)	Bernard Lavery (UK)	1990
Cucumber	12.4 kg (27 lb 5.3 oz)	Alfred J Cobb (UK)	2003
Garlic head	1.19 kg (2 lb 10 oz)	Robert Kirkpatrick (USA)	1985
Gooseberry	61.04 g (2.15 oz)	K Archer (UK)	1993
Gourd	42.8 kg (94 lb 5.7 oz)	Robert Weber (Australia)	2001
Grapefruit	3.065 kg (6 lb 12 oz)	Debbie Hazelton (Australia)	1995
★ Jackfruit	34.6 kg (76 lb 4.4 oz)	George & Margaret Schattauer (USA)	2003
Kohlrabi	29 kg (63 lb 15 oz)	Dave Iles (USA)	2004
Leek	8.1 kg (17 lb 13 oz)	Fred Charlton (UK)	2002
Lemon	5.265 kg (11 lb 9.7 oz)	Aharon Shemoel (Israel)	2003
Mango	1.94 kg (4 lb 4 oz)	John Painter (USA)	1999
Marrow	61.23 kg (135 lb)	John Handbury (UK)	1998
Onion	7.24 kg (15 lb 15.5 oz)	Mel Ednie (UK)	1994
Parsnip	3.8 kg (8 lb 6 oz)	Norman Lee Craven (Canada)	2003
Peach	725 g (25.6 oz)	Paul Friday (USA)	2002
Pear	2.1 kg (4 lb 8oz)	Warren Yeoman (Australia)	1999
Pineapple	8.06 kg (17 lb 12 oz)	E Kamuk (Papua New Guinea)	1994
Potato	3.5 kg (7 lb 11 oz)	K Sloane (UK)	1994
★ Potato (Sweet)	37 kg (81 lb 9 oz)	Manuel Pérez Pérez (Spain)	2004
★ Pumpkin	655.9 kg (1,446 lb)	Allan Eaton (Canada)	2004
Quince	2.34 kg (5 lb 2 oz)	Edward Harold McKinney (USA)	2002
Radish	31.1 kg (68 lb 9 oz)	Manabu Ono (Japan)	2003
Rhubarb	2.67 kg (5 lb 14 oz)	E Stone (UK)	1985
Squash	436 kg (962 lb)	Steve Hoult (Canada)	1997
Strawberry	231 g (8.14 oz)	G Andersen (UK)	1983
Swede	34.35 kg (75 lb 12 oz)	Scott & Mardie Robb (USA)	1999
Tomato	3.51 kg (7 lb 12 oz)	G Graham (USA)	1986

in Aalsmeer, the Netherlands. Every weekday, approximately 19 million flowers and 2 million plants of more than 12,000 varieties are sold, with a daily turnover of €6 million ($7.2 million; £4 million).

The total area of the building covers 999,000 m² (10 million ft²) – equal to 165 football fields.

★ MOST BLOOMS IN ONE NIGHT BY THE SAME PLANT

During the night of 12–13 August 2004, a night-blooming cereus

(*Selenicereus grandiflorus*) produced 40 blooms. The plant is owned by Michie Taylor (USA). Also known as Queen of the Night, *S. grandiflorus* belongs to the cactus family. The buds bloom once a year, during midsummer, and generally wilt before dawn. The following evening, a further 23 bloomed.

★ LARGEST CARPET OF FLOWERS

The largest carpet of flowers measured 7,540.4 m² (81,164 ft²) on 13 July 2004. The union flag

design that formed the carpet was created by The Real Flower Petal Confetti Company using red, white and blue delphiniums grown in Wick, Worcestershire, UK.

TALLEST TOPIARY

Since 1983, Moirangthem Okendra Kumbi (India) has been shaping the shoots of a sky flower bush (*Duranta repens variegata*) in his 'Hedge to Heaven' garden in Manipur, India, which has grown to a height of 18.59 m (61 ft). Overall, with the help of a specially constructed ladder, he has cut 41 structural shapes repeating a design of a rounded umbrella followed by two discs.

★ OLDEST POT PLANT

A prickly cycad (*Encephalartos altensteinii*), which was brought from South Africa to the UK and planted in 1775, is on display in the Palm House, Royal Botanical Gardens, Kew, Surrey, UK. These tree-fern-like cycads are often called 'living fossils', as they are among the oldest surviving species of plants; scientists have established that they were growing more than 200 million years ago, during the Permian era.

TALLEST HOME-GROWN CACTUS

A home-grown cactus (*Cereus uruguayanus*) grown by Pandit S Munji (India) in Dharwad, Karnataka, India, measured 21.3 m (70 ft) on 1 January 2004. The 'hedge cactus' was planted in January 1990 and typically grows to 6 m (19 ft).

TALLEST PLANTS

PLANT	HEIGHT	NAME	DATE
★ Amaranthus	4.61 m (15 ft 1.4 in)	David Brenner (USA)	2004
Brussels sprout	2.8 m (9 ft 3 in)	Patrice and Steve Allison (USA)	2001
Cactus (home-grown)	21.3 m (70 ft)	Pandit S Munji (India)	2004
Celery	2.74 m (9 ft)	Joan Priednieks (UK)	1998
Chrysanthemum	4.34 m (14 ft 3 in)	Bernard Lavery (UK)	1995
★ Coleus	2.5 m (8 ft 4 in)	Nancy Lee Spilove (USA)	2004
Collard	2.79 m (9ft 2 in)	Reggie Kirkman (USA)	1999
Cosmos	3.75 m (12 ft 3 in)	Cosmos Executive Committee, Okayama, Japan	2003
Cotton	7.74 m (25 ft 5 in)	DM Williams (USA)	2004
Daffodil	1.55 m (5 ft 1 in)	M Lowe (UK)	1979
Dandelion	100 cm (39.3 in)	Ragnar Gille and Marcus Hamring (both Sweden)	2001
Fuchsia	6.58 m (21 ft 7 in)	The Growing Place, Lincolnshire, UK	2003
Herba cistanches	1.75 m (5 ft 8 in)	BOC Hong Kong Baptist University, Hong Kong, China	2003
Papaya tree	13.4 m (44 ft)	Prasanta Mal (India)	2003
Parsley	1.39 m (55 in)	Danielle, Gabrielle, Michelle Kassatly (all USA)	2003
Pepper	4.87 m (16 ft)	Laura Liang (USA)	1999
Periwinkle	2.19 m (7 ft 2 in)	Arvind, Rekha, Ashish & Rashmi Nema (all India)	2003
Petunia	5.8 m (19 ft 1 in)	Bernard Lavery (UK)	1994
Potato or brinjal	5.5 m (18 ft 0.5 in)	Abdul Masfoor (India)	1998
★ Rose bush (self-supported)	3.8 m (12 ft 8 in)	Kathleen Mielke-Villalobos (USA)	2004
★ Rose (climbing)	27.7 m (91 ft)	Anne & Charles Grant (both USA)	2004
Sunflower	7.76 m (25 ft 5.5 in)	M Heijms (Netherlands)	1986
Sweet corn (maize)	9.4 m (31 ft)	D Radda (USA)	1946
Tomato	19.8 m (65 ft)	Nutriculture Ltd, Lancashire, UK	2000
Umbrella	8.22 m (27 ft)	Konstantinos Xytakis & Sara Guterbock (both USA)	2002

★ LARGEST VINE

The Great Vine at Hampton Court Palace, Surrey, UK, has a circumference of 3.8 m (12 ft 5 in) and branches typically measuring up to 33 m (108 ft) long. The longest branch measured 75 m (246 ft) as of January 2005. It was planted by the famous gardener Lancelot 'Capability' Brown (UK) in 1768 when he was head gardener to King George III.

★ LARGEST BLOSSOMING PLANT

The Chinese wisteria (*Wisteria sinensis*) at Sierra Madre, California, USA, was planted in 1892 and by 1994 had branches measuring 152 m (500 ft) long, covered a total area of 0.4 ha (1 acre) and weighed 22 tonnes (48,500 lb).

An estimated 1.5 million blossoms were produced during the five-week blossoming period.

★ TALLEST ZINNIA

The tallest zinnia (*Zinnia elegans*) measured 3.81 m (12 ft 6 in) on 16 November 2004 and was grown by Everett W Wallace Jr and Melody Wagner (both USA) in Riegelwood, North Carolina, USA.

LARGEST PERMANENT HEDGE MAZE

The Peace Maze at Castlewellan Forest Park, County Down, UK, is 11,215 m² (2.771 acres) in area and has a total path length of 3.515 km (2.184 miles). It was designed by Beverley Lear (UK) and created by the Forest Service, Northern Ireland, and members of the public. It opened on 12 September 2001.

THE ENVIRONMENT

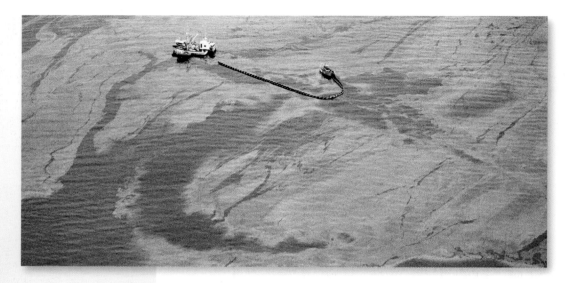

← WORST COASTAL DAMAGE

On 24 March 1989, the *Exxon Valdez* oil tanker ran aground in Prince William sound, Alaska, USA, spilling approximately 41 million litres (9.1 million gal; 11 million US gal) of oil. In total, 2,400 km (1,500 miles) of coast was polluted, and the company was fined $5 billion (£3.2 billion) on top of a clean-up bill of $3 billion (£1.9 billion).

ACID RAIN: MOST ACIDIC

A pH reading of 2.83 was recorded over the Great Lakes, USA/Canada, in 1982, and a reading of 1.87 was recorded at Inverpolly Forest, Highland, Scotland, UK, in 1983. These are the lowest pH levels ever recorded in acid precipitation, making it the most acidic acid rain.

ACID RAIN: MOST SULPHATES

A sulphate reading of 5.52 mg/litre was recorded in Inverpolly Forest, Highland, Scotland, UK in 1983. For the most part, this high level of sulphate was the result of atmospheric fallout from industries in central Scotland.

CHEMICAL POLLUTION: MOST POLLUTED TOWN

The Russian town of Dzerzhinsk (population 285,000 in 1995) is the world's most polluted industrial town. Life expectancy in the town – which is named after the founder of the Soviet secret police – is 42 for men and 47 for women. The town is home to dozens of factories that over the years have produced chlorine, pesticides and chemical weapons.

DEFORESTATION: GREATEST

Between 1990 and 2000, an average area of 22,264 km^2 (8,596 miles^2) of forest was cleared in Brazil every year – a total area equivalent to the entire UK.

A SELECTION OF THE WORST ENVIRONMENTAL DISASTERS

TYPE/LOCATION	DATE	EFFECT
Chemical disaster Bhopal, India	3 December 1984	Toxic cloud of methyl isocyanate (MIC) gas enveloped a settlement. Approximately 3,500 people killed; thousands more left with permanent disabilities.
Industrial explosion Scunthorpe, Flixborough, Lincolnshire, UK	1 June 1974	Chemical plant explosion killed 55 people and injured 75, probably owing to a leak of around 50 tonnes (110,000 lb) of cyclohexane gas. Explosion approximately equivalent to that of 16 tonnes (35,000 lb) of TNT.
Land pollution Arctic Komi Republic, Russia	August–September 1994	14,000–200,000 tonnes (30–400 million lb) of crude oil escaped across tundra. Contaminated area measured 21.1 km^2 (8.1 miles^2).
Marine pollution Minamata Bay, Kyushu, Japan	1953–1967	Fertilizer factory deposited mercury waste into the sea. Up to 20,000 people affected, 4,500 seriously – 43 died from poison; another 800 deaths attributed to mercury poisoning by some sources; 111 others suffered permanent damage.
Nuclear waste accident Kyshtym, Russia	December 1957	Nuclear waste container explosion released radioactive compounds over an area of 23,000 km^2 (8,900 miles^2). A 1992 report suggested that 8,015 people died over a 32-year period as a result.
Oil spill Gulf of Campeche, Gulf of Mexico	Started 3 June 1979	Blow-out beneath drilling rig *Ixtoc I* resulted in oil slick that had extended 640 km (400 miles) by 5 August 1979. Capped on 24 March 1980, after estimated loss of up to 500,000 tonnes (636 million litres; 140 million gal or 168 million US gal) of oil.
River pollution Basel, Switzerland	1 November 1986	Firemen fighting a blaze at Sandoz chemical works flushed 30 tonnes (66,000 lb) of agricultural chemicals into the river Rhine. Resulted in death of half a million fish.
Sulphur dioxide fire Mosul, Iraq	Started 24 June 2003	Released average of 21,000 tonnes (46.3 million lb) of sulphur dioxide gas a day for nearly a month. Resulted in around 600,000 tonnes (1.3 billion lb) of pollution – greatest manmade release of SO_2 in history for a discrete event.

GREATEST SHRINKAGE
OF A LAKE

The Aral Sea, on the border between Uzbekistan and Kazakhstan, has lost more than 60% of its area and approximately 80% of its volume since 1960. From 1960 to 1998, the lake decreased in area from 68,000 km^2 (26,300 miles^2) to 28,700 km^2 (11,000 miles^2) and in volume from approximately 1,040 km^3 (250 miles^3) to 180 km^3 (43 miles^3). The sea level has dropped about 18 m (60 ft) in the same time period.

May 1973

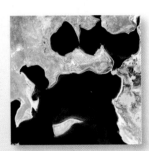

August 1987

July 2000

WORST
NUCLEAR DISASTER

A nuclear reactor disaster at Chernobyl No.4 in the former USSR (now the Ukraine), on 26 April 1986 at 1.23 a.m. local time, resulted in an official death toll of 31 people. No systematic records were kept of subsequent deaths, but over 1.7 million people were exposed to radiation.

RADIOACTIVITY: MOST CONTAMINATED LAKE

Lake Karachay in the Chelyabinsk province of Russia has accumulated 120 million curies of radioactivity and absorbed nearly 100 times more strontium-90 and caesium-137 than was released at Chernobyl. If you were to stand on the shore of the lake you would be contaminated at a radiation exposure rate of 600 roentgens an hour – strong enough to kill you within 60 minutes.

FIRE: WORST DESTRUCTION OF NATURAL ENVIRONMENT

Deliberately lit forest fires in 1997 made this the worst year in recorded history for the destruction of the environment. The largest and most numerous were in Brazil, where they raged on a 1,600-km (1,000-mile) front.

TOXIC CLOUD: LARGEST

In September 1990, a fire at a factory handling beryllium in Ust Kamenogorsk, Kazakhstan (then USSR), released a toxic cloud that extended over an area of 300 km (186 miles) to the Chinese border and an unknown distance beyond.

SULPHUR DIOXIDE: GREATEST AMOUNT OF POLLUTION FROM A FACTORY

The Bulgarian Maritsa power complex releases 350,000 tonnes (770 million lb) of sulphur dioxide into the Maritsa River every single year.

Sulphur dioxide is a pungent-smelling acidic gas, largely produced through volcanic eruptions but also by the burning of fossil fuels. When sulphur dioxide is released into the atmosphere it combines with water vapour in the clouds to form sulphuric acid. This is one of the major causes of acid rain in Europe and North America.

★ LARGEST TREE TRANSPLANT

On 20 January 2004, an oak tree (*Quercus lobata*) named 'Old Glory', aged between 180 and 220 years, was moved 0.4 km (0.25 miles) by the Senna Tree Company (USA) to a new park in Los Angeles, California, USA, where it was successfully replanted. The tree measured 17.6 m (58 ft) tall, 31.6 m (104 ft) wide (branch-span), weighed around 415.5 tonnes (916,000 lb) and had a trunk girth of 5 m (16 ft 2 in).

→ CONTENTS

★ FIRST PRIVATELY FUNDED
MANNED SPACE FLIGHT

On 21 June 2004, *SpaceShipOne* – a spacecraft designed, built and operated by Scaled Composites of Mojave, California, USA, and funded by Paul G Allen (USA) – reached an altitude of 100,124 m (328,492 ft). Piloted by Mike Melvill (USA), it took off from and landed at Mojave Airport.

SpaceShipOne

28KF

and suffocated by the carbon dioxide atmosphere. Venus is

on Io, making her the **discoverer of more active volcanoes** on Io (or on Earth) than anyone else.

Although designed to last just a few months, the *Spirit* and *Opportunity* Mars rovers were still going strong in March 2005, and, hopefully, could pave the way for human exploration of the red planet.

★ FIRST
OBSERVED
← TRANSIT
OF VENUS

The first person to observe, measure and record the transit of the planet Venus across the

→ SCIENCE & TECHNOLOGY
PEOPLE IN SPACE

★ LONGEST
← MOON WALK

On their second excursion on to the surface of the Moon during the *Apollo 17* mission on 12 December 1972, US astronauts Eugene Cernan (pictured) and Harrison Schmitt spent 7 hr 37 min outside their lunar excursion module, *Challenger*. During this time they travelled 20.4 km (12.6 miles) while taking geological samples of the region to the south and west of their landing site in the Taurus-Littrow valley.

NB: in the text, the term USSR stands for Union of Soviet Socialist Republics, the collection of Communist states that existed from 1917 to 1991.

The term CIS stands for Commonwealth of Independent States, a collection of former Communist states that amalgamated on 8 December 1991 after the downfall of the USSR.

STS = Space Transportation System

FIRST MANNED SPACEFLIGHT
Cosmonaut Flight Major Yuri Alekseyevich Gagarin (USSR) flew on *Vostok 1* on 12 April 1961. The maximum altitude during the 40,868.6-km (25,394-mile) flight was recorded at 327 km (203 miles), with a top speed of 28,260 km/h (17,560 mph).

FIRST MEN ON THE MOON
Neil Armstrong (USA), commander of the *Apollo 11* mission, became the first man to set foot on the Moon when he stepped on to the Sea of Tranquillity at 02:56:15 GMT on 21 July 1969 (or 22:56:15 EDT

on 20 July 1969). He was followed out of the lunar module *Eagle* by Edwin 'Buzz' Aldrin (USA), while the command module *Columbia*, piloted by Michael Collins (USA), orbited above.

FIRST SPACEWALK
Lt-Col (now Maj. Gen.) Alexei Arkhipovich Leonov (USSR) was the first person ever to engage in extra-vehicular activity (EVA), commonly known as a spacewalk, on 18 March 1965.

FIRST WOMAN IN SPACE
Junior Lt Valentina Vladimirovna Tereshkova (USSR) was launched in *Vostok 6* from the Baikonur Cosmodrome, Kazakhstan, at 9:30 a.m. GMT on 16 June 1963. She landed at 8:20 a.m. on 19 June after a flight of 2 days 22 hr 50 min and 48 orbits (1,971,000 km; 1,225,000 miles).

GREATEST DISTANCE FROM EARTH
The crew of *Apollo 13* (Jack Swigert, Jim Lovell and Fred Haise, all USA) were an

unprecedented distance of 400,171 km (248,655 miles) from the Earth and 254 km (158 miles) from the Moon on 15 April 1970.

MOST DURABLE SPACE STATION
Mir, the central core module of the *Mir* space station (USSR/Russia), was launched into orbit on 20 February 1986. Over the following 10 years, five modules and a docking port for US space shuttles were added to the complex. On 23 March 2001, the space station was de-orbited and destroyed in a controlled re-entry over the Pacific Ocean. More than 100 people visited the space station in its 15-year operational history.

★ MOST HEAVILY ARMED SPACE STATION
Salyut 3 (USSR, launched 25 June 1974) was the only armed space station. For defensive purposes, it was fitted with a 23-mm Nudelmann aircraft cannon. Although never used in anger, it was test-fired once on 24 January 1975 and destroyed a target satellite.

MOST PEOPLE IN SPACE AT THE SAME TIME
On 14 March 1995, there were seven Americans aboard the space shuttle STS-67 *Endeavour*, three CIS cosmonauts aboard the *Mir* space station, and two cosmonauts and a US astronaut aboard *Soyuz TM21* – making a total of 13 people in space at the same time.

← LARGEST SHUTTLE CREW

Two shuttles have had a crew of eight: the STS-61A *Challenger*, which was launched on 30 October 1985, and STS-71 *Atlantis*, which docked with the *Mir* space station on 7 July 1995. Pictured are members of the *Atlantis* and *Mir* crews.

MOST TIME
SPENT IN SPACE

Russian cosmonaut Sergei Avdeyev (Russia, pictured above) logged a total of 747 days 14 hr 22 min on three spaceflights to the *Mir* space station between July 1992 and July 1999.

Avdeyev also experienced the **most time dilation by an individual**. As a direct consequence of the time he has spent in low Earth orbit, travelling at around 27,000 km/h (17,000 mph) relative to everyone else, he has essentially 'time travelled' 1/50th of a second into the future – consistent with Albert Einstein's Theory of Relativity.

LONGEST MANNED SPACEFLIGHT
Valeriy Poliyakov (Russia) was launched to the *Mir* space station aboard *Soyuz TM18* on 8 January 1994 and landed in *Soyuz TM20* on 22 March 1995 after a spaceflight lasting 437 days 17 hr 58 min 16 sec.

MOST RE-USED SPACECRAFT
Nasa's space shuttle *Discovery* was launched on 10 August 2001 at 4:10 p.m. Central Daylight Time (CDT). Its mission (STS-105) was to deliver a new crew and the *Leonardo* cargo module to the *International Space Station*. This was the 30th mission for *Discovery*, which has operated since 1984.

★ LONGEST SERVING ASTRONAUT
John Young (USA) was selected as a Nasa astronaut in September 1962. He has flown on two *Gemini* Earth-orbital missions and two *Apollo* missions (10 and 16), and commanded STS-1, the first flight of the space shuttle in 1981. His sixth mission was as commander of STS-9 – again on *Columbia*. He remained on active flight status until he retired in December 2004.

MOST REMOTE GOLF SHOT
In February 1971, astronaut Alan Shepard (USA) struck two golf balls in the Fra Mauro region on the surface of the Moon. He used a club made from a sampling tool with a six-iron attached. One of the balls travelled a distance of around 15 m (50 ft).

★ LARGEST ROOM IN SPACE
The largest single habitable volume launched into space was the Nasa (US) space station *Skylab*, which was launched on 14 May 1973. This cylindrical space station had internal dimensions of 14.66 m (48.1 ft) long by 6.7 m (22 ft) in diameter, giving a habitable volume of 295.23 m^3 (10,426 ft^3).

★ LONGEST SOLO SPACEFLIGHT
The longest duration spaceflight with a single person on board was the flight of *Vostok 5*, piloted by Soviet cosmonaut Valery Bykovsky. It was launched on 14 June 1963 and landed on 19 June 1963 with a total mission elapsed time of 4 days 23 hr 7 min.

★ FIRST PRIVATELY FUNDED
MANNED SPACEFLIGHT

SpaceShipOne, designed and built by aviation legend Burt Rutan's company, Scaled Composites, breached the boundary of space on its first sub-orbital flight on 21 June 2004. It was piloted by astronaut Mike Melvill (USA).

SPACE FIRSTS

First person in space:
Yuri Gagarin (USSR), 12 April 1961

First woman in space:
Valentina Tereshkova (USSR), 16 June 1963

First person to walk in space: Alexei Leonov (USSR), 18 March 1965

First rendezvous in space:
Gemini 6 and *7* (USA), 16 December 1965

First docking in space:
Neil Armstrong and David Scott (USA), 16 March 1966

First international space mission:
The *Apollo-Soyuz* Test Project (USA and USSR), 15–24 July 1975

First untethered spacewalk:
Capt. Bruce McCandless II (USA), 7 February 1984

First Briton in space:
Helen Sharman, 18 May 1991

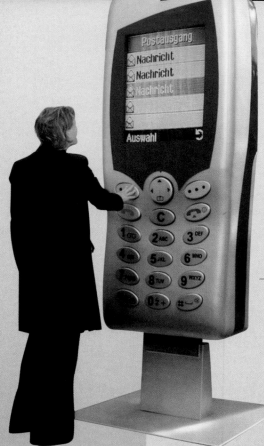

★ ← LARGEST MOBILE TELEPHONE

The Maxi Handy (Maxi Mobile) measures 2.05 x 0.83 x 0.45 m (6.72 x 2.72 x 1.47 ft) and was installed at the Rotmain Centre, Bayreuth, Germany, on 7 June 2004 as part of the 'einfach mobil' infotour. It is made from wood, polyester and metal, and features a colour Thin Film Transistor (TFT) screen. It is fully functional and can send and receive SMS and MMS messages.

The razor-toothed piranhas of the genera *serrasalmus* and *pygocentrus* are the most ferocious freshwater fish in the world. In reality they seldom attack a human.

Can you beat the world record time to type the above text? If you think you can, get in touch with Guinness World Records! Find out how on p.10

FASTEST TEXT MESSAGE
Kimberly Yeo Sue Fern (Singapore) typed a pre-agreed 160-character text on her mobile phone in 43.2 seconds on 27 June 2004 at the Singtel SMS Shootout competition in Singapore. Attempts at this record must be made using text adapted from page 39 of the 1996 *Guinness Book of Records* (displayed on the left).

FIRST MOBILE PHONE
The concept of a portable telephone first appeared in 1947 at Lucent Technologies' Bell Labs in New Jersey, USA, but the first portable telephone handset was invented by Martin Cooper (USA) of Motorola. He made the first call on 3 April 1973 to his rival, Joel Engel, head of research at Bell Labs. The first commercial mobile phone network was launched in Japan in 1979.

MOST CELLPHONE SUBSCRIBERS
Vodafone Group plc has the largest subscriber base, with 151.8 million subscribers globally as of 31 December 2004.

★ MOST DURABLE MOBILE PHONE NUMBER
David Contorno (USA) has owned and used the same mobile telephone number since 2 August 1985. His first mobile phone was an Ameritech AC140, and his carrier has remained Ameritech Mobile Communications.

LARGEST TELEPHONE CONFERENCE CALL
On 29 September 2003, US presidential Democrat candidate Howard Dean (USA) took part in a telephone conference call from Los Angeles, California, USA, with some of his supporters. The total number of people simultaneously connected for at least 10 seconds was 3,466.

★ OLDEST TELETEXT SERVICE
Ceefax was launched in the UK by the BBC on 28 September 1974. It was developed by BBC engineers who were working on a way to provide subtitles for deaf people. They used the 'spare lines' on top of an analogue television signal to incorporate words and simple graphics.

FIRST GEOSTATIONARY COMMUNICATIONS SATELLITE
Syncom 3 was launched from Cape Canaveral, Florida, USA, on 19 August 1964 and manoeuvred to its orbit at an altitude of 35,788 km (22,238 miles) above Earth. At this altitude, the satellite took exactly 24 hours to orbit the planet and so appeared stationary from the ground. Today, more than 200 satellites operate in the geostationary or 'Clarke' orbit, which is named after the science-fiction writer Arthur C Clarke, who was the first person to lay down the principles of satellite communication.

★ LARGEST → COMMUNICATIONS SURVEILLANCE NETWORK

Echelon, the electronic eavesdropping network run by the intelligence organizations of the USA, UK, Australia, New Zealand and Canada, was founded in 1947 by those nations to share intelligence data. Some analysts estimate that it can now intercept some 90% of all Internet traffic, as well as monitoring global telephone and satellite communications. Pictured are the radomes – giant golf ball-like satellite covers – used by Echelon at RAF Menwith Hill, near Narrowgate, North Yorkshire, UK.

The **first form of instant telecommunication** was Morse code. Can you decipher the first message, sent from Washington DC to Baltimore Maryland, USA, in May 1844?

★ LARGEST CIVIL COMMUNICATIONS SATELLITE

Anik F2, constructed by Boeing (USA), was launched in July 2004 to provide broadband Internet services to Canada and the USA. It measures 47.9 m (157 ft) across from the tips of its solar panels, and had a launch mass of 5,950 kg (13,117 lb) and a mass in orbit of 3,805 kg (8,390 lb). *Anik F2* will operate for 15 years.

LARGEST LIVE DIGITAL SATELLITE RADIO BROADCAST

When Ana Ann (UK) performed her debut single 'Ride' on 13 February 2002 at the offices of Worldspace, Soho Square, London, UK, the song was uplinked to Worldspace's AfriStar satellite and then beamed down to Western Europe, the whole of Africa and the Middle East.

★ LONGEST COMMUNICATIONS BASELINE

The unmanned spacecraft *Voyager 1* (USA) was launched in 1977 on a tour of the outer solar system. As of February 2005, the craft was over 14 billion km (8.7 billion miles) from the Sun. At this distance, radio commands

← FIRST COMMUNICATIONS SATELLITE

Echo 1 (sometimes called *Echo 1A*) was launched on 10 July 1962 from Cape Canaveral, Florida, USA. It was a 30-m-diameter (98-ft) balloon with a reflective aluminium coating, allowing radio and television signals to be passively reflected back to Earth. It ceased operations on 24 May 1968.

from Earth travelling at the speed of light take around 13 hours to reach the spacecraft.

★ HIGHEST SPEED TO TRANSMIT MORSE CODE

On 6 May 2003, Andrei Bindasov (Belarus) successfully transmitted 216 Morse code marks of mixed text in one minute.

LARGEST FAX MACHINE

WideCom Group, Inc. of Mississauga, Ontario, Canada, manufacture the WIDEfax 36 – a facsimile machine able to print, copy and transmit documents up to 91 cm (36 in) wide.

STRONGEST RADIO SIGNAL BEAMED INTO SPACE

On 16 November 1974, scientists at the Arecibo Radio Telescope, Puerto Rico, transmitted a binary radio signal to the M13 globular cluster in the constellation of Hercules, in an effort to communicate with extra-terrestrial life. The message, which shows basic data about humanity, lasts for 169 seconds at 2,380 MHz. The message will arrive in around 25,000 years. If there is a reply, it will take another 25,000 years for us to receive it.

★ LONGEST GROUND-LEVEL WI-FI CONNECTION

In July 2004, Ben Corrado, Andy Meng and Justin Rigling (all USA) achieved Wi-Fi wireless contact between two PCs 88.6 km (55.1 miles) apart in the desert outside Las Vegas, USA. They used home-made antennae (pictured) as well as the 802.11b wireless protocol. This feat made them the 2004 winners of the Annual DefCon Wi-Fi Shootout.

★ LARGEST PANORAMIC DIGITAL PHOTO

Imaging experts from TNO (Netherlands) have created a huge online panoramic digital photograph of the city of Delft in the Netherlands. The image is 2.5 gigapixels in size and composed of 600 separate digital shots, taken from the same location, and 'stitched' together over three days in July 2004.

You can view the entire image by going to www.guinnessworld records.com/panorama

★ LARGEST INTERNET TRADING SITE

Founded in 1995, eBay (USA) is a trade website allowing individuals around the world to buy and sell items. In 2004, 56.1 million users bought, sold or bidded for an item on the website. At the end of 2004, eBay had 135.5 million registered users around the world.

★ INTERNET2 LAND SPEED RECORD

On 9 November 2004, a team consisting of the University of Tokyo, Fujitsu Computer Technologies and the WIDE Project (all Japan) successfully transmitted 541 gigabytes of data (equivalent to more than 100 DVD movies) across 20,645 km (12,828 miles) of network in 10 minutes. The resulting value of 148,850 terabit-metres per second was accomplished using IPv4.

HIGHEST CAPACITY INTERCONTINENTAL INTERNET ROUTE

In 2003, the Internet routes between Europe and USA/Canada had a bandwidth capacity of 386,221 Mbps (megabits per second). In second place was the combined routes between USA/Canada and Asia & Pacific, with a bandwidth capacity of 103,282.3 Mbps. The lowest capacity was between USA/Canada and Africa, with a bandwidth capacity of 1,351.5 Mbps.

★ LARGEST ONLINE CONSOLE COMMUNITY

Sony PlayStation 2 had more than 1.4 million registered users in August 2004. The Internet gaming service was launched in August 2002 and continues to grow by roughly 1,400 new users each day.

★ DEEPEST LIVE INTERNET BROADCAST

On 24 July 2001, live footage of HMS *Hood* was broadcast over the Internet from an ROV (remotely operated vehicle) at the bottom of the Denmark Strait (where she sank in 1941), at a depth of 2,800 m (9,200 ft). This followed the discovery of the wreck by David Mearns (UK) of Bluewater Recoveries Ltd (UK), in an expedition organized by ITN Factual for Channel 4 (UK).

★ LARGEST INDEPENDENT INTERNET HUB

The London Exchange (Linx) handles 76 gigabits of data every second at peak times, as of March 2005. It consists of eight high-capacity Internet routing sites around Docklands, London, UK.

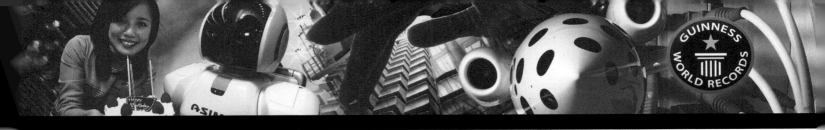

GARY THUERK

On 3 May 1978, Gary Thuerk (USA) sent the first 'spam' (an unsolicited e-mail, usually advertising a product or service) via ARPAnet, a system seen as the predecessor to the Internet.

Why exactly did you send your first spam e-mail?
I wanted to reach people in western USA to tell them about our mainframe-class server.

How many people were on your mailing list?
Over 400, which was about 25% of everyone online in the world at that time. We took the names from a printed phone book and typed them in!

What do think of spam today?
I don't get a lot of spam because I don't leave my contact details

on the Internet – chat rooms, etc. Also, when people forward jokes to friends, they leave the e-mail list in there and spammers can eventually get hold of it.

Does anybody ever blame you for the current volumes of spam today?
Oh yes – I get people who blame me but if I talk to them we normally end up smiling or laughing about it.

Do you feel guilty?
No, of course not. If you take a plane flight and the airline loses your luggage, you don't blame the Wright brothers!

Why exactly are unsolicited e-mails called 'spam'?
It came from a Monty Python's Flying Circus sketch. Somebody

who just watched it was going through his unsolicited e-mails and complained that he was being spammed – and everyone around him began singing the Monty Python spam song!

To receive a copy of the first spam and a message from Gary, send an e-mail – or spam him! – at: garythuerk@ guinnessworld records.com

FIRST JPEGS

A set of four test images created in Copenhagen, Denmark, on 18 June 1987 and entitled 'Boats', 'Barbara' (both pictured), 'Toys' and 'Zelda' were the first to use the jpeg compression method. The jpeg was developed by the Joint Photographic Experts Group in order to standardize techniques for digital image compression, and is used on the Internet and on digital cameras.

★ LARGEST INTERNET SEARCH ENGINE
Google, with over 8 billion pages, has the largest continually refreshed index of web pages of all search engines. Founded by Larry Page (USA) and Sergey Brin (Russia), their first office was a garage in Menlo Park, California, USA, which opened in September 1998 with a staff of four people.

★ LARGEST WIRELESS INTERNET PROVIDER
NTT DoCoMo (Japan) is the world's largest wireless Internet provider, with more than 43.24 million subscribers to their i-mode service as of January 2005.

FIRST E-MAIL
Ray Tomlinson, an engineer at the computer company Bolt, Beranek and Newman in Cambridge, Massachusetts, USA, sent the first ever e-mail in 1971 in an experiment to see if he could get two computers to exchange a message. The message was: 'QWERTYUIOP', and it was Tomlinson who decided to use the '@' symbol to separate the recipient's name from their location.

LARGEST INTERNET JOKE VOTE
Laughlab, an Internet experiment into humour, was conducted by psychologist Richard Wiseman (UK) of the University of

Hertfordshire, UK, and the British Association for the Advancement of Science. Running from September 2001 to October 2002, over 40,000 jokes were submitted from the public worldwide, and around two million votes were cast on what was the funniest. Visit www.guinnessworldrecords.com/ joke to see the winning joke for yourself.

★ FIRST REMOTE COMPUTER CONNECTION →

Pictured is the original sketch showing the plans to connect two computers remotely for the first time in a simple network; this would grow to become the Internet. At around 10:30 a.m. (PST) on 29 October 1969, computer scientists at the University of California, Los Angeles, USA, tried to log in to a computer at the Stanford Research Institute. This first log-in failed, but a second attempt shortly thereafter succeeded.

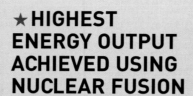

★ LONGEST CHAIN OF ELECTRICAL CABLES

On 14–15 June 2003, a chain of electrical power extension cables measuring 14,690 m (48,195 ft) long was assembled from Thal to Stattegg, Austria. After completion, a current was passed along the cables, illuminating a light panel at the far end.

★ HIGHEST ENERGY OUTPUT ACHIEVED USING NUCLEAR FUSION

The highest energy output achieved using nuclear fusion is 16 mW by the Joint European Torus (JET) tokamak nuclear fusion reactor, Culham, Oxfordshire, UK, in 1997. Pictured is the doughnut-shaped reactor during firing (left) and beforehand (right). →

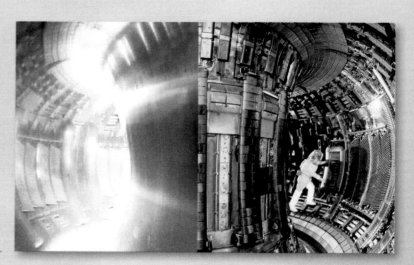

LARGEST...

NATURAL GAS FIELD

The Urengoy gas condensate field in Siberia, Russia, discovered in 1966, has estimated reserves of 8 trillion m³ (280 trillion ft³). The gas field accounts for more than one third of the total annual Russian production of gas.

★ ELECTRICITY SUBSTATION

Shin-noda at Chiba, Japan, has a maximum output of 7,860 MVA, starting commercial operation (at this capacity) on 19 May 1995. The substation, which is run by the Tokyo Electric Power Company, was established in 1961 and supplies the demands of eastern Tokyo and the northern area of the Chiba Prefecture.

★ HYDROELECTRIC POWER STATION

The Itaipu hydroelectric power station on the border between Paraguay and Brazil can generate 12,600 mW of electricity – enough to power the state of California, USA. It began operation in 1985 and was upgraded to its current capacity in March 1991.

★ NUCLEAR POWER STATION

Kashiwazaki Kariwa nuclear power station on the northern coast of Honshu Island, Japan, has a total output of 8,212 mW.

PRODUCER OF ENERGY (COUNTRY)

The USA is the largest producer of commercial energy. In 2001, 75,295 PJ of commercial energy, including solid, liquid and gaseous fuels, was produced, as well as primary electricity.

WIND GENERATOR

The Mod-5B generator in Oahu, Hawaii, USA, has two giant blades measuring 97.5 m (320 ft) from tip to tip, making them as long as a 25-storey building is high. First installed in August 1987, the turbine was built for the US Department of Energy by the Boeing Company at a cost of $55 million (£34 million), and produces 3,200 kW when the wind reaches 51 km/h (32 mph).

MOST POWERFUL...

★ TIDAL POWER STATION

The La Rance tidal barrage, in the mouth of the La Rance river estuary, France, has operated since 1966. It generates 240 mW of electricity from its 24 turbines, which are driven by the rising and falling tides.

★ NEW RECORD ★ UPDATED RECORD

★ BATTERY

The Golden Valley Electric Association (USA) Battery Energy Storage System began operating in Alaska, USA, in November 2003. On 10 December 2003, during a test of its maximum limit, it was discharged at a rate of 46 mW for 5 minutes. It is designed to prevent power loss to local residents during interruptions in the main electricity supply.

★ SOLAR CHIMNEY

Enviromission's (Australia) prototype solar chimney power station in Manzanares, Spain, produced 50 kW of electricity between 1982 and 1989. It consisted of a large area of greenhouses in which air, heated by the Sun, expanded upwards through a 200-m-tall (656-ft) central tower, powering turbines as it escaped into the atmosphere.

MISCELLANEOUS

★ LONGEST HUMAN ELECTRICAL CIRCUIT

The longest human electrical circuit consisted of 250 people, who briefly carried sufficient electrical current (between 200 milliamps and 2 amps) to illuminate a light. The event occurred on 21 November 2004 at the Harrogate International Centre, Harrogate, North Yorkshire, UK, as part of the television show *Zapped*, by YAP Screenhouse Productions (UK).

★ LONGEST CONTINUOUS POWER PLANT OPERATION

Stanwell Corporation's Unit 4 at the Stanwell Power Station in Queensland, Australia, operated continuously from 8 September 1999 to 16 August 2002. This gives a total continuous operation time of 1,073 days and 1 hour.

★ LONGEST OPERATING NUCLEAR POWER STATION

The nuclear reactor in Obninsk, Russia, operated from 27 June 1954 until it was decommissioned on 30 April 2002. It was the world's first operating nuclear reactor.

★ SMALLEST DIRECT METHANOL FUEL CELL

In June 2004, Toshiba (Japan) announced its prototype direct methanol fuel cell designed for use in mobile technology, such as mobile telephones. Measuring just 22 x 56 x 4.5 mm (0.87 x 2.2 x 0.18 in), and weighing 8.5 g (0.29 oz), it can power an MP3 player for around 20 hours on a single charge of 2 cm³ (0.12 in³) of highly concentrated methanol fuel.

★ MOST POWERFUL SOLAR TOWER POWER STATION

Solar II, in the Mojave Desert, California, USA, uses an array of 1,800 curved heliostat mirrors that reflect sunlight on to a central heating element, generating a maximum output of 10 mW of electricity.

LARGEST WIND FARM ↑

At Altamont Pass, California, USA, the Pacific Gas and Electric Company has built a wind farm covering 140 km² (54 mile²) with 7,300 wind turbines. The turbines have produced more than 6 billion kWh of electricity since 1981 – enough to give 800,000 homes in California power for approximately one year.

Glossary of terms:
kWh: kilowatt-hour – 1 kilowatt (1,000 watts) of power used for one hour
MVA: megavolt-amperes – a measurement of electrical current
mW: megawatt (1 million watts)
MWe: megawatts of electrical output
PJ: petajoule = 1,015 joules (a joule is a unit of work, energy and heat)

CUTTING-EDGE SCIENCE

★MOST SPHERICAL MANMADE OBJECT

The most perfect manmade spheres constructed to date are the fused solid quartz gyroscopic rotors built for Nasa's Gravity Probe B spacecraft. There are four spheres on board, each measuring 3.81 cm (1.5 in) across. Their average departure from mathematically perfect sphericity is 1.8×10^{-7} of the diameter. This means that if scaled up to the size of the Earth, the maximum height/depth of topographic features would be 1.5 m (4 ft 6 in).

ACTUAL SIZE

FASTEST...

ATOMIC CLOCK

A team of physicists led by Scott Diddams at the National Institute of Standards and Technology (USA) has built an atomic clock that 'ticks' about a quadrillion (10^{15}) times a second.

Eventually it is hoped that it will be accurate to 1 second in 100 million years, meaning that it would lose just a few minutes of accuracy for the whole of the age of the universe.

★MATTER IN THE UNIVERSE

The fastest objects are blobs of superheated plasma ejected from black holes in the cores of extremely active galaxies known as blazars. These blobs, with as much mass as the planet Jupiter, have been observed moving at 99.99% of the speed of light.

LARGEST...

★CENTRIFUGE

The TsF-18 Centrifuge at the Yuri Gagarin Cosmonaut Training Centre, Star City, Russia, has a rotating arm 18 m (59 ft) long and can simulate up to 30 G with a payload mass of 350 kg (770 lb).

VAN DE GRAAF GENERATOR

A Van de Graaf generator built in 1931 at the Massachussetts Institute of Technology, USA, comprises two columns each with a 4.5-m-diameter (15-ft) hollow aluminium sphere at the top.

←★HEAVIEST OBJECT WEIGHED

On 23 January 2004, the Revolving Service Structure (RSS) of launch pad 39B at Nasa's Kennedy Space Center, Florida, USA, was lifted up on 21 jacking points, which, between them, measured the mass of the RSS as 2,423 tonnes (5,342,000 lb). The work was carried out by Industrial Steel, Inc. (USA) and Buffalo Hydraulic (USA).

★LIGHTEST OBJECT WEIGHED

Scientists at Cornell University (USA) have used a technique involving tiny oscillating cantilevers to physically detect a mass of just 6.3 attograms. (An attogram is a billionth of a billionth of a gram.) The work was carried out by Professor Harold Craighead and Rob Ilic (both USA) and published in April 2004.

LARGEST
← VACUUM CHAMBER

The Space Power Facility, at Nasa's Glenn Research Center, Plum Brook Station, Sandusky, Ohio, USA, measures 30 m (100 ft) in diameter and 37 m (122 ft) in height. It can sustain a high vacuum of 10^{-6} torr and simulate solar radiation using a 4-megawatt quartz heat lamp array, as well as temperatures as low as -195.5°C (-320°F). It is used to test the performance of spacecraft and space hardware prior to launch.

and is virtually invisible to the eye. Aerogel with this density was first created on 10 April 2003.

MISCELLANEOUS

★ LONGEST PENDULUM

The longest pendula were two lengths of number 24 steel piano wire, each 1,353.3 m (4,440 ft) long. They were suspended down the number 4 shaft of the Tamarack Mines, Michigan, USA, in September 1901 by students and staff of the Michigan College of Mining.

★ HIGHEST TEMPERATURE

At the very instant of the Big Bang, 13.7 billion years ago, the universe is thought to have had infinite temperature, as it existed as a single, infinitely small and infinitely dense point. Just 10^{-43} seconds later – the Planck time – it had cooled to roughly 10^{32} K, and expanded to a size of around 10^{-33} cm across.

MOST ACCURATE KILOGRAM

The kilogram is the only base SI (Système International) unit of measurement whose definition is still based on a physical prototype – a cylinder made of platinum and iridium, made in 1889, and maintained at the Bureau International des Poids et Mesures (BIPM) at Sevres near Paris, France. Scientists are currently attempting to change the definition of the kilogram by linking it to more and more precise measurements of Planck's constant.

SMALLEST...

★ ATOMIC CLOCK

In August 2004, the National Institute for Standards and Technology (NIST) in Boulder, Colorado, USA, unveiled a prototype atomic clock the size of a grain of rice. With a volume of less than 10 mm³ (0.000613 in³), and drawing just 75 milliwatts of power, the chip-scale caesium vapour atomic clock is accurate to one second in 300 years.

★ HOMINID

On 28 October 2004, Indonesian and Australian scientists announced in the magazine *Nature* that they had discovered the smallest known member of the hominid family. The remains were discovered in a cave at Liang Bua on the island of Flores, and the scientists named the species *Homo floresiensis*. Standing just 1 m (3 ft) tall, the hominid inhabited Flores as recently as 13,000 years ago. This means that it existed at the same time as modern humans and probably interacted with them.

★ TEST TUBE

A test tube made from a single-walled carbon nanotube measures just 2 micrometres long and 1.5 nanometres wide, giving an internal volume of only 3.5 zeptolitres (3.5 x 10^{-21} litres), or a billionth of a billionth of a millilitre. It was created by a team of scientists from the Department of Materials at Oxford University, Oxford, UK, and announced in December 2004.

★ UNIT OF TIME

The smallest unit of time is known as Planck's time, 10^{-43} seconds. It is the amount of time it takes the **fastest thing** – light, travelling at 3 x 10^{8} m/s – to cross the **smallest distance** – the Planck length, at 1.6 x 10^{-35} m.

WEIGHT

★ LEAST DENSE SOLID

Lawrence Livermore National Laboratory, California, USA, have produced an aerogel with a density of just 1 mg/cm³ (0.25 grains/in³). This aerogel is lighter than air itself (1.2 mg/cm³; 0.3 grains/in³)

CUTTING-EDGE TECHNOLOGY

← ★STRONGEST HUMAN EXOSKELETON

The Berkeley Lower Extremity Exoskeleton (BLEEX) has been developed to provide enhanced strength and endurance. An onboard power source drives hydraulic muscles, allowing the 'wearer' to carry a 32-kg (70-lb) backpack, as well as the 45-kg (100-lb) exoskeleton, while feeling the encumbrance of only 2.2 kg (5 lb).

BLEEX was developed by University of California, Berkeley, California, USA, and funded by the Defense Advanced Research Project Agency (DARPA, USA). It was announced in March 2004.

COMPUTERS

OLDEST COMPUTER MOUSE

The computer mouse was invented by Douglas Engelbart (USA) in 1964. It was described in the patent as an 'X-Y position indicator for a display system' and was nicknamed 'mouse' because of the resemblance of the wire to a tail.

FIRST MICROPROCESSOR

The 4004 chip, designed and built by Intel (USA), was completed in January 1971. The size of a thumbnail, this first single-processor CPU had the same power as ENIAC, the room-sized first electronic computer. The 4004 chip had 2,300 transistors and could perform around 100,000 instructions a second.

★ FASTEST COMPUTER

The Blue Gene/L prototype supercomputer, built by IBM (USA), is capable of 70.72 thousand billion calculations a second (70.72 teraflops). It was announced in November 2004.

SOUND & VISION

★MOST MEMORY IN A MOBILE PHONE

The SPH-V5400, launched by Samsung (South Korea) in September 2004, is capable of holding 1.5 GB of data. It is the first ever mobile phone to contain its own internal hard drive.

★HIGHEST RESOLUTION MOBILE PHONE CAMERA

The highest resolution digital camera integrated into a mobile phone is the SCH-S250, which can take 5-megapixel images. It was launched in South Korea by Samsung (South Korea) in October 2004.

★LARGEST LED SCREEN

The world's largest light-emitting diode (LED) screen measures 57 x 63 m (187 x 206 ft) high, with an area of 3,591 m² (38,522 ft²). It is located on the side of the office building of Aurora Ltd, Shanghai, China, and was completed in September 2003.

★LARGEST TELEVISION DISPLAY

Panasonic SS Marketing Co. Ltd have built a television display with a screen 59.90 x 11.13 m (196.53 x 36.53 ft) in size, giving a total viewable area of 667.09 m² (7,180.49 ft²). Its installation at the Suminoe Boat Race Stadium, Osaka, Japan, was completed on 31 March 2004.

← SMALLEST PC (PERSONAL COMPUTER)

OQO (USA) have developed a fully functioning personal computer with a 1 GHz processor, 10 GB or 20 GB hard drive and 256 MB of RAM, capable of running a full version of Microsoft's Windows XP. Its dimensions are 10.4 x 7.3 x 2.2 cm (4.1 x 2.9 x 0.9 in) and it weighs less than 225 g (9 oz). It was unveiled on 16 April 2002 at the Microsoft Corp. Windows Hardware Engineering Conference 2002 (WinHEC 2002), New Orleans, Louisiana, USA.

ACTUAL SIZE

★ MOST POWERFUL ION ENGINE USED IN SPACE

Nasa's *Deep Space 1* spacecraft, launched on 24 October 1998, was propelled to its target, Comet Borrelly, by a revolutionary type of engine. A beam of ionized xenon atoms were expelled from the engine at 35 km/s (21 miles/s), providing a thrust of 0.09 Newtons (0.02 lb), equivalent to the force exerted by a sheet of paper resting on the palm of a hand. The ion engine was 10 times more efficient than a chemical rocket and was fired for 16,265 hours during the mission.

★ MOST ADVANCED PLANETARIUM PROJECTOR

MEGASTAR-2 Cosmos can simultaneously project 5 million stars on to a planetarium dome. It was developed by Takayuki Ohira (Japan) and installed in the planetarium at the National Museum of Emerging Science and Innovation, Tokyo, Japan, in July 2004. Weighing 50 kg (110 lb) and standing 60 cm (23 in) tall, it can easily be carried in a car.

MISCELLANEOUS

FARTHEST DISTANCE BETWEEN PATIENT AND SURGEON

On 7 September 2001, Madeleine Schaal (France) had her gall bladder removed by a robot in an operating room at Strasbourg, France, while her surgeons Jacques Marescaux and Michel Gagner remotely operated the ZEUS robotic surgical arms on a secured fibre-optic line from New York City, USA. Patient and surgeon were a total distance of 6,222 km (3,866 miles) apart.

★ LARGEST CRIMINAL DNA DATABASE

As of 31 March 2004, the UK's National DNA Database contained 2,527,728 DNA profiles from 2,249,678 individuals. It was set up in April 1995 by the Forensic Science Service (UK) and was the world's first national intelligence DNA database.

★ MOST PATENTS HELD BY AN INDIVIDUAL

Shunpei Yamazaki (Japan), president of Semiconductor Energy Laboratory Co. Ltd (Japan), held a total of 3,245 patents as of 31 May 2004.

★ LONGEST SPACE TETHER

The *SEDS-1* and *SEDS-2* satellites (USA), launched on 29 March 1993 and 10 March 1994 respectively, achieved a space tether 20 km (12.4 miles). Both tethers were eventually severed by orbital debris impact. They were also the first manmade objects in space visible from the ground as a line rather than a point.

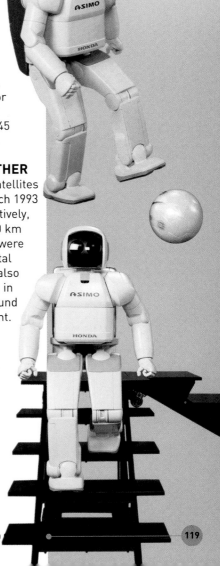

FASTEST RUNNING HUMANOID ROBOT →

ASIMO, which stands for Advanced Step in Innovative Mobility, has been developed and refined by Honda (Japan) since 2000 as the latest in its series of prototype humanoid robots designed to help people in the future. In December 2004, Honda announced that ASIMO had been improved in order to allow it to run at a speed of 3 km/h (1.8 mph).

LARGEST ANNUAL
FOOD FIGHT

On the last Wednesday in August, the town of Buñol, near Valencia, Spain, holds its annual tomato festival, *La Tomatina*. In 1999, about 25,000 people spent one hour at this giant food fight throwing about 125 tonnes (275,500 lb) of tomatoes at each other. From the backs of lorries, attendants dump the red fruit on to the streets for people to scoop up and throw. By the time the food fight is over, the streets and everyone on them are saturated with gloppy tomato paste. Rivers of tomato juice, as much as 30 cm (12 in) deep, run through the town until local fire trucks come in to hose down the streets and the people on them.

→ | **CONTENTS**

BIRTHS, DEATHS & MARRIAGES

← ★ BRIDE WITH THE MOST BRIDESMAIDS

Bride Christa Rasanayagam (Canada) was accompanied by 79 bridesmaids, aged one to 79, when she married Arulanantham Suresh Joachim (Sri Lanka) at Christ the King Catholic Church, Mississauga, Ontario, Canada, on 6 September 2003.

★ GROOM WITH MOST USHERS/ GROOMSMEN →

Accompanied by 47 groomsmen, aged between two and 63, Arulanantham Suresh Joachim (Sri Lanka) married Christa Rasanayagam (Canada) on 6 September 2003 at Christ the King Catholic Church in Mississauga, Ontario, Canada.

FERTILITY RATES
(average number of children per woman, 2000–05)

★ **Highest...**

1	Niger	8.00
2	Somalia	7.25
3	Angola	7.20
4	Guinea-Bissau	7.10
	Uganda	7.10

★ **...and lowest**

1	Hong Kong	1.00
2	Bulgaria	1.10
	Latvia	1.10
	Macau	1.10
5	Russia	1.14

Source: The Economist

BIRTH & DEATH

★ LARGEST POPULATION OF CHILDREN

In 2003, 50.8% of the population of Uganda was aged between 0 and 14 years old. Excluding the Vatican City, Italy has the ★ **smallest population of children** with only 14% aged 0–14 years old in the same year.

BIRTH RATES

Latvia and Georgia both recorded the **lowest birth rates**, with just eight live births per 1,000 population in 2002. The world average for the same year was 21.

The countries with the **highest birth rates** are Somalia and Sierra Leone, both of which recorded 50 live births per 1,000 people in 2002.

★ NATURAL POPULATION INCREASES

The country with the ★ **highest natural population increase** (births minus deaths) is Somalia, with an estimated increase of 32 per 1,000 people in 2002. The world average was 12 per 1,000 for the same year.

Latvia and Ukraine both had the ★ **lowest natural population increase** (or fastest rate of decreasing population) over the same period with an increase of -6 per 1,000 people.

★ INFANT MORTALITY RATES

Sweden has the ★ **lowest infant mortality rate** (that is, the fewest deaths of infants aged under one year), with 3.44 per 1,000 live births as of December 2003.

Angola has the ★ **highest infant mortality rate** with 191.44 deaths per 1,000 live births in the same year.

★ DEATH RATES

According to the most recent data available, both Sierra Leone and Malawi had the ★ **highest death rate**, with an estimated 25 deaths per 1,000 people for 2002. The world average for the same year was nine.

Kuwait and Oman both recorded the ★ **lowest death rate** of just three deaths per 1,000 people for 2002.

LEADING CAUSE OF DEATH

In industrialized countries, diseases of the heart and of blood vessels (cardiovascular disease) account for more than 50% of deaths. The most common of these are heart attacks and strokes, generally due to atheroma (degeneration of the arterial walls) obstructing the flow of blood.

MOST COMMON CAUSE OF SUDDEN DEATH

Coronary heart disease is the most common cause of sudden death. The main factors that put an individual at risk of the disease are smoking, high blood pressure and high levels of cholesterol.

★ SUICIDE RATES

Lithuania had the world's ★ **highest suicide rate**, with 91.7 suicides per 100,000 people in 2000, according to the World Health Organization's latest figures. This breaks down to 75.6 male and 16.1 female suicides per 100,000 people.

According to the World Health Organization, the following countries all recorded the ★ **lowest suicide rates**, with no cases reported in the years shown: Antigua and Barbuda (1995), the Dominican Republic (1994), Saint Kitts and Nevis (1995) and Saint Vincent and the Grenadines (1986).

LONGEST WILL

The will of Frederica Evelyn Stilwell Cook (USA) – proved at Somerset House in London, UK, on 2 November 1925 – consisted of four bound volumes containing a total of 95,940 words and concerning $100,000 (£21,000) worth of property.

★ OLDEST LIVING MARRIED COUPLE

Tadao Watanabe (Japan, b. 3 September 1898) married Minoru Mita (Japan, b. 14 May 1907) on 18 May 1926. Aged 106 years 188 days and 97 years 298 days respectively, they have a record aggregate age of 203 years 285 days. Also, as of 10 March 2005, they had been married for 78 years 296 days, making theirs the ★ **longest marriage for a living couple**.

MARRIAGE

LONGEST MARRIAGE

Sir Temulji Bhicaji Nariman and Lady Nariman were married for 86 years – from 1853 to 1940. The union took place when the two cousins were both five. Sir Temulji (b. 3 September 1848) died, aged 91 years 11 months, in August 1940 at Bombay, India.

Lazarus Rowe and Molly Webber, who were both born in 1725, were recorded as marrying in 1743. Molly died first, in June 1829 at Limington, Maine, USA, at which time the couple had also been married for 86 years.

MOST MARRIAGE VOWS RENEWED (SAME COUPLE)

Lauren Lubeck Blair and David E Hough Blair (both USA) married each other for the 83rd time on 16 August 2004 at the Lighthouse Lounge at the Boardwalk Hotel & Casino, Las Vegas, Nevada, USA.

★ MOST BRIDAL BOUQUETS CAUGHT

Stephanie Monyak (USA) has caught 11 bridal bouquets that were tossed at weddings she has attended since 1983.

MOST MONOGAMOUS MARRIAGES (FEMALE)

Linda Essex (USA) has had a total of 23 monogamous marriages. Her most recent wedding was in June 1996, when she married Glynn 'Scotty' Wolfe, who held the record for the **most monogamous marriages by a male**. He died 10 days before their first wedding anniversary.

HIGHEST DIVORCE RATE

According to the UN, the Maldives has 10.97 divorces per 1,000 inhabitants per year. This is followed by Belarus with 4.63, and the USA with 4.34.

★ BRIDEGROOM MARRIED AT THE HIGHEST ALTITUDE →

On 10 August 2003, Yuri Malenchenko (Ukraine) married Ekaterina Dmitriev (USA) from an altitude of 396 km (214.3 nautical miles). The ceremony was conducted over a video conference link between the bride in Houston, Texas, USA, and the groom who, at the time, was commander of the *Expedition 7* mission to the International Space Station. The closest she got to her husband on the day was standing next to his cardboard cut-out.

★ LOWEST MARRIAGE RATE

In 1994, the latest year for which data is available, the Dominican Republic had just two marriages per 1,000 population.

★ HIGHEST MARRIAGE RATE

Antigua and Barbuda had 22.1 marriages per 1,000 population in 1998. The UK figure from 2000, for comparison, was just 5.1 marriages per 1,000.

★ COUNTRY OF ORIGIN FOR MOST REFUGEES

The country with the most people seeking asylum elsewhere is Afghanistan. According to the provisional figures from the United Nations High Commission for Refugees (UNHCR) for the end of 2003, 2.1 million Afghans applied for political asylum in 74 countries. This represents 22% of the total global refugee population.

Most populous country
China (1,298,847,624)

Least populous country
Vatican City (921)

Largest country
Russia (143,782,338; 17,075,400 km² or 6,592,848 miles²)

Smallest country
Vatican City (0.44 km² or 0.17 miles²)

★ HIGHEST INFLATION

In 2003, Zimbabwe's annual rate of inflation stood at 385%. In 1998, for example, a loaf of bread cost Z$0.70 (less than £0.01; $0.01), rising to Z$3,000 (£0.27; $0.50) in 2003.

The country with the world's **lowest annual inflation** rate is Hong Kong, where consumer prices fell by 2.6% during 2003.

CITIES

OLDEST CAPITAL CITY
Damascus (Dimashq), Syria, has been continuously inhabited since *ca.* 2500 BC.

MOST REMOTE CITY FROM THE SEA
Urumqi, the capital of China's Xinjiang Uygur autonomous region, is 2,500 km (1,500 miles) from the nearest coastline.

★ CITY WITH THE LARGEST FOREIGN-BORN POPULATION
In 2001, 59% of the population of Miami, Florida, USA, was born outside the country.

COST OF LIVING

★ HIGHEST GNI PER CAPITA
According to available data from the World Bank Atlas' figures from September 2004, the country with the highest Gross National Income (GNI) per capita for 2003 was Luxembourg, with $43,940 (£23,692). GNI is the total value of goods and services produced by a country in one year, divided by its population. GNI per capita shows what part of a country's GNI each person would have if GNI were divided equally.

According to the same source, Ethiopia had the ★ **lowest GNI per capita** in 2003, with $90 (£49).

HIGHEST RATE OF TAX
In Denmark, the highest rate of personal income tax is 62.9%, with the basic rate of income tax starting at 43.7% as of June 2003.

The sovereign countries with the **least personal income tax** are Bahrain and Qatar, where the rate, regardless of income, is nil.

★ HIGHEST MILITARY EXPENDITURE PER CAPITA
Israel spent $1,466.51 (£790.74) per capita on military expenditure, according to 2003 figures.

According to the CIA World Factbook, the country with the ★ **lowest military expenditure** is Iceland, with $0 (£0) spent as of December 2003.

GEOGRAPHY

★ FASTEST GROWING COUNTRY THROUGH LAND RECLAMATION (BY PERCENTAGE OF ORIGINAL SIZE)
In 1960, the total area of Singapore was 581.5 km² (224.5 miles²); since then, it has added over 100 km² (38.6 miles²) of land, which represents an increase of 17% of the original area.

★ MOST FORESTED COUNTRY
As of 2000, 95.7% of the Cook Islands in the South Pacific Ocean was covered in forest.

★ HIGHEST COST
← OF LIVING

According to the latest Economist Intelligence Unit's Worldwide Cost of Living Survey – which compares the cost of a wide range of goods and services – the world's most expensive city is Tokyo, Japan. According to the same source, Tehran, the capital of Iran, offers the ★**lowest cost of living**.

★ LARGEST AREA OF LAND NAMED AFTER ONE PERSON

The continents of North and South America, which total 42,495,751 km² (16,407,701 miles²), were both named after the 15th-century Italian explorer Amerigo Vespucci.

POPULATIONS

★ COUNTRY THAT RECEIVES THE MOST REFUGEES

Pakistan receives more asylum seekers than any other country. According to the United Nations High Commission for Refugees (UNHCR), Pakistan received 1.1 million refugees in 2003.

★ HARDEST WORKING CITIZENS (INDUSTRIALIZED NATIONS)

According to the Organization for Economic Co-operation and Development's (OECD) annual Employment Outlook Report 2004, the industrialized country with the hardest working citizens is South Korea, whose working population (excluding self-employed labour) clocked up a total of 2,390 hours per employee for 2003.

LARGEST SHORTAGE OF MEN

The country with the largest recorded shortage of males is Latvia, where 53.97% of the population was female and 46.03% was male in 2002.

The ★**country with the largest recorded shortage of women** is the United Arab Emirates, with the male population numbering 67.63% and female population at 32.37% in 2001.

MISCELLANEOUS

★ HIGHEST UNEMPLOYMENT

According to estimates of 2003, 85% of Liberia's labour force is not in paid employment.

According to available data, in 2002 Nauru and Andorra had the **lowest rate of unemployment** for any country in the world, with 0%.

★ HIGHEST ROAD FATALITY RATE

Mauritius had 43.9 traffic fatalities per 100,000 people in 2000.

★ MOST CORRUPT COUNTRY

As of October 2004, the most corrupt country is Bangladesh, according to Transparency International's Corruption Perceptions Index.

QUALITY OF LIFE
(based on various factors ranging from recreational options to political stability)

★ **Highest...**
1 Zurich, Switzerland
  Geneva, Switzerland
3 Vancouver, Canada
  Vienna, Austria
5 Auckland, New Zealand
  Bern, Switzerland
  Copenhagen, Denmark
  Frankfurt, Germany
  Sydney, Australia

★ **...and lowest**
1 Baghdad, Iraq
2 Bangui, Central African Republic
3 Brazzaville, Republic of the Congo
4 Pointe Noire, Republic of the Congo
  Khartoum, Sudan

Source: The Economist

★ LEAST →
CORRUPT COUNTRY

As of October 2004, the world's least corrupt country is Finland, according to Transparency International's Corruption Perceptions Index. This index compares the misuse of public office for private gain in 146 countries, as perceived by business and country analysts (resident and non-resident).

LARGEST →
CRUISE SHIP LINE

Carnival is the world's largest cruise company, with 12 distinct brands and over 77 ships and 128,000 berths. In 2003, Carnival Corporation merged with P&O Princess plc, and the company's brands now include Carnival Cruise Lines, Princess Cruises, P&O Cruises and Windstar Cruises. Pictured is one of Carnival's ships, the *Carnival Valor*, passing Miami Beach en route to the Port of Miami.

TOP TEN POPULAR INTERNATIONAL TOURIST DESTINATIONS (MOST VISITORS 2003)

10. **Canada** – 17.5 million
9. **Germany** – 18.4 million
8. **Mexico** – 18.7 million
7. **Austria** – 19.1 million
6. **UK** – 24.7 million
5. **China** – 33 million
4. **Italy** – 39.6 million
3. **USA** – 41.2 million
2. **Spain** – 51.8 million

★ 1. MOST POPULAR TOURIST DESTINATION

In 2003, France attracted 75 million international visitors, according to the World Tourism Organization.

LAND

DENSEST ROAD NETWORK

The former Portuguese colony of Macau, today a Special Administrative Region of China, has 19.6 km (12.2 miles) of road per km^2 (0.38 miles^2) of land area. By comparison, the USA, which has the world's **largest road network**, has a density of only 0.69 km (0.43 miles) per km^2 because of its immense size. Of the world's fully sovereign countries, Malta has the densest network of roads, with 7.1 km (4.4 miles) per km^2.

★ MOST CROWDED ROAD NETWORK

Hong Kong, China, has 286.7 registered motor vehicles for every kilometre of road, in theory making its roads the most crowded in the world. The United Arab Emirates is second, with 231.6 vehicles per kilometre, while the USA, because of its vast size and large road network, is in 42nd place, with 34.1 vehicles per kilometre.

COUNTRY WITH THE BUSIEST ROAD NETWORK

Indonesia's roads are the most heavily used in the world, with 8 million km (5 million miles) being driven for every kilometre (0.62 miles) of the country's road network each year.

LONGEST BUS ROUTE

The 'Liberator's Route' is 9,660 km (6,002 miles) long and is operated by Expreso Internacional Ormeño SA of Lima, Peru. It links Caracas, Venezuela and Buenos Aires, Argentina, by bus, passing through the capitals of six South American countries. It takes 214 hours (8 days 22 hours) to complete, including breaks.

SEA

★ BUSIEST PORT BY CARGO VOLUME

In 2004, a total of 393 million tonnes (866 billion lb) of cargo passed through the port of Singapore. Containerized cargo accounted for 223 million tonnes (492 billion lb), with oil at 129 million tonnes (284 billion lb) accounting for the second largest portion. The remainder consisted of 'conventional' and non-oil bulk cargo.

FIRST PUBLIC HOVERCRAFT SERVICE

Between July and September 1962, a hovercraft service was run across the Dee estuary between Rhyl, Denbighshire, and Wallasey, Merseyside, UK.

LARGEST CIVILIAN HOVERCRAFT

The SRN4 Mk III, a British-built civil hovercraft, weighs 310 tonnes (683,400 lb) and can accommodate 418 passengers and 60 cars. It is 56.38 m (185 ft) in length and has a top speed of 65 knots (120 km/h; 75 mph). Service across the English Channel ceased in December 2000 when the hovercraft were replaced by slower but more economical Seacat catamarans.

AIR

★ MOST SCHEDULED FLIGHT JOURNEYS WITHIN 30 DAYS

Brother Michael Bartlett (UK) used a monthly Skypass issued by the Belgian national airline Sabena to fly between London and Brussels 128 times between 18 October and 17 November 1993. He had the individual tickets stapled together to form a 25.3-m-long (83-ft) ticket, and covered a total of 41,771 km (25,955 miles) during the month.

MOST SCHEDULED FLIGHTS IN A WEEK

Tae Oka (Japan) completed 70 flights in seven days on Thai Airways International between 14 and 20 February 2001. The flights were all internal between the Thai cities of Chiang Mai, Chiang Rai and Mae Hong Son airports.

☆ BUSIEST AIRPORT BY NUMBER OF AIRCRAFT

A total of 928,691 take-offs and landings were made during 2003 by aircraft at O'Hare International Airport, Chicago, Illinois, USA, according to the Airports Council International (ACI), making it the world's busiest in terms of the number of aircraft using it.

★ MOST AIRLINES FLOWN ON IN A YEAR

John Bougen and James Irving (both New Zealand) flew on 104 different airlines from 28 August 2002 to 12 February 2003 as part of their All Nations Quest. Their journey started and finished in Auckland, New Zealand, passed through 191 countries, and so also set the record for the **most sovereign countries visited in six months** (191 of the world's 193 sovereign countries in 167 days 15 hr 39 min).

During the same attempt, they took 242 flights on 54 aircraft types, and set a third record, that for ★ **most flights on a single journey**. In accordance with the rules, the 191 airports visited excluded repeat visits to airports and they did not return to New Zealand until the end of the trip.

MAURIZIO GIULIANO

Maurizio Giuliano (Italy/UK, b. 24 February 1975) had visited all 193 of the world's sovereign countries by 20 February 2004, when he was 28 years 361 days old.

Did you set out to be the youngest person to travel to all sovereign countries?
No, although the addiction to crossing borders is interesting... What causes me to travel so much is the passion to learn about different cultures and different mentalities, different peoples.

Is there a country that's been particularly hard to get into?
Yes, North Korea was definitely the most difficult. I went in 2000 after trying for a long time to get a visa. I kept e-mailing and faxing embassies in various parts of the world for a whole year and finally in 2000 I was told that my visa had been approved.

How many passports do you have?
I have a total of 42. Twelve of them are British and 30 are Italian.

Why so many?
It's really helpful to have at least two valid passports because when you send your passport off for a visa, it can take quite a while to get it back. Also, I've been careful to have my visas and stamps in a way that is as aesthetic as possible, so I try not to get all my stamps jammed on to one page. I normally have three or four stamps on a page. I've been to many countries more than once, which means extra stamps.

MOST SUPERSONIC PASSENGER JOURNEYS

By February 2003, Fred Finn (UK) had made 718 Atlantic crossings on Concorde. His first flight was 26 May 1976, for which he still has the special commemorative briefcase tag.

★ LONGEST DISTANCE COMMERCIAL SCHEDULED FLIGHT

A flight operated by Singapore Airlines between Singapore and New York City, USA, covers a distance of some 16,600 km (10,300 miles). The 18-hour flight employs 181-seat Airbus A340-500 aircraft.

BIGGEST TOURIST SPENDERS

In 2003, German citizens spent $64.7 billion (£36.3 billion), excluding airfares, while on holiday abroad, according to the World Tourism Organization.

Americans, the biggest spenders in 2002, were second with $56.5 billion (£31.7 billion), and British citizens were third with $48.5 billion (£27.2 billion).

FOOD FESTIVALS:

February: **Crab festival**, San Francisco, USA

March: **Black pudding festival**, Mortagne au Perche, France

April: **Maple syrup festival**, Saint-Georges, Canada

May: **Cheese rolling festival**, Stilton, UK

July: **Baby food festival**, Freemont, Michigan, USA

September: **Mooncake festival**, Singapore

October: **Truffle festival**, Alba, Italy, and **Date feast**, Erfoud, Morocco

November: **Cherry festival**, Ficksburg, South Africa

December: **Radish night**, Oaxaca, Mexico

← ★ LARGEST
ELEPHANT BUFFET

For the annual elephant parade held in 2003 in the Surin Province, Thailand, a record 269 Asian elephants gathered to eat over 50 tonnes (110,000 lb) of fruit and vegetables that had been laid out for them on tables covered with silk cloth.

RELIGIOUS FESTIVALS

LARGEST GATHERING OF RELIGIOUS LEADERS

The Millennium World Peace Summit of Religious and Spiritual Leaders involved 1,000 delegates. It was held at the UN headquarters in New York, USA, from 28 to 31 August 2000.

LARGEST GATHERING OF SIKHS

Over eight million Sikhs gathered at the Anandpur Sahib gurdwara (Sikh temple), Punjab, India, from 13 to 17 April 1999 to celebrate the 300th anniversary of the Sikh Khalsa, an order of the Sikh religion. More than 3.5 million people gathered there on 13 April, the day of the Vaisakhi festival, to commemorate the day that the Sikh Khalsa was established.

MOST MUSLIM PILGRIMS

The annual Hajj (pilgrimage) to Mecca, Saudi Arabia, attracts greater numbers than any other Islamic mission, an average of 2 million people a year from 140 countries.

MOST CHRISTIAN PILGRIMS

The House of the Virgin Mary at Loretto, Italy, receives 3.5 million pilgrims (as opposed to tourists) a year – over three times the number visiting Lourdes, France.

MOST HINDU PILGRIMS

Every 12 years during the festival of Kumbha Mela, held at the confluence of the Ganges and Jumna (Yamuna) rivers in Uttar Pradesh state, India, worshippers gather to bathe in the waters. In 1995, an estimated 20 million pilgrims attended, the highest recorded total.

FOOD

LARGEST TAMALE FESTIVAL

The annual Indio International Tamale Festival held in Indio, California, USA, to mark the Christmas holiday season, attracted over 154,000 people at its 11th event in December 2002. A tamale is a Mexican dish comprising assorted cheeses, chilli powder, corn masa flour, lard and chicken broth.

LARGEST SILVER SERVICE DINNER

On 28 April 2001, 11,483 people attended a silver service dinner party at Earl's Court, London, UK. The dinner was sponsored by Vodafone Group plc. The event was developed and produced by Skybridge Group plc, and the caterers were Beeton Rumford Ltd.

★ LARGEST BREAKFAST

A breakfast involving 23,291 diners took place at the Chung Shang Stadium, Taiwan, on 13 October 2001. A total of 5,670 litres (1,247 gal; 1,497 US gal) of milk and 1,920 kg (4,232 lb) of bread were consumed.

LARGEST →
FROGS' LEGS FESTIVAL

The Fellsmere Frog Leg Festival held in Fellsmere, Florida, USA, attracted 75,000 visitors from 18 to 21 January 2001. More than 3,000 kg (6,600 lb) of golden battered fried frogs' legs were served during the free, four-day festival to 13,200 diners.

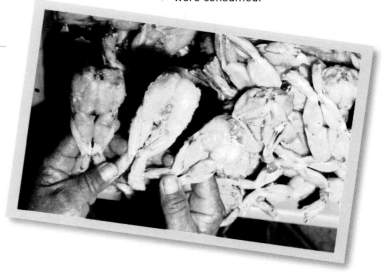

LARGEST DONATION OF HAIR

Pilgrims to the Tirupati temple in Andhra Pradesh, India, donate a tonsure of their hair as a form of sacrifice. An estimated 6.5 million people make donations of their hair every year, and more than $2.2 million (£1.3 million) is raised in temple funds through the annual auction of hair. The temple attracts an average of 30,000 visitors a day. Around 600 barbers are employed 24 hours a day by the temple to shave the pilgrims' heads, and the hair is auctioned to wigmakers as well as chemical and fertilizer factories.

LARGEST RELIGIOUS FEAST

A feast attended by 150,000 guests was held at Ahmedabad, India, on 2 June 1991, as part of the renunciation ceremony of Atul Dalpatlal Shah, when he became a monk.

LARGEST GARLIC FESTIVAL

The three-day Gilroy Garlic Festival, held each summer in Gilroy, California, USA, attracts 130,000 people, who sample garlic flavoured food ranging from meat to ice-cream.

LARGEST WEDDING BANQUET/RECEPTION

Jayalalitha Jayaram (India), former Tamil Nadu chief minister and movie star, hosted a reception banquet for over 150,000 guests at her foster son's wedding in her 20-hectare (50-acre) grounds in Madras, India, on 7 September 1995. The wedding is reported to have cost over 750 million rupees ($21,328,000; £13,759,000).

★ LARGEST PICNIC

At an open-air dinner held during the May Festivals on 2 May 1999, 8,000 people gathered at the Plaza de Espana, Santa Cruz, Tenerife, Spain, to eat prepared meals brought from home.

LONGEST CONTINUOUS TABLE

On 22 March 1998, a team of caterers set places for 15,000 people to eat at a table stretching over 5.05 km (3 miles) along the newly built Vasco da Gama bridge, Lisbon, Portugal – Europe's longest bridge at 18 km (11 miles).

DRINK

LARGEST BEER FESTIVAL

Oktoberfest, the annual beer festival in Munich, Germany (18 September to 5 October), was visited by a record 7 million people in 1999. What they consumed was also a record: 5.8 million litres (1.27 million gal; 1.53 million US gal) of beer was 'tasted' from 11 beer tents that stood on a site as large as 50 football pitches.

LARGEST SPIRIT TASTING

On 24 November 2001 at The World Trade Centre in Stockholm, Sweden, 1,210 people took part in a whisky tasting, each participant sampling five different types.

LARGEST WINE TASTING EVENT

On 22 November 1986, approximately 4,000 wine tasters consumed 9,360 bottles of wine at a single wine tasting. The event was sponsored by local San Francisco television station KQED in California, USA.

LARGEST SIMULTANEOUS TOAST

A total of 462,572 participants gathered in pubs, restaurants, bars and concert venues across the USA on 23 February 2001 at 11.00 p.m. (EST) for The Great Guinness Toast.

→WHERE IS THE WORLD'S LARGEST RELIGIOUS THEME PARK? FIND OUT ON P.206

LARGEST GATHERING →
OF CLOWNS

In 1991, the annual clown convention held at Bognor Regis in West Sussex, UK, attracted 850 clowns, including 430 from North America. The convention has been held since 1946 by Clowns International, which is the **largest** and **oldest clown organization** in the world.

← ★ MOST ELECTION VOTES
CAST IN ONE YEAR

A record total of 58 presidential and parliamentary elections were held in 2004, involving over 1.1 billion voters. The first that year was a presidential election in Georgia, held on 4 January. The last was the third round of Ukraine's presidential elections on 26 December. Pictured are voters in India (top), the Philippines (middle) and South Africa (bottom).

GOVERNMENT

★ MOST VOTES CAST IN A NATIONAL ELECTION

Between 20 April and 10 May 2004, a total of 387.8 million votes were cast in India to elect the 543 members of the 14th Lok Sabha (the House of the People, which is the lower house of the Indian legislature). On 13 May, the Bharatiya Janata Party conceded defeat to the new ruling party, the Indian National Congress under Prime Minister Manmohan Singh.

★ YOUNGEST VOTING AGE

Universal suffrage in Iran is at the age of just 15 years old.

★ HIGHEST PAID PRIME MINISTER

In August 2000, the then prime minister of Singapore, Goh Chok Tong, earned an increase in annual salary of 14% to SG$1.94 million ($1.1 million; £750,000). The current prime minister is Lee Hsien Loong who was sworn in on 12 August 2004.

★ RICHEST PRIME MINISTER

Silvio Berlusconi, prime minister of Italy, has amassed a personal wealth of $10 billion (£5 billion) according to Forbes in 2004.

★ YOUNGEST APPOINTED PRIME MINISTER

Roosevelt Skerritt (b. 8 June 1972) was appointed prime minister of Dominica on 8 January 2004 at the age of 31.

The **oldest living prime minister** is King Fahd bin Abdul Aziz (b. 1921), who became king and prime minister of Saudi Arabia on 13 June 1982.

The **oldest appointed prime minister** was Morarji Ranchhodji Desai (India, 1896–1995), who took up his post in March 1977 aged 81. He served until 1979.

YOUNGEST APPOINTED PRESIDENT

Jean-Claude Duvalier (b. 3 July 1951) succeeded his father, François Duvalier, as president of Haiti for life on 22 April 1971, at the age of 19 years 293 days. He served as president of Haiti until 1986.

LONGEST SERVING HEAD OF STATE

Fidel Castro (b. 13 August 1927), president of Cuba's Council of State, has been the island-state's unchallenged revolutionary and political leader since 26 July 1959, when his guerrilla movement overthrew the military dictatorship headed by Fulgencio Batista.

★ COUNTRY WITH THE MOST SIBLINGS IN POWER

Saudi Arabia has five siblings holding powerful governmental offices. The current head of state is King Fahd bin Abdul Aziz, but owing to illness his half-brother,

Crown Prince Abdullah bin Abdul Aziz, acts as Regent, as well as being First Deputy Prime Minister and Commander of the National Guard. The King's full brother, Prince Sultan bin Abdul Aziz, is Second Deputy Prime Minister and Minister of Defense and Aviation. Other (full) brothers include Prince Nayef bin Abdul Aziz (Interior Minister) and Prince Salman bin Abdul Aziz (Governor of Riyadh).

LONGEST SERVING FEMALE PRIME MINISTER

Sirimavo Bandaranaike was prime minister of Sri Lanka for a total of 17 years 208 days. She served from 21 July 1960 to 25 March 1965; 29 May 1970 to 22 July 1977; and 12 November 1994 to 10 August 2000. Bandaranaike was also the world's **first female prime minister**.

MONARCHY

★ RICHEST MONARCH

King Fahd bin Abdul Aziz (Saudi Arabia) has a personal wealth estimated by Forbes in 2004 to be $25 billion (£13 billion).

★ LARGEST ROYAL FAMILY

In 2002, the house of Al-Saud of Saudi Arabia had over 4,000 royal princes and 30,000 relatives. The

YOUNGEST CURRENT →
HEAD OF STATE

The youngest current republican head of state is Lt Yahya Jammeh (b. 25 May 1965), who became president of the provisional council and head of state of The Gambia following a military coup on 26 July 1994. On 27 September 1996, he was elected president following a return to civilian government. President Jammeh was re-elected on 18 October 2001 for another five years.

kingdom was established by King Abdul Aziz in 1932. His 17 wives bore him 44 sons, four of whom have ruled the kingdom since the king's death in 1953.

SHORTEST REIGN EVER

Crown Prince Luis Filipe was king of Portugal (Dom Luis III) for just 20 minutes on 1 February 1908.

LONGEST REIGN EVER

Minhti, king of Arakan, part of Myanmar, is reputed to have reigned for 95 years between 1279 and 1374.

The **longest documented reign of any monarch** is that of Phiops II (also known as Neferkare or Pepi II), a Sixth-Dynasty pharaoh of ancient Egypt. His reign began c. 2281 BC, when he was six years old, and lasted c. 94 years.

LONGEST REIGN – CURRENT

Bhumibol Adulyadej, king of Thailand, succeeded to the throne following the death of his older brother on 9 June 1946.

The **most durable monarch** is the king of Cambodia, Norodom Sihanouk, who first became king on 16 April 1941. He abdicated on 2 March 1955 and returned to the throne on 24 September 1993.

→ WHICH QUEEN – THE LONGEST SERVING QUEEN ALIVE TODAY – VISITED THE GUINNESS WORLD RECORDS OFFICE IN 2004? FIND OUT ON P.6

KING MSWATI III

King Mswati III of Swaziland was just 18 years and 6 days old when he took the throne. He talks to Guinness World Records about being the world's youngest reigning monarch.

What was it like to become king at such a young age?
It was a great responsibility indeed. I was young with no experience, so I'm grateful to my mother and my advisors for their invaluable support and advice.

What is a typical day like as king?
Always very busy with many problems to solve at both

individual and government levels. A Swazi king must care for and support his people, who must always have access to him.

What is the most difficult thing about being king?
The big responsibility of taking care of your nation and always making the right decision about the future.

If you were not king, what job would you like to do?
I've never seriously thought about any career. I guess I was born to be king. Being king is, to me, a calling from God.

What are the biggest challenges facing Swaziland at this time?
Unemployment, poverty and HIV/Aids are the biggest. We're addressing these problems through job creation programmes aimed at reaching the people at grass roots level. We have traditional and modern programmes, such as the campaign for abstinence from premarital sex, to help our youth protect themselves from HIV/Aids.

★ BUDGET EXPENDITURE

In December 2003, the world's **lowest budget expenditure** was just $878,119 (£455,503) – including capital expenditures – by the Pitcairn Islands in the South Pacific.

The **highest budget expenditure** (based on 2002 figures) was $2.052 trillion (£1.35 billion) by the US government.

CRIME & PUNISHMENT

LONGEST SERVING PRISONER IN SOLITARY CONFINEMENT →

Mordecai Vanunu (Israel) spent nearly 12 years in a total isolation jail cell – the longest known term of solitary confinement in modern times. Born in 1954, Vanunu was convicted of treason for giving information about Israel's nuclear programme to the UK's *Sunday Times* newspaper. He was held in isolation from 1986 until March 1998. However, Vanunu was sentenced to a total of 18 years in prison and remained incarcerated until he was released on 21 April 2004.

SENTENCES

★ LONGEST PRISON SENTENCE FOR HACKING

Brian Salcedo (USA) was sentenced to nine years in prison in Charlotte, North Carolina, USA, on 16 December 2004 for computer hacking. Salcedo had pleaded guilty to conspiracy and numerous hacking charges in August 2004 after attempting to steal credit card information from the computer systems of Loewe's hardware stores (USA).

LONGEST PRISON SENTENCE FOR FRAUD

Chamoy Thipyaso (Thailand) and seven of her associates were each jailed for 141,078 years by the Bangkok Criminal Court, Thailand, on 27 July 1989. The 'Queen of the Underground', as she was known, convinced over 16,000 Thais to put their life savings into a pyramid scheme. The government closed down Thipyaso's business – worth 4.6 billion baht ($204,984,268; £106,513,000) – after it posed a threat to the Thai banking system.

★ SHORTEST JURY DELIBERATION

On 22 July 2004, Nicholas Clive McAllister (New Zealand) was acquitted of cultivating cannabis plants after the jury at Greymouth District Court, West Coast, New Zealand, had deliberated for just one minute. The jury would not have had time to take their seats at the deliberation table.

★ LARGEST SPEEDING FINE

Jussi Salonoja (Finland) was fined €170,000 (£116,000) for driving at 80 km/h (50 mph) in a 40-km/h (25-mph) zone in Helsinki, Finland, in February 2004. In accordance with Finnish law, speeders are fined in proportion to their annual incomes – and Mr Salonoja, heir to a family-owned sausage empire, earned close to £7 million ($11 million) in 2002.

ROBBERY

GREATEST ART ROBBERY

On 14 April 1991, 20 paintings estimated to be worth $500 million (£280 million) were stolen from the Van Gogh Museum in Amsterdam, the Netherlands. However, only 35 minutes later they were found in an abandoned car not far from the museum.

MOST VALUABLE OBJECT STOLEN

It is arguable that Leonardo da Vinci's *Mona Lisa*, though never valued, is the most valuable object ever stolen. It disappeared from the Louvre, Paris, France, on 21 August 1911 and was recovered in Italy in 1913. Vincenzo Perugia (Italy) was charged with its theft.

LARGEST OBJECT STOLEN BY AN INDIVIDUAL

On the moonless night of 5 June 1966, N William Kennedy slashed the mooring lines of the 10,639-dwt SS *Orient Trader* at Wolfes Cove, St Lawrence Seaway, Canada. The vessel drifted to a waiting blacked-out tug, thus evading a ban on any shipping movements during a violent wildcat waterfront strike. It then set sail for Spain.

LARGEST TRAIN ROBBERY

On 8 August 1963, a General Post Office mail train from Glasgow was ambushed at Sears Crossing and robbed at Bridego Bridge near Mentmore, Buckinghamshire, UK. A gang escaped with about 120 mailbags containing £2,631,784 (then $7,369,784) in banknotes that were being taken to London for destruction. Only £343,448 ($961,757) was recovered.

LARGEST JEWEL ROBBERY

An estimated $100 million (£62 million) worth of gems were taken in a raid at the Antwerp Diamond Centre, Belgium, sometime over the weekend of 15–16 February 2003. Although 123 of the 160 vaults were emptied, there was no sign of a break-in, alarms did not go off and the bombproof vault doors were not tampered with.

★ OLDEST BANK ROBBER

At the age of 92, JL Hunter Rountree was sentenced to 151 months in prison on 23 January 2004 after he pleaded guilty to robbing $1,999 (£1,243) from a bank in Texas, USA, on 12 August 2003. In a newspaper interview, he said: 'A bank that I'd done business with had forced me into bankruptcy. I have never liked banks since... I decided I would get even. And I have.' He also claimed that prison food was better than what was served at some nursing homes.

MURDER

MOST PROLIFIC MURDERER

It was established at the trial of Behram, the 'Indian Thug', that he had strangled at least 931 victims with his yellow and white cloth strip or 'ruhmal' in the Oudh district (now in Uttar Pradesh, India) between 1790 and 1840. Thugs ('Thieves') were members of gangs who travelled around India on killing sprees from around 1550 until finally being suppressed in the mid-1800s.

MOST PROLIFIC FEMALE MURDERER

Historically, the most prolific murderer of the western world was Elizabeth Bathori (Hungary), who practised vampirism on girls and young women. Throughout the 15th century, she killed more than 600 virgins in order to drink their blood and bathe in it. When her murderous career was discovered, the countess was locked up in her castle from 1610 until her death in 1614.

MOST PROLIFIC SERIAL KILLER

The most prolific substantiated modern serial killer is Pedro López (Colombia), who confessed to raping and killing 300 girls in Colombia, Peru and Ecuador. Charged on 57 counts of murder in Ecuador, the 'Monster of the Andes' was sentenced to life imprisonment in 1980.

CAPITAL PUNISHMENT

EXECUTIONS

Most executions	China	726 legally sanctioned executions in 2003, according to Amnesty Int.
Most executions per capita	Saudi Arabia	1,409 executions from 1980 to 2002, a figure of 1 per 208,772 citizens
Most popular method of execution	Firing squad	Practised in 73 countries, and sole method in 45; hanging comes next, practised in 58 countries
First execution by injection	7 December 1983	C Brooke (USA), Huntsville, Texas, USA
First execution by electric chair	8 August 1890	William Kemmler (USA), Auburn Prison, New York, USA
Greatest hanging at one gallows	38 Sioux Indians	Hanged on 26 December 1862 outside Mankato, Minnesota, USA
First abolition	1798	Liechtenstein

DEATH ROW

Largest population	3,471	35 states of the USA (2004 figures)
Longest time on death row	39 years	Sadamichi Hirasawa (Japan, 1893–1987) lived out his life on death row in Sendai Prison, Japan, after poisoning 12 bank employees
Longest time on death row for a dog	8 years, 190 days	Word, a Lhasa apso incarcerated for biting in Seattle, Washington, USA

MOST PROLIFIC MURDER PARTNERSHIP

Sisters Delfina and María de Jesús Gonzáles (Mexico) abducted girls to work in brothels and are known to have murdered at least 90 of their victims. The sisters were sentenced to 40 years' imprisonment in 1964.

COUNTRY WITH THE MOST MURDERS

According to the United Nations, from 1998 to 2000 the country with the most murders was India, with 37,170. However, Colombia has the **highest total recorded intentional homicides** per capita, with 65 murders per 100,000.

→ **WHICH IS THE WORLD'S LEAST CORRUPT COUNTRY? FIND OUT ON P.125**

LARGEST ↘
CRIMINAL ORGANIZATION

According to Interpol, the centuries-old Six Great Triads of China has at least 100,000 members scattered around the world. (Pictured are suspected members of a Hong Kong triad gang.)

In terms of profits, the **largest organized crime syndicate** is the Mafia, with an estimated profit in March 1986 of $75 billion (£52 billion). The Mafia has infiltrated the executive, judiciary and legislature of the USA. It consists of up to 5,000 individuals in 25 'families', federated under 'The Commission', involved in gambling, protection rackets, narcotics, bootlegging, loan-sharking and prostitution.

OBJECTS OF DESIRE

MOST EXPENSIVE
COMMERCIALLY AVAILABLE DOMESTIC ROBOT

The Japanese Thames company exhibited their TMSUK IV robot in Tokyo, Japan, on 23 January 2000. The 82-kg (180-lb) robot stands 1.2 m (4 ft) tall and originally cost $44,800 (£30,000), the equivalent of approximately $49,508 (£25,702) today. The robot can run errands, massage humans, is totally obedient and can be controlled remotely by phone.

ACTUAL SIZE

★ MOST EXPENSIVE PINBALL MACHINE

A one-off pinball machine produced in February 1992 is reported to have been sold for $120,000 (£79,000) in Los Angeles, California, USA. This is equivalent to approximately $162,765 (£84,500) today.

MOST COMPLICATED WRISTWATCH

The Piguet/Muller/Gerber Grand Complication watch has 1,116 individual parts and is owned by Willy Ernst Sturzenegger, Territorial Earl of Arran (Switzerland). It was last added to by master watchmaker Paul Gerber (Switzerland).

MOST EXPENSIVE MOBILE PHONE

A mobile phone designed by David Morris International (UK) was sold for £66,629 ($113,256) in 1996. Made entirely from 18-carat gold, the one-off mobile had a keypad that was encrusted with pink and white diamonds.

MOST EXPENSIVE BOARD GAME

A deluxe version of Outrage!, which is based on stealing the Crown Jewels from the Tower of London, UK, retails at £7,995 ($15,400). The set includes mini reproductions of the Crown Jewels, accurately made from solid, 18-carat gold with real diamonds, rubies, emeralds and sapphires. Only 20 sets were ever produced.

MOST EXPENSIVE HOTEL SUITE

In 2003, the Imperial Suite at the President Wilson Hotel in Geneva, Switzerland, could be reserved for CHF45,000 ($36,240; £20,387) a night. This is equivalent to approximately $37,480 (£19,458) today. The suite is accessed by a private lift and fills an entire floor. It has four bedrooms, all overlooking Lake Geneva. The dining room seats 26, the living room can hold 40 people, and all windows and doors are bulletproof.

MOST EXPENSIVE WALLET

A platinum-cornered, diamond-studded crocodile wallet made by Louis Quatorze of Paris, France, and Mikimoto of Tokyo, Japan, sold in September 1984 for $74,816 (£56,000). This is equivalent to approximately $137,030 (£71,140) today.

★ LARGEST CUT
DIAMOND

The world's largest cut diamond is an unnamed Fancy Black containing small red diamond crystals. It weighs 555.55 carats and was polished into 55 facets over several years and completed in June 2004. Ran Gorenstein (Belgium) commissioned this creation.

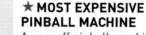

★ NEW RECORD   ☆ UPDATED RECORD

TOP 10 MOST VALUABLE ITEMS FROM THE GUINNESS WORLD RECORDS ARCHIVE

CATEGORY	DESCRIPTION	PRICE PAID	LOCATION OF SALE	DATE OF SALE
1. Jewellery collection	Owned by Duchess of Windsor	£31,380,197 ($50,427,977)	Sotheby's, Geneva, Switzerland	3 April 1987
2. ★Furniture	18th-century Italian Badminton cabinet	£19,045,250 ($36,812,086)	Christie's, London, UK	9 December 2004
3. Illustrated manuscript	Leonardo da Vinci's *Codex Hammer*. Renamed *Codex Leicester*, its original title, after sale	$30,802,500 (£19,246,489)	Christie's, New York City, USA	11 November 1994
4. Jewel	D colour internally flawless pear-shaped diamond weighing 100.10 carats; named 'Star of the Season' after sale	CHF19,858,500 ($16,561,171; £10,548,444)	Sotheby's, Geneva, Switzerland	17 May 1995
5. Car	1931 Bugatti Type 41 'Royale' Sports Coupé	$15 million (£9.13 million)	NA	12 April 1990
6. Watch	Patek Phillipe watch, named *Supercomplication*, that belonged to Henry Graves Jr (USA)	$11,002,500 (£6,882,154)	Sotheby's, New York City, USA	2 December 1999
7. Stamp collection (single sale)	Kanai collection of 183 pages of the classic stamp issues of Mauritius	CHF15,000,000 ($9,982,033; £6,887,052)	Switzerland	3 November 1993
8. Book	An original four-volume subscriber set of J J Audubon's *The Birds of America*	$8,802,500 (£5,567,573)	Christie's, New York City, USA	10 March 2000
9. Dinosaur bones	Largest and most complete *Tyrannosaurus rex* skeleton, known as 'Sue'	$8,362,500 (£5,104,377)	Sotheby's, New York City, USA	4 October 1997
10. Horse	Six-year-old broodmare called Cash Run	$7,100,000 (£4,186,814)	Lexington, Kentucky, USA	3 November 2003

ACTUAL SIZE

MOST VALUABLE BISCUIT

↙

At Christie's in London, UK, on 18 April 2000, a biscuit from Sir Ernest Shackleton's unsuccessful 1907–09 expedition to the South Pole sold for £4,935 (then $7,804). It was bought by art dealer Johnny Van Haeften (UK), whose great-uncle was Sir Philip Brocklehurst, a member of Shackleton's team.

☆ MOST EXPENSIVE HELMET
The highest price paid for an item of headwear is £156,450 ($277,292) when a Phyrgian Chalcidian-type winged bronze helmet from the 4th century BC was sold to a British collector at Christie's of London, UK, on 28 April 2004.

MOST VALUABLE PHILATELIC ITEM
An 1847 letter to wine merchants in Bordeaux – franked with the 1d and 2d first issues of Mauritius – was bought by an anonymous buyer in less than a minute for CHF6,123,750 ($4,075,165;

£2,811,639). The sale was conducted by Geneva-based auctioneer David Feldman (Ireland) in Zürich, Switzerland, on 3 November 1993. Feldman also auctioned the **most valuable stamp**: the Swedish 'Treskilling' Yellow sold for CHF2,870,000 ($2,255,403; £1,367,969) in Geneva, Switzerland, on 8 November 1996.

MOST VALUABLE BASEBALL
A baseball was sold at Guernsey's auction house, New York City, USA, for $3,054,000 (£1,874,655) including commission, to Todd McFarlane on 12 January 1999. The ball had been hit by Mark McGwire (St Louis Cardinals) for his 70th and final home run in his record-setting 1998 season.

☆ MOST VALUABLE GUITAR
Eric Clapton's (UK) 'Blackie' Fender Stratocaster guitar sold for $959,500 (£528,976) to the US chain The Guitar Center at Christie's in New York, USA, on 24 June 2004. 'Blackie' was made from the parts of various Strats bought in Nashville, Tennessee.

MOST VALUABLE BASEBALL CARD

A rare 1909 card, known as T206 Honus Wagner, was sold during an online eBay auction for $1,265,000 (£844,116) to Brian Seigal (USA) on 15 July 2000.

ACTUAL SIZE

HIGHEST GROSSING ANIMATION –
OPENING DAY

The Incredibles (USA, 2004) took $20.5 million (£11.1 million) on its opening day at 3,933 locations across the USA on 5 November 2004, beating the previous record of $11.8 million (£6.6 million) set by *Shrek 2* (USA, 2004) on 19 May 2004.

→ | CONTENTS

The core sample from the Carmichaels' ball of paint!

←★MOST LAYERS
OF PAINT ON A BALL

Michael Carmichael and his wife Glenda of Alexandria, Indiana, USA, have covered a baseball with approximately 18,000 layers of paint. Since first painting the ball in 1977, they have added nearly two coats of paint a day and, as of June 2004, the ball had a circumference of 2.77 m (9 ft 1 in). The number of layers was estimated by taking a core sample (above) and analysing it at a magnification of x1,200.

MOST VALUABLE...

PAINTING SOLD (PRIVATELY)

The seascape *Lost on the Grand Banks*, by Winslow Homer (USA), was sold for over $30 million (£18 million) on 6 May 1998, reportedly to Bill Gates (USA).

★ MOONSCAPE PAINTING

The most expensive moonscape sold was created by US astronaut Alan Bean, who was lunar module pilot on *Apollo 12* (November 1969) and commander of *Skylab 2* (July–September 1973). It depicts a fictional scenario of Bean – who describes himself as an astronaut-explorer-artist – chasing an American football, thrown by *Apollo 12* commander Pete Conrad, on the Moon. The painting, titled *If We Could Do It All Over Again – Are You Ready For Some Football?*, was sold to an unnamed buyer in 2004 for $182,369.60 (£98,415.75).

★ SCULPTURE SOLD (AUCTION)

A bronze sculpture titled *Danaïde* (1913), by Constantin Brancusi (Romania), was sold at Christie's, New York City, USA, for $18,159,500 (£12,366,020) on 7 May 2002. It depicts a figure from Greek mythology – the Danaïdes were the 50 daughters of King Danaos of Argos, Greece.

SCULPTURE BY A LIVING ARTIST

Michael Jackson and Bubbles, a porcelain sculpture created by artist Jeff Koons (USA) in 1988, sold for $5,616,750 (£3,955,903) at Sotheby's, New York City, USA, on 15 May 2001. The gold-and-white sculpture shows Michael Jackson reclining on a bed of roses with his arm around his pet chimp.

POST-IT NOTE

A Post-It Note featuring a pastel and charcoal work called *After Rembrandt* was sold online on 20 December 2000 for £640 ($925). The artist, R B Kitaj (USA), was one of a group of celebrities invited to create mini-masterpieces to mark the 20th anniversary of the famous sticky notelet to raise money for charity.

LARGEST...

★ STONE SCULPTURE

God of Longevity, a carved stone sculpture located in the Meng Shan mountains in Shandong, China, is so large that it can be seen from up to 30 km (19 miles) away. The sculpture is 218 m (715 ft) high and 200 m (656 ft) wide, and is represented with a long stick in one hand and an 'immortal peach' in the other.

ICE LOLLY STICK SCULPTURE

Robert McDonald and his son Robbie (both USA) built *OlaBison* – a Viking ship 3.89 m (12.7 ft) long and 1.18 m (3.8 ft) wide – from 370,000 wooden ice lolly sticks. It floated for an hour in Urk harbour, the Netherlands, on 12 September 2003.

Great balls of...
Alexandria, Indiana, home of the largest painted ball, also lays claim to the world's largest hairball record! In 1992, a 'goat-sized mass of hair' was dredged from the town's sewers. It has since disintegrated, but a replica is often paraded through the town during the festive season. Other record-breaking balls include:

★**Cling film:** Andy Martell (Canada) created a ball of cling film 228.5 cm (89.9 in) in circumference and weighing 70.3 kg (155 lb).

Foil: Richard Roman (USA) made an aluminium foil ball weighing 0.45 kg (1,615 lb) on 17 September 1987.

String: J C Payne (USA) tied a ball of string 12.65 m (41 ft 6 in) in circumference.

LARGEST →
SOAP SCULPTURE

Artist Bev Kirk (USA) carved a winged pig entitled *Sudsie, A Boar of Soap*, in Cincinnati, Ohio, USA, in September 2003. Sudsie was made from a 1.5 x 1.5 x 1.8 m (5 x 5 x 6 ft) bar of Ivory soap and weighs 3,175 kg (7,000 lb) – the equivalent of 26,666 Ivory soap bath bars.

← MOST VALUABLE PAINTING SOLD AT AUCTION

Pablo Picasso's (Spain) *Garçon à la Pipe* (1905) sold to an anonymous buyer for $104 million (£65 million) on 5 May 2004 at Sotheby's, New York City, USA. With buyer's fees and premium, it cost $104,168,000, making it the **first work of art to break the $100 million threshold**. (It is also the most expensive image to reproduce in this book!)

★ INDOOR MURAL

A group of people sentenced to carry out community work completed a mural covering all internal walls and ceilings of the Police and Citizens' Youth Club in Bernie, Tasmania, Australia, on 30 June 2004. The work took 18 months to paint and was coordinated by a mural artist. It is 727.52 m² (7,830.96 ft²) and illustrates a cross-section of the terrain of Tasmania.

The **largest outdoor mural** is the *Pueblo Levee Project*, which measures 3.21 km (2 miles) long and 17.67 m (58 ft) tall, and stretches along the Arkansas River levee (a raised embankment) in Pueblo, Colorado, USA.

★ PERMANENT COIN MURAL

Staff at the PennySaver store in Rancho Cordova, California, USA, created a permanent coin mural consisting of 100,000 pennies. It measures 17.8 m² (191.75 ft²) and was completed in March 2004.

★ PAINTING BY NUMBERS

Great Ormond Street Hospital children's charity completed a 400-m² (4,305-ft²) 'painting by numbers' artwork at the Lindt Easter Bunny Event, Hyde Park, London, UK, on 5 April 2004, in support of the hospital.

★ CHALK PAVEMENT ART

A chalk pavement art 3,298.95 m² (35,509 ft²) in size was created by members of the Oosterhof-Niej Begin Scout Group, in Rijssen, the Netherlands, on 12 June 2004.

LARGEST SAND PAINTING

A sand painting measuring 12.24 m (40 ft 2 in) by 12.24 m (40 ft 2 in) was created by the monks of the Golden Pagoda Buddhist Temple in the Singapore Expo Hall from 15–22 May 2004.

★ JELLY MOSAIC

A vast jelly mosaic measuring 12.8 x 19.8 m (42 x 65 ft) was created by a group of students from the Imperial College Singapore Society, London, UK, on 21 February 2004. The 16,125-piece jelly mosaic depicts the flag of Singapore.

★ BUBBLE-GUM MOSAIC

A mosaic of around 100,000 wrapped bubble gums was completed by TBWA Digerati and ID Productions in association with SABC 1 and Cadbury's Chappies (all South Africa) in Johannesburg, South Africa, on 17 August 2004. The mosaic, which took five days to create, was a portrait of former South African president Nelson Mandela and measured 19.4 m² (209 ft²).

★ CAR MOSAIC

A collection of 192 Mini cars was formed into a mosaic depicting the Mini logo in Villafranca di Verona, Italy, on 17 April 2004, covering an area of 4,950 m² (53,280 ft²).

★ LARGEST CARTOON STRIP

A colossal cartoon strip created by Norm Suchar (USA) and the Gentry High School art department, Indianola, Mississippi, USA, was displayed on 7 June 2003. It measured 41.15 x 14.56 m (135 x 47 ft 9.5 in) and depicted the syndicated comic strip *Lucky Cow*, by Mark Pett (USA).

★ MOST EXPENSIVE ELEPHANT PAINTING

The most expensive painting by a group of elephants is *Cold Wind, Swirling Mist, Charming Lanna I*, which sold for 1.5 million baht ($39,000 or £20,660) to Panit Warin (Sinanta) on 19 February 2005 at Maesa Elephant Camp, Chiang Mai, Thailand.

★ LARGEST CATALOGUE

A replica of the Bon Prix S2 fashion catalogue *Voila!* had 212 pages and measured 1.2 m x 1.5 m (3 ft 11 in x 4 ft 11 in) when unveiled in Hamburg, Germany, on 30 August 2003.

OLDEST AUTHORS

Sarah Louise Delany and A Elizabeth Delany (both USA)
Book: *The Delany Sisters' Book of Everyday Wisdom*
Published: 1994
Age at publication: Sarah Louise, 105; A Elizabeth, 103

Oldest male author:
Constantine Kallias (Greece)
Book: *A Glance of My Life*
Published: 2003
Age at publication: 101

YOUNGEST AUTHOR

Dorothy Straight (USA)
Book: *How the World Began*
Published: 1964
Age at publication: four

Youngest male author:
Dennis Vollmer (USA)
Book: *Joshua Disobeys*
Published: 1987
Age at publication: six

★ OLDEST KNOWN PAPER

A piece of paper thought to date from around AD 150 was found in Wuwei in China's Gansu province. It is made largely of cotton rags.

Paper as we understand it today (that is, a sheet formed on a screen from water suspension) was invented in China around 2,000 years ago. A court official called Ts'ai Lun is traditionally credited with its invention in around AD 100.

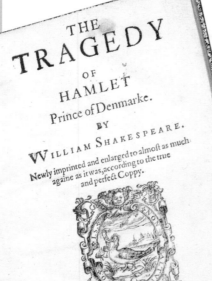

BOOKS

WEALTHIEST AUTHOR

According to the *Forbes World's Richest People 2005*, Harry Potter author J K Rowling (UK) has a total net worth of $1 billion (£548 million). Rowling's annual earnings estimates for June 2003 to June 2004 were $147 million (£79.9 million) — the **highest annual earnings by a children's author**. A total of 60 million Harry Potter books were sold in 2003, and so far 250 million books in the series have been sold worldwide.

★ SMALLEST PRINTED BOOK

An edition of *Chameleon* by the Russian author Anton Chekhov measuring 0.9 x 0.9 mm (0.035 x 0.035 in) was published by Anatoliy Konenko (Russia) in 1996.

Each book consists of 30 pages, has three colour illustrations and 11 lines of text to a page.

The book was printed in a limited edition of 100 copies, half in English, half in Russian. It is bound in gold, silver and leather, and sewn in silk. Each copy retails at $500 (£320).

MOST BLANK PAGES IN A PUBLISHED BOOK

On 9 September 1999, fine art university lecturer Anne Lydiat (UK) published the 52-page *lost for words...* All of its pages are blank and are meant to be 'a feminine place where there is silence,' according to the author.

BEST-SELLING COOKBOOK

Betty Crocker's Quick and Easy Cookbook has sold 50 million copies since 1950.

★ MOST FILMED AUTHOR

The plays and sonnets of William Shakespeare (England, 1564–1616) have been adapted into 420 feature film and TV-movie versions. *Hamlet* has appealed most to film-makers, with 79 versions, followed by *Romeo and Juliet*, with 52, and *Macbeth*, filmed 36 times. The most recent feature film adaptations of Shakespeare plays have been *Huapango* (Mexico, 2004), a modern-day version of *Othello,* and *The Merchant of Venice* (USA/Italy/Luxembourg/UK, 2004), starring Al Pacino (USA) as Shylock.

← ★ LARGEST LIBRARY

The Library of Congress in Washington DC, USA, contains over 128 million items, including approximately 29 million books, 2.7 million recordings, 12 million photographs, 4 million maps and 57 million manuscripts. These items are contained on around 853 km (530 miles) of shelves. The library was founded on 24 April 1800.

★ LARGEST LIBRARY BOOK FINE PAID

A fine of $345.14 (£203.29) was due on the poetry book *Days and Deeds*, checked out of Kewanee Public Library, Illinois, USA, in April 1955 by Emily Canellos-Simms (USA). Emily found it in her mother's house 47 years later and presented the library with a cheque for overdue fines.

MOST OVERDUE LIBRARY BOOK

In 1667–68, Colonel Robert Walpole (England) borrowed a book about the Archbishop of Bremen from Sidney Sussex College, Cambridge, UK. Prof. Sir John Plumb (UK) found the book 288 years later in the library of the then Marquess of Cholmondeley at Houghton Hall, Norfolk, UK. He returned it, but no fine was exacted.

MAGAZINES & NEWSPAPERS

★ LARGEST MAGAZINE

A scaled-up version of *Day & Night Jewellery and Watches Magazine* created by Naiem Jbara (UAE), consisting of 188 pages, measured 70 x 100 cm (27.5 x 39.3 in) on 14 October 2003 at Jewellery Arabia 2003, Manama, Bahrain. In total, 150 copies of the large magazine were printed.

★ MOST SYNDICATED COLUMNIST

Ann Landers's (USA) advice column appeared in over 1,200 newspapers, with an estimated readership of 90 million. She also wrote columns for Internet sites.

★ LONGEST SERVING NEWSPAPER COLUMNIST

Jack Ingram (UK), aka White Eagle, contributed weekly articles on 'Scouts and Scouting' to the *Heywood Advertiser* for 71 years, from 29 December 1933 until his final column on 5 February 2004.

MOST LETTERS PUBLISHED IN A NEWSPAPER

Subhash Chandra Agrawal (India) had 80 of his letters to the editor published in the *Kashmir Times* in 2003. This is also the ★ **most letters published in a single national newspaper in one year**.

Subhash has also had 319 letters published in the *Hindustan Times* since the early 1980s, the ★ **most letters to an editor of one newspaper in a lifetime**.

Madhu Agrawal (India) had 334 of her letters published during the year 2003 in 23 prominent Indian newspapers with circulations over 50,000, the ★ **most letters to editors published in one year in multiple newspapers**.

LIBRARIES

★ MOST SEVERE LIBRARY PENALTY

Beverly Goldman (USA) was jailed in January 2000 on seven counts of failing to return overdue library books. Goldman was arrested after her local library in Clearwater, Florida, USA, had tried for over 16 months to retrieve overdue materials valued at $127.86 (£78).

★ MOST → POSITIONS ON A BEST-SELLER LIST AT ONE TIME

The author Ian Rankin (UK) topped the Scottish best-seller list on 26 February 1999 with his book *Dead Souls* and had a further seven titles in the top 10. In the same year, on 12 March, he had a total of 11 books in the top 20.

LANGUAGE

★ LARGEST FICTIONAL LANGUAGE →

Although it is impossible to know the number of speakers, there is little doubt that the Klingon language, invented for the *Star Trek* series by linguist Mark Okrand (USA), is the most widely used language of its kind. Participants at *Star Trek* conventions frequently converse in the language, and in addition to a Klingon dictionary there are translations of *Hamlet*, *Much Ado About Nothing* and *Gilgamesh*. Amazon.com lists at least four other books written in Klingon or containing large tracts of the language, and the Google search engine is also available in Klingon. The greatest insult in this fictional language is 'Hab SoSll' Quch!' – meaning 'Your mother has a smooth forehead.'

Hab SoSll' Quch!

GORILLA MOST PROFICIENT AT SIGN LANGUAGE
In 1972, a gorilla named Koko was taught Ameslan (American Sign Language for the Deaf) by Dr Francine Patterson (USA). By 2000, Koko had a working vocabulary of over 1,000 signs and understood approximately 2,000 words of spoken English. She can refer to the past and future, argue, joke and lie. When Koko was asked by Dr Patterson whether she was an animal or a person, she replied, 'Fine animal gorilla'.

SHORTEST ALPHABET
Rotokas of central Bougainville Island, Papua New Guinea, has the fewest letters, with 11 (a, b, e, g, i, k, o, p, ř, t and u).

LONGEST ALPHABET
The language with the most letters is Khmer (Cambodian), with 74 (including some without any current use).

★ FASTEST REAL-TIME COURT REPORTER (STENOTYPE MACHINE)
Mark Kislingbury (USA) is the National Court Reporters Association speed and real-time champion. At the association's 2003 summer convention, he typed at a rate of 360 words per minute with 92% accuracy.

LANGUAGE WITH THE MOST CONSONANTS
The language with the largest number of distinct consonantal sounds was that of the Ubykhs in the Caucasus, with 81. Ubykh speakers migrated from the Caucasus to Turkey in the 19th century, and the last fully competent speaker, Tevfik Esenç, died in Istanbul, Turkey, in October 1992.

LONGEST SCIENTIFIC NAME
The tryptophan synthetase A protein, an enzyme consisting of 267 amino acids, has a name 1,913 letters in length.

HARD TO PRONOUNCE AND EVEN HARDER TO SPELL – THE WORLD'S LONGEST WORDS

Japanese – chinchinmogamaga (16) – meaning 'hop on one leg, hopscotch'.

Castilian (Spanish official language) – superextraordinarísimo (22) – meaning 'highly extraordinary'.

French – anticonstitutionnellement (25) – meaning 'anticonstitutionally'.

Italian – precipitevolissimevolmente (26) – meaning 'as fast as possible'.

Portuguese – inconstitucionalissimamente (27) – meaning 'with the highest degree of unconstitutionality'.

Icelandic – hæcstaréttarmalaflutningsmaður (30) – meaning 'supreme court barrister'.

Russian – ryentgyenoelyektrokardiografichyeskogo (33 Cyrillic letters) – transliterating as 38, meaning 'of the X-ray electrocardiographic'.

German – Rechtsschutzversicherungsgesellschaften (39) – meaning 'insurance companies that provide legal protection'.

Hungarian – megszentségtelenithetetlenségeskedéseitekért (44) – meaning 'for your unprofanable actions'.

English – pneumonoultramicroscopicsilicovolcano-coniosis (-koniosis) (45) – meaning 'a lung disease caused by the inhalation of very fine silica dust'.

Dutch – kindercarnavalsoptochtvoorbereidingswerkzaamheden (49) – meaning 'preparation activities for a children's carnival procession'.

Danish – speciallægepraksisplanlægningsstabiliseringsperiode (51) – meaning 'the stabilization period of the planning of medical specialists' practices'.

Finnish – lentokonesuihkuturbiinimoottoriapumekaanikkoaliupseerioppilas (61) – meaning 'apprentice corporal, working as assistant mechanic in charge of aeroplane turbine engines'.

Swedish – nordöstersjökustartilleriflygspaningssimulatoranläggningsmateriel-underhållsuppföljningssystemdiskussionsinläggsförberedelse-arbeten (130) – meaning 'preparatory work on the contribution to the discussion on the maintaining system of support of the material of the aviation survey device within the north-east part of the coast artillery of the Baltic'.

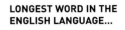

★ LANGUAGE WITH THE FEWEST SPEAKERS

According to the Ethnologue database of languages, over 400 of the world's languages are nearly extinct, meaning that 'only a small number of elderly speakers are still living'. It is thought that languages are disappearing at a rate of one every two weeks.

★ LANGUAGE THAT IS OFFICIAL IN THE GREATEST NUMBER OF COUNTRIES

English is an official language of 56 United Nations member states, more than a quarter of the total UN membership. However, it is not necessarily the most widely spoken language, or the only language, in these countries.

★ LARGEST SCRABBLE BOARD

A Scrabble board with a surface area of 30 m² (323 ft²) was created to celebrate the 50th birthday of the game and was

★ LANGUAGE WITH THE MOST CLICK SOUNDS

The !Xú language, spoken by the Khoisan tribes of southern Africa, has 48 distinct click sounds.

★ EARLIEST ALPHABET

The earliest known example of an alphabet – that is, a writing system in which symbols are used to represent sounds rather than concepts – dates back to around 1800 BC. It was found carved into limestone in Wadi el Hol near Luxor, Egypt, by Yale University archaeologists John and Deborah Darnell in the early 1990s. (Note that this is not the earliest known 'writing'.)

played on 13 October 1998 in Wembley Stadium, London, UK, by teams comprising UK Scrabble champions helping the Army v. the Navy. The letter tiles, made from reinforced fibreglass, measured 1.5 m² (16 ft²) and had to be manoeuvred by two people at a time.

MOST COMMON LANGUAGE

Chinese is spoken by more than 1.1 billion people. The 'common speech' (Pûtônghuà) is the standard form, with pronunciation based on that of Beijing.

MOST AND FEWEST VOWELS

Sedang, a central Vietnamese language, has 55 distinguishable vowel sounds. By contrast, the Caucasian language Abkhazian has only two vowels.

LONGEST PLACE NAME

In its most scholarly transliteration, Krungthep Mahanakhon, the 167-letter official name for Bangkok, the capital of Thailand, has 175 letters. The official short version (without capital letters, which are not used in Thai) is krungthephphramahanakhon bowonratanakosin mahintharayuthaya mahadilokphiphobnovpharad radchataniburirom udomsantisug (six words, 111 letters).

★ MOST COMMON LANGUAGE SOUND

No known language in the world lacks the vowel 'a' (as in the English word 'father').

RAREST SPEECH SOUNDS

The rarest speech sound is 'ř' in Czech and described as a rolled post-alveolar fricative. It occurs in very few languages and is the last sound mastered by Czech children.

MOST SUCCINCT WORD

The most challenging word for any lexicographer to define briefly is the Fuegian (southernmost Argentina and Chile) word mamihlapinatapai, meaning 'looking at each other hoping that either will offer to do something which both parties desire but are unwilling to do'.

LONGEST WORD IN THE ENGLISH LANGUAGE...

...WITH LETTERS ARRANGED IN REVERSE ALPHABETICAL ORDER
Spoonfeed (9 letters).

...CONSISTING ONLY OF VOWELS
Euouae (6). It is formed from the vowels of 'seculorum amen', which is a religious chant.

...CONSISTING STRICTLY OF ALTERNATING CONSONANTS AND VOWELS
Honorificabilitudinitatibus (27). It means 'with honourableness' (a nonsense word from medieval literature).

...WITH LETTERS ARRANGED IN ALPHABETICAL ORDER
Aegilops (8), a plant family.

...WITH ONLY ONE VOWEL
Strengths (9).

...WITHOUT ANY OF THE FIVE MAIN VOWELS
Twyndyllyngs (12), an archaic spelling of the word 'twin'.

SHORTEST WORD IN THE ENGLISH LANGUAGE THAT CONTAINS ALL FIVE MAIN VOWELS
Eunoia (6). A little-used medical term that means 'a normal state of mental health'.

TOP 10 MOST SPOKEN LANGUAGES IN THE WORLD

1.	Mandarin Chinese – 915 million speakers
2.	English – 354 million
3.	Spanish – 325 million
4.	Hindi – 300 million
5.	Arabic – 272 million
6.	Bengali – 194 million
7.	Portuguese – 170 million
8.	Russian – 164 million
9.	Japanese – 125 million
10.	German – 108 million

MOVIE-GOING

LARGEST PERMANENT
← ## CINEMA SCREEN

The Panasonic IMAX Theatre at Darling Harbour, Sydney, Australia, holds the largest fixed projection screen in the world, measuring 35.72 x 29.57 m (117 x 97 ft) – twice the width of a basketball pitch. It can seat 540 people.

→ **WHO EARNED $928,000 (£500,000) PER MINUTE FOR STARRING IN A COMMERCIAL? FIND OUT ON P.154**

CINEMA ATTENDANCE

HIGHEST ANNUAL CINEMA ATTENDANCE

The largest cinema audience in one given year was 4,490 million admissions in the USA in 1929.

★ HIGHEST CINEMA ATTENDANCE TODAY

Cinema admissions reached 2,800 million in India in 2001, based on the most recent figures.

★ HIGHEST ANNUAL CINEMA ATTENDANCE PER CAPITA

In 2004, Iceland registered a greater cinema attendance per capita than any other country,

with an average of 5.45 visits per person at 46 cinemas. This is based on a figure for the Icelandic population of 280,798.

LARGEST...

CINEMA COMPLEX BY SEATS

Kinepolis Madrid, which opened in Spain on 17 September 1998, is the world's largest cinema complex. It has a seating capacity of 9,200 from its 25 screens that can, individually, seat between 211 and 996 people.

DRIVE-IN BY NUMBER OF SCREENS

The Thunderbird Drive-In (also known as the Swap Shop Drive-In), Fort Lauderdale, Florida, USA, which opened with a single screen on 22 November 1963, now has 13 screens of varying sizes.

★ ANNUAL FILM OUTPUT

India produces more feature-length films than any other country. A record 1,200 films were produced in 2002 and, in 1994, a total of 754 films were produced in a record 16 languages.

FIRST...

★ CINEMA IN OPERATION

The Cinématographe Lumière at the Salon Indien, Paris, France, opened under the management of Clément Maurice (France) on 28 December 1895. The opening performance, to an audience of 35 who had paid one franc each, included *L'Arrivée d'un Train en Gare* (France, 1895) by the Lumière brothers.

DRIVE-IN CINEMA

The first patent for a drive-in was issued on 16 May 1933 to Richard Hollingshead (USA), who opened the first one on 6 June 1933 on a site for 400 cars in Camden, New Jersey, USA, to show *Wife Beware* (USA, 1933).

CIRCULAR CINEMA

The first circular cinema is located in the European Park of the Moving Image at Futuroscope, near Poitiers, France. It consists of nine projectors and nine screens covering a total surface area of 272 m² (2,928 ft²). The process enables the projection of nine electronically synchronized films, offering a 360° field of vision.

RECORD-BEATING DRIVE-INS

At 65.8 m (216 ft) wide and 445.9 m² (4,800 ft²) in area, the **largest drive-in cinema screen ever** was the Algiers Drive-In, Detroit, Michigan, USA, which opened on 15 August 1956 and closed in 1985.

With 1,200 seats, the All-Weather Drive-In, Copiague, New York, USA, is the **largest drive-in cinema (patron capacity)**. The Troy Drive-In, Detroit, Michigan, USA, and the Panther Drive-In, Lufkin, Texas, USA, have space for 3,000 cars, making them joint record holders for the **largest drive-in cinema (car capacity)**.

OLDEST PURPOSE-BUILT CINEMA IN OPERATION

The Electric in London, UK, first opened on 24 February 1911. Designed by Gilbert Seymour Valentin in 1910, the cinema had seating for 600 people. The Grade II listed building was closed in the 1980s but re-opened on 22 February 2001 with a seating capacity of 240.

LARGEST CINEMA TODAY

The Radio City Music Hall, New York City, USA (pictured left), opened on 27 December 1932 with 5,945 (now 5,910) seats.

The **largest cinema by seat capacity** is the Roxy in New York City, USA. It was built at a cost of $12 million (then £2.4 million) and had a seating capacity of 6,214 when it opened on 11 March 1927. The cinema employed 16 projectionists, an orchestra of 110 musicians led by four conductors and three organists who rose from the orchestra pit playing simultaneously on Kimball organ consoles. It closed on 29 March 1960 and was demolished later that year.

The **smallest cinema by seat capacity** to operate as a regular commercial venture has 21 seats. The Screen Room on Broad Street, Nottingham, UK, owned by Steven Metcalf (UK), opened on 27 September 2002 with the film *Lost in La Mancha* (Canada, 2002).

LONGEST...

CINEMATIC RELEASE
Titanic (USA, 1997) stayed in the charts from 19 December 1997 to 25 September 1998 in the US market, a total duration of 281 days.

COMMERCIALLY MADE FILM ON GENERAL CINEMA RELEASE
The Burning of the Red Lotus Temple (China, 1928–31) – adapted by the Star Film Co. from a newspaper serial 'Strange Tales of the Adventurer in the Wild Country' by Shang K'ai-jan (China) – was released in 18 feature-length parts over a period of three years. Although never shown publicly in its 27-hour entirety, some cinemas put on all-day performances of half a dozen parts in sequence.

NON-STOP CINEMA SHOW
A 50-hour 'B Movie Marathon' took place at The Variety Arts Center in Hollywood, USA, from 29 to 31 May 1983. A $15 ticket (then £9.53) enabled patrons to see 37 low-budget classics.

MISCELLANEOUS

★ COUNTRY WITH THE LEAST CINEMAS PER POPULATION
Suriname, with a population of 436,494, has only one cinema, found in the capital Paramaribo. In 1997, this cinema saw a total of 103,626 admissions.

★ COUNTRY WITH THE MOST CINEMA SCREENS
According to the most recent statistics, China has 65,500 cinema screens. By way of comparison, the USA has 35,280, India 11,962 and the UK 3,402.

★ MOST EXPENSIVE AVERAGE ADMISSION PRICE TO A CINEMA
The most expensive admission prices in the world are in Japan, where the average price of a cinema ticket is $10.80 (£5.97).

The ★ **lowest admission prices** are in India, with the average price of a cinema ticket at $0.20 (£0.11).

SMALLEST PURPOSE-BUILT CINEMA IN OPERATION

Cinema dei Piccoli was built by Alfredo Annibali (Italy) in 1934 in the park of Villa Borghese, Rome, Italy, and today covers an area of 71.52 m² (769.83 ft²). Originally called the Topolino Cinema, it used a Pathé-Baby 9.5-mm movie projector, had bed-sheets for a screen and played 78s for background music. Restored in 1991, the cinema has 63 seats, a 5 x 2.5-m (16.4 x 8.2-ft) screen, stereo sound and air-conditioning.

★ WIDEST FILM RELEASE ON AN OPENING DAY IN ONE COUNTRY

← *Harry Potter and the Prisoner of Azkaban* (USA, 2004) was given the widest release of any film in history when it opened in the USA on 4 June 2004 at 3,855 cinemas.

★ HIGHEST GROSSING DOCUMENTARY ON AN OPENING WEEKEND

Fahrenheit 9/11 (USA, 2004) took $21.8 million (£11.9 million) in its opening weekend (25–27 June 2004) and is the first documentary to top the US box-office chart in its opening weekend.

★ HIGHEST GROSSING ANIMATION ON AN OPENING DAY

The Incredibles (USA, 2004) took $20.5 million (£11.1 million) on its opening day at 3,933 locations across the USA on 5 November 2004, beating the previous record of $11.8 million (£6.6 million) set by *Shrek 2* (USA, 2004) on 19 May 2004.

HIGHEST GROSSING FILM IN A SINGLE DAY

Spider-Man (USA, 2002) took $43.6 million (£29.8 million) on its second day of opening in the USA on 4 May 2002 from a total of 3,615 screens.

→ WHICH A-LIST HOLLYWOOD SUPERSTAR HOLDS THE RECORD FOR THE HIGHEST OVERALL BOX-OFFICE MOVIE GROSS? FIND OUT ON P.148

RECORD TAKINGS

HIGHEST GROSSING FILM

Titanic (USA, 1997) became the first film to take $1 billion (then £628,535,512) at the international box office, with a total gross of $1.834 billion (£1.297 billion). It also made a record 10-week gross of $918.6 million (£574.1 million) worldwide.

★ HIGHEST GROSSING FILM (INFLATION ADJUSTED)

Rising cinema ticket prices mean that the all-time top-grossing movies are nearly all recent films. However, *Gone with the Wind* (USA, 1939) – which took just $393.4 million (then £88 million) at the international box office – comes top in an inflation-adjusted list with a total gross of $5,362 million (£2,916 million). In the USA alone, *Gone with the Wind* had 283,100,000 admissions compared with 130,900,000 for *Titanic* (USA, 1997).

HIGHEST GROSSING FILM ON AN OPENING DAY

On its opening day, 15 May 2003, *The Matrix Reloaded* (USA, 2003) took a record $42.5 million (£26.2 million) from a total of 3,603 cinemas.

THE DECADES' BOX-OFFICE LEADERS

DECADE	FILM TITLE	BOX OFFICE		RANKING
1910s	*Mickey* (USA, 1918)	*$18,000,000	(£3,777,545)	10th
1920s	*The Big Parade* (USA, 1925)	*$22,000,000	(£4,555,809)	9th
1930s	*Gone with the Wind* (USA, 1939)	$393,400,000	(£88,206,278)	5th
1940s	*Bambi* (USA, 1942)	$268,000,000	(£66,501,241)	6th
1950s	*Lady and the Tramp* (USA, 1955)	*$93,600,000	(£33,428,571)	8th
1960s	*101 Dalmatians* (USA, 1961)	$215,880,014	(£77,036,725)	7th
1970s	*Star Wars* (USA, 1977)	$797,998,007	(£457,174,453)	3rd
1980s	*E.T. the Extra-Terrestrial* (USA, 1982)	$704,804,539	(£402,595,915)	4th
1990s	*Titanic* (USA, 1997)	$1,834,165,466	(£1,249,388,962)	1st
2000s	*The Lord of the Rings: The Return of the King* (USA/NZ, 2003)	$1,129,219,252	(£612,806,888)	2nd

* US domestic total available only

★ HIGHEST GROSSING ANIMATION ON AN OPENING WEEKEND

Shrek 2 (USA, 2004) took an estimated $104.3 million (£58.3 million) over its opening weekend of 22 May 2004, beating the original *Shrek* (USA, 2001), which took $42.3 million (£29.3 million) over the 19 May 2001 weekend. The film opened at 3,737 screens on Wednesday 19 May 2004 and expanded to 4,163 by the weekend (defined as Friday to Sunday, 21–23 May).

★ NEW RECORD   ★ UPDATED RECORD

FILM RELEASE

★ LARGEST SIMULTANEOUS FILM PREMIERE
Matrix Revolutions (USA, 2003) was simultaneously released on 10,013 prints in a record 94 countries by Warner Bros. on 5 November 2003.

★ WIDEST DOCUMENTARY RELEASE ON AN OPENING DAY
Michael Moore's *Fahrenheit 9/11* (USA, 2004) opened at 868 cinemas on 25 June 2004, taking $23,920,637 (£13,105,762) on its first weekend. By comparison, his previous film, *Bowling for Columbine* (USA, 2002), opened at eight cinemas to take an initial weekend gross of $209,148 (£133,983).

★ WIDEST FILM PRINT RUN
Warner Bros. gave *The Matrix Reloaded* (USA, 2003) a print run of 8,517, the largest in history, when the film opened on 15 May 2003 at 3,603 cinemas in the USA.

★ WIDEST ANIMATION RELEASE ON AN OPENING DAY
Shark Tale (USA, 2004) was given the widest film release of any animated movie in history when it opened in the USA on 1 October 2004 at 4,016 cinemas. This beat the previous record – set by *Shrek 2* (USA, 2004) on 19 May 2004 – by 279 cinemas.

★ WIDEST FILM RELEASE IN ONE COUNTRY
Shrek 2 (USA, 2004) was given the widest release of any film in history when, on 21 May 2004 (three days after its opening release), the number of engagements expanded from 3,737 to 4,163 cinemas in the USA.

FASTEST GROSSES

FASTEST $100-MILLION-GROSSING FILM
Two films have surpassed the $100-million mark in three days. The first was *Spider-Man* (USA, 2002; then £68.3 million), which opened on 3 May 2002 at 3,615 cinemas, followed by *The Matrix Reloaded* (USA, 2003; then £62.3 million), which opened on 5 May 2003 at 3,603 cinemas.

FASTEST $100-MILLION-GROSSING ANIMATION
Finding Nemo (USA, 2003), the computer-animated film from Walt Disney and Pixar Animation Studios, reached the $100-million mark (then £60,204,696) at the US box office in just eight days from its release on 30 May 2003 at 3,374 cinemas.

FASTEST $200-MILLION BOX-OFFICE FILM GROSS
From its 3 May 2002 opening, *Spider-Man* (USA, 2002) passed the $200-million mark (then £136.7 million) in 10 days, taking $223.04 million (£152.412 million) by 12 May.

MOST SUCCESSFUL MOVIES

★ RELIGIOUS
The Passion of the Christ (USA, 2004) $604,300,000 (£327,800,000)

★ ANIMATION
Finding Nemo (USA, 2003) $844,400,000 (£455,000,000)

★ MUSICAL
Grease (USA, 1978) $387,713,510 (£230,247,348)

★ DRAMA
Titanic (USA, 1997) $1,834,165,466 (£1,297,000,000)

★ ACTION
Jurassic Park (USA, 1993) $920,067,947 (£577,932,124)

HORROR
The Exorcist (USA, 1973) $292,700,000 (£179,400,000)

★ CRIME/GANGSTER
Ocean's Eleven (USA, 2001) $446,180,493 (£279,439,151)

★ WAR
Saving Private Ryan (USA, 1998) $481,597,636 (£259,663,361)

★ TV ADAPTATION
Mission Impossible II (USA, 2000) $545,400,000 (£384,000,000)

★ THRILLER
The Sixth Sense (USA, 1999) $657,600,000 (£463,900,000)

★ SCIENCE FICTION
Star Wars: Episode I – The Phantom Menace (USA, 1999) $923,136,824 (£583,602,643)

← ★ **PUBLIC APPEARANCES –**
MOST IN 12 HOURS BY A MOVIE STAR

The greatest number of public appearances by a film star at different cities in 12 hours promoting the same film is three by Will Smith (USA). As set out in the rules, he walked the red carpet, signed autographs and introduced the film *Hitch* (USA, 2005) at cinemas in Manchester (bottom), Birmingham (middle) and London (top), UK, on 22 February 2005.

The ★ **highest annual earnings by a film actress** is an estimated $33 million (£17.9 million) earned by Cameron Diaz (USA) in 2003.

★ BOX-OFFICE FILM GROSS FOR AN ACTOR

By February 2005, Harrison Ford (USA) had starred in 27 films with a total box-office gross of $3,369,662,963 (£1,756,496,540), 10 of which took over $200 million (£105.3 million).

The ★ **highest box-office film gross for an actress** is held by Julia Roberts (USA), who has starred in 33 films since 1987 with a total box-office gross of $2,939 million (£1,530 million).

MOST...

★ BEST DIRECTOR OSCAR NOMINATIONS FOR AN ACTOR IN THE SAME FILM

Woody Allen (USA) has been nominated for the category of Best Director on five occasions for films in which he also had a leading role: *Annie Hall* (USA, 1977), *Interiors* (USA, 1978), *Broadway Danny Rose* (USA, 1984), *Hannah and her Sisters* (USA, 1986) and *Crimes and Misdemeanours* (USA, 1989). His sixth Best Director nomination was for *Bullets over Broadway* (USA, 1993), in which he did not have an acting role.

STARS ON THE HOLLYWOOD WALK OF FAME

Gene Autry (USA) – aka the 'Singing Cowboy' – has five stars on the Hollywood Walk of Fame strip, for recording, motion pictures, television, radio and theatre.

★ GOLDEN GLOBE NOMINATIONS FOR AN ACTOR

Jack Lemmon (USA) was nominated for a Golden Globe a total of 22 times between 1960 and 2000. In addition, he was also awarded the Cecil B DeMille Award in 1991 and a Special Award for Best Ensemble Cast – along with the entire cast of *Short Cuts* (USA, 1993) – in 1994.

HIGHEST...

★ ANNUAL EARNINGS BY A FILM ACTOR

Mel Gibson (USA) earned an estimated $210 million (£114 million) in 2003, according to the 2004 *Forbes Celebrity 100* list.

★ BEST DIRECTOR –
MOST OSCAR WINS FOR AN ACTOR

Clint Eastwood (USA) has won the Oscar for Best Director twice for films in which he also starred. The first was on 29 March 1993 for *Unforgiven* (USA, 1992), followed by *Million Dollar Baby* (USA, 2004) on 27 February 2005. In all, he has been nominated in this category three times; the second occasion was in 2004 for *Mystic River* (USA, 2003), a film he did not appear in.

→

OLDEST OSCAR NOMINEES & WINNERS

NAME	AGE	FILM	OSCAR	NOMINEE/WINNER
★ Gloria Stuart (USA)	87 years 221 days	*Titanic* (USA, 1997)	Best Supporting Actress	Nominated 10 February 1998
Ralph Richardson (UK)	82 years 49 days	*Greystoke: The Legend of Tarzan* (UK, 1984)	Best Supporting Actor	Posthumously nominated 6/02/1985
Jessica Tandy (UK)	80 years 295 days	*Driving Miss Daisy* (USA, 1989)	Best Actress	Won 29 March 1990
George Burns (USA)	80 years 68 days	*The Sunshine Boys* (USA, 1975)	Best Supporting Actor	Won 29 March 1976
Richard Farnsworth (USA)	79 years 167 days	*The Straight Story* (USA, 1999)	Best Actor	Nominated 15 February 2000
★ Peggy Ashcroft (UK)	77 years 93 days	*Passage to India* (UK/USA, 1984)	Best Supporting Actress	Won 25 March 1985
Henry Fonda (USA)	76 years 317 days	*On Golden Pond* (USA, 1981)	Best Actor	Won 29 March 1982

YOUNGEST OSCAR NOMINEES & WINNERS

NAME	AGE	FILM	OSCAR	NOMINEE/WINNER
★ Jackie Cooper (USA)	9 years 20 days	*Skippy* (USA, 1931)	Best Actor	Nominated 5 October 1931
Tatum O'Neal (USA)	10 years 148 days	*Paper Moon* (USA, 1973)	Best Supporting Actress	Won 2 April 1974
Keisha Castle-Hughes (NZ)	13 years 309 days	*Whale Rider* (NZ/Germany, 2002)	Best Actress	Nominated 27 January 2004
★ Timothy Hutton (USA)	20 years 227 days	*Ordinary People* (USA, 1980)	Best Supporting Actor	Won 31 March 1981
Marlee Matlin (USA)	21 years 218 days	*Children of a Lesser God* (USA, 1986)	Best Actress	Won 30 March 1987
Adrien Brody (USA)	29 years 343 days	*The Pianist* (France/Germany/UK/Poland, 2002)	Best Actor	Won 23 March 2003

★ GOLDEN GLOBE NOMINATIONS FOR AN ACTRESS

Meryl Streep (USA) has been nominated for a Golden Globe a total of 19 times from 1979 to 2004, winning on five occasions (1980, 1982, 1983, 2003 and 2004).

OLDEST...

★ GOLDEN GLOBE WINNER – ACTOR

Henry Fonda (USA, 1905–82) was aged 76 years 259 days when he was awarded the Golden Globe for Best Actor for playing Norman Thayer Jr in *On Golden Pond* (USA, 1981) on 30 January 1982.

★ GOLDEN GLOBE WINNER – ACTRESS

Jessica Tandy (UK, 1909–94) was aged 80 years 227 days when she won the Golden Globe for Best Actress for her portrayal of Daisy Werthan in *Driving Miss Daisy* (USA, 1989) on 20 January 1990.

MISCELLANEOUS

★ TALLEST ACTOR IN A LEADING ROLE

Two actors hold this title, standing at 1.94 m (6 ft 5 in): Christopher Lee (UK), who has played most of the major horror characters in films since 1958; and Vince Vaughn (USA), who has been in films since the 1990s.

The **tallest actress in a leading role** is a record shared by Margaux Hemingway, Sigourney Weaver, Geena Davis (all USA) and Brigitte Nielson (Denmark), who all stand at 1.82 m (6 ft) tall.

★ FIRST CO-STARS TO WIN TOP ACTING OSCARS

At the 1934 Academy Awards held at the Biltmore Hotel, Hollywood, California, USA, on 27 February 1935, the Best Actress and Best Actor Oscars went to co-stars Clark Gable and Claudette Colbert (both USA) for their performances in *It Happened One Night* (USA, 1934). The most recent ceremony at which this has happened was on 23 March 1998 when both Jack Nicholson and Helen Hunt (both USA) won an Oscar for *As Good as it Gets* (USA, 1997).

★ ONLY NON-PROFESSIONALS TO HAVE WON ACTING OSCARS

World War II veteran Harold Russell (Canada), who played the handless ex-soldier (he had both his arms blown off in combat) in *The Best Years of Our Lives* (USA, 1946), and Cambodian refugee Dr Haing S Ngor, who played a victim of Cambodia's Pol Pot regime in *The Killing Fields* (UK, 1984), both received Best Supporting Actor Oscars for their performance.

YOUNGEST BEST ACTOR OSCAR

Adrien Brody (USA, b. 14 April 1974) won the Best Actor Oscar on 23 March 2003 for his performance as Wladyslaw Szpilman in *The Pianist* (France/Germany/UK/Poland, 2002) aged 29 years 343 days.

STUNTS & SFX

★ LONGEST →
PERFORMANCE CAPTURE FILM

The Polar Express (USA, 2004) – the first film to be created entirely via the performance capture technique, whereby the physical movements of actors are digitally recorded and translated into a computer animation – was released on 10 November 2004 with a running time of 1 hr 33 min. The film, based on Chris Van Allsburg's (USA) children's book, has Tom Hanks (USA) playing five of the characters and was made at a cost of $165 million (£89 million).

STUNTS

★ FIRST FILM STUNTMAN
The first stuntman was ex-US cavalryman Frank Hanaway (USA), who secured himself a part in Edwin S Porter's (Italy/USA) *The Great Train Robbery* (USA, 1903) thanks to his ability to fall off a horse without injuring himself.

MOST PROLIFIC MOVIE STUNTMAN
In a career spanning five decades, Vic Armstrong (UK) has been a stuntman, stunt co-ordinator and director in more than 250 films, and has doubled for every actor to have played the title role in the James Bond series.

LONGEST LEAP IN A CAR PROPELLED BY ITS OWN ENGINE
In a stunt for *Smokey and the Bandit II* (USA, 1980), Gary Davis (USA) raced a stripped-down Plymouth up a ramp, which was butted up against the back of a double-tiered car-carrier, at 128 km/h (80 mph) and cleared 49.6 m (163 ft) before landing again safely.

★ GREATEST HEIGHT RANGE PLAYED BY A STUNTMAN
Stuntman Riky Ash (UK) stands 1.59 m (5 ft 3 in) tall and has doubled for characters with a height differential of 86 cm (34 in).

LARGEST FILM EXPLOSION
An explosion staged for *Blown Away* (USA, 1994) used a scuttled ship beside an old wharf in East Boston, USA, filled with 2,727 litres (600 gal; 720 US gal) of fuel and 32 bombs, each 453 g (16 oz) in weight. The resultant explosion lasted nine seconds.

HIGHEST FREEFALL ON FILM
Dar Robinson (USA) performed a freefall leap of 335 m (1,100 ft) from a ledge at the summit of the CN Tower, Toronto, Canada, in a stunt for *Highpoint* (Canada, 1979). After six seconds of freefalling, his parachute opened just 91 m (300 ft) from the ground.

← SHORTEST STUNTMAN

Kiran Shah (UK) is the shortest professional stuntman working in films, standing 126.3 cm (4 ft 1.7 in) when measured on 20 October 2003. He has appeared in 52 movies since 1976 and has performed stunts in 31 of them, including being perspective stunt-double for Christopher Reeve (USA) in *Superman* (UK, 1978) and *Superman II* (UK, 1980) and more recently for Elijah Wood (USA) in *The Lord of the Rings* trilogy (NZ/USA, 2001–03).

SPECIAL EFFECTS

★ MOST DIGITAL ARTISTS ON A FILM

A team of 320 visual effect artists worked on *Sky Captain and the World of Tomorrow* (USA/UK/Italy, 2004), the first Hollywood feature film shot entirely against a blue screen with digital effects filled in. Directed by Kerry Conran (UK) and starring Jude Law (UK) and Gwyneth Paltrow (USA), the 106-minute movie completed principal photography on the blue set in 26 days. In all, over 2,000 digital shots were produced for the film over a period of eight months.

LARGEST FILM BUDGET FOR SPECIAL EFFECTS

A total of $6.5 million (then £2,246,023) was budgeted for *2001: A Space Odyssey* (USA, 1968), representing over 60% of the total production cost of $10.5 million (then £3,628,191). The modern equivalent of this in the year 2005 is approximately $49.1 million (£25.6 million).

LONGEST STOP-MOTION FEATURE FILM

Chicken Run (UK, 2000), directed by Peter Lord and Nick Park (both UK), was released with a running time of 82 minutes and has 118,080 shots created using the stop-motion special effects technique. A normal live-action feature incorporates between 500 and 1,000 shots.

★ MOST OSCAR NOMINATIONS FOR VISUAL EFFECTS

Dennis Muren (USA) has been nominated for the Academy Award for Visual Effects a record 12 times, starting with *Dragonslayer* (USA, 1981) in 1983 and the most recent in 2004 for *Hulk* (USA, 2003).

In addition to winning the **most Oscars for visual effects**, with a total of six, he has also received two Special Achievement Awards, in 1981 for *Star Wars: Episode V – the Empire Strikes Back* (USA, 1980) and in 1984 for *Star Wars: Episode VI – Return of the Jedi* (USA, 1983), as well as the Technical Achievement Award in 1982.

LARGEST CAMERA CRANE USED ON FILM

In order to cover all angles of the 236-m-long (775-ft) set of the movie *Titanic* (USA, 1997), an Akela crane with a normal reach of 24 m (80 ft) was adapted to have an expanded reach of almost 61 m (200 ft). A gyro-stabilized camera was then mounted on the crane basket and the crane was able to move on tracks along the side of the ship in a water tank.

Titanic also had the **largest stunt budget** – more than $3 million (£1.87 million) of the $200-million (£125-million) budget went towards the stunts.

MOST STILL CAMERAS USED IN A SEQUENCE

When shooting a 'bullet time' sequence in *The Matrix* (USA, 1999), 120 specially modified film cameras were used by directors Larry and Andy Wachowski (both USA) to achieve a panning shot of protagonist Neo (played by Keanu Reeves) as he dodged bullets from a pursuer. The effect is now more commonly called 'time-slicing'.

← ★ MOST BONES BROKEN IN A LIFETIME

Evel Knievel (USA, b. Robert Craig Knievel), the pioneer of motorcycle long-jumping exhibitions, had suffered 433 bone fractures by the end of 1975. In the winter of 1976 he was seriously injured during a televised attempt to jump a tank full of sharks at the Chicago Amphitheater. Knievel, who suffered a brain concussion and two broken arms, decided to retire from major performances as a result.

LONGEST SPEEDBOAT JUMP IN A MOVIE

A stunt sequence by Jerry Comeaux (USA) in *Live and Let Die* (UK, 1973) – in which James Bond is chased down Louisiana's bayou in a 1972 Glastron GT-150 speedboat and leaps over a road – set a world record distance of 36.5 m (120 ft).

TV STARS

★ MOST HOURS ON CAMERA

Presenter Regis Philbin (USA) has logged 15,188 hours on camera. This is an average of almost an hour a day for every year of his 46-year career up to 20 August 2004.

★ YOUNGEST ACTOR TO BE NOMINATED FOR AN EMMY (LEAD CATEGORY)

At 15, Frankie Muniz (USA) was nominated for an Emmy award in the Outstanding Actor in a Comedy Series category for his role of Malcolm in *Malcolm in the Middle* (FOX, USA) in 2001.

FIRST PERSON TO APPEAR ON A BRITISH TV ADVERT

On 22 September 1955 – the opening night of the UK's Independent Television – Meg Smith (UK) beat 80 other actresses to become the UK's first 'plug' girl – starring in a 60-second Gibbs toothpaste advert.

MOST ENDURING TV COMMERCIAL STARS

The PG Tips tea campaign starring chimpanzees began in December 1956. It eventually ran to more than 100 adverts, with the final instalment made in 1994. The chimpanzees, who are said to have earned more than £1,000 ($1,530) each per commercial, have a retirement fund set up by the company.

★ LONGEST BROADCAST CAREER OF A TV PET

George the tortoise, who first appeared on the children's television programme *Blue Peter* (BBC, UK) in May 1982, made his final appearance 22 years later on 14 April 2004.

LONGEST TIME IN THE SAME ROLE IN A TV SERIES

Helen Wagner (USA) has played the character of Nancy Hughes McClosky in *As the World Turns* (CBS, USA) since it premiered on 2 April 1956.

DAVID HASSELHOFF

David Hasselhoff (USA) was the leading man in *Baywatch* – the most widely seen TV show, with a weekly audience of around 1.1 billion in 1996.

How does it feel to be in the book?
It's really cool because it was presented to me by my children, who said, 'Here Dad, you're on page 193.' It meant more to me that it was brought to me by my children. They were really proud.

Why do you think *Baywatch* was so popular?
Someone once said to me, 'The whole world looks to America as the big lifeguard of the world'. I kind of agree. *Baywatch* just came at the right time... The world was looking to America as a symbol of saving lives, and we were communicating that message around the world by television.

What are you most proud of?
The thing that I'm most proud of is that I saved the name 'Hasselhoff' because I took a lot of trouble for that name in High School! I look at my father now and I say, 'The name you gave me – a billion people know that name.' We walk down the street in South Africa or China or Vietnam and people walk by and say 'David Hasselhoff' and I just grin.

If our readers wanted to be like you, what do they have to do?
Whatever you feel you have a talent at, whatever you feel your dream is, go after it with a vision. Focus on what you want and stay focussed. And then go for it.

FIRST VIRTUAL TV PRESENTER

'Maddy' co-presented *Tomorrow's World* (BBC, UK) on 27 March 2002 in real-time alongside the show's human presenters. Maddy was created by Digital Animations Group, Glasgow, UK.

HIGHEST FINE IMPOSED ON A TV BROADCASTER

The Federal Communications Commission (USA) fined the CBS Television network $550,000 (£306,814) for the transmission of the American Super Bowl half-time performance broadcast on 1 February 2004, when singer Janet Jackson (USA) exposed her right breast during a performance.

LONGEST SCREEN KISS IN A TV DRAMA

A kiss lasting for 3 min 15 sec was broadcast on *Hollyoaks* (Channel 4, UK) on 2 July 2002. It was incorporated into the storyline when the characters Ellie Hunter and Ben Davies, played by Sarah Baxendale and Marcus Patric (both UK), won a kissing competition.

LONGEST TV TALK SHOW MARATHON

Both Zoltán Kováry (Hungary) and Vador Lladó (Spain) have each broadcast for 30 hours. Kováry continually interviewed guests and presented from 4.00 p.m. on 13 February 2003 until 10.00 p.m. on 14 February 2003 at the Fix.tv studios, Budapest, Hungary; Lladó of Flaix TV did the same from 3 to 4 May 2002 in Barcelona, Spain.

MOST DURABLE TV PRESENTER

With the exception of two episodes, the monthly *Sky at Night* (BBC, UK) has been presented by Patrick Moore (UK) without a break or a miss since 24 April 1957. By December 2002, 600 shows had been broadcast, making it the world's **longest running TV show with the same presenter**.

LARGEST HOME ↓
IN HOLLYWOOD

The 123-room house at Hollywood's 594 Mapleton Drive occupies an area of 5,253 m² (56,550 ft²) and belongs to Aaron Spelling (USA), producer of such TV series as *Charlie's Angels* and *Beverley Hills 90210*, and the world's **most prolific TV drama producer**. The house is currently valued at $37 million (£26.4 million) and includes a gymnasium, bowling alley and skating rink. Dubbed 'The Manor' by the Spelling family, it was built after purchasing and demolishing the previous house on the site, which was owned by singer Bing Crosby (USA).

TV'S TOP EARNERS

★ TV CHEF
Jamie Oliver (UK), £4.8 million ($8.9 million) in 2004.

TV NEWS BROADCASTER (ANNUAL)
Katie Couric (USA), $13 million (£8 million).

☆ CHILD ACTRESS
Hilary Duff (USA), $8 million (£4.36 million) in 2003.

★ TV TALENT SHOW JUDGE (ANNUAL)
Simon Cowell (UK), £18 million ($34 million) in 2004.

★ REALITY TV HOST
Donald Trump (USA), $7 million (£3.7 million) for appearing on *The Apprentice*, 2003–04.

ACTOR (ANNUAL)
Jerry Seinfeld (USA) earned an estimated $267 million (£159.5 million) in 1998.

★ REALITY TV STARS (OWN SHOW)
Jessica Simpson (pictured with husband), $4 million (£2.12 million) in 2003.

★ TV STYLISTS
Kyan Douglas, Ted Allen, Carson Kressley, Jai Rodriguez and Thom Filicia (all USA), stars of *Queer Eye for the Straight Guy*, $4 million (£2.12 million) in 2003.

TV ACTRESS (ANNUAL)
Helen Hunt, $31 million (£18.7 million) in 1999.

CHAT SHOW HOST
Oprah Winfrey (USA), $210 million (£114.68 million) in 2003.

★ TV PRODUCER EVER
David E Kelley (USA), creator of *Ally McBeal*, $300 million (£185 million) for a six-year deal in 2000.

TV ACTOR
Ray Romano (USA), $1.8 million (£1.2 million) per episode of *Everybody Loves Raymond* in 2004/05.

TV SHOWS & ADVERTISING

MOST EXPENSIVE
TV DOCUMENTARY SERIES PER MINUTE

Walking with Dinosaurs, the series depicting how dinosaurs lived, reproduced and became extinct, cost over £37,654 ($61,112) a minute to produce. It took more than two years to make the six 27-minute episodes at a total cost of £6.1 million ($9.9 million).

★ MOST WEDDINGS IN A TV SOAP OPERA

British soap *Coronation Street* has celebrated 59 weddings since it was first aired in December 1960.

★ LONGEST CONTINUOUS TV SHOT

A continuous shot lasting 111 minutes – the entire episode of *C.I.D.* – was filmed by B P Singh (India) in Mumbai, India, on 8 October 2004 and broadcast on 7 November 2004.

LONGEST RUNNING...

ANIMATED SERIES
The Simpsons (FOX, USA)
First aired: 17 December 1989
Episodes: 352 as of
15 May 2005

CHILDREN'S PROGRAMME
Bozo the Clown (WGN TV, USA)
First aired: 1949
Episodes: over 150,000
as of August 2001

★ SCIENCE FICTION SERIES
Doctor Who (BBC, UK)
First aired: 23 November 1963
Episodes: 709 (173 stories)
as of 18 June 2005

SOAP OPERA
Guiding Light (CBS, USA)
First aired: 30 June 1952
Episodes: 14,613 as of
25 February 2005

TALENT SHOW
Opportunity Knocks
(ITV, UK/BBC, UK)
First aired: 1956
Episodes: unknown

MAGIC SHOW
Magicland (WMC-TV, USA)
First aired: January 1966
Episodes: 1,200 as of
January 1989

COMEDY SERIES
Last of the Summer Wine
(BBC, UK)
First aired: 12 November 1973
Episodes: 235 as of
18 April 2004

TV SHOWS

★ FIRST PRIME-TIME ANIMATION SHOW

The Flintstones, created by William Hanna and Joseph Barbera, was first aired on the ABC Television network (USA) in September 1960.

LARGEST PRODUCERS OF SOAP OPERAS

Brazil, Mexico and Puerto Rico dominate the trade in 'telenovelos', with the average running for more than 100 episodes. They supply them for stations throughout Latin America, Italy and Portugal.

★ MOST CONSECUTIVE WINS ON A GAME SHOW

Ian Lygo (UK) celebrated 75 victories on UK game show *100%* in December 1998. Lygo also holds the record for the ★ **most opponents defeated on a single TV game show**, with 150.

MOST GAME SHOW CONTESTANTS ON A SINGLE TV SHOW

A record 80,799 people took part in the All-Japan High-School Quiz Championship televised by NTV on 31 December 1983.

MOST GAME SHOW CONTESTANTS IN A SERIES

The quiz show *Trans-America Ultra Quiz* featured a total of 213,430 contestants throughout its 16-year run from 1977 to 1993. Only 31 contestants ever made it to the final stage.

LARGEST AUDIENCE FOR A COMEDY PROGRAMME

The final episode of *M*A*S*H* had an estimated audience of 125 million people when it was transmitted on 28 February 1983.

LARGEST AUDIENCE FOR A TV SERIES

At its peak of popularity in 1996, *Baywatch* had an estimated weekly audience of more than 1.1 billion in 142 countries. Covering every continent except Antarctica, the show has since been seen in 148 countries and translated into 44 languages.

★ EARLIEST TV SERIES PRODUCED IN COLOUR

The World Is Yours began transmission on 26 June 1951. However, the predominance of black-and-white receivers in most US homes at the time meant that many households did not receive it until colour broadcasting was introduced in December 1953.

★ MOST EXPENSIVE →
TV ADVERTISEMENT (PRODUCTION)

A four-minute feature film made by director Baz Luhrmann (Australia) advertising Chanel No.5 perfume cost £18 million ($33 million) to produce. Starring Nicole Kidman (Australia) as a Marilyn Monroe-style actress who is pursued by paparazzi, the advert made its debut on the big screen in cinemas throughout the USA on 1 November 2004 and subsequently premiered on US television on 11 November 2004. Kidman reportedly earned $3.71 million (£2 million) for this ad, the **highest fee per minute by an actor for a TV commercial** at $928,800 (£500,000) a minute.

GOODBYE, FRIENDS.
SERIES FINALE MAY 6

★HIGHEST
ADVERTISING
RATE FOR
A TV SERIES

An average of $2 million
(£1.1 million) was paid for a
30-second slot during the hour-
long final episode of *Friends*, which
aired in the USA on 6 May 2004.

ADVERTISEMENTS

LARGEST SIMULTANEOUS TV ADVERT PREMIERE

The Ford Motor Company aired
its Global Anthem advertisement
on over 140 pan-regional or local
market networks in 190 countries
on 1 November 1999 at 9.00 p.m.
local time. Featuring Charlotte
Church (UK) and all seven of
Ford's automobile brands, the
advert was shot in nine countries.

★ MOST TV COMMERCIALS SHOWN FOR ONE PRODUCT – SINGLE PROGRAMME

On 17 August 1996, Castlemaine
XXXX screened nine different
adverts during the course of a
programme shown on ITV (UK).
Three different versions of the
advert were shown during each
of three advertising breaks.

HIGHEST ADVERTISING RATE EVER

The highest TV advertising
rate ever paid is $2.4 million
(£1.6 million) for 30 seconds'
airtime during the NBC network
prime-time transmission of the
Super Bowl XXXV game on
28 January 2001.

FIRST COMMERCIAL FILMED IN SPACE

An advertising campaign for
Tnuva Milk, showing cosmonaut
Vasily Tsibliyev (Russia) drinking
milk on board the
Russian *Mir* space

station, was
first broadcast on
22 August 1997.

MOST COMMERCIALS STARRING A COMPANY FOUNDER

Between 1989 and 2002, Dave
Thomas (USA), the founder of
Wendy's Old Fashioned Hamburger
Restaurants, made over
700 television commercial
appearances for his company.

FIRST PUBLIC TV ADVERT

On 27 June 1941, the first open
public TV advertisement was
broadcast on NBC's WNBT
station in New York, USA, for
a Bulova watch.

LONGEST RUNNING POP SHOW

The first edition of *Top of
the Pops* (BBC, UK) was
presented by Jimmy
Savile (top) on 1 January
1964. Artists featured
were Dusty Springfield,
the Rolling Stones, the
Dave Clark Five, the
Swinging Blue Jeans
and the Hollies. The
Beatles and Cliff Richard
and the Shadows were
shown on film. The
weekly show celebrated
its 41st year on air in
January 2005. Other
presenters have included
Bruno Brooks, Anthea
Turner and Gary Davis
(centre, left to right)
and Fearne Cotton and
Reggie Yates (bottom).

★LARGEST CASH PRIZE
WON ON A TV GAME SHOW

Ken Jennings (USA) won $2,520,700 (£1,352,597)
on *Jeopardy!* by winning 74 games during 75
episodes aired between 2 June and 30 November
2004. Jennings defeated 149 opponents, correctly
answering over 2,000 questions in total.

DIGITAL MUSIC

WHAT IS DIGITAL MUSIC?

• Traditionally, music has been recorded and stored physically on **solid objects, such as in the grooves** on vinyl records or in the magnetized areas on audio cassettes.

• Digital music exists in a **binary digital format,** which is a series of **zeros and ones** that does the same job as the grooves on a record.

• Because digital music exists as data, you can **store it and play it on a computer** – often as an MP3 file.

• Development in personal computers, combined with the growth of the Internet, has meant that digital songs can be **easily transferred** around the world and from one type of playback device to another.

• It is **easier than ever** to get hold of your favourite tunes, but there are complex legal and copyright issues associated with this new way of buying and listening to music.

SALES

★ BIGGEST SELLING DOWNLOAD SINGLE IN A WEEK IN THE UK

'Dogz Don't Kill People Wabbits Do' by Mouldy Looking Stain sold over 7,000 copies in the UK in a single week in October 2004.

★ BIGGEST SELLING DOWNLOAD SINGLE IN THE USA

'Hey Ya' by OutKast (USA) is the only downloaded track to have received a multi-platinum Recording Industry Association of America (RIAA) award for sales of over 400,000 (as of October 2004).

★ FIRST DOWNLOAD-ONLY HIT SINGLE

The first single to enter the US Hot 100 chart on download singles sales alone was 'Peacekeeper' by Fleetwood Mac (UK/USA) in March 2003.

FIRST MILLION-SELLING CD

The first CD to sell a million copies worldwide was Dire Straits' *Brothers in Arms* in 1986. It subsequently topped a million sales in Europe alone, including over 250,000 in the UK.

★ BIGGEST ← SELLING DOWNLOAD SINGLE IN THE UK

'(Is This The Way To) Amarillo' by Tony Christie (UK, left) featuring Peter Kay (UK, right) was released on 14 March 2005. To date, it has recorded download sales of 57,804.

★ LARGEST ILLEGAL ← FILE-SHARING SERVICE

Before being shut down in 2001 after legal action by the RIAA, the illegal file-sharing service Napster (USA) had over 70 million users. Created by US student Shawn Fanning, the service enabled members to swap MP3 music files online for free. The picture shows Shawn (far left) with his attorney David Boiesat at a press conference outside the Federal court building in San Francisco, California, USA, on 2 March 2001. Napster re-launched as a legal service in 2003.

TECHNOLOGY

★ OLDEST MULTI-TRACK DIGITAL RECORDING STUDIO

Sound 80 Studios, Minneapolis, Minnesota, USA, was constructed in 1970 and – in a collaboration with the 3M Company, the developer of multi-track digital recording – became the world's first multi-track digital recording studio. The studio complex is now part of Orfield Laboratories.

FIRST COMPACT DISC

The standard for the compact disc was first proposed by Philips (Netherlands) and Sony (Japan) in 1980, and agreed upon in 1981 by the Compact Disc Standard Digital Audio Disc Committee. The first CDs became available to the public in Europe and Japan in the autumn of 1982, and the USA in 1983, where 800,000 discs were sold in the first year alone. Optical discs, which are written and read with a laser, have become the standard medium for home entertainment and computing.

★ LARGEST →
ONLINE MUSIC STORE

The largest online collection of legally downloadable music is Apple's iTunes, which launched in May 2003. Since then, its catalogue of songs has grown to over 1 million individual tracks, which can be paid for and downloaded over the Internet.

★ FIRST ARTIST-CREATED INTERNET SERVICE PROVIDER

BowieNet (www.davidbowie.com, USA) is the first musician-created ISP (Internet Service Provider) and was launched by David Bowie (UK) and Ultrastar Internet Services on 1 September 1998.

★ FIRST MP3

The term MP3 is short for MPEG audio layer-3 and is a widely used digital music file type. It is audio-only and is a direct descendent of the MPEG-1, which is low-bandwidth video compression, commonly used over the Internet. The development of MP3 began in 1987 at the Fraunhofer Institut Integrierte Schaltungen in Germany, and in 1992 it became recognized as the global standard by the International Standards Organization.

HIGHEST CAPACITY
MULTIMEDIA JUKEBOX

The highest capacity multimedia jukebox to date is the AV380, with 80 GB of storage space on its internal hard drive. Created by Archos (France), the AV380 can store and play MP3 music tracks as well as MPEG4 video files. It was launched in August 2003.

The 80-GB capacity of the AV380 is enough to hold around 2,000 CDs of music, or 160 hours of television, or around 120 full-length DVD movies.

★ BEST SELLING SYNTHESIZER

The most popular digital synthesizer of all time is the Korg M1 Music Workstation, which had a production run of 250,000 beginning in 1988.

INTERNET RADIO

★ FIRST INTERNET RADIO SHOW

The earliest Internet radio show was 'Geek of the Week', produced by Internet Talk Radio (USA), which first aired on 1 April 1993. The show was developed by Carl Malumud (USA) using MBONE (IP Multicast Backbone on the Internet) technology. The show was interview based, involved members of the nascent Internet community and was made available to listeners via FTP (File Transfer Protocol).

★ FIRST INTERNET RADIO STATION

The first full-time Internet-only radio station was Radio HK (USA), which began broadcasting music by independent bands in February 1995. The station, created by Norman Hajjar (USA) in California, USA, used a CU-SeeMe web conferencing reflector connected to a custom-created audio CD in endless loop.

★ BIGGEST SELLING DOWNLOAD SINGLE IN A WEEK IN THE USA

'Hollaback Girl' by Gwen Stefani (USA) recorded sales of 58,500 in the week ending 7 May 2005.

★ MOST EXPLETIVES
IN A NO.1 SINGLE

Topping the singles charts in the US, UK, Australia and numerous European charts in early 2004, Eamon's (Eamon Doyle, USA) single 'F*** It (I Don't Want You Back)' contained 33 expletives.

★ LOWEST-SELLING US NO.1 SINGLE

American Idol 3 runner-up Diana DeGarmo's (USA) single 'Dreams' hit the No.1 spot on the US singles sales chart in September 2004 with a record-low weekly sale of under 3,000 copies.

★ LOWEST-SELLING UK NO.1 SINGLE

'Call On Me' by Eric Prydz (Sweden) sold just 21,749 copies in the week ending 30 October 2004 when it was the UK No.1 hit single.

★ FASTEST-SELLING COMPILATION ALBUM

The 57th volume of the world's **most successful album series** *Now!* sold a record 334,345 units in its first week on sale in the UK in April 2004.

★ OLDEST RECORD TO REACH NO.1 ON THE US SINGLES CHART

In July 2004, the best-selling single in the US was 'That's Alright' by Elvis Presley (USA). The track, which also made the UK Top 3, had been recorded and released (without success) 50 years earlier in 1954.

★ HIGHEST DEBUT POSITION ON US SINGLES CHART

The only artist to make their first chart appearance at No.1 on the Hot 100 in the USA is Fantasia Barrino (USA), the winner of *American Idol 3*, with 'I Believe' on 10 July 2004.

MOST WEEKS AT NO.1 & 2 SPENT SIMULTANEOUSLY ON US SINGLES CHART

OutKast (USA) simultaneously spent eight weeks at No.1 & 2 on the US singles chart, with 'Hey Ya!' and 'The Way You Move', from 20 December 2003 to 7 February 2004.

MOST UK SINGLES TO DEBUT AT NO.1

Westlife, comprising Shane Filan, Nicky Byrne, Bryan McFadden,

BIGGEST-SELLING ALBUM

Thriller by Michael Jackson (USA) has achieved global sales of over 51 million copies since 1982.

ANDRE '3000' BENJAMIN

Andre 3000 (born Andre Benjamin, USA) is one half of OutKast, who hold a record for the most weeks at No.1 & 2.

Did you always want to be a music artist?
No, I'm a visual artist first. I wasn't interested in music until high school.

What's the best part of your job?
Being able to hear and see an idea, and to bring it to the masses.

When you began your musical career did you think it would be as successful as it is?
No, you hope your music resonates with people, but you never know how popular it will be.

What is your greatest achievement in music?
Reaching the point where the audience was just as excited about something new and challenging as I was.

What advice would you give to youngsters wanting to make music their career?
Make sure you're having fun or getting enjoyment from what you're doing. Learn the business as well as the craft. Know your worth. Diversify. Let the music almost be your hobby because in today's climate it's hard to make real money from it.

MOST UK NO.1s
BY A CHRISTMAS SONG

'Do They Know It's Christmas?' has topped the UK singles chart at Christmas on three separate occasions – in 1984, 1989 and 2004. The first version sold a then-record 3.6 million copies in the UK alone, and the latest version by Band Aid 20 was the UK's top selling single in 2004, with over 1 million sold. It was written by Bob Geldof (Ireland) and Midge Ure (UK).

Mark Feehily and Kian Egan (all Ireland), had a record-breaking 12 singles debut at the No.1 spot between 1 May 1999 and 22 November 2003.

★ MOST NEW ENTRIES ON UK SINGLES CHART

On 16 October 2004 there were a record 17 new entries in the UK Top 40 singles chart.

★ MOST NEW ENTRIES ON US ALBUM CHART

On 16 October 2004 there were a record 11 new entries in the USA Top 20 album chart.

★ MOST ENTRIES ON US ADULT CONTEMPORARY CHART

In September 2004, Elton John (UK) achieved a 64th entry on the US adult contemporary chart with the track 'Answer in the Sky'. Barbra Streisand (USA) has 63 entries, making her the **female singer with the most appearances in the chart**.

LONGEST SINGLES CHART STAY

'How Do I Live' by LeAnn Rimes (USA) entered the Top 25 US country singles sales chart on 21 June 1997 and was still there in February 2003 – a record breaking 291 weeks (over 5.5 years) later.

LONGEST US CHART SPAN FOR A SINGLE

Louis Armstrong (USA, 1901–71) first appeared on a Billboard chart on 6 April 1946. His most recent entry to the listings came in 1988, a full 17 years after his death, with 'What a Wonderful World' from the film soundtrack to *Good Morning Vietnam* (USA, 1987). Armstrong also had over 50 hits before the 'official' chart started in 1940, his first being 'Muskrat Ramble' in 1926, thus taking his span of hits to more than 61 years.

★ MOST MULTINATIONAL UK NO.1 ALBUM GROUP

The group Il Divo had four different nationalities making up their numbers when their album *Il Divo* reached the No.1 spot on 13 November 2004. The quartet is made up of Carlos Marin (Spain), David Miller (USA), Urs Buhler (Switzerland) and Seb Izambard (France). The album features both classical and pop numbers and is sung in English, Spanish and Italian.

★ MOST SUCCESSFUL UK SONG TITLE

The most successful song title to appear on the UK singles chart is 'Angel', with 11 appearances in the Top 40, the latest coming from The Corrs (Ireland) in September 2004.

→ **WHERE IS THE WORLD'S LARGEST JAZZ FESTIVAL HELD EACH YEAR? FIND OUT ON P.173**

★ LONGEST TIME SPENT AT NO.1 ON US SINGLES CHART IN A YEAR

Usher (Usher Raymond IV, USA) spent a total of 28 weeks at the top of the US singles chart in 2004.

★ BURGER →

The largest hamburger commercially available weighs 4 kg (9 lb) and is available on the menu at Denny's Beer Barrel Pub, Inc., Clearfield, Pennsylvania, USA. It costs $23.95 (£13.42), and anyone who can finish it within three hours receives a refund, together with their name on a plaque and a $65 (£36) gift certificate to use for a future visit. To date, no one has managed the feat.

★ GOLF TEE

HARIBO GmbH & Co. KG created a wooden golf tee measuring 3.30 m (10 ft 9.25 in) long with a head diameter of 74.5 cm (29.25 in) and a shaft width of 30 cm (11.75 in). It was made of spruce wood and was completed in July 2004 as part of the HARIBO Children and Young Persons Golf Series.

★ SURFBOARD

A surfboard made by Nev Hyman (Australia) was 12 m (39 ft 4 in) long, 3 m (9 ft 10 in) wide and 30 cm (11.8 in) thick and was launched at Snapper Rocks, Queensland, Australia, on 5 March 2005. It took 300 litres (79 US gal; 66 UK gal) of resin and nearly half a tonne (1,102 lb) of foam to make, and weighed nearly 800 kg (1,760 lb).

★ SKATEBOARD →

The Foundation Skateboards WBS (World's Biggest Skateboard) is 3.66 m (12 ft) long, 1.2 m (4 ft) wide and 0.76 m (2 ft 6 in) high, and was designed and produced by Tod Swank, Greg Winter, Dana Hard and Damon Mills (all USA) in San Diego, California, USA. Its wheels are car tyres and it has scaled-up trucks that turn when the board is tilted, as on a regular-sized skateboard.

★ POPCORN MACHINE

Greg Scott Abbott (aka Rev Gadget), Wink Eller, Lisa Lejohn, Eric Scarlett, Christoff Koon and Charles Cretors (all USA) built a popcorn machine measuring 6.77 m (22 ft 2.75 in) tall, 2.92 m (9 ft 7 in) wide and 2.46 m (8 ft 1.1 in) deep in Santa Clarita, California, USA. It took five days to construct and was unveiled in June 2004 on Discovery Channel's BIG! television show.

★ SCISSORS →

The world's largest pair of functional scissors were created in July 2001 by Mike Stephenson (USA), and measure 0.9 m (36 in) tip to handle when closed, and 0.82 m (32.5 in) blade tip to blade tip when fully open.

RUBBER BAND BALL →

John J Bain (USA) constructed a ball made of rubber bands that weighed 1,415.2 kg (3,120 lb) when measured on 22 October 2003 in Delaware, USA. It has a circumference of 4.59 m (15 ft 1 in).

← ★ BOOT

The largest leather boot measures 6 m (20 ft) long, 2.1 m (7 ft) wide and 4.8 m (16 ft) tall, and was made by the staff of the Red Wing Shoe Company at their premises in Red Wing, Minnesota, USA, and unveiled on 5 February 2005. It weighs 1,043 kg (2,300 lb), used 80 hides of leather and is equivalent to a size 638 (US size 638½; European size 850).

THE WORLD'S LARGEST LEATHER BOOT

★ MOUSE-TRAP ↘

A mousetrap built by Truly Nolen, a US-based pest control company, measured 3.53 m (11 ft 7 in) long and 1.67 m (5 ft 6 in) wide when unveiled in Miami Gardens, Florida, USA, on 5 November 2003.

X GAMES

★ MOST MEDALS WON BY AN INDIVIDUAL ↗

Dave Mirra (USA) has won a total of 18 X Games medals in the Bike Stunt discipline.

X GAMES HISTORY

The X Games (originally called Extreme Games) were first held in Rhode Island and Vermont, USA, in July 1995, and have been staged annually ever since. In 1997, the first Winter X Games were held at Snow Summit Mountain Resort in California, USA.

The X Games are the brainchild of the sports TV network ESPN (Entertainment and Sports Programming Network), who were looking to create an international forum for action sport athletes. Its popularity has continued to grow around the world, with top athletes now battling it out in various qualifying rounds for limited spots in the X Games.

X GAMES – SUMMER EVENTS

SKATEBOARD
★ STREET PARK – a concrete course with stairs, rails, banks and ledges
★ BIG AIR – a roll-in from a height of 18–24 m (60–80 ft), launching over a gap to land in an 8-m (27-ft) quarterpipe
★ VERT – big air and tricks performed off a halfpipe
★ VERT BEST TRICK – best halfpipe trick

MOTO X
(125cc/250cc DIRT BIKES)
★ STEP-UP – a 7.6-m (25-ft) run-up to a vertical dirt face used as a launch pad for a high jump over a bar
★ FREESTYLE – tricks using ramp-to-dirt and dirt-to-dirt jumps

★ BEST TRICK – a jump trick off a giant dirt ramp
★ SUPER MOTO – a combination of street racing, motocross and freestyle on a dirt and asphalt track

BIKE STUNT (BMX)
★ VERT – big air and tricks off a halfpipe
★ PARK – tricks using launch and sub boxes, wall rides and rails

AGGRESSIVE INLINE SKATE
★ VERT – big air and tricks off a halfpipe
★ SURFING THE GAME – two teams compete for overall score
★ WAKEBOARD – jumps and tricks performed off a boat's wake around a course of water obstacles

★ SNOWBOARD SUPERPIPE – MOST MEDALS WON →

Danny Kass (USA) has won a total of four medals in the snowboard Superpipe discipline: gold in 2001, silver in 2003 and 2004, and bronze in 2005.

★ MOST GOLD MEDALS WON BY AN INDIVIDUAL

Dave Mirra (USA) also holds the record for the most X Games gold medals won by an individual, with 13 in the Bike Stunt category.

→ **FOR A COMPLETE LIST OF X GAMES MEDAL RECORDS, PLEASE REFER TO THE SPORTS REFERENCE SECTION, P.276**

SNOWBOARDING MOST MEDALS WON (WOMEN)

The most X Games snowboarding medals won by a woman is 10 by Barrett Christy (USA).

→SEE P.1▮
INTERVIEW▮
RYAN SHEC▮
THE YOUNG▮
X GAMES GOL▮
MEDALLIST

FIRST '9▮ ON A SKATEBO▮

Skateboard legend Tony Ha▮ the first person to achieve a ▮ airborne rotations) in competit▮ in San Francisco, California, US▮ The '900' (so-called because the ▮ through 900°) is one of the most ▮ skateboarding. Hawk was successf▮ attempt of the evening.

★ MOTO X
MOST MEDALS WON BY AN INDIVIDUAL

Brian Deegan (USA), known as the Metal Mulisha, has won a total of nine X Games medals (two of them gold) during his career in the discipline of Moto X.

★ YOUNGEST ATHLETE

Takeshi Yasutoko (Japan) was 11 years 50 days old when he made his X Games debut in the 1998 Aggressive Inline Skate Vert.

'900'
...OARD

...wk (USA) became ...900' (two and a half ...on at the X Games ...A, on 27 June 1999. ...skater spins ...ficult tricks in ...d on his 11th

TONY HAWK

'Birdman' Tony Hawk (USA, left) has won a record 16 X Games skateboard medals, and was also the first to pull off a '900' (see left).

How does it feel to be a Guinness World Record holder?
It's huge! I would never have believed it if you'd told me when I was a kid that I would be included in the book, especially for skate-boarding. It's a big honour.

What's been your greatest achievement so far?
Making the '900' for the first time in any contest was a great feat for me, because it was the one trick I had pursued for the longest – probably about five years up to that point. But I'd had the idea

long before that without having the guts to try it. It'd been this thorn in my side since I'd thought about trying it.
Beyond that, being on The Simpsons was a major event for me. It's such a measure of pop-culture status, especially if they have you play yourself.

Did you ever expect to be where you are now?
I'm still in disbelief that I get to skateboard for a living. Even when skateboarding wasn't very big and when it was difficult to make a living, I was still doing it. Now it's bigger and better than ever and I still get to do it – just on a bigger scale!

What advice do you give to kids who are starting out?
Don't get too frustrated with yourself – these things take a long time to learn. Also, enjoy it. Don't do it if you think it's some tool to get fame or fortune, because you have to be enjoying it to be successful.

★ SNOCROSS →
MOST MEDALS WON (MEN)

Blair Morgan (Canada) has won a record seven medals for snocross. He took gold in 2001, 2002, 2003 and 2005, silver in 1999 and 2000, and bronze in 2004. He came back to win the gold in 2005 after recovering from a broken back and leg.

X GAMES – WINTER EVENTS

MOTO X
★ BEST TRICK – mid-air trick performed over a gap between take-off and landing ramp

SKI
★ SKIER X – racers follow a downhill course
★ SLOPESTYLE – tricks performed through a course of obstacles, rails and jumps
★ SUPERPIPE – tricks performed off a halfpipe

SNOCROSS
A race combining oval-track racing and cross country

SNOWBOARD
★ SNOWBOARDER X – racers follow a downhill course
★ SLOPESTYLE – (see SKI)
★ SUPERPIPE – (see SKI)

ULTRACROSS
A downhill relay race in pairs of one skier and one snowboarder

★ MOST SKIING MEDALS

Jon Olsson (Sweden) has won eight Winter X Games skiing medals: four in the Superpipe discipline and four in the Slopestyle, 2002–05.

MOTO X
HIGHEST STEP-UP JUMP

The greatest height achieved in the X Games Moto X Step-Up event is 10.67 m (35 ft), by Tommy Clowers (USA) in August 2000. Essentially a 'high jump' on a motorcycle, riders must try to clear a bar placed at the top of a steep take-off ramp. The height obtained is the equivalent of jumping on to the roof of a two-storey building.

★ HIGHEST CHART POSITIONS FOR SIMULTANEOUS US ALBUM RELEASES

Two albums by rap artist Nelly (USA, b. Cornell Haynes) – *Suit* and *Sweat* – simultaneously entered the US album chart at No.1 and No.2 in October 2004.

→ **WHAT ALBUM HAS SOLD MORE THAN 51 MILLION COPIES SINCE ITS RELEASE IN 1982? FIND OUT ON P.158**

BIGGEST SELLING...

★ CONTEMPORARY JAZZ ALBUM

The Norah Jones (USA) album *Come Away With Me* headed the US contemporary jazz chart for 143 successive weeks, selling 16 million copies around the world. It debuted at No.1 in March 2002, before finally slipping to No.2 in December 2004.

WORLD MUSIC ALBUM

The 1998 Grammy Award-winning album *Buena Vista Social Club* (Cuba, 1997) has sold more than 4 million copies.

FEMALE LATIN ARTIST

Gloria Estefan (Cuba) has achieved world sales estimated at more than 70 million by her record company. She amassed eight gold albums in the USA, four of which have passed the 3 million sales mark: *Primitive Love* (1985), *Let It Loose* (1987), *Cuts Both Ways* (1989) and *Greatest Hits* (1992).

MALE LATIN ARTIST

Vocalist Julio Iglesias (Spain) has achieved reported global sales of more than 200 million albums. His album *Julio* (1983) was the first foreign-language

album to sell more than 2 million copies in the USA, and the only foreign-language record to go double platinum there.

RAP ARTIST

Rap legend 2Pac (USA, b. Tupac Shakur) has certified US album sales of 36 million. He has had more hits since he died (at the age of 25 in September 1996) than he managed to amass while he was alive, including three No.1 albums.

COUNTRY ARTIST

Garth Brooks (USA) has achieved album sales of over 100 million since 1989.

MUSIC VIDEO

The Making of Michael Jackson's Thriller, released in December 1983, has sold over 900,000 units.

★ MOST PUBLIC APPEARANCES BY A POP ARTIST IN 24 HOURS

Rachel Stevens (UK) made seven public appearances on 8 and 9 September 2004. The cities visited were, in order: Salford, Liverpool, Stoke-on-Trent, Birmingham, Bristol, Oxford and London. All appearances lasted a minimum of 15 minutes.

★ MOST ALBUMS ← CONSECUTIVELY SIGNED BY THE ARTIST

Yahir Othön Parra (Mexico) signed a record 2,852 copies of his album *Otra historia de amor* at Plaza Cuicuilco, Mexico City, on 6 and 7 July 2004. He signed CDs non-stop for 8 hr 13 min 49 sec.

★ LONGEST CREDIT ON A SINGLE

The single 'Was Ist Passiert?' released by PUR (Germany) on 20 October 2003 lists the names of 1,491 people. Those credited are fans who registered via the band's website.

MOST...

★ BRIT AWARDS WON BY AN INDIVIDUAL

Robbie Williams (UK) has won 15 BRIT (British Record Industry Trust) Awards. His most recent win was for Best Song (of the last 25 years) Award, received for 'Angels', at the ceremony held on 10 February 2005.

BRIT AWARDS WON IN A YEAR BY A GROUP

Blur won four BRIT Awards in 1995. At the time, the group – which formed in 1988 – comprised Damon Albarn, Graham Coxon, Alex James and Dave Rowntree (all UK).

GRAMMY AWARDS WON BY AN INDIVIDUAL

The classical music conductor Sir Georg Solti (UK) won 31 Grammy Awards (including a special Trustees award in 1967) between 1958 and 1997.

GRAMMY AWARDS WON BY A FEMALE ARTIST

Aretha Franklin (USA) has won 15 Grammys since receiving her first in 1967 for Best R&B Vocal Performance with 'Respect'. She then went on to win the female category of the same award 11 times from 1967 to 1987.

GRAMMY AWARDS WON BY A SOLO POP PERFORMER

Stevie Wonder (USA) has won 19 Grammy Awards, including Best Male R&B Vocal Performance six times, since 1973.

GRAMMY AWARDS WON IN A YEAR BY A GROUP

Rockgroup Santana, formed in the 1960s, won eight Grammy Awards on 23 February 2000.

GRAMMY AWARDS WON IN A YEAR BY AN INDIVIDUAL

Michael Jackson (USA) won eight Grammy Awards in 1984.

PEOPLE TO SHARE A GRAMMY AWARD

The 46 members of the Chicago Symphony Orchestra won a Grammy Award in February 1978 for Best Choral Performance –Classical with its recording of Verdi's *Requiem*.

MOST EXPENSIVE...

POP STAR CLOTHING

An outfit worn by Geri Halliwell (UK) for the Spice Girls' 1997 BRIT Awards performance was bought for £41,320 (then $66,112) at Sotheby's, London, UK, on 16 September 1998. The outfit had been made by the singer's sister, Karen Davis, who, on a budget, made a corset on to which she stitched a union flag.

MUSIC VIDEO

Directed by Mark Romanek (USA), the video for Michael and Janet Jackson's hit single 'Scream' (1995) cost $7 million (£4.4 million) to make.

★ YOUNGEST FEMALE TO TOP UK ALBUM CHART

Joss Stone (UK) reached No.1 with her second album *Mind, Body & Soul* on 9 October 2004, aged 17 years and 181 days.

MUSIC FACTS & FEATS

Human vocal range (all note names relative to piano keyboard)

1. ★Greatest range (female): Nine octaves, G2–G10, Georgia Brown (Brazil), 18 August 2004

2. Highest vocal note (female): Georgia Brown's G10 – a frequency rather than a note, verified using a piano, violin and Hammond organ

3. Greatest range (male): Six octaves, Tim Storms (USA)

4. Highest vocal note (male): D7 (four Ds above Middle C), Adam Lopez (Australia), 17 March 2003

5. Highest note in classical repertoire: G6 (3 Gs above Middle C) in 'Popoli di Tessaglia', a concert aria by Mozart (Austria, 1756–91)

6. ★Lowest classical note: Low D (three Ds below Middle C) in Osmin's aria in Mozart's *Die Entführung aus dem Serail*

7. Lowest vocal note: Tim Storms' B-2, nearly two octaves below piano's lowest note

Note: the pale keys on the keyboard (left) indicate the range of a standard 88-key piano. The areas in grey represent pitches outside this range.

★ LONGEST CONCERT
BY A GROUP

From 20 to 22 February 2004, the Grand Boys – aka Paul Bromley, John Griffin, Bob and Robert Kelly, Alan Marshall, Adrian Robertson, Colin Sinclair and Alan Stewart (all UK) – played for 42 hr 38 min at Smith's Restaurant in Stirling, Scotland, UK.

CLUB DJ
DJ Martin Boss (USA) held a 74-hour mixing session at Vinyl Frontier in Orlando, Florida, USA, from 1 to 4 February 2002.

★ KARAOKE
Mark Pearson (UK) sang for 25 hr 45 min at Keighley Cougars Rugby Club, Keighley, UK, on 25–26 June 2004. The ★ longest group karaoke session featured 399 acts and lasted for 100 hours in an event held at the Guangzhou Victory Plaza, China, from 26 to 30 December 2004.

VOCAL POWER

FASTEST RAP MC
Rebel XD, otherwise known as Seandale Price (USA), is the world's fastest rap artist. On 24 June 1998 he rapped 683 syllables in 54.501 seconds, which works out at just over 12.5 syllables a second, beating his own previous record of 674 syllables in 54.9 seconds, or 12.2 syllables a second, which was set in 1992.

★ LONGEST CONTINUOUS VOCAL NOTE
David McFetridge (Ireland) held a single vocal note continuously for 29.03 seconds on the children's radio programme *Big Toe Radio Show* in London, UK, on 29 July 2003. David was placed exactly 1 m (3ft 2 in) from the measuring instrument and chose his own pitch, which was checked for deviation from the original starting note by two qualified musical experts.

MARATHONS

★ ELVIS
Franz Nübel (Germany), the 'Eifel-Elvis', held an Elvis Presley singing marathon lasting 42 hr 16 min 8 sec in Kall, Germany, between 29 and 30 January 2004.

★ RADIO DJ
Arulanantham Suresh Joachim (Australia) broadcast for 120 hours on Geethavaani Tamil Radio in Scarborough, Ontario, Canada, between 23 and 28 June 2003.

LARGEST MUSICAL INSTRUMENT ENSEMBLES

INSTRUMENT	NUMBER	PLACE	DATE
Bell (campanology)	10,000	Gdansk, Poland	31 December 2000
Violin	4,000	London, UK	15 June 1925
Recorder	3,337	Hong Kong, China	4 March 2001
Drum	3,140	Hong Kong, China	13 July 2003
★ Panpipes	2,317	La Paz, Bolivia	24 October 2004
Kazoo	1,791	Quincy, USA	30 June 2004
★ Erhu	1,490	Jiangsu, China	17 October 2004
Guitar	1,322	Vancouver, Canada	7 May 1994
Cello	1,103	Kobe, Japan	29 November 1998
★ Harmonica	851	Poznan, Poland	13 September 2003
Shamisen	815	Tokyo, Japan	27 November 1999

MOST...

★ DJS IN RELAY

The most DJs to consecutively mix one record each is 59 at D-Train, Bridge & Tunnel Club, London, UK, on 18 June 2003. Each DJ played one record, one after the other, with every mix being continuous, synchronous and to a professional standard.

★ TURNTABLES IN A MIX

DJ Trixta (Andrew Cooper, UK) used six records on six turntables in a synchronous mix at the Phoenix Centre, Exeter, Devon, UK, on 26 September 2002.

★ INSTRUMENTS IN A PIECE OF MUSIC

A total of 147 different musical instruments were played by children from Caistor Primary School in a recital held on 3 July 2002 at Caistor, Lincolnshire, UK. The piece – entitled *Caistor Symphony* – lasted 30 minutes.

DRUMBEATS IN A MINUTE

Oliver Butterworth (UK) played 1,080 single-stroke drumbeats in one minute on 13 June 2002 at the University of Lincoln, UK.

LARGEST...

BAND

On 28 June 1964, a total of 20,100 bandsmen from Norges Musikkorps Forbund assembled at the Ullevaal Stadium in Oslo, Norway.

★ CARILLON

A carillon consists of brass bells fixed to a frame, played by keyboard and pedals. The largest

LARGEST
DRUM ENSEMBLE →

The largest drum ensemble consisted of 3,140 participants who gathered to play at the opening ceremony of the Hong Kong Drum Festival at Victoria Park, Hong Kong, China, on 13 July 2003. Among those leading the group were the 100-piece drum troupe of the Hong Kong Chinese Orchestra.

(minimum 23 bells) is the five-octave Hyechon College Carillon in Seo-ku, Taejon, South Korea, with 78 bells, which took two years to build. The heaviest bell, the Bourdonbell, weighs 10 tonnes (22,046 lb).

CHOIR

A choir of 60,000 sang at a choral contest finale in Breslau, Germany, on 2 August 1937.

★ HUMAN BEATBOX

A human beatbox comprising 106 people, mostly residents of Laburnham Road, Maidenhead, Berkshire, UK, came together on 3 June 2002. They kept to a set rhythm for over three minutes.

★ JAZZ FESTIVAL

The world's largest jazz festival is the *Festival International de Jazz de Montréal* in Québec, Canada. For its 25th anniversary festival in July 2004 it attracted 1,913,868 people.

★ MUSIC LESSON

Len Collins (UK) held a guitar class for 211 students at Middleton Hall, Milton Keynes, Buckinghamshire, UK, on 11 May 2004.

ORGAN

The largest and **loudest musical instrument** ever constructed is the now-only-partially-functional Auditorium Organ in Atlantic City, New Jersey, USA. Completed in 1930, it had two consoles, 1,477 stop controls and 33,112 pipes. It had a range of seven octaves and the volume of 25 brass bands.

ORCHESTRA

A total of 6,452 musicians – comprising the Vancouver Symphony Orchestra and music students from British Columbia, Canada – played *Ten Minutes of Nine* for 9 min 44 sec at Place Stadium, Vancouver, Canada, on 15 May 2000.

★ SING-ALONG (ONE VENUE)

On 9 May 2004, Freddy Quinn (Germany) led 88,600 people in a rendition of *La Paloma* from the museum ship *Rickmer Rickmers* at Hamburg, Germany.

★ LARGEST PLAYABLE BAR CHIMES

Bar chimes built by George Barbar (Lebanon) and played at the Byblos-off Festival in Byblos, Lebanon, on 17 June 2004, measured 15 m (49 ft) in length and consisted of 1,000 chimes. They varied in lengths from 5.1 cm (2 in) to 105 cm (41 in), and were attached to 20 wooden bars fixed to 20 cymbal stands.

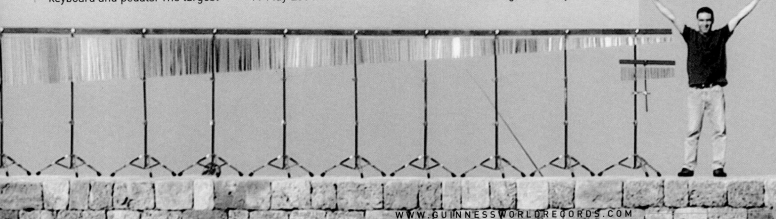

THE STAGE

★ MOST CONCURRENT
MUSICAL PRODUCTIONS

As of February 2005, the musical *Mamma Mia!* had the most global productions playing at the same time with 12, consisting of nine resident productions (UK; two in the USA; Spain; Japan; Sweden; Germany; Canada; Holland) along with three tours in Europe, South Africa and the USA.

Cameron Mackintosh's production of *Les Misérables* had the **most concurrent productions ever**, with 15 being staged around the world at one time.

Broadway production of *Dance of the Vampire*. The show opened on 9 December 2002 at the Minskoff Theater, New York City, USA, and closed on 25 January 2003 after playing more previews (61) than performances (56), securing the record for the **greatest theatrical loss**.

MOST EXPENSIVE STAGE PRODUCTION IN THE WEST END

Eon Productions' *Chitty Chitty Bang Bang*, which opened on 16 April 2002 at the London Palladium, UK, starring Michael Ball (UK), cost £6.2 million ($8.9 million) to stage, beating the previous record set by *Cats* of £6 million ($12.69 million) on 11 May 1981.

MOST TONY AWARDS WON BY A MUSICAL

The Producers won a record 12 awards from 15 nominations – including Best Musical – at the 2001 Tony Awards. Directed by Susan Stroman (USA), it broke the previous record of 10 wins held since 1964 by *Hello Dolly!*

MUSICALS

★ SHORTEST THEATRICAL RUN IN THE WEST END

A production of *Oscar Wilde* closed after its opening night performance on 22 October 2004 due to only five seats having been booked for the second night at the 466-seater Shaw Theatre in London, UK.

★ HIGHEST PAID ACTOR IN A BROADWAY MUSICAL

Michael Crawford (UK) was given a reported $180,000-a-week (£114,018) contract for the role of Count Von Krolock in the

★ MOST PROLIFIC COMPOSER

With various collaborators, Richard Rodgers (USA) wrote 51 musicals for theatre and film in a career that spanned seven decades, beginning with *You'd Be Surprised* (1920) and ending with *I Remember Mama* (1979). Perhaps the most popular production was *South Pacific*, first produced in 1949 and made into a film in 1958. The soundtrack holds the record for the **most weeks at No.1 on the UK album chart**, with 70.

HIGHEST THEATRICAL BOX OFFICE GROSS

Since first opening in London on 9 October 1986, Andrew Lloyd Webber's musical *The Phantom of the Opera* has played over 65,000 performances in 20 countries and has taken over £2 billion ($3.2 billion) at the box office.

MOST TONY AWARD NOMINATIONS

★ **Actor:** eight, Jason Robards (USA), 1957–1978

★ **Actress:** 10, Julie Harris (USA), 1952–1997

Play: nine for *Angels in America: Millennium Approaches* (1993) and *Indiscretions* (1995)

★ **Play (without winning):** nine for *Indiscretions* (1995)

★ **Musical (without winning):** 11 for *Chicago* (1976) and *Steel Pier* (1997)

→ WHICH POP STAR MADE THE MOST PUBLIC APPEARANCES IN 24 HOURS? FIND OUT ON P.170

★ LARGEST BUDGET
(PRE-PRODUCTION)

The largest pre-production budget allocated to a stage show before its world premiere has so far been in excess of £11.7 million ($22.3 million) for the musical *The Lord of the Rings*. Directed by Matthew Warchus (UK) and produced by Kevin Wallace Ltd, the show is due to premiere at the Prince of Wales Theatre, Toronto, Ontario, Canada, in 2006.

THEATRE

★ MOST CHARACTERS PLAYED BY ONE ACTOR IN A SINGLE PRODUCTION

Laxman Deshpande (India) plays all 52 parts in the three-hour one-man play *Varhad Nighalay Londonla*. He has performed 2,125 times since the first paying production in December 1979 at Aurangabad, India.

★ FASTEST PRODUCTION

On 27 September 2003, the cast and crew of Dundee University Musical Society, in association with Apex Productions, produced and performed *Seven Brides for Seven Brothers* at the Gardyne Theatre, Dundee, UK, in a time of 23 hr 30 min from first receiving the script. The time includes auditions, casting, rehearsals, publicity design, rigging, stage and set design, and construction.

★ MOST PLAYS BY ONE WRITER RUNNING SIMULTANEOUSLY ON BROADWAY

For a period of 186 days from 21 December 1966 to 25 June 1967, Neil Simon (USA) had four plays running on Broadway: *Barefoot in the Park* at the Biltmore (23 October 1963 to 25 June 1967), *The Odd Couple* at the Eugene O'Neill (1 August 1966 to 2 July 1967), *The Star-Spangled Girl* at the Plymouth (21 December 1966 to 5 August 1967) and *Sweet Charity* at the Palace (9 January 1966 to 15 July 1967).

★ LONGEST THEATRICAL RUN OF A COMEDY

Since first opening at the Edinburgh Festival Fringe, Scotland, UK, on 18 August 1979, *NewsRevue* has continued its run in London, UK, at the Kings Head Theatre (1979), Gate Theatre (1980–85) and the Canal Café Theatre (1985 to present) as well as producing a concurrent production every August for the Edinburgh Festival Fringe.

MOST THEATRICAL APPEARANCES ON A SINGLE NIGHT

On 24 February 2004, Jerry Hall (USA) took on recognized scripted roles in six different London West End theatre productions during the course of a single night. →

★ YOUNGEST THEATRE PRODUCER IN THE WEST END

Gary Sullivan (UK) was 20 years 152 days old when his variety showcase, *Energy*, played at Her Majesty's Theatre, London, UK, on 18 March 2001. It featured 200 performers, comprising solo singers, dance groups, bands and choirs.

★ LARGEST LIVE ENTERTAINMENT COMPANY

Clear Channel Entertainment Inc. is the world's largest producer, promoter and operator of live entertainment events such as concerts, touring Broadway shows and sports events. It operates in 65 countries, with sales of $2,646.9 million (£1,600.7 million) in 2003.

LARGEST THEATRE CAST

A total of 2,100 children appeared in the finale of the Rolf Harris Schools Variety Spectacular, which was held in Sydney, Australia, in November 1985.

★ MOST EXPENSIVE STAGE PRODUCTION ON BROADWAY

The stage adaptation of Disney's 1994 film *The Lion King* is the most expensive theatrical production ever, with the Broadway show – which opened on 13 November 1997 – costing an estimated $15 million (£9.3 million).

↖

JERRY HALL'S THEATRE SCHEDULE, 24 FEBRUARY 2004

Phantom of the Opera
Character: Monsieur André
On stage: 7.30 p.m.
Off stage: 7.40 p.m.

Les Misérables
Character: a prostitute
On stage: 7.59 p.m.
Off stage: 8.04 p.m.

Fame
Character: Mr Myers
On stage: 8.30 p.m.
Off stage: 8.35 p.m.

Blood Brothers
Character: Brenda
On stage: 8.55 p.m.
Off stage: 9.00 p.m.

Anything Goes
Character: one of six 'Swings'
On stage: 9.25 p.m.
Off stage: 9.40 p.m.

Chitty Chitty Bang Bang
Character: one of the 24 members of the ensemble
On stage: 10.09 p.m.
Off stage: 10.18 p.m.

Total time: 2 hr 42 min

CIRCUS SKILLS

JUGGLING - DURATION

Three objects:
Terry Cole (UK)
11 hr 4 min 22 sec (1995)

★ Three objects underwater:
Ashrita Furman (USA)
48 min 36 sec (2002)

★ Three shot-puts (male):
Milan Roskopf (Slovakia)
52.02 sec (2002)

Five clubs:
Anthony Gatto (USA)
45 min 2 sec (1989)

LARGEST...

TRAVELLING CIRCUS TENT
The Ringling Bros and Barnum & Bailey Circus (USA) travelled with a circus tent covering 8,492 m² (91,407 ft²). Consisting of a round top 61 m (200 ft) in diameter with five middle sections each 18 m (59 ft) wide, it was used on tours from 1921 to 1924. The biggest circus tents now in use have a floor area just over half this size.

★ MOST PEOPLE
STILT-WALKING SIMULTANEOUSLY

As part of Cirque du Soleil's 20th anniversary celebrations on 16 June 2004, 544 of their employees simultaneously walked a distance of 100 m (328 ft) on stilts at their headquarters in Montreal, Quebec, Canada.

BIG TOPS
The two largest big tops measure 120.7 x 37.8 m (396 x 124 ft) – slightly longer and narrower than an American football field – and are used by Carson and Barnes Circus, and Clyde Beatty-Cole Brothers' Circus, both in the USA. The Carson and Barnes tent is moved seven days a week for a record 36 consecutive weeks every year. The Clyde Beatty-Cole Brothers' tent seats 3,000 people.

CIRCUS TENT AUDIENCE
An audience of 16,702 (15,686 paid) assembled for the Ringling Bros and Barnum & Bailey Circus at Concordia, Kansas, USA, on 13 September 1924.

ANIMAL CIRCUS ACT: LIONS
'Captain' Alfred Schneider (UK) mastered and fed 70 lions in a cage, unaided, at Bertram Mills' Circus, London, UK, in 1925.

ANIMAL CIRCUS ACT: POLAR BEARS
Willy Hagenbeck (Germany) worked with 70 polar bears in a presentation at the Paul Busch Circus, Berlin, Germany, in 1904.

CLOWN BOOTS
Circus clown Coco (Latvia, b. Nicolai Poliakoff) took an enormous size 58 boot.

LONGEST...

★ RUNNING CIRCUS
The Ringling Bros and Barnum & Bailey Circus' 'Greatest Show on Earth' has run for 135 years. Barnum started the show in 1870 and merged with the Ringling Brothers in 1919.

SERVING CIRCUS BANDMASTER
Merle Evans (USA) served with the Ringling Bros and Barnum & Bailey Circus for 50 years. From 1919 to 1969 he led the band for about 30,000 performances.

★ MOST CONSECUTIVE FOOT-JUGGLING FLIPS

Stiv and Roni Bello (Italy) performed 45 consecutive foot-juggling flips during their performance in 'Varekai', Cirque du Soleil's North American tour at San Jose, California, USA, on 15 February 2003.

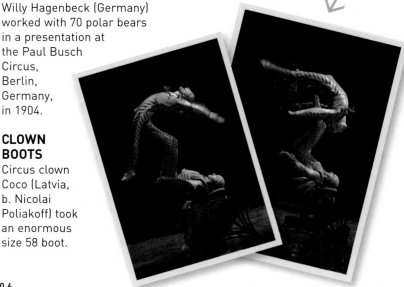

MOST...

★ FOOT-JUGGLING FLIPS IN 30 SECONDS
Cirque du Soleil's Bello Brothers – Stiv and Roni Bello (Italy, pictured below) – achieved 38 consecutive foot-juggling flips in 30 seconds during a performance in California, USA, on 15 February 2003.

★ ELEPHANTS PERFORMING AT A CIRCUS
The Ringling Bros and Barnum & Bailey Circus toured 55 elephants around the USA in the 1920s and 1930s. The **most performers in a circus act** ever was 263 people plus around 175 animals, in the 1890 Barnum & Bailey Circus tour of the USA.

★ INVENTIVE CLOWN
Between 1927 and 1937, Charlie Cairoli (Italy) and his father devised over 700 different routines at the Cirque Medrano in Paris, France. He then played 40 consecutive seasons without repeating a routine.

★ SADDLE ROLLS IN ONE MINUTE
Ami Miller (UK) and the Funky Fools achieved 19 saddle rolls on horseback in Newcastle-Upon-Tyne, UK, on 1 September 2004.

JUGGLING AND FLASHING

OBJECTS	NUMBER	HOLDER	DATE
Balls (juggled)	10	Enrico Rastelli (Italy)	1920
		Bruce Sarafian (USA)	1996
Balls (flashed)	12	Bruce Sarafian (USA)	1995
Balls (bounced)	10	Tim Nolan (USA)	1998
Flaming torches	7	Anthony Gatto (USA)	1989
Clubs	7	Albert Petrovski (USSR)	1963
		Sorin Munteanu (Romania)	1975
		Jack Bremlov (Czechoslovakia)	1985
		Albert Lucas (USA)	1996
		Anthony Gatto (USA)	1988
		Bruce Tiemann (USA)	1995
Clubs (flashed)	8	Anthony Gatto (USA)	1989
		Scott Sorensen (USA)	1995
Batons	7	Françoise Rochais (France)	1999
Rings	11	Albert Petrovski (USSR)	1963
		Eugene Belaur (USSR)	1968
		Sergei Ignatov (USSR)	1973
Rings (flashed)	13	Albert Lucas (USA)	2002

Note: In **juggling**, the number of catches made equals the number of objects multiplied by the number of hands. When **flashing**, the number of catches made equals at least the number of objects but less than a juggle.

★ CONSECUTIVE SKIPS ON A TIGHTROPE
Juan Pedro Carrillo (USA) managed 1,323 consecutive skips with a rope on an 8.2-m-high (27-ft) wire at the Big Apple Circus Big Top in Massachusetts, USA, on 26 April 2004.

☆ SWORDS SWALLOWED
Natasha Verushka (USA) swallowed 13 swords at the Third Annual Sideshow Gathering and Sword Swallowers Convention at Wilkes-Barre, Pennsylvania, USA, on 3 September 2004.

FARTHEST...

★ HUMAN ARROW SHOT
Vesta Gueschkova (Bulgaria) was fired 22.9 m (75 ft) from a crossbow at the Ringling Bros and Barnum & Bailey Circus at Tampa, Florida, USA, on 27 December 1995.

★ FASTEST 10 KM JOGGLE WITH THREE OBJECTS
Paul-Erik Lillholm (Norway) jogged 10 km (6.2 miles) while juggling three beanbags without dropping them in 41 min 18 sec in Skansemyrer, Bergen, Norway, on 9 July 2000.

FIRE BREATHING
Robert Milton (UK, pictured) blew a flame 4.1 m (13 ft 5 in) high to achieve the ★**highest flame blown**. The **greatest distance blown** by a fire-breather is 9.4 m (31 ft) by Reg Morris (UK) on 29 October 1986.

Matthew 'Matt the Knife' Cassiere (USA) held a lit torch vertically in his teeth for 23 seconds on 30 October 2004 – the **longest duration for fire torch teething**. Antti Karvinen (Finland) extinguished 36 torches by mouth on 9 October 2000 to claim the record for ★**most torches extinguished in one minute**.

MAGIC & ILLUSION

★ MOST PROLIFIC QUICK-CHANGE ILLUSION ARTIST

Arturo Brachetti (Italy) changed costume 22,500 times during 250 performances of the show *L'Homme Aux Mille Visages*, Paris, France, in 2001–02. His quickest costume change, including shoes, took two seconds, from black tail suit to white in full view of the audience.

★ MOST VALUABLE MAGIC POSTER

There are two holders of this record. A Houdini *Water Torture Cell* lithograph by Strobridge was sold by CRG Auctions in Las Vegas, USA, on 30 October 2004 for $55,000 (£29,930) to David Copperfield (USA).

Houdini's *Water Torture Cell* (pictured), a lithograph printed by Dangerfield (UK), was auctioned on 25 May 2000 at Christie's, London, UK, and purchased by Norm Nielsen (USA) for £30,000 ($44,669).

★ FIRST MAGIC SOCIETY TO BE FEATURED ON A NATIONAL STAMP

The UK's Royal Mail issued a series of five interactive stamps on 15 March 2005, marking the centenary of The Magic Circle (UK), one of the oldest societies of magicians in the world. The issue features another first – a 'scratch and reveal' first-class stamp. Rubbing it with a coin reveals either a 'heads' or 'tails' image.

★ MOST MAGIC SHOWS PLAYING AT ONE TIME IN ONE CITY

Excluding review and variety shows, as of 1 March 2005 there were 11 magic shows playing in Las Vegas, Nevada, USA.

★ LARGEST DISPLAYED MAGIC POSTER COLLECTION

There are 587 stone lithograph magic posters on display within the collection belonging to Norm and Lupa Nielsen (both USA). The collection, which was started in 1991, includes 34 Houdini posters – 14 of which are coloured lithographs – and 64 different Chung Ling Soo lithographs.

★ LARGEST STONE LITHOGRAPH MAGIC POSTER

A 28-sheet poster printed in 1895 by the Strobridge Lithograph Company (USA) for Frederick Bancroft (USA) measured 2.74 x 7.62 m (9 x 25 ft).

★ HIGHEST SUSPENSION STRAITJACKET ESCAPE

Scott Hammell (Canada) escaped from a regulation straitjacket while suspended by a rope hanging inverted below the basket of a hot-air balloon travelling at a height of 2,194.5 m (7,200 ft) over Knoxville, Tennessee, USA, on 13 August 2003. The rope hung 15.24 m (50 ft) from the basket.

★ DEADLIEST MAGIC TRICK

At least 11 people have been killed during the bullet-catching trick, where at least one gun loaded with a marked bullet is fired at a magician, who appears to catch the bullet in his teeth or on a plate. Although the feat involves illusionary elements, it is fraught with danger. The most famous death has been Chung Ling Soo (USA, b. William Elsworth Robinson), who was shot on stage at the Wood Green Empire, London, UK, on 23 March 1918.

★ MOST CONSECUTIVE MULTI-COIN ROLLS

Jeff McBride (USA) simultaneously rolled eight silver dollars around the fingers of both his hands (four coins per hand) using the classic coin-roll technique, each completing 18 consecutive revolutions in a time of 5 min 43 sec at the Magical Arts Center, Las Vegas, Nevada, USA, on 17 July 2004.

MOST
LIVING CREATURES PRODUCED DURING A MAGIC PERFORMANCE

Penn & Teller (USA) produced more than 80,000 bees during their television special, *Don't Try This at Home*, filmed in 1990.

DAVID COPPERFIELD

David Copperfield (USA) has 11 Guinness World Records – more than any other magician. He talks to us about his achievements.

Who inspired you to become a magician?
Magic was something that I always had a feeling for, and I just seemed to be good at it. I love movies and all the fantasy and wonder that they create, but magic is what I did well. So I tried to combine the two. So the answer would be lot of people who were working in film, including Walt Disney, Orson Welles, Frank Capra and Victor Fleming.

What is your favourite magic illusion of all time?
I'm very proud of Flying, especially flying into the Plexiglas box. I also like the Death Saw and the Lottery piece with the car that appears surrounded by the audience.

Of your career so far, what are you most proud of?
The one thing I'm proudest of is Project Magic. It's a programme that I created which uses magic as a form of therapy for people who have disabilities. It's currently being used in 1,000 hospitals in 30 countries around the world.

Can you see yourself ever retiring or slowing down?
Why? My work is my play. I get to enjoy one of my passions every time I do a show. Why would I want to give that up?

What's it like to be a Guinness World Record holder?
It's a great honour to be in the same company as the fastest baked bean eater! I remember reading *Guinness World Records* as a kid. To be recognized by it is amazing.

CAN HE DO IT?
The Illusion of the Century.

David COPPERFIELD

★ MOST TICKETS SOLD WORLDWIDE BY A SOLO ENTERTAINER
From the period 1984 to 2004, the magician David Copperfield (USA) sold approximately 39,690,000 tickets to his shows.

★ MOST GENERATIONS OF MAGICIANS
The Bamberg family consisted of six generations who excelled in the art of magic for over 200 years.

LONGEST RUNNING THEATRE OF MAGIC
John Nevil Maskelyne and George Cooke (both UK) founded, produced and starred in the Maskelyne & Cooke magic theatre at the Egyptian Hall, Piccadilly, London, UK, from 26 May 1873 to 10 December 1904. After Maskelyne and business partner David Devant moved the show to St George's Hall, Langham Place,

London, UK, the daily shows were continued by the Maskelyne family until 14 October 1933.

MOST EXPENSIVE MAGIC SHOW EVER STAGED
Siegfried and Roy at the Mirage, Las Vegas, Nevada, USA, starring Siegfried Fishbacher and Roy Horn (both Germany), cost over $28 million (then £16 million) to stage when it opened on 1 February 1990. The show, which featured dozens of wild animals, a giant mechanical dragon that breathed fire and a cast of 60, closed after its 5,750th performance on 3 October 2003.

FASTEST TRANSFORMATION ILLUSION
Internationally renowned illusionists The Pendragons (USA) present Houdini's

metamorphosis illusion at a speed that would have fooled its inventor. Jonathan Pendragon is locked in a trunk on top of which his wife, Charlotte, stands. She conceals herself behind a curtain, which drops after just 0.25 seconds to reveal her husband. Charlotte is now locked in the trunk.

DAVID COPPERFIELD'S GUINNESS WORLD RECORDS

1. ★ Most tickets sold worldwide by a solo entertainer
2. ★ Highest career earnings as a magician
3. ★ Highest Broadway gross in a week
4. ★ Largest Broadway attendance in a week
5. ★ Largest international television audience for a magician
6. ★ Most magic shows performed in a year
7. ★ Largest private collection of magic artifacts
8. ★ Most valuable magic poster
9. ★ Largest work archive by a magician
10. Highest annual earnings by a magician
11. Largest illusion ever staged

LOWEST DEATH-DIVE ESCAPE →

In 1997, Robert Gallup (USA) was leg-manacled, handcuffed, chained, sealed in a secured mail bag and locked in a 0.74-m² (8-ft²) jail cell cage before being thrown out of a plane at 5,485 m (18,000 ft) above the Mojave Desert, California, USA. A minute before impact, and travelling at 240 km/h (150 mph), he escaped to reach his parachute – secured on the outside of the cage – and deployed it safely at 366 m (1,200 ft), just five seconds before impact.

COMPUTER GAMES

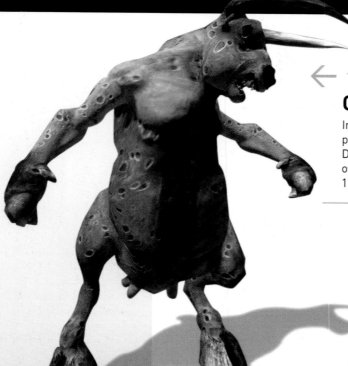

← ★ MOST COMPLEX
CHARACTER IN A COMPUTER GAME

In *Black and White II* by Lionhead Studios, due for release in late 2005, the player controls a character that trains an artificially intelligent creature. During the game, the creature learns from the player and develops its own distinct personality. The mind of a mature creature can take up to 1.2 MB of physical hard-drive space.

★ MOST VALUABLE VIRTUAL OBJECT ↓

On 11 December 2004, David Storey (Australia), aka Deathifier, paid 265,000 PEDs (Project Entropia Dollars) for an island in the MMORPG (massively multi-player online role-playing game) *Project Entropia*. Because the game allows a real exchange rate between virtual and real money, the Amethera Treasure Island was sold to Deathifier by auction for the equivalent of $26,500 (£13,700).

★ MOST PORTED COMPUTER GAME

Tetris, invented by Alexey Pajitnov (Russia) in 1987, is regarded as one of the most original yet simple ideas in game history. Since launch, its code has been translated on to more than 70 different platforms, including mobile phones.

★ LARGEST GAME OF TETRIS

In November 1995, students at Delft University of Technology, Delft, Netherlands, temporarily converted the building of the university's Faculty of Electrical Engineering into a huge version of the computer game *Tetris*. They installed a series of lights (which turned on and off to represent falling blocks) in each room of the 96-m-tall (314-ft) building. In total, the giant Tetris game used 15 storeys, each 10 rooms wide, to create a playable area of around 2,000 m² (21,500 ft²).

★ LARGEST VIDEO ARCADE

The Gran Prix Race-O-Rama Arcade in Fort Lauderdale, Florida, USA, contained 844 individual video arcade games in 1984, increasing to around 950 before being demolished in 1986 to make way for a new highway. Afterwards, it was rebuilt at a new location in Fort Lauderdale, where it contained around 1,200 games in separate buildings.

★ LARGEST CASH PRIZE WON BY AN INDIVIDUAL IN A GAMING EVENT

On 19 October 2004, Meng 'RocketBoy' Yang (China) won $125,000 (£64,894) for defeating Jonathan 'Fatal1ty' Wendell in the ACON Fatal1ty Shootout at the Great Wall of China.

★ LARGEST LAN PARTY

DreamHack Winter 2004 was the world's largest Local Area Network party. It was hosted in Jönköping, Sweden, from 25 to 28 November 2004. A total of 5,272 gamers attended, and the maximum number of computers on the LAN during the party was 5,852. It was organized by Martin Öjes and Kenny Eklund (both Sweden).

★ LONGEST SERVING PROFESSIONAL GAMING REFEREE

Walter Day (USA), founder of Twin Galaxies, has been refereeing world computer game high scores since 1982, when his database of high-score statistics was first made available to the public. He has refereed high scores ever since and has been recognized by most of the major games manufacturers.

★ LARGEST CASH PRIZE FOR A TOURNAMENT

The Cyberathlete Professional League (CPL) began hosting professional game tournaments in 1997. The CPL tournament, held in Texas, USA, in August 2004, awarded $250,000 (£129,789) to gamers as prize money.

★ MOST ACTION GAMERS PLAYING ON A SINGLE SERVER

On 27 November 2004 a team from Microsoft and Unisys (both Sweden) sustained 1,073 computer gamers playing *Counterstrike* on a single Unisys ES7000 server. The event took place as part of DreamHack Winter 2004 in Jönköping, Sweden.

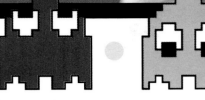

★ NEW RECORD ★ UPDATED RECORD

★ LARGEST ONLINE GAME ECONOMY

According to research by Prof. Edward Castronova at Indiana University, USA, the Kingdom of Norrath in the game *Everquest* has a gross national product per capita of $2,266 (£1,176). This is based on a market exchange rate between virtual Norrath gold coins sold on online auction sites and real world currency. This places the Kingdom of Norrath as the world's 73rd largest economy, between the actual economies of Turkey (GNP per head: $2,451, or £1,272) and Ghana (GNP per head: $2,174, or £1,128).

MOST ADVANCED BATTLEFIELD SIMULATOR

The most sophisticated battlefield computer simulator is the Combined Arms Tactical Trainer. Situated at Warminster, UK, and Sennelager, Germany, it is capable of training more than 850 personnel at once in an integrated, realistic combat scenario involving vehicles, aircraft, soldiers and weapons.

★ BEST SELLING CONSOLE GAMES

PlayStation 2: According to *Screen Digest*, the best selling game is *Grand Theft Auto Vice City* (pictured), which had sold 9 million units as of December 2003. **GameCube**: *Mario Sunshine* had sold a record 3.5 million units as of December 2003. **Xbox**: *Halo* had sold 4 million units as of December 2003.

Simulated combat arenas of more than 10,000 km² (3,800 miles²) are used. It became operational on 1 September 2002.

★ MOST EXPENSIVE COMPUTER GAME DEVELOPMENT

Enter the Matrix, published by Atari in 2003, has a story that runs in parallel to the *Matrix* movies, and features original material written and directed by brothers Andy and Larry Wachoski (USA), who wrote and directed the movies. The game includes two hours of original live action footage not seen in the movie series. Its development was reported to have cost more than $30 million (£16,873,840).

★ LONGEST RUNNING ONLINE SUBSCRIPTION GAME

Ultima Online was first launched in May 1997 by Electronic Arts, and helped define the emerging category of MMORPGs. It is now played by millions of gamers in more than 100 countries.

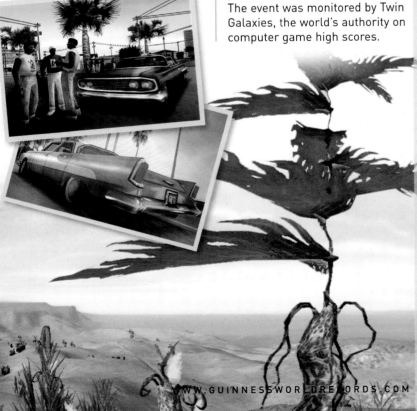

MOST SUCCESSFUL COIN-OPERATED GAME

From its launch in 1981 until 1987, a total of 293,822 *PAC-MAN* arcade machines were built and installed around the world. Designed by Tohru Iwatani (Japan) of Namco, it is estimated that *PAC-MAN* has been played more than 10 billion times in its 25-year history.

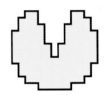

★ FIRST PERFECT PAC-MAN SCORE

The first person ever to achieve a perfect score on *PAC-MAN* was Billy Mitchell (USA). On 3 July 1999, he played the game for nearly six hours continuously, on one quarter coin, eating every dot, energizer, blue man and fruit on each of the 256 boards, after which the game runs out of memory and ends with a split screen. Billy used only one life and his final perfect score was 3,333,360 points. The event was monitored by Twin Galaxies, the world's authority on computer game high scores.

FIRST...

COMPUTER GAME
Spacewar! (1961–62)
MIT, USA (below)

VIDEO ARCADE GAME
Computer Space (1971)
By Nolan Bushnell (USA), founder of Atari

PLATFORM ARCADE GAME
Donkey Kong (1981)
Nintendo

★ MULTI-USER DUNGEON (MUD)
MUD1 (1980)
Conceived by Roy Trubshaw (UK) of Essex University

★ FULL-ANIMATION LASER DISK GAME
Dragon's Lair (1983)
Cinematronics (above)

★ 'GOD' GAME
Populous (1989) by Peter Molyneux (UK) of Bullfrog

★ REAL-TIME STRATEGY (RTS)
Dune 2 (1992) by Westwood, USA

★ FIRST-PERSON SHOOTER (PC VERSION)
Wolfenstein 3D (1992/3) by ID Software, USA

★ MMORPG (MASSIVELY MULTI-PLAYER ONLINE ROLE-PLAYING GAME)
Meridian 59 (1996) by 3DO Studios, USA

★ TALLEST BRIDGE
FROM GROUND TO HIGHEST POINT

The Millau Viaduct in France was constructed to relieve heavy traffic in the old town of Millau. Stretching for 2,460 m (8,070 ft) across the river Tarn in the Massif Central mountains, the road deck is supported by seven concrete piers, the tallest of which measures a record 343 m (1,125 ft) from the ground to the tip – more than twice the original height of the Great Pyramid at Giza, Egypt. The bridge was designed by Foster and Partners (UK) and opened to the public in December 2004.

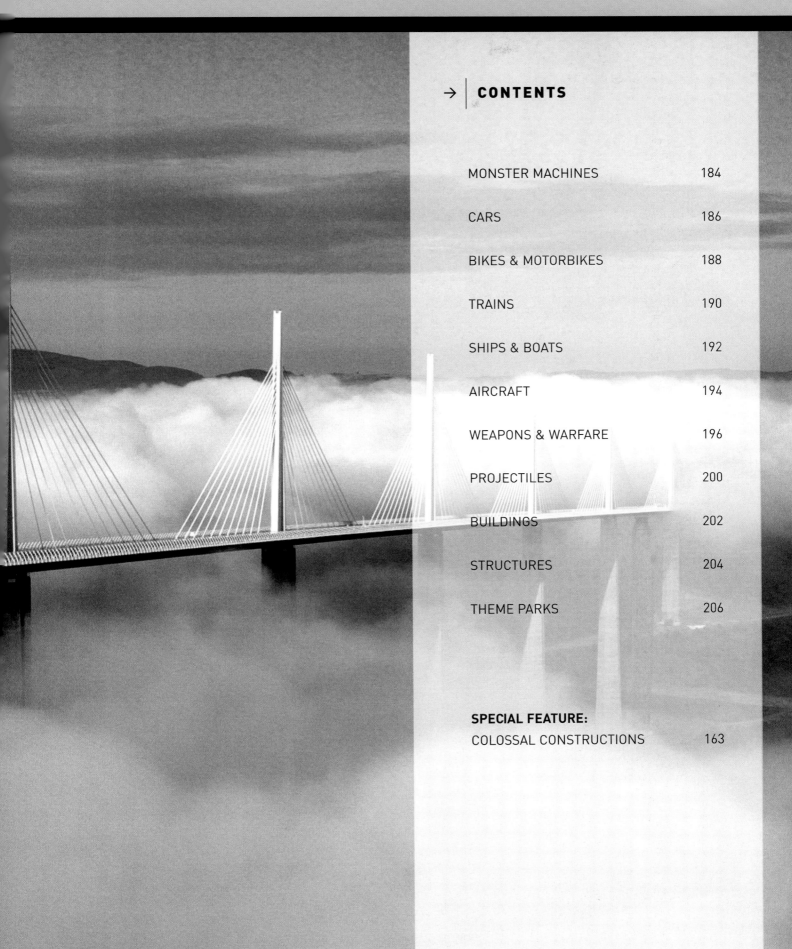

→ | **CONTENTS**

MONSTER MACHINES

← LAND VEHICLE

The 14,196-tonne (31.3 million-lb) RB293 bucket wheel excavator is an earthmoving machine 220 m (722 ft) long and 94.5 m (310 ft) tall at its highest point. It is capable of shifting 240,000 m³ (8.475 million ft³) of earth a day. The 18 buckets – each with a volume of 6,600 litres (1,452 gal; 1,743 US gal) – are fitted to the outside of a massive wheel (the bucket wheel) at the front of the vehicle, which is as tall as a four-storey building. At the scale shown opposite, a person would be only slightly larger than the full stop at the end of this sentence.

→ WHAT'S THE MOST POWERFUL PRODUCTION MOTORCYCLE IN THE WORLD? FIND OUT ON P.188

LARGEST...

AMBULANCE
Articulated Alligator Jumbulances are 18 m (59 ft) long. Operated by the Across Trust (UK), these outsized vehicles are designed to convey the sick and disabled on holidays and pilgrimages across Europe.

CAR ENGINE
The greatest engine capacity of a production car was 13.5 litres (823.8 in³) for the US Pierce-Arrow 6-66 Raceabout of 1912–18, the US Peerless 6-60 of 1912–14 and the Fageol of 1918. Despite their size, these giants from the early days of automobiles were very inefficient compared with their modern counterparts.

The ★ **largest production car engine currently in use** is the 8.275-litre (505-in³) V10 engine of the Dodge Viper SRT-10. It produces 373 kW (500 hp) of power and 712 Nm (525 lb-ft) of torque – enough to power it to 96.5 km/h (60 mph) in four seconds.

CRANE (REVOLVING PEDESTAL)
The revolving pedestal crane at the Yantai Raffles shipyard in Yantai, China, can lift 2,000 tonnes (4.4 million lb) to a height of 95 m (311 ft) from its main hook, and 200 tonnes (440,000 lb) to 135 m (443 ft) from its secondary arm. It is used in the construction of oil rigs and tall vessels.

The **largest tower crane** is the Kroll K-10000, which is capable of lifting a weight of 120 tonnes (264,500 lb) at an 82-m (269-ft) radius (i.e. the distance from the central supporting column to the weight being lifted). The Kroll K-10000 tower crane stands 120 m (393 ft) high on a rotating cylinder 12 m (39 ft 4 in) in diameter without support wires, but has 223 tonnes (491,630 lb) of counterweights to balance its 84-m-long (275-ft) boom.

★ DIESEL ENGINE
The 14-cylinder Wärtsila Sulzer RTA96C two-stroke diesel engine has a rated maximum output of 80,080 kW (108,920 hp), weighs 2,300 tonnes (5.07 million lb), and is 13.5 m (44 ft 4 in) tall and 27.3 m (89 ft 6 in) wide. Each of the engine's pistons is 960 mm (37.8 in) in diameter and has a 2.5-m (8-ft 2-in) stroke. The Wärtsila Sulzer RTA96C is designed to be used in the world's largest container ships.

← ★ RACING VEHICLES

The trucks in the FIA European Truck Racing Championship weigh at least 5,500 kg (12,125 lb). They typically sport 12-litre (732-in³) turbocharged engines that generate over 746 kW (1,000 hp) of power and 3,000 Nm (2,200 lb-ft) of torque. Despite this massive power, their top speed is limited to 160 km/h (99 mph) for safety reasons.

★ AUTOMATED PARKING FACILITY

The two 48-m-tall (157-ft) 'car towers' at Volkswagen's Autostadt in Wolfsburg, Germany, can each store 400 cars. Car buyers at the Autostadt are treated to the sight of their new car being retrieved and delivered to them from one of the 20-storey towers (inset, left) by an automated system that travels at up to 2 m/s (6.6 ft/s).

DRAGLINE EXCAVATOR

Big Muskie, a walking earthmoving machine weighing 13,200 tonnes (29.1 million lb) – nearly as much as 10,000 saloon cars – moved 3.6 million m³ (127 million ft³) of earth during its operational life. That's nearly twice the amount excavated in the creation of the Panama Canal.

★ DUMPER TRUCK

The Liebherr T 282 B has a payload capacity of 363 tonnes (800,000 lb). It is 14.5 m (47 ft 6 in) long, 8.8 m (28 ft 10 in) wide, 7.4 m (24 ft 3 in) high and weighs over 200 tonnes (441,000 lb) empty. Its tyres are twice as tall as an average man.

MONSTER TRUCK

Bigfoot 5 is 4.7 m (15 ft 6 in) tall with 3-m-tall (10-ft) tyres and weighs 17,236 kg (38,000 lb). Built in 1986 as one in a series of 17 created by Bob Chandler of St Louis, USA, *Bigfoot 5* is now permanently parked in St Louis, USA, and makes occasional appearances at local shows.

★ TRACTOR

In 1978, Northern Manufacturing of Havre, Montana, USA, built a tractor weighing around 43 tonnes (95,000 lb) without ballast. A one-off vehicle, the 670-kW (900-hp) Big Bud 16V-747, is powered by a 16-cylinder, 24-litre (1,46-in³) dual turbo Detroit Diesel engine and has eight giant tyres, each 2.4 m (7 ft 10 in) in diameter.

The ★**most powerful tractor** record is held by the John Deere 9620T and the Caterpillar Challenger MT865, both of which have a claimed power output of 373 kW (500 hp).

The 9620T has four-wheel drive, with four sets of double wheels, and weighs 17.69 tonnes (39,000 lb) without ballast. The MT865 is powered by a 14.6-litre (890-in³) engine and runs on tracks.

TUNNEL BORING MACHINE

The boring machine being used to carve the 7-km-long (4.3-mile) Groene Hart Tunnel from Amsterdam to Rotterdam, the Netherlands, measures 14.87 m (48 ft 9 in) in diameter by 120 m (393 ft) long and weighs 3,520 tonnes (7,760,271 lb).

★ LONGEST TRIKE

Anaconda measures 5.94 m (19 ft 6 in) long and sits up to 10 riders. It was constructed by Stephen McGill (USA), weighs 644 kg (1,420 lb) and consists of a 1998 Harley Davidson Electra-Glide with a custom-built rear end. It is licensed for road use.

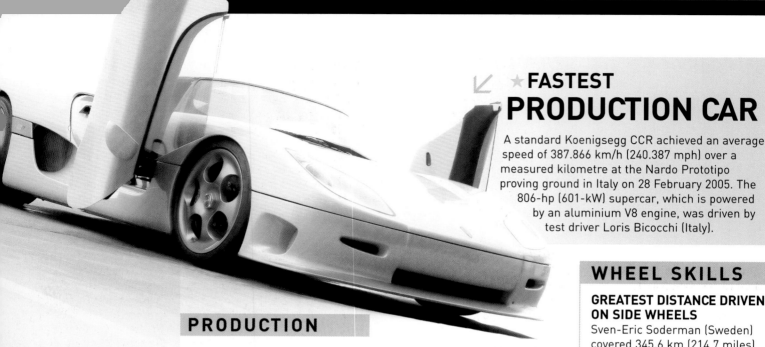

FASTEST PRODUCTION CAR

A standard Koenigsegg CCR achieved an average speed of 387.866 km/h (240.387 mph) over a measured kilometre at the Nardo Prototipo proving ground in Italy on 28 February 2005. The 806-hp (601-kW) supercar, which is powered by an aluminium V8 engine, was driven by test driver Loris Bicocchi (Italy).

WHEEL SKILLS

GREATEST DISTANCE DRIVEN ON SIDE WHEELS
Sven-Eric Soderman (Sweden) covered 345.6 km (214.7 miles) driving a car on two side wheels at Mora Siljan Airport, Dalarna, Sweden, on 25 September 1999. In an event lasting 10 hr 38 min, he covered 108 laps of a circuit 3.2 km (1.9 miles) long.

★ LONGEST RAMP JUMP WITH CARAVAN
Professional stuntman Derek Lea (UK) jumped a distance of 57.2 m (187 ft 8 in) in a car towing a full-size caravan at Bentwaters Parks, Suffolk, UK, on 5 May 2004 for the TV motoring show *5th Gear*.

LONGEST HORIZONTAL POWER SLIDE
On 29 July 2001 at the MIRA Proving Ground, Nuneaton, UK, Simon de Banke (UK) performed a slide that lasted 2 hr 11 min 18 sec. He was driving a standard Subaru Impreza WRX 2001. The road surface was Bridgeport pebbles, which, when wet, have similar handling characteristics to compacted snow.

★ FASTEST TIME TO DO 10 DONUTS IN A CAR
On 11 September 2004, Russ Swift (UK) performed 10 donuts (360° spins) in 16.07 seconds in a Mitsubishi Lancer Evo VIII on the set of *Guinness World Records: 50 Years, 50 Records* at London Studios, UK.

PRODUCTION

★ MOST FUEL-EFFICIENT CAR
Team FANCY CAROL-NOK (Japan) achieved a fuel consumption of 0.0245 litres/100 km (11,524.915 mpg) around a 19.2-km (11.9-mile) course during the Super Mileage Car Contest 2004 at the Hiroshima License Centre, Japan, on 29 August 2004.

★ MOST PRODUCED AUTOMOBILE
The Ford F-series nameplate has appeared on more vehicles than any other, with more than 29.3 million F-series pick-up trucks having been produced. The first in the series, the F1, was first produced in 1948, and an F-150 truck provided the bodywork for the original *Bigfoot* monster truck.

Between 800,000 and 900,000 F-series trucks are sold annually, largely in North America, accounting for nearly one eighth of Ford's global sales.

★ MOST PRODUCED CAR
Toyota Corolla is the name that has appeared on more cars than any other, with in excess of 28.2 million units produced worldwide.

However, the vehicle itself has undergone a total of nine transformations since it was first produced in 1966 and cannot, strictly speaking, be said to be the same car.

★ BEST-SELLING HYBRID (DUAL-FUEL) CAR
Over 250,000 Toyota Prius hybrid cars have been sold globally since 1997. In 2004, Toyota announced that global production would rise from 10,000 to 15,000 units a month to meet growing demand, especially in the US market where around 100,000 were expected to be sold in 2005 alone.

★ BEST-SELLING TWO-SEATER SPORTS CAR
Mazda Motor Corporation (Japan) has produced in excess of 700,000 units of the Mazda roadster (known as the Miata in North America and the MX-5 in Europe), an open two-seater sports car, since production began in April 1989 at Mazda's production plant in Hiroshima, Japan.

★LONGEST OWNERSHIP OF VEHICLE

John P O'Hara (USA) bought a new 1953 Chevrolet Bel-Air in Detroit, Michigan, USA, in June 1953 and has owned the vehicle ever since. It remains in mint condition.

MOST EXPENSIVE REGISTRATION

Licence plate No.9 was sold at a Hong Kong, China, government auction for HK\$13 million (US\$1.7 million; £1.1 million) on 19 March 1994 to Albert Yeung Sau-shing (China). In Cantonese, the pronunciation of the word 'nine' is identical to the word 'dog' and was considered lucky because 1994 was the Year of the Dog.

★MOST SIMULTANEOUS DONUTS BY THE SAME DRIVER

Terry Grant (UK) had three cars performing donuts at the MPH'04 show at Earl's Court, London, UK, on 20 November 2004.

FASTEST...

★CARAVAN TOW

On 24 October 2003, a Mercedes Benz S600 driven by Eugene Herbert (South Africa) reached a speed of 223.881 km/h (139.113 mph) while towing a standard caravan at Hoedspruit Air Force Base, South Africa. The record attempt was organized by Risk Administrative Consultants.

★DIESEL-ENGINED CAR

Virgil W Snyder (USA) reached a speed of 379.4 km/h (235.7 mph) in a streamliner called *Thermo King-Wynns* at Bonneville Salt Flats, Utah, USA, on 25 August 1973.

★WHEEL-DRIVEN VEHICLE

Al Teague (USA) reached an average speed of 659.808 km/h (409.986 mph) over two runs, with a peak speed of 696.331 km/h (432.692 mph), in *Spirit of '76*, at Bonneville Salt Flats, Utah, USA, on 21 August 1991.

MISCELLANEOUS

LARGEST PRODUCTION CAR

The Bugatti 'Royale' type 41, known in the UK as the 'Golden Bugatti', was built in 1927 and measures over 6.7 m (22 ft) in length, with the hood itself more than 2.13 m (7 ft) long.

LONGEST CAR

Jay Ohrberg (USA) designed a 30.5-m- (100-ft-) long, 26-wheeled limo. The car incorporates many features, including a swimming pool with diving board, a king-sized water bed and a helipad.

★MOST POWERFUL PRODUCTION CAR

The Bugatti Veyron, due to go into production in September 2005, has a claimed output of 736 kW (988 hp) from its 8-litre (488-in³), 16-cylinder engine. The engine has four turbochargers. The top speed has not been officially tested, but Bugatti claims it is capable of speeds of over 400 km/h (248 mph).

★LONGEST RUNNING CAR POOL

M te Lindert, A Hogendoorn, J Kalisvaart and JJ Kooy (all Netherlands) belong to a car pool that began on 1 January 1972 and has been running ever since between their homes and their workplace.

★LARGEST PRODUCTION PICK-UP TRUCK

The International Truck & Engine Company's (USA) 7300 CXT is the world's largest standard pick-up truck, weighing in at 6,577 kg (14,500 lb). Although it is 6.55 m (21 ft 6 in) long and 2.74 m (9 ft) high, it can be driven with a standard driving licence.

BIKES & MOTORBIKES

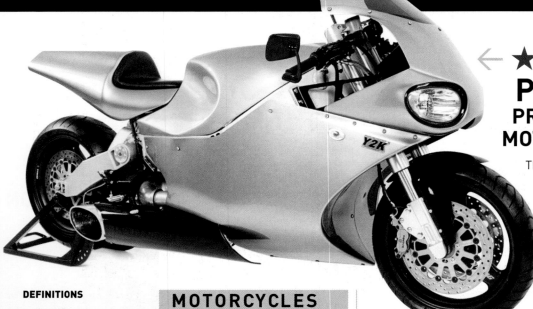

★ MOST POWERFUL PRODUCTION MOTORCYCLE

The $185,000 (£101,000) MTT Turbine Superbike's Rolls-Royce Allison gas-turbine engine is claimed by its manufacturer to supply 213 kW (286 hp) of power at the rear wheel, with 576 N.m (425 lb-ft) of torque at 2,000 rpm.

This makes the Superbike the most powerful motorcycle ever to enter series production.

DEFINITIONS

cc (cu in): cubic cm (cubic inch). A measure of volume capacity used to define engine size.

kW (hp): kilowatts (horsepower). A measure of power.

N.m (lb-ft): Newton metres (foot-pounds). A measure of torque. One Newton metre is the force required to give a mass of 1 kilogram an acceleration of 1 metre per second per second at a distance of 1 metre from the fulcrum.

Torque: A measure of the 'twisting' force an engine can apply to its crankshaft (and therefore to a vehicle's wheels).

MOTORCYCLES

★ LONGEST SIDE-WHEEL RIDE ON A QUAD BIKE

Ron Flerlage (USA) covered a distance of 19.3 km (12.8 miles) on two side wheels of his quad bike around an athletics track at Scott High School, Covington, Kentucky, USA, on 5 October 2003.

★ HIGHEST SPEED ON A QUAD BIKE

Graham 'G-Force' Hicks (UK) reached a speed of 214.07 km/h (133.02 mph) on a quad bike at RAF Wittering, UK, on 14 August 2004. Because Hicks is deaf-blind, Brian Sharman (UK) rode pillion and communicated steering instructions to him through a touch system.

★ HIGHEST MOTORCYCLE SPEED (RIDING BACKWARDS)

Dave Coates (UK) reached a speed of 244.1 km/h (151.7 mph) on a motorcycle sitting with his back to the handlebars at Elvington airfield, Yorkshire, UK, on 28 October 2002.

★ FASTEST MOTORCYCLE WHEELIE OVER A KILOMETRE

Dave Rogers (UK) reached a speed of 220.3 km/h (136.9 mph) while performing a motorcycle wheelie over 1 km (3,281 ft) at Elvington airfield, Yorkshire, UK, on 28 October 2002.

★ MOST POWERFUL PRODUCTION MOTORCYCLE WITH A PISTON ENGINE

Based on manufacturers' claims, the most powerful piston-powered motorcycle in production is the 1,198-cc (73.1-cu-in) Kawasaki Ninja ZX-12R, which has a power output of 131 kW (175.6 hp) without a forced-air system (RAM), and 140 kW (187.7 hp) with RAM air. However, rivals Honda, Suzuki and Yamaha all produce sports bikes with claimed power outputs in excess of 127 kW (170 hp).

★ MOST EXPENSIVE PRODUCTION MOTORCYCLE

The MTT Turbine Superbike, powered by a Rolls-Royce Allison gas turbine engine, went on sale in 2004 for $185,000 (£101,000).

★ LARGEST SIMULTANEOUS MOTORCYCLE BURN-OUT

A total of 37 motorcycles took part in a 'burn-out' organized by IBM Klub Motobiking at Heidesheim, Germany, on 28 August 2004. A burn-out consists of spinning the rear wheel of the motorcycle while it is stationary, burning rubber and creating smoke.

★ MOST PEOPLE ON A QUAD BIKE WHEELIE

Roger LeBlanc (Canada) wheelied an unmodified Honda 350 Fourtrax ATV carrying 16 people for over 50 m (165 ft) at Riverglade Speedway, New Brunswick, Canada, on 15 May 2004.

SPEED RECORDS
all records: Fédération Internationale de Motocyclisme   ** all speeds average over 1 km (flying start)

CLASS*	RIDER	MOTORCYCLE	PLACE	DATE	SPEED**
★ 50 cc	Jan Huberts (Netherlands)	Casal Plompen	Lelystad, Netherlands	03/08/81	224.580 km/h (139.547 mph)
★ 125 cc	AJ Smit (Netherlands)	Cagiva Plompen	Lelystad, Netherlands	03/08/81	257.113 km/h (159.762 mph)
★ 250 cc	Fabrizio Braccini Lazari (Italy)	Aprilia	Nardo, Italy	27/08/95	254.021 km/h (157.841 mph)
★ 500 cc	Ron Haslam (UK)	Honda Elf 3	Nardo, Italy	14/09/86	278.853 km/h (173.271 mph)
★ 1,000 cc	Christian Le Liard (France)	Holda Elf	Nardo, Italy	14/09/86	306.491 km/h (190.444 mph)
★ 1,300 cc	Nicolas Brisset (France)	Suzuki GSX	Nardo, Italy	23/06/02	338.221 km/h (210.160 mph)
'Absolute'	Dave Campos (USA)	Easyriders	Bonneville, USA	14/07/90	518.450 km/h (322.150 mph)

★ FASTEST → MONOWHEEL

Kerry McLean (USA) reached 91.7 km/h (57 mph) on a monowheel at Irwindale Speedway, California, USA, on 10 January 2001. His 1.22-m-diameter (48-in) monowheel was powered by a 340-cc (20.7-cu-in) snowmobile engine generating 30 kW (40 hp). A monowheel consists of a wheel that revolves around a track, which houses the rider and engine.

★ LONGEST FORKS

William Longest, Rick Dozer, Bill Decker and Rob Moore (all USA) built a rideable chopper-style motorcycle – the world's **longest motorcycle** – with 4.57-m-long (15-ft) forks. It is 1.8 m (6 ft) tall at its highest point and measures 8.9 m (29 ft 3 in) wheel to wheel. William Longest rode it on a public road near Georgetown, Kentucky, USA, on 15 June 2003.

★ MOST PIROUETTES ON A MOTORCYCLE IN 30 SECONDS

Horst Hoffman (Germany) pulled off 16 pirouettes (360° spins) on the rear wheel of his motorcycle in 30 seconds on the set of *Guinness World Records: Die Grössten Weltrekorde* in Cologne, Germany, on 23 January 2004.

BICYCLES

★ LONGEST BICYCLE

The longest true bicycle – one with only two wheels and no stabilizers – is 28.1 m (92 ft 2 in) long, and was built by engineering students at Delft University of Technology. It was ridden in excess of 100 m (328 ft) at Delft, the Netherlands, on 11 December 2002.

★ TALLEST BICYCLE

Terry Goertzen (Canada) rode a true bicycle 5.55 m (18 ft 2.5 in) tall – without stabilizers – for over 300 m (1,000 ft) at North Kildonan Mennonite Brethren Church, Canada, on 26 June 2004.

★ LARGEST PEDAL-POWERED VEHICLE

Jacques Frechette (Canada) built a pedal-powered vehicle capable of carrying 74 riders. It was ridden for 3.5 km (2.17 miles) through the town of Laurierville in Quebec, Canada, on 31 July 2004. Also, 72 of the 74 passengers shared the same surname: Bergeron.

★ GREATEST DEPTH CYCLED UNDERWATER

Vittorio Innocente (Italy) cycled to a depth of 52.5 m (172.2 ft) on the ocean floor off Genoa, Italy, on 23 July 2002. He used scuba gear and a standard mountain bike modified with small lead weights and a plastic wing behind the seat. The tyres were also flooded to reduce buoyancy.

On 4 May 2003, Innocente also set the ★ **farthest underwater cycling** record by pedalling for 2 km (1.24 miles) on the bottom of the Naviglio canal in Milan, Italy. It took him 36 min 38.15 sec.

★ LIGHTEST RACING BIKE

Sub 4.0 is a rideable full-size racing bicycle – built by Mirko Glöckner (Germany) – weighing just 3.89 kg (8 lb 9.2 oz). It has a carbon-fibre frame weighing 873 g (1 lb 14.7 oz) and components made largely of aluminium, titanium and carbon fibre.

★ FASTEST BICYCLE WHEELIE

Bobby Root (USA) reached a speed of 138.56 km/h (86.1 mph) while riding on the rear wheel of his bicycle at Palmdale, California, USA, on 31 January 2001 for *Guinness World Records: Primetime*. The **highest speed ever** achieved on a bicycle is 268.831 km/h (166.944 mph).

FARTHEST DISTANCE CYCLED (NO HANDS) IN ONE HOUR

Shai Hadar (Israel) cycled a distance of 20.8 km (12.92 miles) in one hour without his hands touching the handlebars at the Wingate Institute near Netanya, Israel, on 18 October 2002.

BICYCLE BALANCING

Rudi Jan Jozef De Greef (Belgium) stayed stationary on his bicycle – without any means of support – for a total of 10 hours at Meensel-Kiezegem, Belgium, on 19 November 1982.

★ FASTEST DOWNHILL WHEELIE (FLYING START)

Gilles Cruchaud (Switzerland) covered 500 m (1,640 ft) of a downhill course on the back wheel of is bicycle in 26.341 seconds, averaging a speed of 68.33 km/h (42.45 mph) at Col de l'Aiguillon, Switzerland, on 12 July 2004.

LONGEST STRAIGHT RAILROAD

The Trans-Australian line over the Nullarbor Plain runs dead straight, though not level, for 478 km (297 miles). The section runs from Mile 496 – between Nurina and Loongana, Western Australia – to Mile 793 – between Ooldea and Watson, South Australia. The word 'nullarbor' literally means 'no trees', and is a reflection of the lack of vegetation on this virtually uninhabited limestone plateau.

★ BUSIEST NATIONAL RAILWAY SYSTEM

Japan's railways carried an estimated 8.6 billion passengers during 2003, making the system the world's busiest in terms of the number of people using it, according to the International Union of Railways (UIC). India was second with nearly 5.2 billion passengers, and Germany third with nearly 1.7 billion passengers.

★ BUSIEST RAILWAY COMPANY

In 2003, the East Japan Railway Company carried 5.846 billion passengers, with an average of 16 million a day. The company operates 7,530 km (4,679 miles) of network in the east of Japan, including the busy Tokyo metropolitan area.

★ BUSIEST UNDERGROUND RAILWAY

The Moscow Metro in Russia carries 8–9 million passengers each day. By comparison, the New York City Subway, the world's **largest urban railway system**, carries 4.5 million people each day, and the London Underground – the **oldest metro system** – just under 3 million.

★ MOST FREQUENT TRAVELLERS BY TRAIN

Swiss citizens cover an average distance of 2,077 km (1,290 miles) by train each year, closely followed by the Japanese, who travel 1,900 km (1,180 miles) on railways annually.

★ SMALLEST ARMOURED TRAIN

During World War II, the 381-mm-gauge (15-in) Romney, Hythe & Dymchurch Railway, which runs between Hythe and Dungeness along the coast of Kent, UK, was requisitioned by the British government. One steam locomotive, *Hercules*, and several carriages were given steel armour, and machine guns were mounted on the train, both as a defence against invasion and to protect trains transporting war goods. With a track gauge roughly one quarter the width of standard gauge, the locomotives and carriages were correspondingly diminutive.

★ HIGHEST ALTITUDE RAILWAY TUNNEL

The Fenghuo Mount railway tunnel is situated at 4,905 m (16,092 ft) on the Qinghai-Tibet Railway as it passes over the Qinghai-Tibet Highland between China and Tibet. It is 1,338 m (4,390 ft) long and was built between 18 October 2001 and 30 September 2003.

★ LARGEST HIGH-SPEED RAIL NETWORK

According to the UIC, Japan has the world's largest high-speed rail network, with 2,700 km (1,678 miles) of high-speed lines in operation or under construction. The country opened the world's first dedicated high-speed line – between Tokyo and Osaka – in 1964.

FASTEST STEAM LOCOMOTIVE

The London North Eastern Railway 'Class A4' No 4468 *Mallard* recorded a speed of 201 km/h (125 mph) while hauling seven coaches weighing 243 tonnes (535,722 lb) down Stoke Bank, near Essendine, between Grantham, Lincolnshire, and Peterborough, Cambridgeshire, UK, on 3 July 1938.

★ FASTEST PROPELLER-DRIVEN TRAIN

The 'Rail Zeppelin' built by the German engineer Franz Kruckenberg reached a speed of 230 km/h (143 mph) during a test run on 21 June 1931 between Hamburg and Berlin, Germany. The vehicle received its nickname because of the large propeller mounted behind the passenger compartment and its lightweight steel and canvas construction. It was powered by a 433-kW (580-hp) BMW aircraft engine but never entered regular service.

★ NEW RECORD   UPDATED RECORD

LONGEST TRAIN JOURNEY WITHOUT CHANGING TRAINS

A continuous 10,214-km (6,346-mile) train journey can be taken from Moscow, Russia, to Pyongyang, North Korea. One train a week makes the journey by this route, which includes sections of the famous Trans-Siberian line. It is scheduled to take 7 days 20 hr 25 min. Pictured right, the Trans-Siberian stretch is shown as a thin lateral line; the dark area near the centre of this line is the Russian city of Omsk.

FASTEST TRAIN JOURNEY (AVERAGE SPEED)

The West Japan Railway Company operates its 500-Series-Nozomi bullet trains (Shinkansen) at an average speed of 261.8 km/h (162.7 mph) on the 192-km (119-mile) line between Hiroshima and Kokura on the island of Honshu, Japan.

FASTEST TRAIN IN REGULAR PUBLIC SERVICE

The magnetically levitated (maglev) train linking China's Shanghai International Airport and the city's financial district reaches a top speed of 431 km/h (267.8 mph) on each 30-km (18.6-mile) run. The train had its official maiden run on 31 December 2002.

FASTEST MAGLEV TRAIN

The MLX01, a manned maglev train, reached a speed of 581 km/h (361 mph) on 2 December 2003. It was operated by the Central Japan Railway Company and Railway Technical Research Institute and ran on the Yamanashi Maglev Test Line, Yamanashi Prefecture, Japan.

★ FIRST MAGLEV TRAIN TO ENTER PUBLIC SERVICE

A maglev train ran for 600 m (1,968 ft) between Birmingham International Airport and the nearby Birmingham International Interchange in West Midlands, UK, from 1984 to 1995. It was taken out of service owing to the high cost of replacing worn parts.

FASTEST TRAIN ON A NATIONAL RAIL SYSTEM

On 18 May 1990, a French SNCF high-speed TGV Atlantique train (No.325) reached 515.3 km/h (320.2 mph) on a national rail system (as opposed to a dedicated test track) between Courtalain and Tours, France.

FASTEST DIESEL TRAIN

A British Rail InterCity 125 train achieved a speed of 238 km/h (148 mph) on a test run between Darlington and York, UK, on 1 November 1987.

HEAVIEST FREIGHT TRAIN

On 21 June 2001, a train assembled by BHP Iron Ore (Australia) was weighed at 99,732.1 tonnes (220 million lb). At 7.35 km (4.5 miles) long, it was also the **longest freight train ever**.

FASTEST RAILED VEHICLE (ROCKET SLED)

A four-stage rocket sled system accelerated an 87-kg (192-lb) payload to a speed of 2,886 m/s (9,468 ft/s) in 6.031 seconds at Holloman High Speed Test Track, Holloman Air Force Base, New Mexico, USA, on 30 April 2003. This is equivalent to 10,385 km/h (6,453 mph).

SHIPS & BOATS

←★LONGEST SLOOP

The 75.2-m (246.7-ft) luxury vessel *Mirabella V* is the world's longest sloop, or single-masted yacht. The state-of-the-art ship has a composite hull, a 150-tonne (330,000-lb) lifting keel and, at 90 m (295 ft) high, the world's **tallest mast**.

LARGEST...

★PASSENGER-CARRYING CAPACITY FOR A SHIP

The vessels with the largest standard passenger loads are the Staten Island ferry (New York City, USA) sister ships *Andrew J Barberi* and *Samuel I Newhouse*. Each can carry 6,000 passengers and is 95 m (310 ft) long and 21 m (69 ft 10 in) wide with a speed of 16 knots (30 km/h, or 19 mph).

★DRY BULK CARRIER SHIP

The *Berge Stahl* can carry 364,767 tonnes (804.1 million lb) of cargo (typically iron ore). The vessel, owned by Bergesen of Norway, is 343 m (1,125 ft) long and 63.5 m (208 ft) wide.

PASSENGER LINER

The Cunard Line's *Queen Mary 2*, which made its maiden voyage in January 2004, is 345 m (1,132 ft) long, and has a beam of 41 m (135 ft). At around 150,000 gross registered tons (grt), *Queen Mary 2* is nearly three times larger than *Titanic* (46,000 grt), with space for 2,620 passengers and 1,253 crew.

★DRILLSHIP

Discoverer Enterprise, Discoverer Spirit and *Discoverer Deep Seas* each displace 103,000 tonnes (227 million lb). The vessels are owned by Transocean, Inc. (USA) and are capable of drilling in more than 3,050 m (10,000 ft) of water, and to depths of 10,650 m (35,000 ft). The ships are 255 m (835 ft) long and 38 m (125 ft) wide.

ICEBREAKER

The 306.9-m-long (1,007-ft) SS *Manhattan* was converted into a 152,407-tonne (335 million-lb) icebreaker, fitted with steel armour 2.7 m (9 ft) thick, 9.1 m (30 ft) deep and 204 m (670 ft) long. It made a double voyage through the North-West Passage in arctic Canada in August 1969.

★RESCUE OPERATION BY A SINGLE SHIP

During the Korean War, the freighter SS *Meredith Victory* evacuated 14,000 civilian refugees to safety from Hungnam, North Korea, to Pusan, South Korea, in a single voyage between 22 and 25 December 1950.

CARGO VESSEL

The oil tanker *Jahre Viking* (formerly the *Happy Giant* and *Seawise Giant*) can carry 564,763 tonnes (1,245 billion lb) of cargo, fuel and stores (deadweight tonnage). It is 458.45 m (1,504 ft) long, has a beam of 68.8 m (226 ft) and a draught of 24.61 m (80 ft 9 in).

PRIVATE YACHT

The Saudi Arabian royal yacht *Abdul Aziz* is 147 m (482 ft) long. Completed on 22 June 1984 at Vospers Yard, Southampton, UK, it was estimated in 1987 to be worth more than $100 million (£53.8 million).

★RACING TRIMARAN (YACHT)

The trimaran *Geronimo*, skippered by Olivier de Kersauson (France), is 34 m (111 ft) long and has a 22-m (72-ft) beam. It was built at the Multiplast yard at Vannes, France, between 1999 and 2001.

WATER SPEED RECORDS

RECORD	PILOT/CAPTAIN (NATIONALITY)	VESSEL NAME (DATE)	SPEED
Human-powered vessel	Mark Drela (USA)	*Decavitator* (1991)	18.5 knots (34.2 km/h; 21.2 mph)
Passenger liner	USA	*United States* (1952)	44 knots (81.4 km/h; 50.63 mph)
Destroyer (warship)	France	*Le Terrible* (1935)	45.25 knots (83.42 km/h; 52 mph)
Sailing vessel	Simon McKeon (Australia)	*Yellow Pages Endeavour* (1993)	46.5 knots (86.1 km/h; 53.5 mph)
Windsurfer	Finian Maynard (Ireland)	--	46.82 knots (86.71 km/h; 53.87 mph)
Aquabike (PWC)	Forrest Smith (USA)	Yamaha GP1200R (2002)	122.79 km/h (76.17 mph)
Propeller power boat	Dave Villwock (USA)	*Miss Budweiser* (2004)	354.84 km/h (220.49 mph)
Overall water speed	Ken Warby (Australia)	*Spirit of Australia* (1977)	275.97 knots (511.1 km/h; 317.5 mph)

★LARGEST OPEN-DECK TRANSPORT SHIP

The semi-submersible *Blue Marlin* has a flat open cargo deck 178.2 m (584 ft) long and 63 m (206 ft 8 in) wide and is capable of carrying oversized cargo weighing 76,061 tonnes (167.6 million lb). The giant carrier, which is operated by Dockwise of the Netherlands, is able to submerge its deck to a depth of 16 m (52 ft 6 in) to allow it to load its giant cargoes – typically oil and gas platforms – by floating underneath them. →

FASTEST...

★PASSENGER LINER

The SS *United States* reached speeds in excess of 44 knots (81.4 km/h; 50.63 mph) during sea trials and cruised across the Atlantic at an average speed of 34.51 knots (63.9 km/h; 39.7 mph) in 1952. It was 301.9 m (990 ft 6 in) long, but its speed was due to its light weight (aluminium was used in its construction) and powerful 180,000-kW (241,000-hp) engines.

★HIGHEST SPEED UNDER SAIL ON WATER

The highest speed reached under sail on water is 46.82 knots (86.71 km/h; 53.87 mph) by Finian Maynard (Ireland) on a windsurfer at Saintes-Maries-de-la-Mer, France, on 13 November 2004. By way of comparison, the fastest animal on land over long distances, the pronghorn (*Antilocapra americana*), reaches speeds of 56 km/h (35 mph).

★GREATEST DISTANCE COVERED IN A MONOHULL IN 24 HOURS

The monohull yacht *Mari-Cha IV*, captained by Robert Miller (UK) and sailed by a crew of 24, covered a distance of 525.7 nautical miles (973.59 km; 604.96 miles) under sail on 6–7 October 2003.

DISTANCE SAILED IN 24 HOURS

The greatest distance covered by sail power alone in a 24-hour period is 694.78 nautical miles (1,286.73 km; 799.5 statute miles) – more than 1.2 times the entire length of the UK – by the 33.5-m (110-ft) maxi catamaran *Maiden 2* in the North Atlantic on 12 and 13 June 2002.

★PROPELLER-DRIVEN BOAT

Dave Villwock (USA) reached a top speed of 354.849 km/h (220.493 mph) in *Miss Budweiser*, an unlimited-class hydroplane, on 13 March 2004 at Thermalito Afterbay, Oroville, California, USA. The boat is powered by a Lycoming T-55 L-7 turbine engine from a Chinook helicopter, which is rated at 1,976 kW (2,650 hp).

←★OLDEST COMMISSIONED WARSHIP AFLOAT

The USS *Constitution* – also known as 'Old Ironsides' – was commissioned on 21 October 1797 and remains on the US navy ship roster with a crew of between 50 and 80 active duty navy sailors. *Constitution*'s home port is Charlestown, Massachusetts, USA, and it makes occasional trips to sea.

SHIP SIZE COMPARISONS
1 cm = 130 m

Abdul Aziz
Largest private yacht
Length: 147 m (482 ft)

Blue Marlin
Largest open-deck transport ship
Length: 178.2 m (584 ft)

Titanic
Length: 269 m (882 ft)

Queen Mary 2
Largest passenger ship
Length: 345 m (1,132 ft)

Jahre Viking
Largest cargo vessel
Length: 458.45 m (1,504 ft)

AIRCRAFT

LARGEST CARGO
AIRCRAFT BY VOLUME

The Airbus A300-600ST Super Transporter 'Beluga' has a cargo deck with a volume of 1,400 m³ (49,440 ft³), and is 37.7 m (123 ft 8 in) long, with a maximum height and width of 7.1 m (23 ft 3 in). Its maximum payload weight is 47 tonnes (103,610 lb). The schematic (inset) shows how the plane is front-loaded.

SPEED RECORDS

★ **Paraglider**: Edel Energy 30/Patrick Berod (France) 28.26 km/h (17.55 mph)

★ **Hang-glider**: Moyes Delta Gliders Litespeed 4/Tomas Suchanek (Czech Republic) 50.81 km/h (31.57 mph)

★ **Microlight**: B-612/Pavel Skarytka (Czech Republic) 194.2 km/h (120.67 mph)

★ **Glider**: Jantor STD11/ Horacio Miranda (Argentina) 249.09 km/h (154.77 mph)

Helicopter: Westland Lynx/ John Trevor Eggington (UK) 400.86 km/h (249.08 mph)

Production jet aircraft: Lockheed Martin SR-71/ Capt. E Joersz and Maj. G Morgan (both USA) 3,529.56 km/h (2,193.17 mph)

Rocket aircraft: X-15A2/ Pete Knight (USA) 7,274 km/h (4,520 mph)

★ **Air-breathing (jet) aircraft**: X-43A/unmanned 10,300 km/h (6,400 mph)

FLIGHTS

HIGHEST ALTITUDE BY AN AIRCRAFT

The Fédération Aéronautique Internationale (FAI) altitude record is 37,650 m (123,523 ft), by Alexandr Fedotov (USSR) flying a highly modified MIG-25 'Foxbat' (designated E266M) from Podmoskovnoe Aerodrome, Russia, on 31 August 1977.

HIGHEST ALTITUDE FLIGHT BY A HELICOPTER

Jean Bouletan (France) reached an altitude of 12,442 m (40,820 ft) in an Aérospatiale SA315B 'Lama' helicopter over Istres, France, on 21 June 1972.

★ FASTEST AIR-BREATHING AIRCRAFT

On 16 November 2004, Nasa's unmanned Hyper-X (X-43A) aircraft reached Mach 9.68, almost 10 times the speed of sound. It was boosted to an altitude of 33,000 m (115,000 ft) by a Pegasus rocket launched from beneath a B52-B aircraft. The 'scramjet' aircraft then burned its engine before crashing into the Pacific Ocean.

★ LONGEST FLIGHT BY A MODEL AIRCRAFT

Maynard Hill, Barrett Foster and David Brown (all USA) flew a piston-engined radio-controlled model aircraft a distance of 3,030 km (1,882.7 miles) from Cape Spear, Newfoundland, Canada, to Mannin Beach, Ireland, without refuelling or landing, in 38 hours from 9 to 11 August 2003.

LIGHTEST AEROPLANE TO CROSS THE ATLANTIC

On 7 May 1933, Capt. Stanislaw Skarzynski (Poland) flew a RWD-5bis 3,582 km (2,225 miles) from St Louis, Senegal, to Maceio, Brazil, in 20 hr 30 min. At the time this was an FAI record for straight-line distance for single-seater aircraft with a top weight of 450 kg (992 lb), less than half the weight of a new Mini Cooper.

HIGHEST HOT-AIR BALLOON FLIGHT

On 6 June 1988, Per Lindstrand (UK) rose to a height of 19,811 m (64,997 ft) over Laredo, Texas, USA, in a Colt 600 hot-air balloon.

HIGHEST ALTITUDE REACHED BY A BALLOON

The greatest altitude ever reached by a manned balloon is 34,668 m (113,740 ft), by Commander Malcolm D Ross and Lieutenant Commander Victor A Prather of the US navy over the Gulf of Mexico, USA, on 4 May 1961. Their gas-filled, non-pressurized, polyethylene balloon was called *Lee Lewis Memorial*.

HEAVIEST AIRCRAFT

The aircraft with the highest standard maximum take-off weight is the Antonov An-225 'Mriya' (Dream), at 600 tonnes (1.32 million lb). Only two of these behemoths were ever built. With a wing-span of 88.4 m (290 ft) – almost as long as four tennis courts – it was designed to 'piggyback' the Russian Buran space shuttles into launch position. The 'Mriya' is a heavy-lift version of the standard Antonov An-124 'Ruslan' cargo plane.

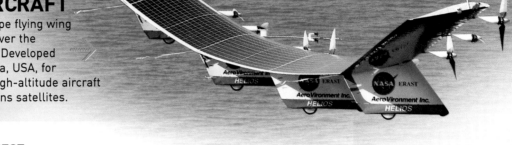

HIGHEST FLIGHT BY
PROPELLER-DRIVEN AIRCRAFT

The unmanned solar-powered *Helios* prototype flying wing achieved an altitude of 29,524 m (96,863 ft) over the Hawaiian island of Kauai on 13 August 2001. Developed by AeroVironment, Inc. of Monrovia, California, USA, for Nasa, *Helios* is a new breed of slow-flying, high-altitude aircraft that could be an alternative to communications satellites.

SIZE & WEIGHT

★ LARGEST BIPLANES

The largest ever biplanes were four aircraft built for the US navy in 1918 by the Curtiss company (designated NC 1-4). They had a wing-span of 38.4 m (126 ft), were 20.8 m (68 ft 3 in) long and had an operational weight of around 12,000 kg (26,400 lb).

The ★ **biggest double-wing aircraft currently in common use** is the Antonov An-2/An-3, first manufactured in 1947, which has a wing-span of 18.8 m (61 ft 7 in) and a maximum take-off weight of 5,800 kg (12,790 lb). It has a 12-person capacity in typical configuration and was first manufactured in 1947.

★ LARGEST FLYING BOAT

The Martin JRM-3 'Mars' has a wing-span of 61 m (200 ft) and a maximum take-off weight of 73,500 kg (162,000 lb). Five were built by the Glenn L Martin Company for the US navy in the 1940s, and two remain in service as water bombers with the Canadian company Flying Tankers.

HEAVIEST PRODUCTION AIRCRAFT

The Ukrainian Antonov An-124 'Ruslan' has a maximum take-off weight of 405 tonnes (893,000 lb). Its cargo hold has a usable volume of 1,014 m³ (35,800 ft³).

LONGEST PASSENGER AIRCRAFT IN SERVICE

The Airbus A340-600 is 75.3 m (246 ft 11 in) long. It has a maximum take-off weight of 365 tonnes (804,700 lb), a wing-span of 63.45 m (208 ft 2 in) and can carry up to 419 passengers.

★ LARGEST AIRBORNE TELESCOPE

Nasa's Stratospheric Observatory for Infrared Astronomy (Sofia) is a Boeing 747SP fitted with an infrared telescope with a 2.7-m-wide (8-ft 10-in) primary mirror. 'First light' (the moment it was first successfully tested) occurred on 18 August 2004.

LARGEST PASSENGER AIRCRAFT

The Boeing 747-400 has a wing-span of 64.4 m (211 ft 3 in), a length of 70.6 m (231 ft 7 in) and a maximum take-off weight of 396.89 tonnes (875,000 lb).

However, the Airbus A380, unveiled on 18 January 2005 and due to enter service by 2007, will have a wing-span of 79.8 m (261 ft 10 in), a length of 73 m (239 ft 6 in) and a maximum take-off weight of 560 tonnes (1.23 million lb).

★ LARGEST WORKING AIRSHIP

Manufactured by Zeppelin Luftschifftechnik of Germany, the 75-m-long (246-ft) Zeppelin NT has an envelope volume of 8,225 m² (290,463 ft²) and can carry 14 people. The **largest airships ever** were the 213.9-tonne (471,500-lb) German *Hindenburg* (LZ 129) and *Graf Zeppelin II* (LZ 130). Each had a length of 245 m (803 ft 10 in).

LARGEST PRODUCTION HELICOPTER

The five-man Russian Mil Mi-26 has a maximum take-off weight of 56,000 kg (123,460 lb). Unladen it weighs 28,200 kg (62,170 lb) and it is 40.03 m (131 ft 4 in) long. The eight-bladed rotor has a diameter of 32 m (105 ft) and is powered by two 8,500-kW (11,400-hp) turbine engines.

AIRCRAFT SIZE COMPARISONS
1 cm = 10 m

Antonov An-2/An-3
Largest biplanes in service
Wing-span: 18.8 m (61 ft 7 in)

Avro B2 'Vulcan'
Largest delta-wing aircraft
Wing-span: 33.8 m (111 ft)
(See Weapons & Warfare, p.198)

Airbus A380
Largest passenger aircraft
Wing-span: 79.8 m (261 ft 10 in)

Antonov An-225
Heaviest aircraft
Wing-span: 88.4 m (290 ft)

Hindenburg (LZ 129), above, and *Graf Zeppelin II*
Largest airship
Length: 245 m (803 ft 10 in)

WEAPONS & WARFARE

← ★ LARGEST DELTA WING

The RAF's Avro B2 'Vulcan' delta-wing nuclear bomber had a wing-span of 33.8 m (111 ft) and a top speed of 1,038 km/h (645 mph) thanks to its four Bristol Siddeley Olympus 201 engines. The B2 version of the Vulcan first entered service in 1958 and the last was retired by the RAF in 1986.

INTERNATIONAL WARS

Shortest: 9:00 a.m. to 9:45 a.m. on 27 August 1896 between Zanzibar and Britain

Longest: Thirty Years War between various European countries from 1618 to 1648, after which the map of Europe was radically changed

LARGEST AMPHIBIOUS SHIP

The US navy's Wasp-class vessels have a full load displacement of 36,500 tonnes (80.5 million lb) and a length of 257 m (844 ft). Capable of carrying aircraft, landing vessels of various kinds and large numbers of personnel, their primary role is to put troops on to enemy shores.

★ MOST AIRCRAFT ON A SUBMARINE

The three Japanese I-400 Sen Toku-class submarines built during World War II each carried three Aichi M6A1 'Sieran' seaplanes, which were stored folded in a 35-m-long (115-ft) hangar on the submarines' decks and launched along the deck by catapult. The subs displaced around 6,000 tonnes (13,228,000 lb) submerged and were 122 m (400 ft) long, making them the largest ever at that time.

★ LARGEST GUN ON A SUBMARINE

The three British Royal Navy M-Class submarines developed towards the end of World War I were fitted with a deck-mounted 30-cm (12-in) gun, a weapon more commonly found on battleships. The diesel-electric-powered submarines were 90.5 m (297 ft) long, had a surface displacement of 1,600 tonnes (3.5 million lb), and could travel at 8 knots (15 km/h; 9 mph) submerged and at 14 knots (26 km/h; 16 mph) on the surface.

★ MOST PRODUCED MILITARY JET AIRCRAFT

It is estimated that over 8,000 Russian MIG-21 'Fishbed' jet fighters have been produced since the first prototype flew in 1955, making it the most common jet-powered military aircraft ever and the military aircraft produced in the greatest numbers in the post-World War II era. The aircraft has been produced in over 30 different variants and has seen service with around 50 air forces around the world.

LARGEST EVER BOMBER WING-SPAN

The American 10-engined Convair B-36J 'Peacemaker' had a wing-span of 70.1 m (230 ft). The aircraft had a maximum take-off weight of 185 tonnes (410,000 lb) – equivalent to the weight of 120 average cars, and around 15 such cars could be parked end to end along its wings. Its top speed was 700 km/h (435 mph).

★ FIRST USE OF MILITARY BALLOONS IN WARFARE

Military balloons were first used by the French in 1794 for reconnaissance observations of their enemy, Austria, during the French Revolutionary Wars of 1792–1801.

★ FIRST USE OF A FIXED-WING AIRCRAFT IN WARFARE

On 22 October 1911, during the Italo-Turkish War of 1911–12, Captain Carlo Piazza of the Italian army flew a Blériot monoplane from Tripoli to Azzia in Libya during a reconnaissance mission over Turkish forces.

★ FIRST OFFENSIVE STRIKE BY AN UNMANNED AERIAL VEHICLE (UAV)

On 3 November 2002 in Yemen, an AGM-114 Hellfire missile was fired from a CIA-operated General Atomics RQ-1 'Predator' at six alleged Al-Qaeda operatives travelling in a car.

HEAVIEST
TANKS →

The M1A2 Abrams main battle tank, produced by General Dynamics Land Systems (USA), has a combat weight of 63 tonnes (138,900 lb), making it the **★heaviest tank currently in operational service**. Equipped with a 120-mm (4.7-in) gun, it has a top speed of 68 km/h (42 mph).

The **heaviest operational tank ever** was the 75.2-tonne (165,780-lb) 13-man French Char de Rupture 2C bis of 1922. It carried a 15.5-cm (6.1-in) howitzer and was powered by two 186-kW (250-hp) engines giving a top speed of 12 km/h (7.5 mph).

LARGEST TANK BATTLE

The Battle of Kursk was fought on 12 July 1943 in the Prokhorovka region near the Russian town of Kursk. A total of 1,500 German and Russian tanks amassed for close-range fighting. By the end of the day both sides had lost more than 300 tanks each.

★ LONGEST RANGE TANK HIT

The longest documented range at which a tank has scored a hit on another is 4.1 km (2.54 miles) by a British Challenger tank of the Royal Scots Dragoon Guards during the land offensive of the Gulf War (24 to 28 February 1991). The Iraqi tank was a Russian-made T-55.

★ LONGEST RANGE HIT BY SHIP'S GUNS

On two occasions during World War II, one ship's guns hit another vessel at a distance of 24 km (15 miles). On 8 June 1940 the German 'pocket battleship' *Scharnhorst* hit the British aircraft carrier HMS *Glorious* at that range in the North Atlantic, while a month later on 9 July, during the battle of Calabria, the British battleship HMS *Warspite* hit the Italian flagship *Guilio Cesare* at a similar distance. Both are remarkable feats of gunnery, considering that in each case both vessels involved in the exchange were moving at high speed.

MOST WIDELY USED FIREARM

During the Cold War, the USSR supplied Automatic Kalashnikov 1947s (AK-47s) to anti-Western insurgents and thus the rifle became a popular symbol of left-wing revolution. Between 50 and 80 million copies and variations of the AK-47 have been produced globally.

★ FASTEST WORLD WAR II FIGHTER AIRCRAFT

Germany's Messerschmitt ME 163 was a rocket-powered aircraft with a top speed of 960 km/h (597 mph). It entered service with the Luftwaffe in May 1944 but, because of its very limited flight time, was never a great success operationally.

↓

WEAPONS & WARFARE

★ MILITARY ROBOTS:
FIRST USE IN COMBAT

The first time robots were used in ground combat occurred during the war in Afghanistan in July 2002. A robot named Hermes was deployed to search a network of caves in Qiqay, Afghanistan. Hermes – and the other three prototypes, Professor, Thing and Fester – are heavy enough (19 kg; 42 lb) to trigger mines, tall enough (30 cm; 1 ft) to trip booby-traps at foot level and long enough (1 m; 3 ft) to carry 12 cameras, a grenade launcher and a 12-gauge shotgun.

★ FIRST AERIAL BOMBARDMENT

The first aerial bombardment was attempted in 1849 when Austrians launched 200 pilotless hot-air balloons to drop timed-release bombs over enemy defences in Venice, Italy. Unpredictable winds meant that there were few casualties.

The ★ **first aerial bombardment by aeroplane** occurred on 1 November 1911 during the Italo-Turkish War of 1911–12. Second Lieutenant Giulio Gavotti of the Italian Air Flotilla, threw four small 2-kg (4.5-lb) grenades over a Turkish camp stationed in Ain Zara, Libya, from his Taube monoplane, which was flying at an altitude of 185 m (600 ft).

★ HEAVIEST CANNON

A cannon built in 1868 at Perm, Russia, weighs 144.1 tonnes (317,685 lb), has a bore of 50.8 cm (20 in) and a barrel 4.6 m (15 ft 1 in) long. Its cannonballs weighed approximately half a tonne. Known as the Tsar Cannon, it is on display in Moscow, Russia.

★ FASTEST TORPEDO

Russia's rocket-propelled Shkval (Squall) torpedo releases a stream of bubbles from its nose and skin, surrounding it with a sheath of gas and dramatically reducing its friction with sea water. This allows it to reach velocities estimated at 360 km/h (220 mph), with a range of around 6.8 km (4.2 miles).

★ MOST POWERFUL ↓
LASER WEAPON

The Airborne Laser (ABL), developed by Boeing, Lockheed Martin and Northrop Grumman, is designed to fit inside a modified Boeing 747 and will ultimately be used to track and destroy ballistic missiles. Although still in development, its power output measures about one megawatt. The ABL's chemical oxygen iodine laser (COIL) was first fired in a ground-test at Edwards Air Force Base, California, USA, in November 2004; the first aerial test of shooting a ballistic missile is scheduled for late 2005.

★ FIRST FILMING OF A WAR

The first war to be filmed was the Battle of Volo in Thessaly, Greece, in April 1897. This war between Turkey and Greece was filmed by the British war correspondent and cinematographer Frederick Villiers (UK), but never publicly broadcast. The earliest footage of war that still exists was filmed on 12 November 1899 by John Bennett (UK) during the British campaign at Orange River, South Africa, during the Boer War (pictured).

★ SMALLEST MAMMAL
USED IN DETECTING LANDMINES

The Gambian (or African) giant pouch rat (*Cricetomys gambianus*) measures 76 cm (30 in) long (including the tail) and weighs 1.35 kg (3 lb), i.e. light enough not to trigger an explosion. According to APOPO, the Belgian company that developed this idea, a single rat and its handler can search 150 m² (1,614 ft²) in a day. The rats are trained to respond to the smell emitted by the explosive by biting or scratching at the location until they are rewarded with food.

HEAVIEST NUCLEAR BOMB

The MK 17, which was carried by US B-36 bombers in the mid-1950s, weighed 19,050 kg (41,998 lb) and was 7.49 m (24 ft 6 in) long.

★ FIRST TEST OF A LASER WEAPON

In a test that took place in November 1973, a 100-kW carbon dioxide laser destroyed a 3.6-m (12-ft) airborne drone above the Sandia Optical Test Range of Kirtland Air Force Base, New Mexico, USA.

HIGHEST RATE OF FIRE BY A BALLISTIC WEAPON

A prototype 36-barrel gun built by Metal Storm of Brisbane, Australia, has a firing rate in excess of one million rounds a minute. Such high rates of fire are possible because the rounds are stacked in the barrels of the gun and fired electronically by computer, rather than by a hammer detonator.

LARGEST NON-NUCLEAR CONVENTIONAL BOMB IN EXISTENCE

The Massive Ordnance Air Blast (MOAB) is a guided weapon weighing 9,752 kg (21,500 lb). It was first tested at the Eglin Air Force Armament Center, Florida, USA, on 11 March 2003.

★ LONGEST RANGE MISSILE EVER

The US Atlas missile entered service in 1959 and had a range of 16,669 km (10,357 miles) – about 4,828 km (3,000 miles) more than was needed to hit any point in Soviet territory from launch sites in the West.

HIGHEST RATE OF FIRE BY A MACHINE GUN IN SERVICE

The 7.62-mm (0.3-in) calibre M134 Minigun has a firing rate of 6,000 rounds a minute, or 100 a second – about 10 times that of an ordinary machine gun.

★ COUNTRY WITH THE MOST TROOPS DEPLOYED OVERSEAS

As of May 2004, the USA had approximately 370,000 land-based military personnel on active duty. This is out of a global total of over 500,000 soldiers from 47 countries serving abroad in all capacities, including war, peacekeeping and disaster relief.

FIRST USE OF A CROSSBOW

The earliest use of a crossbow was in 341 BC at the Battle of Ma-Ling, Linyi, China.

MOST INTELLIGENT HANDGUN →

The O'Dwyer Variable Lethality Law Enforcement (VLe) prototype pistol, made by Metal Storm Limited of Brisbane, Australia, has no moving parts. Instead, projectiles are fired electronically by a built-in computer processor. It can only be fired by someone wearing an authorized transponder ring, and is capable of firing up to three shots in extremely quick succession (within 1/500th of a second).

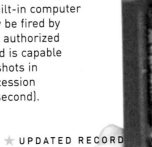

PROJECTILES

MOST POTATOES
LAUNCHED IN 3 MINUTES

Tom Pringle (UK), aka Dr Bunhead, successfully fired eight potatoes manually from a potato launcher in three minutes. The attempt occurred on 14 December 2004 in London, UK. Dr Bunhead is a professional science communicator dedicated to 'bringing science out of the laboratory and into the classroom, theatres and TV'.

Paper aircraft
Made from a single sheet of A4 (8.5 x 11 in quarto paper), and a specified length of standard sticky tape
63.19 m (207 ft 4 in)
Stephen Krieger (USA)
Near Moses Lake,
Washington, USA
6 September 2003

FARTHEST DISTANCE...

The objects on this spread represent those that have been hurled, spat, tossed, popped or thrown farther than any others.

House brick throw
2.27-kg (5-lb) house brick
44.54 m (146 ft 1 in)
Geoff Capes (UK)
Orton Goldhay,
Cambridgehire, UK
19 July 1978

★ **Rubber band shot**
30.16 m (98 ft 11 in)
Leo Clouser (USA)
Wyomissing,
Pennsylvania, USA
18 June 1999

Rolling pin throw
Weighing 907 g (2 lb)
53.47 m (175 ft 5 in)
Lori La Deane Adams (USA)
Iowa State Fair, USA
21 August 1979

Champagne cork flight
Cork from an untreated and unheated Champagne bottle
54.18 m (177 ft 9 in)
Heinrich Medicus (USA)
Woodbury Vineyards
Winery, New York, USA
5 June 1988

Haggis hurl
Minimum weight of 680 g (1 lb 8 oz)
55.11 m (180 ft 10 in)
Alan Pettigrew (UK)
Inchmurrin, Argyll and Bute, Scotland, UK
24 May 1984

Cherry stone spit
28.51 m (93 ft 6.5 in)
Brian 'Young Gun' Krause (USA)
2004 International Cherry Pit-Spitting Championships,
Eau Claire,
Michigan, USA

Tobacco spit
Wad (mouthful) of tobacco
16.23 m (53 ft 3 in)
David O'Dell (USA)
World Tobacco Spitting Championships,
Calico Ghost Town,
California, USA
22 March 1997

Watermelon seed spit
22.91 m (75 ft 2 in)
Jason Schayot (USA)
De Leon, Texas, USA
12 August 1995

MOST PAINTBALLS →
CAUGHT IN TWO MINUTES

Fired from a distance of 20 m (65 ft), Anthony Kelly (Australia) caught 28 in tact in two minutes at Ultimate Skirmish paintball field, Helensburgh, New South Wales, Australia, on 30 May 2003.

Gumboot throw (man)
Size 8 Challenger Dunlop boot
63.98 m (209 ft 9 in)
Teppo Luoma (Finland)
Hämeenlinna, Finland
12 October 1996

Gumboot throw (woman)
Size 8 Challenger Dunlop boot
40.87 m (134 ft 1 in)
Sari Tirkkonen (Finland)
Hämeenlinna, Finland
19 April 1996

Flying disc throw (man)
250 m (820 ft)
Christian Sandstrom (Sweden)
El Mirage, California, USA
26 April 2002

Flying disc throw (woman)
138.56 m (454 ft 6 in)
Jennifer Griffin (USA)
Fredericksburg, Virginia, USA
8 April 2000

Object with no tail
Flying ring
406.29 m (1,333 ft)
Erin Hemmings (USA)
Fort Funston, California, USA
14 July 2003

Egg throw
Fresh, raw hen's egg – must remain intact when caught
98.51 m (323 ft 2 in)
Johnny Fell to Keith Thomas (both USA)
Jewett, Texas, USA
12 November 1978

Cow pat toss
Not moulded into a spherical shape, 100% 'organic'
81.1 m (226 ft)
Steve Urner (USA)
Mountain Festival
Tehachapi,
California, USA
14 August 1981

Baseball pitch (man)
135.88 m (445 ft 10 in)
Glen Edward Gorbous
(Canada)
1 August 1957

Baseball pitch (woman)
90.2 m (296 ft)
Mildred Ella 'Babe'
Didrikson (USA)
25 July 1951

★ LARGEST TREBUCHET WITH A PROJECTILE WEIGHT OF 20 KG AND OVER

The *Car Thrower* threw a 3,400-kg (7,496-lb) steel block over a distance of 15.32 m (50 ft 3 in), creating a power output of 52,088 kg-m (376,623 lb-ft). The trebuchet was built by Angus Robson and team of Rocktec Ltd (New Zealand) and fired on 19 February 2004 in Matamata, New Zealand. Pictured is the *Car Thrower* throwing a car!

TALLEST ← HOTEL

The all-suite Burj Al Arab ('The Arabian Tower'), situated 15 km (9 miles) south of Dubai, UAE, was 320.94 m (1,052 ft) high from ground level to the top of its mast when measured on 26 October 1999. Pictured is its helipad, which was temporarily converted into a tennis court in 2005 for a non-competition match between Roger Federer (Switzerland) and Andre Agassi (USA).

★ TALLEST UNOCCUPIED BUILDING

Although it had reached its full height of 330 m (1,082 ft), the Ryugyong Hotel in Pyongyang, North Korea, was not finished when construction was halted in 1992. It is the world's 18th tallest building, and would be the world's tallest hotel if completed.

★ FIRST BUILDING TO HAVE A SAFETY LIFT

On 23 March 1857, the first modern 'safety elevator' went into service at the Haughwout Department Store in New York City, USA. It was installed by Elisha Otis and was powered by a steam engine.

★ LARGEST DOME STRUCTURE

Although not a true 'dome', in the sense that it is not self-supporting, the Millennium Dome at Greenwich in London, UK, is the largest dome-shaped structure. It has an overall diameter of 365 m (1,181 ft), an internal diameter of 320 m (1,050 ft) and a roof height of 50 m (164 ft). It consists of a polytetrafluoroethylene- (PTFE-) coated fibreglass membrane, suspended from twelve 95-m-tall (312-ft) steel masts, and covers 80,000 m² (861,000 ft²).

LARGEST ADMINISTRATIVE BUILDING

The Pentagon in Arlington, Virginia, USA, has a floor area of 604,000 m² (6.5 million ft²). Each of the outermost sides is 281 m (921 ft) long and the perimeter of the building is about 1,405 m (4,610 ft). Its corridors total 28 km (17.5 miles) in length and there are 7,754 windows to be cleaned. More than 26,000 military and civilian employees work in the building.

★ FASTEST LIFT

Two high-speed lifts installed by Toshiba Elevator and Building Systems (Japan) in Taipei 101, the world's **tallest building**, situated in Taipei, Taiwan, have a maximum speed of 1,010 m/min (3,313 ft/min), equivalent to 60.6 km/h (37.6 mph). The lifts take just 40 seconds from ground level to the 89th floor, situated at 382 m (1,253 ft), and have atmospheric pressure regulatory systems to avoid discomfort (ear popping) for the occupants.

★ LARGEST MIXED-USE BUILDING

Berjaya Times Square KL in Kuala Lumpur, Malaysia, has a total floor area of 678,000 m² (7.3 million ft²) and features a 320,000-m² (3.45 million-ft²) shopping mall, an indoor theme park and two 48-storey towers containing offices and a hotel. It opened in 2003.

★ HEAVIEST BUILDING MOVED INTACT

The 10-storey, 13,254-tonne (29.2 million-lb) Talent Exchange Centre in Wuzhou, Guangxi, China, was moved 30.2 m (99 ft) on a specially built roller system, from 25 May to 3 June 2004. Dalian Jiuding Special Construction Engineering carried out the move, which happened at a rate of 3–7 m (10–23 ft) a day. The building's occupants continued to live and work in it during the move.

★ HIGHEST MOSQUE ABOVE GROUND LEVEL

The Prince Abdulla Mosque on the 77th floor of the Kingdom Centre building in Riyadh, Saudi Arabia, is 183 m (600 ft) above ground level and was completed on 5 July 2004.

★ LARGEST UNDERGROUND SHOPPING COMPLEX

The PATH Walkway in Toronto, Canada, has 27 km (16.7 miles) of shopping arcades with 371,600 m² (4 million ft²) of retail space for around 1,200 shops and services. Over 50 buildings, five subway stations and a rail terminal are accessible through the complex.

★ LARGEST KALEIDOSCOPE

The Nagoya City Pavilion 'Earth Tower', erected for the Aichi Expo 2005 near Nagoya, Japan, stands 47 m (154 ft) tall and projects a kaleidoscopic image 40 m (131 ft) to viewers at the base of the triangular tower.

★ TALLEST HOSPITAL BUILDING

The 34-storey Guy's Tower at Guy's Hospital in London, UK, is 142.6 m (468 ft) tall.

★ LARGEST SINGLE FREE-SPAN WOODEN STRUCTURE

The Odate Jukai Dome in Odate, Japan, is a dome-shaped building that measures 178 m (584 ft) on its longest axis and 157 m (515 ft) on its shortest axis. It consists of an opaque membrane stretched over a frame constructed from 25,000 Akita cedar trees.

LARGEST PYRAMID

The Quetzalcóatl pyramid at Cholula de Rivadavia, 101 km (63 miles) southeast of Mexico City, Mexico, is both the largest pyramid and the **largest monument** ever built. It is 54 m (177 ft) tall, and its base covers nearly 18.2 ha (45 acres). Its total volume has been estimated at 3.3 million m³ (116.5 million ft³), compared with the current volume of 2.4 million m³ (84.7 million ft³) for the Great Egyptian Pyramid of Khufu or Cheops, the **tallest pyramid**.

LARGEST RELIGIOUS STRUCTURE

The Angkor Wat (City Temple) in Cambodia encloses 162.6 ha (401 acres). It was built in honour of the Hindu god Vishnu by the Khmer King Suryavarman II in the period AD 1113–50. Its curtain wall measures 1,280 m (4,200 ft) and its population, before it was abandoned in 1432, was 80,000. The temple forms part of a complex of 72 major monuments that extends across 24.8 km (15.4 miles).

LARGEST SURVIVING ZIGGURAT

Although not the largest ever ziggurat (rectangular stepped pyramid), the largest surviving ziggurat is the Ziggurat of Ur (now Muqayyar, Iraq) with a base 61 x 45.7 m (200 x 150 ft), built to three storeys and surmounted by a summit temple. The first storey and part of the second storey now survive to a height of 18 m (60 ft).

The ziggurat was constructed during the reign of Ur-nammu (ca 2113–2095 BC).

★ LONGEST SINGLE-SPAN ROOF STRUCTURE

The giant steel arch supporting the roof of the north stand of the new Wembley Stadium in London, UK, has a span of 315 m (1,033 ft), making it the world's longest unsupported roof structure. It weighs 1,750 tonnes (3.85 million lb) and is 7 m (23 ft) in diameter. The Eiffel Tower (324 m; 1,063 ft) is just a shade taller than the steel arch's span.

→ COMPARE THE WORLD'S TALLEST STRUCTURES BY TURNING TO P.163

LONGEST ↑ TIBETAN BRIDGE

The bridge connecting the islands of Procida and Vivara, Italy, has a span of 362 m (1,187 ft). It was completed on 15 July 2001.

HIGHEST...

BRIDGE

The bridge over the Royal Gorge of the Arkansas River in Colorado, USA, is 321 m (1,053 ft) above water level. It is a suspension bridge with a main span of 268 m (880 ft) and was finished on 6 December 1929 after six months' construction.

DAM

The Nurek dam, 300 m (984 ft) high, on the river Vakhsh, Tajikistan, is currently the highest dam, but this should be surpassed by the Rogunskaya dam, at 335 m (1,098 ft), also across the river Vakhsh. However, the break-up of the former Soviet Union has delayed its completion.

CONCRETE DAM

Grande Dixence, on the river Dixence in Switzerland, was built between 1953 and 1961 to a height of 285 m (935 ft), with a crest length of 700 m (2,297 ft), using 5,960,000 m³ (210,400,000 ft³) of concrete.

CAUSEWAY

Once the road bridge at the highest altitude in the world at 5,602 m (18,380 ft), Bailey bridge, erected in August 1982 over Khardungla Pass, Ladakh, India, was replaced by a causeway – a raised road – in the mid-1990s owing to damage from avalanches.

LARGEST...

★ TIDAL BARRIER

The Oosterscheldedam, a storm-surge barrier in the southwest of the Netherlands, is the world's largest tidal river barrier. It has 65 concrete piers and 62 steel gates and covers a total length of 9 km (5.6 miles).

RESERVOIR (BY VOLUME)

The most voluminous fully man-made reservoir is the Bratskoye reservoir on the river Angara in Russia, with a volume of 169.3 km³ (40.6 miles³) and an area of 5,470 km² (2,112 miles²).

RESERVOIR (BY SURFACE AREA)

The world's largest artificial lake is Lake Volta in Ghana, formed by the Akosombo dam, completed in 1965. By 1969, the lake had filled to an area of 8,482 km² (3,275 miles²), with a shoreline 7,250 km (4,500 miles) in length.

COOLING TOWER

The largest cooling tower is 180 m (590 ft) tall and stands adjacent to the nuclear power plant at Uentrop, Germany. It was completed in 1976.

ROAD TUNNEL (DIAMETER)

The road tunnel blasted through Yerba Buena Island, San Francisco, California, USA, is 24 m (79 ft) wide, 17 m (56 ft) high and 165 m (541 ft) long. More than 280,000 vehicles pass along its two decks every day.

LONGEST WALL →

The Great Wall of China has a main-line length of 3,460 km (2,150 miles) – nearly three times the length of Britain – plus 3,530 km (2,195 miles) of branches and spurs. Construction began during the reign of Qin Shi Huangdi (221–210 BC). Its height varies from 4.5 to 12 m (15 to 39 ft) and it is up to 9.8 m (32 ft) thick. It runs from Shanhaiguan to Yumenguan and Yangguan, and was kept in repair up to the 16th century. Some 51.5 km (32 miles) of the wall have been destroyed since 1966, and part of the wall was blown up to make way for a dam in July 1979.

LONGEST...

ROAD AND RAIL BRIDGE SYSTEM

The Seto-Ohashi bridge in Japan consists of six bridge sections and stretches across a total distance of 9.4 km (5.8 miles).

BRIDGE

The Second Lake Pontchartrain causeway bridge, which joins Mandeville and Metairie, Louisiana, USA, is 38.42 km (23.87 miles) long.

CABLE SUSPENSION BRIDGE (ROAD AND RAIL)

The Tsing Ma bridge in Hong Kong opened to the public in May 1997. It has a main span of 1,377 m (4,518 ft), a width of 40 m (130 ft) and a length of 2.2 km (1.36 miles), making it the longest suspension-bridge span for combined road and railway traffic.

Its shipping clearance reaches 62 m (203 ft) and the tower height is 206 m (675 ft).

CANTILEVER BRIDGE

The Quebec bridge (Pont de Quebec) over the St Lawrence River in Canada has a cantilever truss span measuring 549 m (1,800 ft) between the piers and 987 m (3,239 ft) overall. It carries a railway track and two carriageways. Work started in 1899 and it was finally opened to traffic on 3 December 1917.

CONCRETE GIRDER BRIDGE

The Raftsundet bridge in Norway is 298 m (978 ft) long – approximately the length of four 747 jumbo jets laid end to end. It links the main islands of the Norwegian Lofoten group and was completed in 1997.

FLOATING BRIDGE

Second Lake Washington bridge, Washington State, USA, has a total length of 3.8 km (2.39 miles), with its floating section measuring 2,291 m (7,518 ft). It was completed in August 1963.

STEEL ARCH BRIDGE

The Lupu bridge in Shanghai, China, has a span of 550 m (1,804 ft) over the Huangpu river. It was constructed over a period of three years and opened on 28 June 2003.

LONGEST WOODEN BRIDGE

Lake Pontchartrain Railroad Trestle, Louisiana, USA, made of creosoted yellow pine timber, spans 9.36 km (5.82 miles). Construction began in February 1882 and finished in September of that year. When it opened in 1883, it originally spanned 34.6 km (21.49 miles).

LARGEST CONCRETE DAM

The Grand Coulee (begun in 1933 and operational on 22 March 1941) dam on the Columbia River, Washington State, USA, had a concrete volume of 8,092,000 m³ (285,760,000 ft³) to a weight of 19,595,000 tonnes (43.2 billion lb). It was finally completed in 1942 at a cost of $56 million (£14 million). It has a crest length of 1,272 m (4,173 ft) and is 168 m (550 ft) high.

LONGEST SPAN OF A CABLE SUSPENSION BRIDGE

The main span of the Akashi-Kaikyo road bridge, which links Honshu and Shikoku, Japan, is 1,990.8 m (6,532 ft; 1.24 miles) long. The overall suspended length with side-spans totals 3,911.1 m (12,831 ft 8 in or 2.43 miles).

THEME PARKS

← OLDEST
CONTINUALLY OPERATING
ROLLERCOASTER

The Scenic Railway at Luna Park, St Kilda, Melbourne, Australia, opened to the public on 13 December 1912 and has remained in operation ever since.

OBSERVATION WHEEL

The British Airways London Eye, designed by architects David Marks and Julia Barfield (both UK), has a diameter of 135 m (443 ft). Constructed at Jubilee Gardens on London's South Bank, it made its first 'flight' on 1 February 2000, with regular services commencing the following month.

WAVE POOL

According to the World Waterpark Association, the largest wave pool (often called an artificial sea) covers 16,000 m² (172,000 ft²) and can be found at Siam Park, Bangkok, Thailand.

LONGEST...

ROLLERCOASTER

Steel Dragon 2000 at Nagashima Spaland, Mie, Japan, is 2,479 m (8,133 ft) long. A steel-track out-and-back coaster, it has a maximum height of 95 m (311 ft 8 in) and a top speed of 149 km/h (92.5 mph). It opened on 1 August 2000.

★ FLYING ROLLERCOASTER

Batwing at Six Flags America in Maryland, USA, and X-Flight at Geauga Lake, Ohio, USA, are both 1,018 m (3,340 ft) long. Flying rollercoasters are rides in which the occupants are suspended horizontally beneath the coaster parallel to the track, giving the sensation of flying.

★ STAND-UP
ROLLERCOASTER

Riddler's Revenge at Six Flags Magic Mountain in California, USA, is 1,332 m (4,370 ft) long. Riders stand rather than sit during the ride, which is also the fastest of its kind, reaching a top speed of 104.6 km/h (65 mph).

WOODEN ROLLERCOASTER

Beast, built in 1979 at Paramount's Kings Island in Ohio, USA, is the longest traditional wooden laminated track rollercoaster at 2,286 m (7,400 ft). Rides last 3 min 40 sec and reach a top speed of 104 km/h (65 mph).

LARGEST...

★ THEME PARK OPERATOR

Walt Disney Parks & Resorts is the world's largest operator of theme parks, with an estimated 101 million people visiting its attractions in 2004, according to *Amusement Business* magazine. By comparison, France, the ★ **most popular tourist destination**, only receives around 75 million international tourists each year. In 2004, eight of the world's top 10 theme parks were operated by Disney.

INDOOR AMUSEMENT PARK

Galaxyland, located in West Edmonton Mall, Alberta, Canada, covers 37,200 m² (400,000 ft²). It has 30 skill games and 27 rides and attractions.

LARGEST RELIGIOUS THEME PARK

The Holy Land Experience, a 6.07-ha (15-acre) site in Orlando, Florida, USA, opened on 5 February 2001 and is a re-creation of Jerusalem, Israel, during the period from 1450 BC to AD 66.

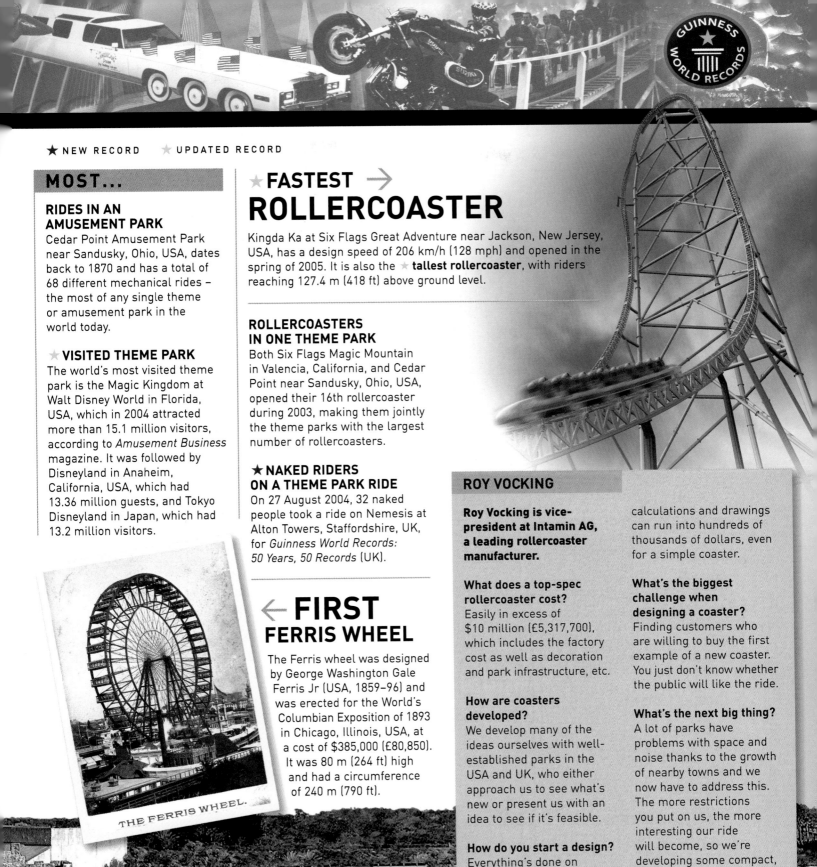

MOST...

RIDES IN AN AMUSEMENT PARK

Cedar Point Amusement Park near Sandusky, Ohio, USA, dates back to 1870 and has a total of 68 different mechanical rides – the most of any single theme or amusement park in the world today.

★ VISITED THEME PARK

The world's most visited theme park is the Magic Kingdom at Walt Disney World in Florida, USA, which in 2004 attracted more than 15.1 million visitors, according to *Amusement Business* magazine. It was followed by Disneyland in Anaheim, California, USA, which had 13.36 million guests, and Tokyo Disneyland in Japan, which had 13.2 million visitors.

★ FASTEST → ROLLERCOASTER

Kingda Ka at Six Flags Great Adventure near Jackson, New Jersey, USA, has a design speed of 206 km/h (128 mph) and opened in the spring of 2005. It is also the ★ **tallest rollercoaster**, with riders reaching 127.4 m (418 ft) above ground level.

ROLLERCOASTERS IN ONE THEME PARK

Both Six Flags Magic Mountain in Valencia, California, and Cedar Point near Sandusky, Ohio, USA, opened their 16th rollercoaster during 2003, making them jointly the theme parks with the largest number of rollercoasters.

★ NAKED RIDERS ON A THEME PARK RIDE

On 27 August 2004, 32 naked people took a ride on Nemesis at Alton Towers, Staffordshire, UK, for *Guinness World Records: 50 Years, 50 Records* (UK).

← FIRST FERRIS WHEEL

The Ferris wheel was designed by George Washington Gale Ferris Jr (USA, 1859–96) and was erected for the World's Columbian Exposition of 1893 in Chicago, Illinois, USA, at a cost of $385,000 (£80,850). It was 80 m (264 ft) high and had a circumference of 240 m (790 ft).

THE FERRIS WHEEL.

ROY VOCKING

Roy Vocking is vice-president at Intamin AG, a leading rollercoaster manufacturer.

What does a top-spec rollercoaster cost?
Easily in excess of $10 million (£5,317,700), which includes the factory cost as well as decoration and park infrastructure, etc.

How are coasters developed?
We develop many of the ideas ourselves with well-established parks in the USA and UK, who either approach us to see what's new or present us with an idea to see if it's feasible.

How do you start a design?
Everything's done on computers, and the calculations and drawings can run into hundreds of thousands of dollars, even for a simple coaster.

What's the biggest challenge when designing a coaster?
Finding customers who are willing to buy the first example of a new coaster. You just don't know whether the public will like the ride.

What's the next big thing?
A lot of parks have problems with space and noise thanks to the growth of nearby towns and we now have to address this. The more restrictions you put on us, the more interesting our ride will become, so we're developing some compact, high-impact thrill rides.

→ SPORTS & GAMES

→ | **CONTENTS**

★LONGEST
SKATEBOARD RAMP JUMP

Professional skateboarder Danny Way (USA) performed a 24-m (79-ft) 360º air on his Megaramp at X Games X in Los Angeles, California, USA, on 8 August 2004. He also holds the record for the ★ **highest skateboard air off a quarterpipe**, with a 7.1-m (23-ft 6-in) method air performed off an 8.2-m (27-ft) pipe at Point X Camp near Aguanga, California, USA, on 19 June 2003. *For more X Games records, see the special feature on p.167.*

MOST PEOPLE
← TO TANDEM PARACHUTE IN 24 HOURS

A total of 128 tandem parachute jumps were made from Hibaldstow Airfield, Lincolnshire, UK, on 28 June 2004, at a charity event for the Echo Trust children's charity.

Fédération Aéronautique Internationale (FAI) definitions of aircraft:

Hang-glider
A glider capable of being carried, foot-launched and landed solely by the use of the pilot's legs

Paraglider
A hang-glider with no rigid primary structure

Microlight
A one or two-seat aeroplane with a specified maximum mass and a very low wing loading

Glider
A fixed-wing aerodyne (a heavier-than-air aircraft deriving lift from motion) capable of sustained flight and having no means of propulsion

AEROBATICS

MOST WORLD CHAMPIONSHIP WINS
Petr Jirmus (Czechoslovakia, now Czech Republic) is the only man to become world champion twice, in 1984 and 1986.

★ OLDEST WORLD CHAMPION
Henry Haigh (USA, b. 12 December 1924) was aerobatics world champion at the age of 64 in 1988.

BALLOONING

★ LONGEST DURATION FLOWN BY A BALLOON (SOLO)
Steve Fossett (USA) flew for 14 days 19 hr 50 min, from 19 June to 4 July 2002, while piloting his balloon, *Bud Light Spirit of Freedom*, around the world solo.

GLIDING

HIGHEST SPEED
James and Thomas Payne (both USA) recorded an FAI average top speed of 247.49 km/h (153.78 mph) over a course of 500 km (310.6 miles) when setting the out-and-return speed record in California, USA, on 3 March 1999.

The **highest speed in a glider by a woman** was reached by Pamela Kurstjens-Hawkins (UK), with an FAI average top speed of 159.06 km/h (98.83 mph) over a triangular course of 100 km (62 miles) at McCaffrey's Airfield, Australia, on 14 December 2002.

HANG-GLIDING

GREATEST HEIGHT GAIN
Larry Tudor (USA) rose to an altitude of 4,343 m (14,250 ft) over Owens Valley, California, USA, on 4 August 1985.

The **greatest height gain in a hang-glider by a woman** was achieved by Judy Leden (UK), who reached 3,970 m (13,025 ft) in Kuruman, South Africa, on 1 December 1992.

★ HIGHEST SPEED
Thomas Suchanek (Czech Republic) achieved a top speed of 50.81 km/h (31.57 mph) over a 25-km (15.5-mile) triangular course at Riverside, Australia, on 15 December 2000.

The ★ **highest speed for a hang-glider by a woman** over the same distance was achieved by Jenny Ganderton (Australia), who reached a top speed of 26 km/h (16.15 mph) at Forbes, New South Wales, Australia, on 14 February 1990.

★ FIRST HOT-AIR BALLOON WORLD CHAMPIONSHIPS

This form of ballooning was revived in the USA in 1961, and the first World Championships were held in Albuquerque, New Mexico, USA, from 10 to 17 February 1973. The greatest mass ascent of hot-air balloons took place at the 2000 event when 329 balloons were launched in the space of an hour.

←

MOST PARACHUTISTS TO JUMP FROM A BALLOON SIMULTANEOUSLY

A group of 20 members of the Paraclub Flevo of Lelystad (Netherlands) jumped simultaneously at 2,000 m (6,500 ft) over Markelo, the Netherlands, on 10 May 2003.

PARAGLIDING

★ LONGEST FLIGHT (DISTANCE) – TANDEM
André Luis Grosso Fleury and Claudia Otila Guimaraes Ribeiro (both Brazil) travelled 299.7 km (186.2 miles) without landing from Patu to Varzea da Cacimba, Brazil, on 17 October 2003.

★ MOST POWERED PARAGLIDERS AIRBORNE SIMULTANEOUSLY
A total of 78 powered paragliders were airborne above the Fantasy of Flight Museum, Polk City, Florida, USA, on 12 April 2003.

SKYDIVING

SPEED SKYDIVING – GREATEST SPEED
Speed skydiving involves jumping from an aircraft at 4,000 m (13,000 ft) and accelerating in a near vertical head-first position into the 'measuring zone', which extends from 2,700 m (8,850 ft) altitude to 1,700 m (5,570 ft).

ESTRID GEERTSEN

Estrid Geertsen (Denmark, b. 1 August 1904) became the oldest tandem parachute jumper on 30 September 2004, leaping from an altitude of 4,000 m (13,100 ft) over Roskilde, Denmark, at the age of 100 years 60 days.

What was it like?
There was a lot of noise from the parachute but it was still a great experience.

What inspired you to make your first jump?
After reading in a newspaper that the record belonged to an American woman, I wanted to do everything I could to get Denmark the record.

Do you get scared before you make your jumps?
Not at all – don't forget, I'm 100 years old!

What do your family think about your hobby?
They think it's wonderful. At first I wasn't going to tell them – I thought they would try to talk me out of it.

Do you intend to keep making parachute jumps?
Only if my record is taken by somebody else!

Michael Brooke (France) reached a speed of 524.13 km/h (325.67 mph) at the Millennium Speed Skydiving Competition over Gap, France, on 19 September 1999.

The **fastest female speed skydiver** is Lucia Bottari Italy), who reached 432.12 km/h (268.5 mph) at Bottens, Switzerland, on 16 September 2002.

LARGEST FREEFALL EVENT
The World Freefall Convention 2000, held in Quincy, Illinois, USA, from 4 to 13 August, attracted 5,732 registered skydivers from 55 countries, who made in excess of 63,000 jumps.

PARACHUTING

LARGEST FAI-APPROVED FREEFALL FORMATION
A group of 357 skydivers from over 40 countries formed above Takhli, Thailand, on 6 February 2004. The event was organized by World Team 04 and formed part of the Thailand Royal Sky Celebration, in honour of the Thai royal family.

LONGEST FREEFALL JUMP (UNOFFICIAL)
Capt. Joseph W Kittinger (USA) dropped 25,820 m (84,700 ft) from a balloon at 31,330 m (102,800 ft) above Tularosa, New Mexico, USA, on 16 August 1960. The maximum speed reached in rarified air was 1,006 km/h (625.25 mph) – just faster than the speed of sound – at 27,400 m (90,000 ft). He fell for 4 min 37 sec before his parachute was deployed automatically.

★ MOST PARACHUTE JUMPS IN 24 HOURS

Jay Stokes (USA) made 534 successful parachute jumps in a 24-hour period on 11 and 12 November 2003 above Lake Elsinore, California, USA. This required Jay to make a parachute jump every two-and-a-half minutes.

★ NEW RECORD   ★ UPDATED RECORD

AMERICAN FOOTBALL

★ MOST → CONSECUTIVE GAME WINS

The New England Patriots had 18 consecutive regular season game wins between 28 September 2003 and 24 October 2004. Head coach Bill Belichick (USA, pictured) holds the Vince Lombardi trophy after the team won Super Bowl XXXVIII on 1 February 2004 at the Reliant Stadium in Houston, Texas, USA.

NFL

HIGHEST SCORE IN AN NFL REGULAR SEASON GAME

The Washington Redskins scored 72 against the New York Giants (41) at Washington, USA, on 27 November 1966. The aggregate score of 113 is also a record.

★ LONGEST NFL INTERCEPTION RETURN

The longest interception return in an NFL game is 106 yards by Ed Reed (USA) for the Baltimore Ravens against the Cleveland Browns on 7 November 2004.

★ MOST POST-SEASON WINS BY A HEAD COACH

Two National Football League head coaches have won ten post-season games – Vince Lombardi (USA), coach of the Green Bay Packers between 1961 and 1967; and Bill Belichick (USA), coach of the New England Patriots between 1994 and 2005. Of the two coaches, Belichick has the better overall record with 10 victories and one loss to Lombardi's 10 victories and two losses.

MOST NFL CAREER INTERCEPTIONS

Paul Krause (USA), a free safety from the University of Iowa, USA, is the leading pass interceptor of all time with 81 steals during a 16-season career, playing for Washington Redskins (1964–67) and Minnesota Vikings (1968–79).

LONGEST PASS COMPLETION

A pass completion of 99 yd has been achieved on eight occasions and has always resulted in a touchdown. The most recent was a pass from Brett Favre to Robert Brooks of the Green Bay Packers against the Chicago Bears on 11 September 1995.

★ HIGHEST PAID AMERICAN FOOTBALL PLAYER

The highest paid NFL player is Atlanta Falcons quarterback Michael Vick (USA), who signed a ten-year $130-million (£67.9-million) deal on 23 December 2004, which included a $27-million (£14.1-million) signing bonus.

MOST NFL TITLES

The Green Bay Packers have won 12 titles (1929–31, 1936, 1939, 1944, 1961–62, 1965–67 and 1996).

★ MOST PASSES RECEIVED IN A GAME

Terrell Owens (USA) received a record 20 passes in an NFL game playing for San Francisco 49ers v. Chicago Bears on 17 December 2000.

MOST FIELD GOALS BY AN INDIVIDUAL IN A CAREER

Gary Anderson (USA) playing for Pittsburgh Steelers (1982–94), Philadelphia Eagles (1995–96), San Francisco 49ers (1997) and Minnesota Vikings (1999–2001) scored 465 field goals in his NFL career.

MOST YARDS GAINED RECEIVING IN A SEASON

Jerry Rice (USA) gained 1,848 yd receiving in the 1995 NFL season, playing for the San Francisco 49ers.

MOST GAMES PLAYED BY AN INDIVIDUAL

George Blanda (USA) played in a record 340 games in a record 26 seasons in the NFL (Chicago Bears 1949–58, Baltimore Colts 1950, Houston Oilers 1960–66 and Oakland Raiders 1967–75).

MOST PASSES RECEIVED IN A SUPER BOWL GAME

Three players share the record of 11 passes received: Dan Ross (USA) for the Cincinnati Bengals in 1982, Jerry Rice (USA) for the San Francisco 49ers in 1989, and Deion Branch (USA, pictured) for the New England Patriots in 2005.

Bowl career records for **most points scored** (48), **most yards gained receiving** (589) and **most passes received** (33).

MOST YARDS GAINED RUSHING BY A QUARTERBACK IN A GAME

The most yards rushed by a quarterback in a single NFL game is 173 yd by Michael Vick (USA) for the Atlanta Falcons against the Minnesota Vikings in the 30-24 victory on 1 December 2002 at Minneapolis, Minnesota, USA.

★ MOST YARDS GAINED RUSHING IN A CAREER

Emmitt Smith (USA) gained 18,355 yd in a career spanning from 1990 to 2004 playing for the Dallas Cowboys and Arizona Cardinals.

MOST TOUCHDOWNS IN A GAME

The most touchdowns scored in an NFL game is six by Ernie Nevers (USA) playing for Chicago Cardinals v. Chicago Bears on 28 November 1929; William Jones (USA) for Cleveland Browns v. Chicago Bears on 25 November 1951; and Gale Sayers (USA) for Chicago Bears v. San Francisco 49ers on 12 December 1965.

★ MOST TOUCHDOWNS IN A CAREER

Jerry Rice (San Francisco 49ers, Oakland Raiders and the Seattle Seahawks) scored a record 197 touchdowns between 1985 and 2004. He also holds the Super

★ MOST POINTS →
SCORED IN A SUPER BOWL QUARTER

The most points scored by both teams in a quarter of Super Bowl play is 37 by the New England Patriots and Carolina Panthers in the fourth quarter of Super Bowl XXXVIII held in Houston, Texas, USA, on 1 February 2004.

★ WORST START BY AN NFL FRANCHISE

The worst start by a new National Football League franchise is 26 consecutive regular season losses by the Tampa Bay Buccaneers after they joined the League in 1976.

SUPER BOWL

HIGHEST TEAM SCORE

The highest team score and record victory margin was achieved when the San Francisco 49ers beat the Denver Broncos 55-10 at New Orleans, Louisiana, USA, on 28 January 1990.

LONGEST TOUCHDOWN IN A SUPER BOWL

Muhsin Muhammad (USA) scored from 85 yd playing for the Carolina Panthers in Super Bowl XXXVIII on 1 February 2004.

MOST SUPER BOWL MVPs (MOST VALUABLE PLAYER)

Joe Montana, quarterback with the San Francisco 49ers, was voted Most Valuable Player in three Super Bowls: 1982, 1985 and 1990.

↑
★ MOST TOUCHDOWN PASSES IN A SEASON

Peyton Manning (USA) threw a record 49 touchdown passes playing for the Indianapolis Colts in 2004.

← ★ LONGEST RIDE
ON A MECHANICAL RODEO

Jamie Manning (Australia, pictured) rode a mechanical rodeo for 2 min 4.49 sec on the set of *Guinness World Records* at Seven Network Studios, Sydney, Australia on 2 April 2005. This record involves staying on the bull at level 1 for 8 seconds, and if successful, progressing to level 2 for 8 seconds, and every subsequent level for 8 seconds until the top level is reached. At this point, the participant must stay on at the top level – which must be set at 50 Hz – for as long as possible.

DOG RACING

★ MOST CONSECUTIVE WINS
From 15 April 1985 to 9 December 1986, Ballyregan Bob (UK) won a total of 32 consecutive greyhound races.

★ MOST MONEY WON AT A RACE
The richest greyhound race in the world is the Great American Greyhound Futurity Race, held every year at The Woodlands Racetrack, Kansas, USA. On 28 May 2001 (the eighth year of the race), it had a net purse of $344,762.25 (£242,449), of which $155,143 (£109,102) was claimed by the winner, Tom S Green Mile.

FASTEST GREYHOUND
The highest speed at which any greyhound has been timed is 67.32 km/h (41.83 mph) by Star Title at Wyong, New South Wales, Australia, on 5 March 1994.

DRESSAGE

★ MOST INDIVIDUAL WORLD CHAMPIONSHIP WINS
Dr Reiner Klimke (West Germany) won two titles on Mehmed in 1974 and Ahlerich in 1982. Isabell Werth (Germany) achieved the same feat on Gigolo in 1994 and 1998.

MOST TEAM WORLD CHAMPIONSHIP WINS
Germany won nine times between 1966 and 2002 (as West Germany between 1968 and 1990).

★ LARGEST PARADE OF HORSE-DRAWN CARRIAGES
A total of 208 horse-drawn carriages rode in a 5.7-km (3.5-mile) parade through the streets of Lingen, Germany, on 1 August 2004. The event was organized by the Dressurclub Hanekenfähr as part of the city's International Dressage Festival.

HORSE RACING

MOST CAREER WINS
Laffit Pincay Jr (USA) won 9,531 races in his career, from his first winner on 16 May 1964 to 1 March 2003.

OLDEST RACE-WINNING HORSE
Al Jabal, a pure-bred arab ridden by Brian Boulton and owned by Andrea Boulton (both UK), won The Three Horseshoes Handicap Stakes (over 6 furlongs) on 9 June 2002 at Barbury Castle, Wiltshire, UK, aged 19 years.

MOST RUNNERS IN A RACE
There were 66 runners in the Grand National at Aintree, Merseyside, UK, on 22 March 1929. The record for a race on the flat is 58 in the Lincolnshire Handicap at Lincoln, UK, on 13 March 1948.

★ MOST STEEPLECHASE WINS IN A CAREER
Tony McCoy (UK) won 2,211 races between 1992 and 2004. He also holds the record for **most steeplechase wins in a season**, with 289 in 2001/02.

RODEO

★ HIGHEST EARNINGS AT A SINGLE RODEO
Ty Murray (USA) earned $124,821 (£79,716) at the National Finals Rodeo in Las Vegas, Nevada, USA, in 1993.

← HIGHEST EARNINGS IN A RODEO CAREER

Ty Murray (USA) amassed career earnings of $2,931,227 (£1,870,624) from 1989 to 2002.

FLAT-RACING RECORDS

RACE (FIRST RUN)	FASTEST TIME/HORSE	MOST WINS/JOCKEY	MOST WINS/TRAINER
Epsom Derby (1780)	2 min 32.3 sec, Lammtarra (1995)	9, Lester Piggott (UK), 1954–83	7, Robert Robson (UK), 1793–1823
Prix de L'Arc de Triomphe (1920)	2 min 24.6 sec, Peintre Célèbre (1997)	4, Jacques Doyasbère (France), 1942–51 4, Frédéric Head (France), 1966–79 4, Yves Saint Martin (France), 1970–84 4, Pat Eddery (Ireland), 1980–87	5, Andre Fabre (France), 1987–98
Dubai World Cup (1996)	1 min 59.5 sec, Dubai Millennium (2000)	4, Jerry Bailey (USA), 1996–2003	4, Saeed bin Suroor (UAE), 1999–2003
VRC Melbourne Cup (1861)	3 min 16.3 sec, Kingston Rule (1990)	4, Bobby Lewis (Australia), 1902–27 4, Harry White (Australia), 1974–79	11, Bart Cummings (Australia), 1965–99
Kentucky Derby (1875)	1 min 59.4 sec, Secretariat (1973)	5, Eddie Arcaro (USA), 1938–52 5, Bill Hartack (USA), 1957–69	6, Ben Jones (USA), 1938–52

MOST ALL-AROUND WORLD CHAMPIONSHIP WINS

Ty Murray (USA) won seven all-around titles (awarded to the leading money winner in a single season in two or more events) in the Professional Rodeo Cowboy Association (PRCA) World Championships between 1989 and 1998.

★ MOST COMBINED WORLD CHAMPIONSHIP TITLES WON

Jim Shoulders (USA) won 16 combined events at PRCA World Championships from 1949 to 1959.

★ MOST MONEY WON BY A ROOKIE IN A YEAR

Will Lowe (USA) won $149,690 (£90,902) in 2002 (his debut year) in the bareback competition.

★ MOST WORLD CHAMPIONSHIP WINS

Guy Allen (USA) won 18 championships in steer roping in 1977, 1980, 1982, 1984, 1989, a record 11 consecutively from 1991 to 2001, and 2003–04.

SHOW JUMPING

HIGHEST JUMP

The official Fédération Equestre Internationale (FEI) record for high jump is 2.47 m (8 ft 1.25 in) by Huaso ex-Faithful, ridden by Alberto Larraguibel Morales (Chile) at Viña del Mar, Santiago, Chile, on 5 February 1949.

FARTHEST JUMP

The official FEI record for a long jump over water is 8.4 m (27 ft 6.7 in). The feat was achieved on 25 April 1975 by Something, ridden by André Ferreira (South Africa) in Johannesburg, South Africa.

MOST WORLD CHAMPIONSHIP WINS

Two men have won a total of two titles each – Hans Günter Winkler (Germany), who won in 1954 and 1955, and Raimondo d'Inzeo (Italy) in 1956 and 1960.

The **most show-jumping world championships won by a woman** is also two. The feat was achieved by Janou Tissot (née Lefebvre, France), who won two titles on Rocket in 1970 and 1974.

MOST TEAM WORLD CHAMPIONSHIP WINS

Three teams each hold two show-jumping World Championship titles: France in 1982 and 1990, Germany in 1994 and 1998, and the USA in 1986 and 2002.

★ MOST WORLD THREE-DAY EVENTING WINS BY AN INDIVIDUAL

Bruce Davidson (USA) has won two World Championship titles, on Irish Cap in 1974 and Might Tango in 1978. Blyth Tait (New Zealand, above) matched this record on Messiah in 1990 and Ready Teddy in 1998.

LARGEST PRIZE
FOR A SINGLE HORSE RACE

The Dubai World Cup, held in Dubai, United Arab Emirates, has a total purse of $6 million (£4 million), $3.6 million (£2.5 million) of which goes to the race winner. Pictured is jockey Jerry Bailey (USA), riding atop Balletto from the United Arab Emirates.

FARTHEST TRIPLE JUMP (WOMEN)

During the International Association of Athletics Federations (IAAF) World Indoor Championships at the Budapest Sportarena in Budapest, Hungary, on 6 March 2004, Tatyana Lebedeva (Russia) won the triple-jump final with a jump that measured 15.36 m (50 ft 4.5 in).

→ HOW YOUNG IS THE YOUNGEST OLYMPIC GOLD MEDALLIST? FIND OUT ON P.247

CROSS COUNTRY

MOST WORLD CHAMPIONSHIP INDIVIDUAL WINS (MEN)

John Ngugi (Kenya) won five World Championships from 1986 to 1989 and in 1992. Paul Tergat (Kenya) also won five times, between 1995 and 1999.

MOST WORLD CHAMPIONSHIP INDIVIDUAL WINS (WOMEN)

Grete Waitz (Norway) won five times between 1978 and 1981 and in 1983.

★ MOST WORLD CHAMPIONSHIP TEAM WINS (MEN)

Kenya won 18 team victories in the official World Championships between 1986 and 2003.

MOST WORLD CHAMPIONSHIP TEAM WINS (WOMEN)

The USSR won a total of eight women's team victories, in 1976–77, 1980–82 and 1988–90.

OLYMPIC GAMES

MOST ATHLETICS MEDALS (MEN)

Paavo Nurmi (Finland) has won a total of 12 medals (nine gold and three silver), which he secured at the Games of 1920, 1924 and 1928.

MOST ATHLETICS MEDALS (WOMEN)

Merlene Ottey (Jamaica) won eight medals – three silver and five bronze – over the course of the Games in 1980, 1984, 1992, 1996 and 2000.

MOST ATHLETICS GOLD MEDALS WON (WOMEN)

Four athletes have won four golds. Francina 'Fanny' Elsje Blankers-Koen (Netherlands) in the 100 m, 200 m, 80 m hurdles and 4 x 100 m relay in 1948; Elizabeth 'Betty' Cuthbert (Australia) in the 100 m, 200 m and 4 x 100 m relay in 1956 and 400 m in 1964; Bärbel Wöckel (née Eckert, GDR) in the 200 m and 4 x 100 m relay in 1976 and 1980; and Evelyn Ashford (USA) in the 100 m in 1984 and 4 x 100 m relay in 1984, 1988 and 1992.

WORLD ATHLETICS CHAMPIONSHIPS

MOST GOLD MEDALS

The World Championships – which are distinct from the Olympic Games – were inaugurated in 1983, when they were held in Helsinki, Finland. The most golds won is nine by Michael Johnson (USA): the 200 m in 1991 and 1995; the 400 m in 1993, 1995, 1997 and 1999; and the 4 x 400 m relay in 1993, 1995 and 1999.

Gail Devers (USA) has won the **most gold medals by a woman** with five: the 100 m in 1993, the 100 m hurdles in 1993, 1995 and 1999, and the 4 x 100 m in 1997.

★ MOST GOLD MEDALS FOR INDIVIDUAL EVENTS

Iván Pedroso (Cuba) has won five gold medals, in the long jump in 1993, 1995, 1997, 1999 and 2001.

The **most individual golds won by a woman** is five by Stefka Kostadinova (Bulgaria) in the high jump of 1985, 1987, 1989, 1993 and 1997, and Maria Mutola (Mozambique) in the 800 m races of 1993, 1995, 1997, 2001 and 2003.

FOR A FULL LIST OF ATHLETICS RECORDS, SEE P.266–75

★ MOST COMPETING COUNTRIES AT THE HALF MARATHON WORLD CHAMPIONSHIPS →

Athletes from 64 nations attended the 13th International Association of Athletics Federations (IAAF) World Half Marathon Championships in New Delhi, India, on 3 October 2004.

★ MOST MARATHON COMPETITORS

A total of 36,562 out of an initial 37,257 starters in the New York City Marathon, New York, USA, managed to complete the race on 7 November 2004. Pictured is the Verrazano Narrows Bridge at the start of the marathon in the Brooklyn borough of New York City. The first race in 1970 had only 55 finishers, who completed just over four laps of Central Park. The race increased in popularity following the decision in 1976 to move the route on to the city's streets.

MOST MEDALS (MEN)

Carl Lewis (USA) won 10 medals: eight gold (the 100 m, long jump and 4 x 100 m relay in 1983; the 100 m, long jump and 4 x 100 m relay in 1987; the 100 m and 4 x 100 m relay in 1991), one silver (the long jump in 1991) and one bronze (the 200 m in 1993).

MOST MEDALS (WOMEN)

Merlene Ottey (Jamaica) won 14 medals – three gold, four silver and seven bronze – in the 100 m, 200 m and 4 x 100 m from 1983 to 1997.

MISCELLANEOUS

★ OLDEST ROAD RACE

The Red Hose Five Mile Race has been held annually in Carnwath, UK, since 1508. It is named after its original prize – a pair of hose, or stockings, traditionally red.

MOST PARTICIPANTS IN AN ATHLETICS RELAY RACE

On 24 April 2004, the Batavierenrace relay race (an annual race from Nijmegen to Enschede, the Netherlands) featured a total of 7,375 runners.

FASTEST 100 MILE RELAY (TEAM OF 10)

On 21 September 2003, 10 cadets from the 2331 (St Ives) Squadron Air Training Corps (UK) set a time of 10 hr 21 min 35 sec in the 100 mile relay at the St Ivo Outdoor Centre, Cambridgeshire, UK.

MOST ATHLETICS WORLD RECORDS SET ON ONE DAY

Jesse Owens (USA) set six world records in 45 minutes at Ann Arbor, Michigan, USA, on 25 May 1935. In order, by times, they were:
1 3:15 p.m.: 100 yd in 9.4 seconds
2 3:25 p.m.: 8.13-m (26-ft 8.25-in) long jump
3 & 4 3:45 p.m.: 220 yd (and 200 m) in 20.3 seconds
5 & 6 4:00 p.m.: 220 yd low hurdles (and 200 m) in 22.6 seconds.

LONGEST WINNING SEQUENCE IN A TRACK EVENT

Edwin Corley Moses (USA) won 122 consecutive races at the 400 m hurdles. The winning sequence began on 2 September 1977 and ended when Moses was beaten by Danny Lee Harris (USA) at Madrid, Spain, on 4 June 1987.

MOST FINISHERS IN A 5 KM ROAD RACE

A total of 35,957 people finished the 5 km Race for the Cure, held in Washington DC, USA, on 6 June 1998. The race is organized by the Susan G Komen Breast Cancer Foundation.

★ LONGEST ANNUAL RUNNING RACE

The longest race staged annually is the Sri Chinmoy 4,989-km (3,100-mile) race, which is held at Jamaica, New York, USA. The fastest time to complete the race is 42 days 13 hr 24 min 3 sec, a feat achieved by Wolfgang Schwerk (Germany) in 2002.

LONGEST WINNING STREAK IN A FIELD EVENT

Iolanda Balas (Romania) won 150 consecutive competitions at the high jump from 1956 to 1967.

OLDEST WOMAN TO SET AN ATHLETICS WORLD RECORD

Marina Styepanova (USSR, b. 1 May 1950) was 36 years 139 days old when she set the record of 52.94 seconds for the 400 m hurdles at Tashkent, USSR, on 17 September 1986.

FASTEST 10 KM RUN WEARING A PANTOMIME COSTUME (TWO PERSON)

Simon Wiles and Les Morton (both UK) ran the Percy Pud 10 km race in a time of 44 min 2 sec at Loxley, Sheffield, South Yorkshire, UK, on 2 December 2001 while wearing a pantomime camel costume.

HIGHEST ALTITUDE MARATHON

The highest start to a marathon is that of the Everest Marathon, first run on 27 November 1987. It begins at Gorak Shep, 5,212 m (17,100 ft), ending at Namche Bazar, 3,444 m (11,300 ft). The fastest time to complete this race by a man is 3 hr 50 min 23 sec by Hari Roka (Nepal) in 2000. The record for a woman is 5 hr 16 min 3 sec, by Anne Stentiford (UK) in 1997.

← HIGHEST POLE VAULT

The **highest pole vault by a man** is 6.15 m (20 ft 2 in) by Sergei Bubka (Ukraine) in Donetsk, Ukraine, on 21 February 1993. Yelena Isinbayeva (Russia, pictured) cleared 4.9 m (16 ft 0.75 in) in Madrid, Spain, on 6 March 2005 to take the record for the ★ **highest indoor pole vault by a woman.**

ENDURANCE

★ GREATEST LIFETIME MILEAGE RUN BY A MAN

Dr Ron Hill (UK), who is the 1969 European and 1970 Commonwealth marathon champion, has trained every day since 20 December 1964. His training log shows a total of over 234,177 km (145,511 miles) from 3 September 1956 to 23 March 2005. He has competed in 115 marathons, with all but his last sub 2:52, and has raced in 88 nations.

★ GREATEST LIFETIME MILEAGE RUN BY A WOMAN

Kathy Pycior (USA) has not missed a day's training since 31 December 1980. She has kept a detailed log of route and distance for every single run between 1 January 1981 and 30 June 2004, and has run a total distance of 48,656.5 miles (78,305 km).

LONGEST EVER RUNNING RACE

The 1929 transcontinental race from New York City to Los Angeles, California, USA, was competed over a total of 5,850 km (3,635 miles). Finnish-born Johnny Salo was the winner, in 79 days from 31 March to 17 June. In a 'two horse' race, his elapsed time of 525 hr 57 min 20 sec (averaging a speed of 11.12 km/h, or 6.91 mph) put him only 2 min 47 sec ahead of Pietro 'Peter' Gavuzzi (UK).

★ MOST 100 KM RACES IN A LIFETIME

Henri Girault (France) ran 517 races at 100 km – an International Association of Athletics Federations (IAAF) recognized distance – from 1979 to 6 November 2004.

HALF MARATHONS

FASTEST (MEN)

The world best time on a properly measured course is 59 min 5 sec by Paul Tergat (Kenya) at Lisbon, Portugal, on 26 March 2000. The official world best recognized by the IAAF is 59 min 17 sec, also by Paul Tergat, at Milan, Italy, on 4 April 1998.

FASTEST (WOMEN)

Masako Chiba (Japan) ran a half marathon in 66 min 43 sec in Tokyo, Japan, on 19 January 1997.

LARGEST

The BUPA Great North Run, between Newcastle upon Tyne and South Shields, Tyne and Wear, UK, had 36,822 finishers out of 50,173 entries for the event held on 22 October 2000.

★ DEEPEST

On 4 March 2004, 11 participants made 8.5 circuits of a 2,438-m (7,999-ft) running track at a depth of 212 m (695 ft) in Bochnia salt mine, Poland.

★ MOST INDIVIDUAL WINS AT THE WORLD CHAMPIONSHIP

Two runners have won three times: Tegla Loroupe (Kenya) in 1997, 1998 and 1999, and Paula Radcliffe (UK) in 2000, 2001 and 2003.

LONGEST ESTABLISHED MAJOR MARATHON

The Boston marathon (USA) was first held on 19 April 1897, when it was run over a distance of 39 km (24 miles). John A Kelley (USA) finished the Boston marathon 61 times between 1928 and 1992, winning in 1935 and 1945.

FASTEST TIME TO COMPLETE THE HAWAIIAN IRONMAN (WOMEN)

Paula Newby-Fraser (Zimbabwe) completed the Hawaiian Ironman in a time of 8 hr 55 min 28 sec in 1992. She has also achieved the **most wins in the Hawaiian Ironman**, with a total of eight victories in 1986, 1988–89, 1991–94 and 1996.

★ MOST TEAM MEDALS AT THE WORLD CHAMPIONSHIPS

Kenya has won eight medals in the men's World Championships, from 1992 to 1995, 1997, 2000, 2002 and 2004.

The **most medals in the women's World Championships** is six, by Romania, from 1993 to 1997 and in 2000.

★ MOST INDIVIDUAL MEDALS AT THE WORLD CHAMPIONSHIPS

Lidia Simon-Slavuteanu (Romania) won eight medals – three team gold, one team silver, one individual silver and three individual bronze – between 1996 and 2000.

FASTEST SPEED MARCH WITH 40-LB PACK

William Hugh MacLennan (UK) ran a half marathon wearing full military combat gear and carrying an 18-kg (40-lb) backpack in 1 hr 43 min 42 sec at the Redcar Half Marathon, North Yorkshire, UK, on 25 March 2001.

MARATHONS

FASTEST AGGREGATE TIME TO RUN A MARATHON ON EACH CONTINENT (MEN)

Tim Rogers (UK) ran a marathon on each continent in 34 hr 23 min 8 sec between 13 February and 23 May 1999. He also holds the record for the **shortest duration to complete a marathon on each continent (men)**: 99 days, from 13 February to 23 May 1999.

★ FASTEST AGGREGATE TIME TO RUN A MARATHON ON EACH CONTINENT (WOMEN)

Amie Dworecki (USA) completed a marathon on all seven continents in a total time of 32 hr 24 min 29 sec between 25 February 2002 and 2 August 2003. She also holds the record for the **★ shortest duration to complete a marathon on each continent (women)** – 523 days, between 25 February 2002 and 2 August 2003.

★ MOST COMPLETED

Horst Preisler (Germany) has run 1,305 races of 42.195 km (26 miles 385 yd) or longer from 1974 to 31 December 2004.

★ MOST TRIATHLON WORLD CHAMPIONSHIP VICTORIES (MEN) ↗

Simon Lessing (UK) has won the triathlon World Championships a total of four times, in 1992, 1995, 1996 and 1998. In addition to his victories, he has also won the greatest number of medals overall to date in the World Championships, with two silver medals (in 1993 and 1999) and one bronze (in 1997).

★ MOST NORTHERLY

The North Pole Marathon has been held annually since 2002, and the course at the geographic North Pole has been certified by the Association of International Marathons and Road Races (AIMS). The fastest men's time is 3 hr 43 min 17 sec by Sean Burch (USA); the fastest woman is Stevie Matthews (UK), with a time of 7 hr 55 min 32 sec.

FASTEST TIME TO COMPLETE THREE MARATHONS IN THREE DAYS

Raymond Hubbard (UK) ran three marathons in three days with a total time of 8 hr 22 min 31 sec. He ran in Belfast in 2 hr 45 min 55 sec, London in 2 hr 48 min 45 sec, and Boston in 2 hr 47 min 51 sec from 16 to 18 April 1988.

TRIATHLON

MOST WINS IN THE HAWAIIAN IRONMAN (MEN)

Dave Scott (USA) won six races, in 1980, from 1982 to 1984 and 1986–87. He shares this record with Mark Allen (USA), who has also won six races in 1989–93 and in 1995.

FASTEST TIME TO COMPLETE THE HAWAIIAN IRONMAN (MEN)

Luc van Lierde (Belgium) set a time of 8 hr 4 min 8 sec in 1996.

Note: The triathlon is a race comprising three different events, which are performed consecutively.

Competitors at the Hawaiian Ironman triathlon begin with a 3.8-km (2.4-mile) swim, then a 180-km (112-mile) bike ride and end with a 42-km (26.2-mile) marathon. (Despite its name, women can also enter the Ironman!)

The triathlon is considered to be a separate discipline from athletics.

BALL SPORTS

MOST WOMEN'S HOCKEY CHAMPIONS' TROPHY WINS ←

Australia (Wendy Alcorn, far left) has won this trophy a record six times, in 1991, 1993, 1995, 1997, 1999 and 2003. The trophy was first contested in 1987.

★ MOST WORLD TOUR TITLES BY A PAIR

Sinjin Smith and Randy Stoklos (both USA) won four men's titles, in 1989–90 and 1992–93.

Shelda Bede and Adriana Behar (both Brazil) won six titles, from 1997 to 2001 and, in 2004, the ★ **most women's world tour titles by a pair**.

CANADIAN FOOTBALL (CFL)

★ HIGHEST SCORING GREY CUP FINAL

In 1989, the Saskatchewan Roughriders beat the Hamilton Tiger-Cats 43-40, to give an aggregate score of 83.

LONGEST FIELD GOAL

Paul McCallum (Canada) scored a goal from 62 yards for the Saskatchewan Roughriders v. Edmonton Eskimos on 27 October 2001.

★ MOST YARDS RECEIVING IN ONE GAME

Hal Patterson (USA) received passes totalling 338 yards for the Montreal Alouettes v. Hamilton Tiger-Cats on 29 September 1956.

AUSTRALIAN FOOTBALL (AFL)

THE BROWNLOW MEDAL

The Brownlow medal has been awarded since 1924 and is given to the fairest and best player in the Australian Football League (AFL) each season.

★ MOST BROWNLOW MEDAL WINS

A record three wins is shared by Haydn Bunton, in 1931, 1932 and 1935; Dick Reynolds, in 1934, 1937 and 1938; and Ian Stewart, in 1965, 1966 and 1971 (all Australia).

★ MOST PREMIERSHIPS WON BY A PLAYER

Michael Tuck (Australia) won seven titles with Hawthorn, from 1972 to 1991.

MOST GAMES PLAYED

Michael Tuck (Australia) played 426 games for Hawthorn from 1972 to 1991.

MOST PREMIERSHIP TITLES

Two teams have amassed 16 AFL Premiership titles: Carlton between 1906 and 1995, and Essendon between 1897 and 2000.

BEACH VOLLEYBALL

★ MOST MEN'S WORLD CHAMPIONSHIPS

The Brazil men's pair has won the title three times, in 1997, 1999 and 2003.

DISCIPLINARY FINES ←
LARGEST FOR A SINGLE AFL MATCH

A fine of AUS$67,500 (£28,163; $49,773) was imposed in an AFL match between Western Bulldogs and St Kilda on 4 May 2003. Nine players from each side were fined, but only one player was suspended. Bulldogs' Ryan Hargrave (left) was banned for three games for kicking St Kilda's Heath Black (both Australia) in the face during a brawl.

★ AFL GRAND FINAL WINS – MOST CONSECUTIVE →

From 2001 to 2003, the Brisbane Lions had three consecutive wins. The Lions were formed in the first ever union of two AFL clubs, when the Brisbane Bears merged with the Fitzroy Lions. The new club was formed in 1996, before entering national competition in 1997.

★ MOST TOUCHDOWNS BY A PLAYER IN ONE GAME

Two players have scored six touchdowns: Eddie James (Canada) for Winnipeg St Johns v. Winnipeg Garrison on 28 September 1932; and Bob McNamara (USA) for the Winnipeg Blue Bombers v. British Columbia Lions (aka BC Lions) on 13 October 1956.

FIELD HOCKEY

MOST MEN'S CHAMPIONS' TROPHY WINS

The greatest number of wins is eight by Germany, in 1986–88 (as West Germany), 1991–92, 1995, 1997 and 2001.

HIGHEST SCORE IN AN INTERNATIONAL MATCH (WOMEN)

England defeated France 23-0 at Merton, Greater London, UK, on 3 February 1923.

★ MOST GOALS SCORED IN INTERNATIONAL HOCKEY

Sohail Abbas (Pakistan) scored a total of 274 goals between 1998 and 2004.

HIGHEST ATTENDANCE AT A MATCH

A total of 65,165 people attended the game between England and the USA at Wembley, London, UK, on 11 March 1978.

GAELIC FOOTBALL

★ HIGHEST COMBINED SCORE IN AN ALL-IRELAND FINAL

The highest combined score by both teams is 45 points, when Cork (26, 3-17)* beat Galway (19, 2-13) in 1973.

★ MOST ALL-IRELAND FINAL WINS

Kerry won 33 All-Ireland Championships from 1903 to 2004.

★ MOST CONSECUTIVE ALL-IRELAND FINAL WINS

Wexford had four wins between 1915 and 1918. Kerry equalled the feat twice, between 1929 and 1932, and 1978 and 1981.

HANDBALL

HIGHEST SCORE IN AN INTERNATIONAL MATCH

The USSR beat Afghanistan 86-2 in the 'Friendly Army Tournament' at Miskolc, Hungary, in August 1981.

TARGET SHOOTING

Jonas Källman (Sweden) hit eight handball targets in 30 seconds in Stockholm, Sweden, on 27 November 2001.

*Note: In the Gaelic football records, the aggregate score is listed first. The goals and points, respectively, are given separately afterwards.

← MOST MEN'S HANDBALL WORLD CHAMPIONSHIPS

Romania has won four times, in 1961, 1964, 1970 and 1974; Sweden matched this achievement with their fourth victory in 1999 to follow wins in 1954, 1958 and 1990. Pictured is the Swedish captain, Stefan Lovgren, celebrating Sweden's victory in 1999.

→ WHICH BALL SPORT IS CONSIDERED TO BE THE FASTEST IN THE WORLD? FIND OUT ON P.223

→ HOW FAST WAS THE FASTEST SHUTTLECOCK EVER STRUCK? FIND OUT ON P.248

MOST COMMONWEALTH NETBALL TITLES

Netball has been contested twice at the Commonwealth Games, first in Kuala Lumpur, Malaysia, in 1998 and then in Manchester, UK, in 2002. Australia won both times. Pictured are Sherelle McMahon (Australia, left) battling Sherly Clarke (New Zealand) in the 2002 final of the Commonwealth Games.

Note: in the hurling records, the aggregate score is listed first. The goals and points, respectively, are given separately afterwards, in brackets.

HURLING

★ **HIGHEST COMBINED SCORE IN AN ALL-IRELAND FINAL**
The greatest aggregate score is 64 points, achieved when Cork beat Wexford 39 (6-21) 25 (5-10) in the 1970 final in Dublin, Ireland.

HIGHEST TEAM SCORE IN AN ALL-IRELAND FINAL
This stands at 41 and was created by Tipperary (4-29) when they beat Antrim's score of 18 (3-9) at Croke Park, Dublin, Ireland, in 1989.

★ **LOWEST COMBINED SCORE IN AN ALL-IRELAND FINAL**
The lowest total is 4, scored when Tipperary 4 (1-1) beat Galway (nil) in the first championship held at Birr, Ireland, in 1887.

★ **MOST ALL-IRELAND FINAL VICTORIES**
Cork has won 29 championships between 1890 and 2004.

MOST CONSECUTIVE ALL-IRELAND FINAL WINS
Cork had four successive wins from 1941 to 1944, all at Croke Park, Dublin, Ireland.

KORFBALL

HIGHEST SCORE IN A WORLD CHAMPIONSHIP FINAL
The highest team score is 23, by the Netherlands against Belgium (11) in 1999.

★ **LARGEST TOURNAMENT**
On 14 June 2003, 2,571 men and women participated in the Kom Keukens/Ten Donck international youth korfball tournament in Ridderkerk, the Netherlands.

MOST VICTORIES AT THE WORLD CHAMPIONSHIPS
The Netherlands has won six times, in 1978, 1984, 1987, 1995, 1999 and 2003.

LACROSSE

LONGEST THROW
Barnet Quinn of Ottawa, Canada, achieved a throw of 148.91 m (488 ft 6 in) on 10 September 1892.

★ **MOST INDOOR WORLD CHAMPIONSHIP WINS**
The inaugural indoor lacrosse World Championships held in Ontario, Canada, in 2003 were won by Canada, who beat the Iroquois Nationals 21-4 for the gold medal. The winning team were undefeated in the competition.

← CANADIAN FOOTBALL – MOST GAMES PLAYED

Lui Passaglia (Canada) played in 408 CFL games for the British Columbia Lions (aka the BC Lions) from 1976 to 2000. He also scored a CFL career record 3,991 points for the BC Lions during that time.

← FASTEST SPORT

The fastest projectile speed in any ball game is 302 km/h (187.6 mph) in jai-alai. This compares with 273 km/h (169.6 mph) for an electronically timed golf ball driven off a tee.

NETBALL

HIGHEST TEAM SCORE AT A WORLD CHAMPIONSHIP
On 9 July 1991 during the World Championships at Sydney, Australia, the Cook Islands beat Vanuatu 120-38.

MOST WORLD CHAMPIONSHIP WINS
Australia has won a record eight times, in 1963, 1971, 1975, 1979, 1983, 1991, 1995 and 1999.

MOST POINTS SCORED BY ONE PLAYER AT A WORLD CHAMPIONSHIP
Irene van Dyk (South Africa) scored 543 goals in the 1995 tournament.

SHINTY

★ MOST CONSECUTIVE CAMANACHD CUP WINS
Kingussie (Scotland) won seven times between 1997 and 2003.

HIGHEST TEAM SCORE IN A CAMANACHD FINAL
This record was set in 1997 when Kingussie beat Newtonmore 12-1 at Fort William, Highland, UK.

BEACH VOLLEYBALL – MOST WORLD TITLE WINS (WOMEN) →

The Brazil women's pair has won the World Championships three times, in 1997, 1999 and 2001. Pictured are Shelda Bede (left) and Adriana Behar (both Brazil) celebrating their victory in a 2004 World Tour semi-final match in Rio de Janeiro, Brazil, in September 2004.

VOLLEYBALL

★ MOST WORLD CHAMPIONSHIP WINS (MEN)
The USSR has won six titles, in 1949, 1952, 1960, 1962, 1978 and 1982.

★ MOST WORLD CHAMPIONSHIP WINS (WOMEN)
The USSR have won five titles, in 1952, 1956, 1960, 1970 and 1990.

★ MOST CONSECUTIVE WORLD CHAMPIONSHIP WINS (MEN)
Italy has won three times – in Brazil (1990), Greece (1994) and Japan (1998).

★ MOST WORLD CUP WINS (MEN)
The USSR have won the volleyball World Cup four times, in 1965, 1977, 1981 and 1991. Russia also won the title in 1999.

★ MOST WORLD CUP WINS (WOMEN)
Cuba had four consecutive victories in the volleyball World Cup, in 1989, 1991, 1995 and 1999.

★ BEACH VOLLEYBALL: MOST CONSECUTIVE PASSES
The most consecutive passes of a beach volleyball – one touch per person – is 29, on the set of *L'Été de Tous les Records*, Biscarrosse, France, on 1 July 2004.

MOST CFL GREY CUPS

The Toronto Argonauts have won 15 Grey Cups, in 1914, 1921, 1933, 1937–38, 1945–47, 1950, 1952, 1983, 1991, 1996–97 and 2004. Damon Allen (USA) is pictured above, holding the Grey Cup after the win in 2004.

★ MOST HITS
IN A MAJOR LEAGUE SEASON

Ichiro Suzuki (Japan) achieved 262 base hits playing for the Seattle Mariners in 2004.

WORLD SERIES – MOST WINS

Played annually between the winners of the National League and the American League, the World Series was first staged unofficially in 1903, and officially from 1905. The most wins to date is 26 by the New York Yankees, between 1923 and 2000.

MOST CONSECUTIVE GAMES

Cal Ripken Jr (USA, Baltimore Orioles) played 2,632 consecutive games from 30 May 1982 to 19 September 1998.

MOST RUNS IN A MAJOR LEAGUE SEASON

Billy Hamilton (USA, Philadelphia Phillies) scored 192 runs in 1894.

MOST RUNS BATTED IN IN A MAJOR LEAGUE SEASON

Hack Wilson (USA, Chicago Cubs) batted in a total of 191 runs in the 1930 season. The **most runs batted in in a major league career** is 2,297, by Henry 'Hank' Aaron (USA) for the Milwaukee Braves from 1954 to 1976.

★ MOST DOUBLES HIT IN A MAJOR LEAGUE SEASON

Earl Webb (USA) hit 67 playing for the Boston Red Sox in 1931.

MOST DOUBLES HIT IN A MAJOR LEAGUE CAREER

Tris Speaker (USA, Boston Red Sox, Cleveland Indians, Washington Senators and Philadelphia Athletics) hit 792 doubles from 1907 to 1928.

★ MOST TRIPLES HIT IN A MAJOR LEAGUE SEASON

Chief Wilson (USA) hit 36 triples in a season playing for the Pittsburgh Pirates in 1912.

MOST TRIPLES HIT IN A MAJOR LEAGUE CAREER

Sam Crawford (USA, Cincinnati Reds and Detroit Tigers) hit 309 triples from 1899 to 1917.

LONGEST HOME RUN HIT

On 10 September 1960, Mickey Mantle (USA) hit a home run of 193 m (633 ft) for the New York Yankees against the Detroit Tigers at Briggs Stadium, Detroit, Michigan, USA.

MOST HOME RUNS IN A SEASON

Barry Bonds (USA) scored an unsurpassed 73 home runs playing for the San Francisco Giants in 2001.

MOST HOME RUNS IN A CAREER

Hank Aaron (USA) hit 755 in his career: 733 for the Milwaukee (1954–65) and Atlanta (1966–74) Braves in the National League, and 22 for the Milwaukee Brewers in the American League, 1975–76. On 8 April 1974, he beat the previous record of 714 set by George Herman 'Babe' Ruth (USA) in 1935.

MOST RUNS IN A CAREER

At the close of the 2003 season, Rickey Henderson (USA) had scored 2,295 runs.

★ HIGHEST SLUGGING PERCENTAGE IN A SEASON

A batter's slugging percentage is calculated by dividing the total number of bases gained by the total number of 'at bats'. Barry Bonds (USA) registered an unprecedented .863 playing for the San Francisco Giants in 2001.

★ HIGHEST SLUGGING PERCENTAGE IN MAJOR LEAGUE HISTORY

Babe Ruth (USA) recorded .690 playing for the Boston Red Sox and the New York Yankees between 1914 and 1935.

HISTORY OF BASEBALL

Baseball is descended from the English games of cricket and rounders, although the exact origins of America's national pastime are unclear.

The first set of rules were published for the Knickerbocker Club of New York in 1845 by Alexander Cartwright (USA), often referred to as 'The Father of Modern Baseball'.

The professional game began in 1865 in the United States, with the first World Series contested between the National and American Leagues in 1903.

★ FASTEST TIME
TO VISIT ALL MAJOR LEAGUE BASEBALL STADIUMS

Joe Pfeiffer of Irvine, California, USA, watched a complete baseball game at all 30 Major League stadiums in the USA and Canada in 30 days, from 22 July to 20 August 2004. He began in San Francisco, California, and finished in Houston, Texas, USA.

HIGHEST BATTING AVERAGE IN A MAJOR LEAGUE CAREER

Tyrus Raymond 'Ty' Cobb (USA, Detroit Tigers, Philadelphia Athletics) had a batting average of .367 between 1905 and 1928.

MOST BASE HITS IN A MAJOR LEAGUE CAREER

Peter Rose (USA, Cincinnati Reds, Philadelphia Phillies, Montreal Expos, Cincinnati) had a total of 4,256 base hits from 1963 to 1986.

MOST TOTAL BASES IN A CAREER

Between 1954 and 1976, Hank Aaron (USA) achieved the highest number of total bases in a career, with 6,856.

MOST INNINGS PITCHED IN A CAREER

Denton True 'Cy' Young (USA) pitched a record total of 7,356 innings between 1890 and 1911.

MOST GAMES WON BY A PITCHER IN A CAREER

Cy Young (USA) won 511 games playing for the Cleveland Spiders, St Louis Perfectos/Cardinals, Boston Americans/Somersets/Pilgrims/Red Sox, Cleveland Naps and Boston Braves between 1890 and 1911.

★ MOST GAMES LOST BY A PITCHER IN A CAREER

Cy Young (USA) lost 316 games from 1890 to 1911.

MOST MAJOR LEAGUE GAMES PITCHED →

By the end of the 2003 season, Jesse Orosco (USA) had pitched 1,251 games for the New York Mets, LA Dodgers, Cleveland Indians, Milwaukee Brewers, Baltimore Orioles, St Louis Cardinals, Minnesota Twins, New York Yankees and San Diego Padres.

★ MOST GAMES SAVED BY A PITCHER

A save is credited to a relief pitcher if he is the last pitcher in a game won by his team. Lee Smith (USA) saved 478 games between 1980 and 1997 playing for the Chicago Cubs, Boston Red Sox, St Louis Cardinals, New York Yankees, Baltimore Orioles, California Angels, Cincinnati Reds and Montreal Expos.

★ MOST BATSMEN HIT BY A PITCHER

Gus Weyhing (USA) hit 277 batters between 1887 and 1901 while pitching for the Philadelphia Athletics, Brooklyn Ward's Wonders, Philadelphia Phillies, Louisville Colonels, Pittsburgh Pirates, Washington Senators, St Louis Cardinals, Brooklyn Superbas, Cincinnati Reds and Cleveland Blues.

★ MOST WILD PITCHES

A 'wild pitch' is a ball pitched beyond the area usually covered by the catcher. Tony Mullane (USA) threw 343 wild pitches playing for the Detroit Wolverines, Louisville Eclipse, St Louis Browns, Toledo Blue Stockings, Cincinnati Red Stockings/Reds, Baltimore Orioles and Cleveland Spiders from 1881 to 1894.

→ HOW MUCH DID THE MOST VALUABLE BASEBALL CARD SELL FOR? FIND OUT ON P.135

MOST WINS
OF THE MOST VALUABLE PLAYER AWARD

Barry Bonds (USA) has won more Most Valuable Player (MVP) awards than anyone else in Major League baseball, with seven. He won in 1990, 1992, 1993 and 2001–03, winning his seventh award while playing with the San Francisco Giants in the 2004 season.

BASKETBALL

★ LONGEST SUSPENSION
FOR AN ON-COURT INCIDENT

The longest non-drug-related suspension given out by the NBA to an individual player is 72 days to Ron Artest (USA, pictured far left) of the Indiana Pacers following their game at the Detroit Pistons on 19 November 2004. Artest was banned from playing the rest of the 2004/05 season after sparking a mêlée in which Pacers players brawled with Pistons fans.

MOST FIELD GOALS IN AN NBA SEASON

Wilt Chamberlain (USA) – voted in 1996 as one of the 50 greatest players in NBA history – scored a record 1,597 field goals for the Philadelphia Warriors in the 1961/62 season.

MOST POINTS SCORED BY A TEAM IN AN NBA GAME

The Detroit Pistons – the 2003/04 NBA Champions – scored a record 186 points in a match against the Denver Nuggets (who scored an impressive 184) at Denver, Colorado, USA, on 13 December 1983.

HISTORY OF BASKETBALL

Basketball was invented in 1891 by Dr James Naismith (Canada) in Springfield, Massachusetts, USA, in an attempt to provide sporting activity for his charges at the local YMCA during the long winter months. Using a football, he established some basic rules and nailed a peach basket to the wall of the indoor gym.

One of his students then came up with the name 'basket ball' and, after the first official game on 20 January 1892, the new sport spread quickly across the USA.

HIGHEST POINT SCORING AVERAGE IN AN NBA CAREER

For players exceeding 10,000 points (the minimum at which an average can be calculated), the record average points per game is 30.1 by Michael Jordan (USA), who scored 32,292 points in 1,072 games for the Chicago Bulls (1984–98) and the Washington Wizards (2001–03).

HIGHEST SCORING AVERAGE IN AN NBA SEASON

Wilt Chamberlain (USA) scored an average of 50.4 points a game for the Philadelphia Warriors in the 1961/62 season.

MOST REBOUNDS IN AN NBA CAREER

Wilt Chamberlain (USA) recorded 23,924 rebounds in 1,045 games playing for the Philadelphia Warriors (1959–62), San Francisco Warriors (1962–64), Philadelphia 76ers (1964–68) and Los Angeles Lakers (1968–73).

MOST BLOCKS IN AN NBA CAREER

Hakeem Olajuwon (USA) achieved 3,830 blocks in 1,238 games while playing for the Houston Rockets (1984–2001) and the Toronto Raptors (2001–02).

MOST ASSISTS IN AN NBA CAREER

John Stockton (USA) has the most assists in an NBA career, with 15,806 in 1,504 games playing for 19 seasons for the Utah Jazz (1984–2003).

MOST CONSECUTIVE NBA GAMES PLAYED

A C Green (USA) played 1,177 games for the Los Angeles Lakers, Phoenix Suns, Dallas Mavericks and Miami Heat from 19 November 1986 to 20 March 2001.

★ MOST THREE-POINTERS IN AN NBA CAREER →

Reggie Miller (USA) scored 2,491 three-point field goals for the Indiana Pacers from 1987 to 2005. He also broke the record for the most three-pointers in a rookie season with 61 in 1987/88.

MOST CAREER MINUTES →
PLAYED IN THE NBA

Kareem Abdul-Jabbar (USA) played for a record 57,446 minutes during the course of his career from 1969 to 1989.

MOST CONSECUTIVE NBA WINS

The Los Angeles Lakers won 33 NBA games in succession from 5 November 1971 to 7 January 1972.

★ MOST FREE THROWS IN AN NBA CAREER

Karl Malone (USA) made 9,787 free throws in 1,476 games playing for Utah Jazz from 1985 to 2003 and the Los Angeles Lakers in 2003/04.

MOST POINTS IN NBA ALL-STAR GAMES

Michael Jordan (USA) scored 262 points in NBA All-Star games, scoring 20 points in his 14th appearance in Atlanta, Georgia, USA, on 9 February 2003.

MOST POINTS SCORED BY AN INDIVIDUAL IN AN NBA GAME

Wilt Chamberlain (USA) scored 100 points when he played for the Philadelphia Warriors against the New York Knicks on 2 March 1962.

MOST GAMES PLAYED IN AN NBA CAREER

Robert Parish (USA) played 1,611 regular season games from 1976 to 1997.

MOST NBA CHAMPIONSHIP TITLES

The Boston Celtics have won 16 titles, in 1957, 1959–66, 1968–69, 1974, 1976, 1981, 1984 and 1986.

★ LONGEST GOAL THROWN IN A WOMEN'S GAME

Allyson Fasnacht (USA) scored a field goal measured at 24.85 m (81 ft 6 in) for Glenvar Highlanders against JJ Kelly at Salem Civic Center, Salem, Virginia, USA, on 6 December 2002.

★ MOST MINIATURE BASKETBALL SHOTS MADE IN ONE MINUTE

Jay Kletecka (USA) made 139 miniature basketball shots in one minute at Willoughby Hills, Ohio, USA, on 11 July 2004.

★ FARTHEST DISTANCE SLAM-DUNKED FROM A TRAMPOLINE

Jonathon Thibout (France) slam-dunked a basketball from a trampoline placed 5.86 m (19 ft 2 in) from the backboard on 3 August 2004.

LONGEST TIME TO SPIN A BASKETBALL ON ONE FINGER

Zhao Guang (China) spun a regulation basketball on one finger for a total time of 3 hr 59 min on 29 January 2003 in Shenyang, China.

★ GREATEST DISTANCE TO DRIBBLE A BASKETBALL IN 24 HOURS

Tyler Curiel (USA) dribbled a basketball for a distance of 174.46 km (108.4 miles) in 24 hours at Tulane University, New Orleans, Louisiana, USA, on 15–16 December 2003.

→ WHAT'S THE FASTEST TIME FOR ONE PERSON TO WATCH COMPLETE GAMES AT ALL THE MAJOR LEAGUE BASEBALL STADIUMS? FIND OUT ON P.224

★ MOST NBA GAMES
WON BY A COACH

During the NBA's golden anniversary celebrations in 1996, Lenny Wilkens (USA) was named one of the 10 greatest coaches in NBA history. To date, he has won a record 1,315 games as an NBA coach. He is also one of only two men to be inducted into the Hall of Fame as both a player and a coach.

↑ ★ MOST MEN'S TEAM KARATE KUMITE WORLD TITLES

Two nations have won six World Championships (instituted 1970) at the men's kumite team event: the UK in 1975, 1982, 1984, 1986, 1988 and 1990; and France in 1972, 1994, 1996, 1998, 2000 and 2004. Karate is Japanese for 'open hand'; kumite means 'sparring'.

Pictured are the French team after winning the title at the 17th Championships on 19 November 2004.

BOXING

LONGEST REIGN BY A WORLD HEAVYWEIGHT
Joe Louis (USA) was champion for 11 years 252 days, from 22 June 1937, when he knocked out James Joseph Braddock (USA), until announcing his retirement on 1 March 1949.

MOST KNOCKDOWNS
Vic Toweel (South Africa) knocked down Danny O'Sullivan (UK) 14 times in 10 rounds in their world bantamweight fight in Johannesburg, South Africa, on 2 December 1950.

SHORTEST WORLD TITLE FIGHT
Gerald McClellan (USA) beat Jay Bell (USA) in 20 seconds in a World Boxing Council (WBC) middleweight bout at Puerto Rico on 7 August 1993.

OLDEST → WRESTLING COMPETITION

The Kirkpinar Wrestling Festival has been held since 1460. The event is currently staged on the Sarayici Peninsula, near Edirne, Turkey.

MOST WORLD TITLE RECAPTURES
The only boxer to win a world title five times at one weight is 'Sugar' Ray Robinson (USA), who beat Carmen Basilio (USA) in the Chicago Stadium on 25 March 1958 to regain the world middleweight title for the fourth time.

MOST ROUNDS
Jack Jones defeated Patsy Tunney (both UK) in a boxing match that lasted 276 rounds in Cheshire in 1825. The fight lasted 4 hr 30 min.

★ BOXING ANNOUNCER: MOST BOUTS IN ONE WEEK
Hank Kropinski (USA) announced 240 bouts during the 1998 US Championships at Colorado Springs, Colorado, USA, from 16 to 21 March 1998.

JUDO

MOST THROWS IN ONE HOUR BY A PAIR
Dale Moore and Nigel Townsend (both UK) completed 3,786 judo throws in one hour at Esporta Health Club, Chiswick Park, London, UK, on 23 February 2002.

MOST THROWS IN 10 HOURS
Csaba Mezei and Zoltán Farkas (both Hungary) of the Szany Judo Sport Team completed 57,603 judo throws in a 10-hour period at the Szany Sports Hall, Szany, Hungary, on 1 May 2003. The pair threw 27 members of their club.

MOST WOMEN'S WORLD CHAMPIONSHIPS
Ingrid Berghmans (Belgium) won six women's world titles: the Open in 1980, 1982, 1984 and 1986, and the Under 72 kg in 1984 and 1989.

KARATE

MOST COMPETITORS AT A WORLD CHAMPIONSHIPS
A total of 1,157 competitors took part in the ninth staging of the World Championships, in Cairo, Egypt, in 1988.

MOST KICKS IN ONE MINUTE USING ONE LEG
Fabian Cuenca Pirroti (Spain) completed 128 karate kicks in one minute, using only one leg, on 11 November 2001 on the set of *El Show de los Records* in Madrid, Spain.

★ LARGEST MONGOLIAN WRESTLING TOURNAMENT →

A total of 2,048 competitors participated in a Mongolian Wrestling tournament that took place in Bayanwula, Xiwuzhumuqinqi, Inner Mongolia, China, between 28 July and 1 August 2004.

MOST INDIVIDUAL KUMITE WORLD CHAMPIONSHIP TITLES

Guusje van Mourik (Netherlands) has won a total of four karate kumite World Championship titles – in the Female Over 60 kg category – in 1982, 1984, 1986 and 1988.

KICKBOXING

MOST WORLD TITLES

Don 'The Dragon' Wilson (USA) won 11 world titles in three weight divisions (light-heavyweight, super light-heavyweight and cruiserweight) and for six sanctioning organizations between 1980 and 1999. The organizations are the World Kickboxing Association (WKA), Standardized Tournaments And Ratings (STAR), Karate International Council of Kickboxing (KICK), International Sport Karate Association (ISKA), Professional Kickboxing Organization (PKO) and International Kickboxing Federation (IKF).

WRESTLING

★ LARGEST ATTENDANCE

A total of 190,000 people attended the Pyongyang Stadium, Pyongyang, North Korea, for the International Sports and Cultural Festival for Peace on 29 April 1995.

LARGEST SUMO WRESTLER (*YOKOZUNA*)

In January 1993, Chad Rowan (Hawaii), alias Akebono, became the first foreign *rikishi* (sumo wrestler) to be promoted to the top rank of *yokozuna*. He is also the **tallest *yokozuna*** – at 204 cm (6 ft 8 in) – and **heaviest *yokozuna*** – at 227 kg (501 lb) – in sumo history.

MOST CONSECUTIVE WINS AT SUMO WRESTLING (*YOKOZUNA*)

The *yokozuna* Sadaji Akiyoshi (Japan), alias Futabayama, had 69 consecutive wins, 1937–39.

MISCELLANEOUS

★ MOST PLATES BROKEN IN ONE MINUTE BY NUNCHAKU

Thierry Guyon (France) broke 51 clay sporting targets in one minute using nunchaku (Japanese martial arts weapons comprising two hardwood sticks linked by a chain or strap) on the set of *L'Été de Tous les Records* in Bénodet, France, on 2 August 2004.

★ MOST SPEEDBALL HITS IN ONE MINUTE

Michael Benham (Australia) registered 373 hits in one minute at Melbourne's Crown Casino, Australia, on 7 May 2001.

★ MOST FULL-CONTACT KICKS IN ONE HOUR

Suzanne Nobles (USA) performed 2,180 full-contact kicks in one hour in Deep Creek Baptist Church Gymnasium, Chesapeake, Virginia, USA, on 22 May 2004.

★ GREATEST COMBINED WEIGHT FOR A WORLD TITLE FIGHT

On 11 December 2004, at the Mandalay Bay Resort, Las Vegas, Nevada, USA, defending champion Vitali Klitschko (Ukraine, below right) met Danny Williams (UK, below left) for the World Boxing Council heavyweight title. The combined weight of both fighters was 235.8 kg (520 lb), with Klitschko weighing in at 113.3 kg (250 lb) and Williams at 122.4 kg (270 lb). Klitschko retained his title, knocking out Williams in the eighth round.

CRICKET

←★ MOST CENTURIES
IN A CAREER (ONE-DAY INTERNATIONALS)

Sachin Tendulkar (India) has scored 37 centuries, having played 342 matches between 1989 and 2005.

MOST RUNS BY AN INDIVIDUAL IN A TEST MATCH

Graham Gooch (UK) scored 456 runs in the 1st Test against India at Lords, Middlesex, UK, between 26 and 31 July 1990. Gooch, who was England captain at the time, scored 333 in the first innings and 123 in the second.

★ MOST RUNS OFF A TEST MATCH OVER

Brian Lara (Trinidad and Tobago) scored 28 off one over playing for the West Indies against South Africa at the Wanderers, Johannesburg, South Africa, on 14 December 2003. The runs were taken off the bowling of Robin Peterson (South Africa), and the scoring sequence ball by ball was 466444. Lara scored 202 in his innings.

HIGHEST CRICKET INNINGS SCORE

Brian Lara scored 501 not out in 7 hr 54 min for Warwickshire v. Durham at Edgbaston on 3 and 6 June 1994. His innings included the **most runs in a day** (390 on 6 June) and the **most runs from strokes worth four or more** (308, 62 fours and 10 sixes).

★ HIGHEST PARTNERSHIP IN CRICKET (ONE-DAY INTERNATIONALS)

Indian captain Sachin Tendulkar (186*) and Rahul Dravid (153) scored 331 runs against New Zealand in Hyderabad, India, on 8 November 1999, with both batsmen making their highest scores in limited-overs internationals.

HIGHEST PARTNERSHIP IN TEST CRICKET

Sanath Jayasuriya (340) and Roshan Mahanama (225) put on a stand of 576 for the second wicket for Sri Lanka v. India at Colombo on 4–6 August 1997.

BATTING

HIGHEST BATTING AVERAGE IN TEST CRICKET

After playing for Australia in 52 Tests from 1928 to 1948, Sir Don Bradman finished his career with a batting average of 99.94 (6,996 runs in 80 innings).

MOST DUCKS IN TEST CRICKET

The player who has the dubious honour of scoring the most ducks in Test cricket is Courtney Walsh (Jamaica) with 43 in 185 innings for the West Indies, between November 1984 and April 2001.

MOST RUNS IN TEST CRICKET

Allan Border (Australia) scored 11,174 runs in 156 Tests (averaging 50.56) between 1978 and 1994.

★ MOST RUNS IN A CAREER (ONE-DAY INTERNATIONALS)

Sachin Tendulkar (India) scored 13,497 runs in 342 one-day international matches (at an average of 44.84) from 1989 to 2005.

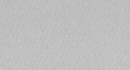

→ **WHO HAS SCORED THE MOST GOALS IN INTERNATIONAL SOCCER – A MAN OR A WOMAN? FIND OUT ON P.234**

←★ MOST TEST MATCHES UMPIRED BY AN INDIVIDUAL

Steve Bucknor (Jamaica) umpired 102 Test matches between 1989 and 2005.

★ NEW RECORD   ★ UPDATED RECORD

★ HIGHEST INNINGS IN A LIMITED-OVERS MATCH (TEAM) ↑

Surrey scored 438 in a limited 50-over Cheltenham and Gloucester Trophy match against Glamorgan at The Oval, London, UK, on 19 June 2002. Pictured is Surrey batsman Alistair Brown (UK), whose score of 268, shown on the scoreboard, is the **highest innings by an individual in a limited-overs match**.

★ MOST CENTURIES IN TEST CRICKET

Two Indian batsmen have scored 34 Test match centuries: Sunil Gavaskar between 1971 and 1987, and Sachin Tendulkar between 1989 and 2005.

★ HIGHEST TEST INNINGS

Brian Lara (Trinidad and Tobago) scored 400* for West Indies v. England at the Antigua Recreation Ground, St John, Antigua, from 10 to 12 April 2004. The innings included four sixes and 43 fours in a team total of 751-5.

BOWLING

FASTEST BALL BOWLED

The highest electronically measured speed for a ball bowled by any bowler is 161.3 km/h (100.23 mph) by Shoaib Akhtar (Pakistan) against England on 22 February 2003 in a World Cup match at Newlands, Cape Town, South Africa. The World Cup communications director has stated: 'ICC has always said there is not enough uniformity in the various speed guns around the world for any one performance to be designated official.' Many believe this to have been the fastest ball bowled, though.

MOST WICKETS IN A CAREER (ONE-DAY INTERNATIONALS)

Wasim Akram (Pakistan) took 502 wickets (at an average of 23.52) in 356 matches, from 1984 to 2003.

WICKET-KEEPING

MOST CATCHES BY A WICKET-KEEPER IN TEST CRICKET

Ian Healy (Australia) took 366 catches in 119 Tests, playing for Australia between 1988 and 1999.

MOST DISMISSALS BY A WICKET-KEEPER IN TEST CRICKET

Ian Healy made 395 dismissals in 119 Tests – 366 caught and 29 stumped – playing for Australia between 1988 and 1999.

MOST STUMPINGS BY A WICKET-KEEPER IN TEST CRICKET

William Oldfield (Australia) claimed 52 stumpings in 54 Tests between 1920 and 1937.

TEAMS

HIGHEST CRICKET TEST SCORE

Sri Lanka scored 952-6 against India at Colombo on 4 to 6 August 1997. England scored 903-7 declared in 15 hr 17 min against Australia at The Oval, London on 20, 22 and 23 August 1938.

LOWEST INNINGS TOTAL IN TEST CRICKET

New Zealand scored 26 against England at Auckland on 28 March 1955.

MOST WORLD CUP VICTORIES

Australia won in 1987, 1999 and 2003. The cricket World Cup competition began in 1975, and is held every four years.

MISCELLANEOUS

★ MOST DURABLE CRICKET SCORER

Mike Garwood (UK, b. 24 February 1928) has been keeping score regularly for Old Minchendenians Cricket Club, Southgate, UK, for 50 years.

★ MOST MATCHES PLAYED IN A CAREER (ONE-DAY INTERNATIONALS)

Wasim Akram (Pakistan) played 356 one-day international matches from 1984 to 2003.

MOST EXTRAS IN A ONE-DAY INTERNATIONAL

Two teams have conceded 59 extras in a one-day international: West Indies (8 byes, 10 leg byes, 4 no-balls and 37 wides) v. Pakistan at Brisbane, Australia, on 7 January 1989; and Scotland (5 byes, 6 leg byes, 15 no-balls and 33 wides) v. Pakistan at Chester-le-Street, Durham, UK, on 20 May 1999.

The **most extras conceded in a test match** is 71 by West Indies in Pakistan's first innings at Georgetown, Guyana, on 3–4 April 1988 (21 byes, 8 leg byes, 4 wides and 38 no-balls).

CRICKET TERMINOLOGY

* indicates a 'not out' score
bye: a run scored other than by using the bat
duck: a score of zero by a batsman
leg-bye: a run scored off the batsman's body
no-ball: a ball that has been bowled illegally. It must be bowled again; 1 run is added to the batting team's score
wide: a ball that is bowled too far away from the batsman for him to strike it. It must be bowled again; 1 run is added to the batting team's score

★ MOST TEST MATCH WICKETS ↓

Shane Warne (Australia) is the leading Test match wicket-taker, with 583 (at an average of 25.51 runs a wicket) in 123 matches, from August 1992 to March 2005.

← ★MOST WINS – KING OF THE MOUNTAINS

The 'best climber' in the Tour de France is awarded a polka-dot jersey and the title King of the Mountains. Richard Virenque (France) has won the polka-dot jersey seven times between 1994 and 2004.

TOUR DE FRANCE

MOST STAGE WINS
Eddie Merckx (Belgium) won 34 stages between 1969 and 1978.

CLOSEST RACE
The closest Tour de France race was in 1989, when after 3,267 km (2,030 miles) over 23 days (1 to 23 July), Greg LeMond (USA) – who completed the Tour in 87 hr 38 min 35 sec – beat Laurent Fignon (France) in Paris by only 8 seconds.

→ WHAT'S THE FASTEST BICYCLE WHEELIE? FIND OUT ON P.189

YOUNGEST WINNER
Henri Cornet (France) was 19 years 350 days when he won in 1904. He actually finished fifth, but was awarded victory after the first four riders – Maurice Garin, Lucien Pothier, César Garin and Hippolyte Aucouturier (all France) – were disqualified.

OLDEST WINNER
Firmin Lambot (Belgium) was 36 years 4 months when he won the Tour de France in 1922.

FASTEST AVERAGE SPEED
During the 1999 Tour, Lance Armstrong (USA) cycled at an average speed of 40.276 km/h (25.026 mph). The **fastest average speed in a single stage** was 50.355 km/h (31.29 mph) by Mario Cipollini (Italy) on 7 July 1999 (during stage 4).

LARGEST ATTENDANCE FOR A SPORTING EVENT
An estimated 10 million people gather over a period of three weeks to watch the annual Tour de France race.

BIGGEST WINNING MARGIN
The greatest gap between winner and runner-up at the finish of a Tour de France is 28 min 27 sec, between Fausto Coppi (Italy) and Stan Ockers (Belgium) in 1952.

GREAT DISTANCES

★FASTEST TIME TO CYCLE THE LENGTH OF SOUTH AMERICA
Giampietro Marion (Italy) cycled the South American portion of the Pan-American Highway, starting in Chigorodo, Colombia, and finishing in Ushuaia, Argentina, in a time of 59 days between 17 September and 15 November 2000.

GREATEST DISTANCE CYCLED IN 24 HOURS
The 24-hour record behind pace is 1,958.196 km (1,216.8 miles) by Michael Secrest (USA) at Phoenix International Raceway, Arizona, USA, on 26–27 April 1990. Solo and unpaced, he achieved a distance of 857.36 km (532.74 miles) at the Olympic Velodrome, California State University, Carson, USA, on 23–24 October 1997.

GREATEST DISTANCE (BACKWARDS) IN ONE HOUR
Markus Riese (Germany) cycled 29.1 km (18 miles) backwards in one hour at the VC Darmstadt 1899 eV cycling club, Darmstadt, Germany, on 24 May 2003.

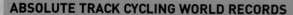

ABSOLUTE TRACK CYCLING WORLD RECORDS

MEN	TIME/DISTANCE	NAME & NATIONALITY	PLACE	DATE
200 m	9.865	Curt Harnett (Canada)	Bogota, Colombia	28 September 1995
500 m	25.850	Arnaud Duble (France)	La Paz, Bolivia	10 October 2001
1 km	58.875	Arnaud Tournant (France)	La Paz, Bolivia	10 October 2001
4 km	4:11.114	Chris Boardman (UK)	Manchester, UK	29 August 1996
Team 4 km	3:56.610	Australia (Graeme Brown, Brett Lancaster, Bradley McGee, Luke Roberts, pictured right)	Athens, Greece	22 August 2004
1 hour	49 km 441 m	Chris Boardman (UK)	Manchester, UK	27 August 1996
WOMEN	TIME/DISTANCE	NAME & NATIONALITY	PLACE	DATE
200 m	10.831	Olga Slioussareva (Russia)	Moscow, Russia	25 April 1993
500 m	29.655	Erika Saloumiaee (USSR)	Moscow, USSR	6 August 1987
3 km	3:24.357	Sarah Ulmer (New Zealand)	Athens, Greece	22 August 2004
1 hour	48 km 159 m	Jeannie Longo-Ciprelli (France)	Mexico City, Mexico	26 October 1996

LANCE ARMSTRONG

Between 1994 and 2004, Lance Armstrong (USA) won the Tour de France a record six times. In October 1996, he was diagnosed with testicular cancer and given less than 50% chance of survival. Against all the odds, he returned to claim the yellow jersey on his first Tour out of recovery.

Who inspired you most when you were growing up?
Easy answer – my mom! If I had to name the cyclists I most admire, I'd have to say Eddy Merckx... my idol and the greatest cyclist of all time.

When you began your cycling career, did you think it would be so successful?
I knew I'd be successful, but never to the level that I'm fortunate to be at now.

Did you always want to be a professional cyclist?
I started off in triathalons but switched to cycling as a teenager.

What's been your greatest achievement in cycling?
Without a doubt, winning the Tour de France six times. It's my favourite race.

How do you motivate yourself each season after the amazing successes you've had?
I look at each season as a new one. Whatever's happened in the previous years doesn't matter when the new season starts.

What advice would you give to young sportsmen and women?
Just never take anything for granted!

MOUNTAIN BIKING

★ MOST CROSS-COUNTRY WORLD CUPS (MEN)
Swiss cyclist Thomas Frischknecht won three cross-country World Cup titles, in 1992–93 and 1995.

★ MOST CROSS-COUNTRY WORLD CUPS (WOMEN)
Juli Furtado (USA) won three cross-country mountain-bike World Cup titles from 1993 to 1995, equalled by Alison Sydor (Canada) between 1996 and 1999.

☆ MOST DOWNHILL WORLD TITLES (WOMEN)
Anne-Caroline Chausson (France) won 11 World Championships – three in the junior championship from 1993 to 1995, and eight in the senior class from 1996 to 2003.

★ MOST DOWNHILL WORLD CUPS (MEN)
Nicolas Vouilloz (France) won five downhill World Cup titles, in 1995–96 and 1998–2000.

★ MOST WORLD CUP TITLES BY A WOMAN
Anne-Caroline Chausson (France) won five titles from 1998 to 2002.

MISCELLANEOUS

★ MOST CYCLO-CROSS WORLD TITLES (WOMEN)
Two women have won the World Championships twice: Hanka Kupfernagel (Germany) in 2000 and 2001, and Laurence Leboucher (France) in 2002 and 2004.

★ MOST VERTICAL METRES IN 24 HOURS
Alessandro Forni (Italy) cycled 17,612 vertical metres (57,782 ft) on 19–20 October 2002 at Trento, Italy. The height – nearly twice the height of Mt Everest – was gained by completing 23 laps of a 22.8-km (14.16-mile) circuit with a 770.5-m (2,528-ft) difference between its lowest and highest points.

★ LONGEST STATIC CYCLING MARATHON
The Netherlands' Niels Rietveld and Edwin Snijders continuously and simultaneously cycled for 77 hr 15 min at Sportstudio Buiten, Almere, the Netherlands, from 30 April to 3 May 2004.

★ MOST GYRATOR SPINS IN ONE MINUTE – BMX
Sam Foakes (UK) executed 33 spins in one minute at the offices of Guinness World Records in London, UK, on 20 July 2004.

MOST MEN'S TRIALS
WORLD CHAMPIONSHIPS

Two riders have won a record two elite trials cycling World Championships: Marco Hösel (Germany) in 1999 and 2002, and Benito Ros Charral (Spain, pictured) in 2003 and 2004.

★ NEW RECORD   ☆ UPDATED RECORD

MOST INTERNATIONAL GOALS SCORED BY A WOMAN

Mia Hamm (USA) has scored 144 international goals. Widely regarded as the best female football player ever, her senior international career began in 1987 aged just 15 years old. In 2001 she was voted FIFA World Footballer of the Year and currently plays for the Washington Freedom in WUSA, the US Women's Professional League.

GOALS & CAPS

MOST INTERNATIONAL CAPS

The most international appearances for a national side is officially 270 by Kristine Lilly (USA) from 1987 to 2004.

The **most international caps by a man** is 171 by Claudio Suarez (Mexico) between 1992 and 2003.

HIGHEST SCORE IN AN INTERNATIONAL FOOTBALL MATCH

Australia won 31-0 against American Samoa in a World Cup qualifying match at Coffs Harbour, New South Wales, Australia, on 11 April 2001.

The **highest score in an international women's football match** is 21-0 and has occurred on four occasions: Japan v. Guam at Guangzhou, China, on 5 December 1997; Canada v. Puerto Rico at Centennial Park, Toronto, Canada, on 28 August 1998; and Australia v. American Samoa and New Zealand against Samoa, both at Mt Smart Stadium, Auckland, New Zealand, on 9 October 1998.

INTERNATIONAL TOURNAMENTS

MOST EUROPEAN CHAMPIONSHIP WINS

Germany has won the European Championships three times, in 1972, 1980 and 1996 (the first two as West Germany). A women's version was first held in 1984 and the **most wins in women's football** is four, also by Germany (1989, 1991, 1995 and 1997).

MOST AFRICA CUP OF NATIONS WINS

The most wins is four by Ghana (1963, 1965, 1978 and 1982), Egypt (1957, 1959, 1986 and 1998) and Cameroon (1984, 1988, 2000 and 2002).

MOST SOUTH AMERICAN CHAMPIONSHIP WINS

Argentina has won the South American championship (Copa America since 1975) a record 15 times between 1910 and 1993.

FASTEST INTERNATIONAL HAT-TRICK

Japanese international Masashi 'Gon' Nakayama scored a hat-trick in 3 min 15 sec against Brunei during an Asian Cup qualifying match played on 16 February 2000. Nakayama netted on 1 min, 2 min and 3 min 15 sec, bettering the 62-year-old mark set by England's George William Hall, who scored three in 3 min 30 sec against Ireland at Old Trafford, Manchester, UK, on 16 November 1938.

Football v. soccer
The world's first governing body for football was founded in 1863 with the formation of the Football Association in England after the split between rugby football and association football. The international organization *Fédération Internationale de Football Association* (FIFA) was established in 1904 with seven founder members: France, Belgium, Denmark, the Netherlands, Spain, Sweden and Switzerland.

The name soccer, as the sport is known in some parts of the world, derives from the shortening of 'association' to 'assoc' and then 'soccer'.

★ MOST → INTERNATIONAL GOALS SCORED BY A MAN

The most football international goals scored by a man is 103 by Ali Daei (Iran, pictured right) between 1993 and 2005.

★ MOST →
ASIAN CUP WINS

The most wins in the Asian Cup is three by Iran (1968, 1972 and 1976), Saudi Arabia (1984, 1988 and 1996) and Japan (1992, 2000 and 2004, pictured).

WORLD CUPS

★ MOST PENALTY SHOOT-OUT SAVES

Two goalkeepers have saved four penalties in World Cup finals match penalty shoot-outs: Harald Schumacher playing for West Germany in 1982 and 1986, and Sergio Goycochea playing for Argentina in 1990.

LARGEST FOOTBALL MATCH ATTENDANCE

A record 199,854 people attended the Brazil v. Uruguay World Cup match in the Maracanã Municipal Stadium, Rio de Janeiro, Brazil, on 16 July 1950.

MOST GOALS IN A WORLD CUP FINALS

Just Fontaine (France) scored a record 13 goals during the 1958 World Cup finals in Sweden.

★ MOST GOALS SCORED BY AN INDIVIDUAL IN A GAME

Oleg Salenko (Russia) scored five goals playing for Russia against Cameroon in a 1994 finals match at Stanford Stadium, San Francisco, USA, on 28 June 1994.

★ LONGEST WORLD CUP FINALS CLEAN SHEET

The longest time played in World Cup finals matches by a goalkeeper without conceding a goal is 518 minutes by Walter Zenga playing for Italy in the 1990 tournament staged in Italy.

MOST GOALS SCORED IN AN INTERNATIONAL BY AN INDIVIDUAL

During Australia's record breaking 31-0 defeat of American Samoa in a World Cup qualifying match at Coffs Harbour, New South Wales, Australia, on 11 April 2001, Archie Thompson (Australia) scored an international record 13 goals.

↑ ★ MOST WORLD CUP FINALS APPEARANCES BY A TEAM

Brazil appeared in a record 17 World Cup finals tournaments between 1930 and 2002. Pictured above is the 1958 team lining up for the national anthems on 29 June 1958, before the final where Brazil defeated Sweden, attaining their first title.

FOOTBALL CONTROL

RECORD	DURATION/TOUCHES	HOLDER	PLACE	DATE
Feet, legs, head (male)	19 hr 30 min	Martinho Eduardo Orige (Brazil)	Ararangua, Brazil	2–3 August 2003
Feet, legs, head (female)	7 hr 5 min 25 sec	Cláudia Martini (Brazil)	Caxias do Sul, Brazil	12 July 1996
Head	8 hr 12 min 25 sec	Goderdzi Makharadze (Georgia)	Tbilisi, Georgia	26 May 1996
Head, seated	3 hr 59 min	Andrzej Kukla (Poland)	Biala Podlaska, Poland	20 March 1998
Chest	30.29 sec	Amadou Gueye (France)	Paris, France	7 September 2001
★ Lying down	8 min 27 sec	Tomas Lundman (Sweden)	Bankery, Sweden	31 October 2004
★ Spinning, forehead	12.9 sec	Tommy Baker (UK)	Newcastle, UK	4 December 2004
Fastest marathon distance	7 hr 18 min 55 sec	Jan Skorkovsky (Czech Republic)	Prague, Czech Republic	8 July 1990
Most touches 1 min (male)	266	Ferdie Adoboe (USA)	Blaine, Minnesota, USA	19 July 2000
Most touches 1 min (female)	269	Tasha-Nicole Terani (USA)	Atlanta, Georgia, USA	4 September 2003
Most touches 30 sec (male)	141	Ferdie Adoboe (USA)	New York City, USA	27 August 2003
Most touches 30 sec (female)	137	Tasha-Nicole Terani (USA)	New York City, USA	27 August 2003
Most people, simultaneous	446	FA Centres of Excellence Festival	Warwick, UK	19 June 1999

←★HIGHEST AGGREGATE SCORE IN A CHAMPIONS LEAGUE MATCH

The most goals scored by both teams is 11, when French side Monaco beat Deportivo La Coruña of Spain 8-3 at the Stade Louis II, Monaco, France, on 5 November 2003. Pictured are Monaco forward Dado Prso (Croatia, right) and Deportivo La Coruna defender Jorge Andrade (Portugal).

FASTEST CHAMPIONS LEAGUE GOAL
Gilberto Silva (Brazil) scored in 20.07 seconds playing for Arsenal against PSV Eindhoven in Eindhoven, the Netherlands, on 25 September 2002. Arsenal went on to win the game 4-0.

★ MOST FA CUP WINS
The greatest number of wins is 11 by Manchester United (UK) in 1909, 1948, 1963, 1977, 1983, 1985, 1990, 1994, 1996, 1999 and 2004.

★LONGEST FA CUP TIE
The FA Cup tie between Alvechurch and Oxford City (both UK) in November 1971 lasted for six games and 11 hours. The match results sequence was 2-2, 1-1, 1-1, 0-0, 0-0 with Alvechurch finally winning 1-0.

OTHER COMPETITIONS

★LONGEST PREMIERSHIP CLEAN SHEET
The longest time played by a Premiership goalkeeper without conceding a goal is 781 minutes by Peter Cech (Czech Republic) playing for Chelsea FC (UK) between 27 November 2004 and 2 February 2005.

MOST DOMESTIC LEAGUE TITLES WON
Rangers FC (UK) won 50 titles in the Scottish Division 1 and Premier Division Championships between 1891 and 2003.

HIGHEST SCORE IN A NATIONAL CUP FINAL
In 1935, Lausanne-Sports beat Nordstern Basel 10-0 in the Swiss Cup Final. Two years later they suffered defeat by the same scoreline at the hands of Grasshopper-Club (Zurich) in the 1937 Swiss Cup Final.

★LONGEST RUNNING CHARITY GAME
The Football Association Charity Shield was inaugurated in 1908 and has been played annually since 1924 at Wembley Stadium, London, UK, and more recently the Millennium Stadium in Cardiff, Wales.

EUROPEAN

MOST EUROPEAN CUP WINS
The European Champions Cup has been won nine times by Real Madrid (Spain) in 1955/56, 1956/57, 1957/58, 1958/59, 1959/60, 1965/66, 1997/98, 1999/2000 and 2002/03.

MOST CONSECUTIVE CHAMPIONS LEAGUE MATCH VICTORIES
The longest winning streak in UEFA Champions League matches is 11 games by FC Barcelona in the 2002/03 season. The Catalan team posted a perfect record from the start of the competition before registering a goalless draw with Inter Milan (Italy).

→ WHO IS THE HIGHEST PAID NFL FOOTBALLER? FIND OUT ON P.212

★MOST GOALS IN ↘ THE ENGLISH PREMIERSHIP

The most goals scored in the English Premiership is 250 by Alan Shearer (UK). Shearer began his career with Southampton before moving to Blackburn Rovers and finally to Newcastle United in July 1996 for a record fee (at that time) of £15.6 million ($22.4 million). Shearer continues to play for Newcastle United and is still scoring goals.

← ★LONGEST
UNBEATEN PREMIERSHIP RUN

The most games unbeaten in the English Premier League is 49 by Arsenal between 7 May 2003 and 16 October 2004. This total comprises the last two games of the 2002/03 season, 38 games unbeaten for the whole of the 2003/04 season and the first nine games of the 2004/05 season.

This also means that Arsenal have the record for the **★longest unbeaten run in top-division English football**.

MISCELLANEOUS

★ LONGEST SERVING FOOTBALL CLUB MANAGER

Roly Howard (UK) of Marine Football Club managed his first game on 12 August 1972 and continued to 2004/05, his 33rd and final season.

MOST EXPENSIVE FOOTBALL PLAYER

The highest transfer fee for a player is 13 billion Spanish pesetas (£47 million; $66 million) for Zinédine Zidane (France) for his transfer from Juventus to Real Madrid on 9 July 2001.

FASTEST TIME TO VISIT ALL FOOTBALL LEAGUE GROUNDS

Ken Ferris (UK) watched a league match at all 92 League grounds in England and Wales (including Berwick Rangers) in just 237 days, between 10 September 1994 and 6 May 1995. He began at Carlisle Utd and finished at Everton.

MOST FOOTBALL MANAGEMENT REJECTION LETTERS

Richard Dixon (UK) applied for – and received rejection letters for – 29 jobs as a football manager. Richard applies only for jobs that are available and has received official letters from clubs such as Tottenham Hotspur, Manchester United, Atlético de Madrid and the English and Cypriot national sides. The hobby began in 2000 when physical education teacher Dixon contracted glandular fever and applied for the Millwall job.

★ LONGEST TOUR

Between 3 July and 3 August 2004, Lenton Griffins Football Club (UK) visited a total of 12 countries. The team played fixtures in Wales, Belgium, Luxembourg, Germany, Austria, Liechtenstein, Switzerland, Italy, France, Andorra, Spain and Morocco. There were also inadmissable fixtures played in England and Ireland.

★ YOUNGEST HAT-TRICK SCORER IN WOMEN'S FOOTBALL

Amy Wilding (UK) was 15 years 220 days old when she scored three goals for Camberley Town Ladies against CTC Ladies in Croydon, Surrey, UK, on 30 March 2003.

FASTEST GOAL

Goals scored in 3 seconds and less after the kick-off have been claimed by a number of players. From video evidence, Ricardo Olivera (Uruguay) scored in 2.8 seconds for Río Negro against Soriano at the José Enrique Rodó stadium, Soriano, Uruguay, on 26 December 1998.

MOST MAJOR LEAGUE CHAMPIONSHIP WINS

The most Major League soccer titles won by a team is four by DC United (USA) in 1996, 1997, 1999 and 2004. Pictured is star player Freddy Adu (USA, middle).

★MOST ROUNDS OF GOLF PLAYED
IN DIFFERENT COUNTRIES ← IN ONE DAY

Eric Kirchner and Patrick Herresthal (both Germany) played six rounds of golf in six different countries on 19 June 2004. The pair played a full 18-hole round at the following courses: Golfpark Riefensberg (Austria), Golfclub Waldkirch (Switzerland), Golf de Soufflenheim (France), Five Nations Golfclub (Belgium), Golf de Clervaux (Luxembourg) and the Golfclub Heddesshiem (Germany).

MOST WORLD CUP TEAM WINS

The World Cup (instituted as the Canada Cup in 1953) has been won by the USA 23 times between 1955 and 2000.

→ **HOW TALL IS THE WORLD'S LARGEST GOLF TEE? FIND OUT ON P.160**

MOST US OPEN TITLES

Four US golfers have won the US Open four times: Willie Anderson (1901, 1903–05); Bobby Jones Jr (1923, 1926, 1929 and 1930); Ben Hogan (1948, 1950, 1951 and 1953); and Jack Nicklaus (1962, 1967, 1972 and 1980).

MOST BRITISH OPEN TITLES

Harry Vardon (UK) won six British Open titles (1896, 1898, 1899, 1903, 1911 and 1914).

MOST US MASTERS WINS

Jack Nicklaus (USA) won the Masters title six times (1963, 1965, 1966, 1972, 1975 and 1986).

In 1973, Nicklaus became the **first player ever to have career earnings of $2 million**, and in 1986 he became the **oldest player to win the Masters**, aged 46.

★MOST WORLD MATCH PLAY CHAMPIONSHIPS WON BY AN INDIVIDUAL

Ernie Els (South Africa) won six championships (1994–96 and 2002–04).

MOST SOLHEIM CUP WINS BY A TEAM

The female equivalent of the Ryder Cup is contested every two years between the top professional players of Europe and the USA. The USA has won five times (1990, 1994, 1996, 1998 and 2002), with Europe winning in 1992, 2000 and 2003.

MOST INDIVIDUAL CURTIS CUP TIES AND WINS

Carole Semple-Thompson (USA) has played in 12 ties and won 18 matches from 1974 to 2002.

HIGHEST CAREER EARNINGS ON US PGA TOUR

The all-time top career earner on the US PGA circuit is Tiger Woods (USA) who won $46,356,737 (£24,692,835) between August 1996 and January 2005.

★ BIGGEST MARGIN OF VICTORY IN A MAJOR GOLF TOURNAMENT

Tiger Woods (USA) won the 2000 US Open by 15 shots. He finished with a round of 67 to add to rounds of 65, 69 and 71 for a 12-under-par total of 272.

LOWEST SCORE OVER 18 HOLES (WOMEN)

Annika Sorenstam (Sweden) scored 59 in the 2001 Standard Register PING at Moon Valley Country Club, Phoenix, Arizona, USA, on 16 March 2001.

RYDER CUP – MOST WINS BY A TEAM

The biennial Ryder Cup professional match between the USA and Europe was instituted in 1927. The USA has won 24 to 9 (with 2 draws) to 2004. Pictured is US Ryder Cup team captain Ben Crenshaw accepting the trophy on 26 September 1999 in Brookline, Massachusetts, USA. →

LOWEST BELOW-AGE SCORE

At the age of 89, James D Morton (USA) hit a 72 at Valleybrook Golf and Country Club, Hixson, Tennessee, USA, on 21 April 2001, setting the lowest score below a player's age at 17.

★ FASTEST ROUND BY A FOURBALL

A fourball consisting of Kenny Crawford, Colin Gerard, John Henderson and Joe McParland (all UK) completed 18 holes in 1 hr 32 min 48 sec on the Torrance Course at St Andrews Bay Golf Resort & Spa, St Andrews, Fife, UK, on 12 June 2004.

MOST PARTICIPANTS IN A LESSON

A total of 478 people were taught by Andrew Carnall (UK), a PGA-qualified golf professional, at Chesterfield, Derbyshire, UK, on 26 September 2003.

FASTEST ROUND OF GOLF BY A TEAM

The WBAP News/Talk 820 team of golfers completed 18 holes in 8 min 47 sec at Bridlewood Golf Club, Flower Mound, Texas, USA, on 12 August 2003.

MOST CONSECUTIVE HOLES-IN-ONE

There are at least 20 cases of people achieving two aces consecutively, but the greatest was Norman L Manley's unique double albatross on the par-4 301-m (330-yd) seventh and par-4 265-m (290-yd) eighth holes on the Del Valle Country Club course, Saugus, California, USA, on 2 September 1964. The first woman to achieve this feat was Sue Prell (Australia) on the 13th and 14th holes at Chatswood GC, Sydney, Australia, on 29 May 1977.

★ GREATEST DISTANCE BETWEEN TWO ROUNDS OF GOLF PLAYED ON THE SAME DAY

John Knobel (Australia) played two full 18-hole rounds – the first at The Coast Golf Club, Sydney, Australia, and the second 14,843 km (9,223 miles) away at White Pines Golf Club, Bensenville, Illinois, USA, on 15 September 2004.

LONGEST GOLF CARRY AT AN ALTITUDE BELOW 1,000 M

Karl Woodward (UK) drove a ball a distance of 373 m (408 yd) at Golf del Sur, Tenerife, on 30 June 1999.

★ MOST HOLES IN SEVEN DAYS WITH A CART

Using a golf cart for transport, Troy Grant, aka Rusty Gate, (Australia) completed 1,800 holes at Tenterfield Golf Club, New South Wales, Australia, from 3 to 10 February 2004.

★ LARGEST GOLF CART PARADE

A total of 1,138 golf carts took part in a parade at the Timber Pines retirement community in Spring Hill, Florida, USA, on 15 March 2004.

GOLF TERMINOLOGY

albatross: three strokes under par for a specific hole. Also called a double eagle

handicap: the number of strokes given to a player to enable him or her to complete a round on scratch

hole-in-one: a ball that is holed directly from the tee in one shot. Also called an 'ace'

par: the number of strokes it should take a golfer with a low handicap to complete a hole or a round. The par for a hole is made up of the number of strokes taken to reach the green, plus two strokes to putt the ball

scratch: a player who has no handicap, and can therefore complete a course in par

★ LARGEST GOLF FACILITY

Mission Hills Golf Club, China, has had 10 fully operational 18-hole courses since April 2004. In addition, the extensive changing rooms can accommodate up to 3,000 guests.

← MOST HAT-TRICKS IN AN NHL CAREER

Wayne Gretzky (Canada) scored 50 hat-tricks during his NHL career, playing for the Edmonton Oilers, Los Angeles Kings, St Louis Blues and New York Rangers between 1979 and 1999.

MOST GOALS SCORED BY AN INDIVIDUAL IN A GAME

Joe Malone (Canada) scored seven goals for the Quebec Bulldogs in their game against the Toronto St Patricks in Quebec City, Canada, on 31 January 1920.

★ FASTEST HAT-TRICK

Bill Mosienko (Canada) scored a hat-trick within 21 seconds for the Chicago Blackhawks against the New York Rangers on 23 March 1952.

MOST CAREER WINS BY A GOALTENDER

Up to the end of the 2003 regular season, Patrick Roy (Canada) achieved 551 wins, playing for the Colorado Avalanche (having begun his career with the Montreal Canadiens in 1985).

NHL HISTORY & AWARDS

An ice hockey league began in Canada in 1885 and featured four teams. The Stanley Cup (named after the English Governor General of Canada, Lord Stanley of Preston) was introduced in 1892, and was awarded to the team that won the play-offs. The National Hockey League (NHL), as it is known today, played its first game on 19 December 1917.

Today, the NHL awards many different cups and trophies, including:

Art Ross Trophy: Top point scorer in the NHL

Bill Masterton Memorial Trophy: Qualities of perseverance and sportsmanship

Calder Memorial Trophy: Rookie of the year

Clarence S Campbell Bowl: Western Conference champion

Conn Smythe Trophy: Most Valuable Player in the Stanley Cup play-offs

Continued →

NHL

★ MOST GOALS SCORED BY A TEAM IN A GAME

The Montreal Canadiens scored 16 goals in their 16-3 victory over the Quebec Bulldogs on 3 March 1920.

MOST GOALS SCORED BY A TEAM IN A SEASON

The Edmonton Oilers scored 446 goals in the 1983/84 season. The Oilers also achieved a record 1,182 scoring points the same season.

★ MOST NHL → TEAMS PLAYED FOR

Two players who began their careers with the Vancouver Canucks have played for 10 National Hockey League (NHL) teams. J J Daigneault (Canada, pictured) left the Canucks at the end of the 1985/86 season and went on to play for the Philadelphia Flyers, Montreal Canadiens, St Louis Blues, Pittsburgh Penguins, Anaheim Mighty Ducks, New York Islanders, Nashville Predators, Phoenix Coyotes and Minnesota Wild.

Michael Petit (Canada) left the Canucks during the 1987/88 season and went on to play for the New York Rangers, Quebec Nordiques, Toronto Maple Leafs, Calgary Flames, Los Angeles Kings, Tampa Bay Lightning, Edmonton Oilers, Philadelphia Flyers and Phoenix Coyotes.

MOST GOALS SCORED BY AN INDIVIDUAL IN A SEASON

Wayne Gretzky (Canada) scored a record 92 goals for the Edmonton Oilers in the 1981/82 season.

MOST GOALS SCORED BY A ROOKIE IN A SEASON

Teemu Selanne (Finland) scored 76 goals playing for the Winnipeg Jets in the 1992/93 season.

MOST GOALTENDING SHUTOUTS IN A CAREER

Terry Sawchuk (Canada) achieved 103 goaltending shutouts for Detroit Red Wings, Boston Bruins, Toronto Maple Leafs, Los Angeles Kings and New York Rangers from 1949 to 1970.

★ MOST LADY BYNG TROPHIES

Frank Boucher (Canada) has won seven times, in 1928–31 and in 1933–35, playing for the New York Rangers.

MOST PENALTY MINUTES IN A CAREER

The player with the most penalty minutes in NHL history is Dave 'Tiger' Williams (Canada) with 3,966, in 17 seasons (1971–88), playing for the Toronto Maple Leafs, Vancouver Canucks, Detroit Red Wings, Los Angeles Kings and the now defunct Hartford Whalers.

← ★ MOST MEN'S
ICE HOCKEY WORLD CHAMPIONSHIPS

Canada won 23 World Championships, in 1920–32 (held irregularly), 1934–35, 1937–39, 1948, 1950–52, 1958–59, 1961, 1994, 1997 and 2003–04.

MISCELLANEOUS

★ LARGEST ICE HOCKEY TOURNAMENT BY PLAYERS

The Quikcard Edmonton Minor Hockey Week, held from 10 to 19 January 2003 in Edmonton, Canada, was contested by 471 teams totalling 7,127 players.

★ MOST DURABLE ICE HOCKEY PLAYER

John Burnosky (USA) began playing in 1929 and continued for a total of 76 years.

HIGHEST SCORE IN AN ICE HOCKEY MATCH

Australia beat New Zealand 58-0 at Perth on 15 March 1987.

★ MOST WOMEN'S ICE HOCKEY WORLD CHAMPIONSHIPS

World Championships for women have been held since 1990, and have been won eight times by Canada, in 1990, 1992, 1994, 1997, 1999, 2000, 2001 and 2004.

Frank J Selke Trophy: Top defensive forward in the NHL

Hart Memorial Trophy: NHL Most Valuable Player

Jack Adams Award: Coach of the year

James Norris Memorial Trophy: Top defenceman in the NHL

King Clancy Memorial Trophy: Leadership and humanitarian contribution

Lady Byng Memorial Trophy: Player who displays gentlemanly conduct

Lester B Pearson Award: Most Valuable Player as selected by the NHLPA

Lester Patrick Trophy: Outstanding service to hockey in the USA

Maurice Richard Trophy: Top goal scorer in the NHL

Presidents' Trophy: Best overall record

Prince of Wales Trophy: Eastern Conference champion

Vezina Trophy: Top goaltender in the NHL

William M Jennings Trophy: Goaltender(s) with the fewest goals scored against them

MOST STANLEY CUP WINS BY A TEAM

The Montreal Canadiens won the cup 24 times from a record 32 finals, in 1916, 1924, 1930–31, 1944, 1946, 1953, 1956–60, 1965–66, 1968–69, 1971, 1973, 1976–79, 1986 and 1993.

MOST ALL-STAR SELECTIONS

Gordie Howe (Canada) was selected 21 times for the NHL All-Star game while playing for the Detroit Red Wings from 1946 to 1979. He was selected for the first team on 12 occasions and the second team on nine.

★ MOST PENALTY MINUTES IN A SEASON

Dave 'The Hammer' Schultz (Canada) had 472 minutes playing for the Philadelphia Flyers in 1974/75.

MOST PENALTIES AGAINST AN INDIVIDUAL IN A GAME

Chris Nilan (USA), playing for the Boston Bruins against the Hartford Whalers on 31 March 1991, had 10 penalties called against him, made up of six minors, two majors, one 10-minute misconduct and one game misconduct.

★ MOST PENALTY MINUTES IN A PLAY-OFF GAME

The most penalty minutes accrued by an individual player in a Stanley Cup play-off match is 42 by Dave 'The Hammer' Schultz (Canada) for the Philadelphia Flyers against the Toronto Maple Leafs on 22 April 1976.

MOST GOALS →
SCORED IN A STANLEY CUP GAME

Five goals were scored in a Stanley Cup game by Newsy Lalonde (Canada) for Montreal against Ottawa on 1 March 1919; by Maurice Richard in Montreal's 5-1 win over Toronto on 23 March 1944; by Darryl Glen Sittler for Toronto (8) v. Philadelphia (5) on 22 April 1976; by Reggie Leach for Philadelphia (6) v. Boston (3) on 6 May 1976; and by Mario Lemieux (pictured) for Pittsburgh (10) v. Philadelphia (7) on 25 April 1989.

MOTOR SPORTS

★ MOST WINS
BY A CONSTRUCTOR
IN A SEASON

McLaren (UK, 1988) and Ferrari (Italy, 2002 and 2004) have both had 15 wins by a constructor in a single F1 season.

similar displacement engine running petrol, and produces at least 8,000 horsepower.

★ LOWEST ELAPSED TIME
IN A FUNNY CAR

John Force (USA) covered 440 yd in 4.665 seconds driving a Ford at Yorba Linda, California, USA, on 10 March 2004.

★ FASTEST SPEED IN A DRAG
RACING PRO STOCK CAR

For a petrol-driven piston-engined car (Pro Stock), the highest terminal velocity is 334.34 km/h (207.75 mph), set by Greg Anderson (USA) in a Pontiac at Concord, North Carolina, USA, on 10 February 2004.

★ LOWEST ELAPSED TIME
IN A DRAG RACING
PRO STOCK CAR

Greg Anderson (USA) covered 440 yd in 6.661 seconds in a Pontiac Grand Am at Concord, North Carolina, USA, on 10 February 2004.

FASTEST SPEED
ON A DRAG RACING
PRO STOCK MOTORBIKE

Matt Hines (USA) reached 312.37 km/h (194.10 mph) on a Suzuki at Englishtown, New Jersey, USA, in May 2001.

★ LOWEST ELAPSED TIME
ON A DRAG RACING
PRO STOCK MOTORBIKE

Andrew Hines (USA) covered 440 yd in 7.016 seconds on his Harley V-rod, at Brownsburg, Indiana, USA, on 19 June 2004.

DRAG RACING

★ FASTEST SPEED IN A
TOP FUEL DRAG RACER

The highest terminal velocity at the end of a 440-yd run is 536.57 km/h (333.41 mph) by Brandon Bernstein (USA) at Lake Forest, California, USA, on 22 May 2004 in a McKinney dragster.

LOWEST ELAPSED TIME
IN A TOP FUEL DRAG RACER

Anthony Schumacher (USA) covered 440 yd in 4.441 seconds in a McKinney dragster at Long Grove, Illinois, USA, on 4 October 2003. Top Fuel cars run on 90% nitro-methane and 10% methanol, also known as racing alcohol. As a result, the engine is about 2.4 times as powerful as a

DRAG RACING

Drag racing is a form of motorsport where cars and motorcylces compete on short tracks, usual a quarter of a mile (440 yd), with the objective of finishing the course as quickly as possible. The National Hot Rod Association, or NHRA, was founded in 1951 in California by Wally Parks (USA) to provide a governing body for the sport.

↙ ★ GRAND
PRIX:
MOST WINS
BY A DRIVER

Michael Schumacher (Germany) won 83 races, 1991–2004. He has also won the **most World Championships** in Formula One with seven (1994–95, 2000–04).

★ FASTEST SPEED
BY A FUNNY CAR (DRAG RACING)

John Force (USA) reached a terminal velocity of 536.84 km/h (333.58 mph) from a standing start over 440 yd in a Ford at Yorba Linda, California, USA, on 10 March 2004.

FORMULA ONE

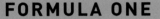

★ FASTEST AVERAGE SPEED IN A GRAND PRIX

Michael Schumacher achieved an average speed of 247.585 km/h (153.842 mph) in a Ferrari at Monza in the Italian Grand Prix on 14 September 2003.

★ MOST CONSECUTIVE GRAND PRIX VICTORIES

Alberto Ascari (Italy), driving for Ferrari, won nine consecutive Formula One Grands Prix in 1952–53. He won all six races of the 1952 season and the first three of 1953, winning the World Championship in both years.

★ MOST CONSTRUCTORS' WORLD CHAMPIONSHIP TITLES

Ferrari won 14 Formula One constructors' World Championship titles (1961, 1964, 1975–77, 1979, 1982–83 and 1999–2004).

★ MOST POINTS BY A CONSTRUCTOR IN A SEASON

In the 2004 Formula One season, the Ferrari team amassed an overall total of 262 World Championship points.

★ MOST POINTS BY A DRIVER IN A SEASON

Michael Schumacher scored 148 points in the 2004 Formula One season.

★ MOST GRAND PRIX WINS BY A MANUFACTURER

Ferrari has had 166 Grand Prix race wins.

★ MOST POINTS SCORED BY A DRIVER

Michael Schumacher scored a record 1,186 points from 1991 to 2004. (This total includes 78 points from the 1997 season when he was excluded from the final standings.)

★ YOUNGEST DRIVER TO CLAIM A WORLD CHAMPIONSHIP POINT

Jenson Button (UK, b. 19 January 1980) was 20 years 67 days old when he finished in sixth place in the Brazilian Grand Prix on 26 March 2000.

MOTORCYCLE WORLD CHAMPIONSHIPS

MOST 50-CC TITLES

Angel Roldán Nieto (Spain) won six 50-cc titles (1969, 1970, 1972, 1975–77).

MOST 80-CC TITLES

Jorge Martinez (Spain) won three 80-cc motorcycle World Championships between 1986 and 1988.

MOST 125-CC TITLES

Angel Roldán Nieto won seven 125-cc titles (1971, 1972, 1979 and 1981–84).

MOST 250-CC TITLES

Phil Read (UK) won four 250-cc titles (1964, 1965, 1968 and 1971). Max Biaggi (Italy) equalled this record from 1994 to 1997.

MOST 350-CC TITLES

Giacomo Agostini (Italy) won seven 350-cc titles between 1968–74.

MOST 500-CC TITLES

Giacomo Agostini won eight titles in 1966–72 and 1975.

→ HOW FAST IS THE WORLD'S FASTEST PRODUCTION CAR? FIND OUT ON P.186

★ YOUNGEST DRIVER TO WIN A WORLD CHAMPIONSHIP RACE →

Fernando Alonso (Spain, b. 29 July 1981) was 22 years 26 days old when he won the Hungarian Formula One Grand Prix on 24 August 2003, driving for Renault. He is pictured here, in April of the same year, holding the third-place trophy that he won in the Brazilian Grand Prix.

MOTOR SPORTS

←★ MOST RACE WINS BY A MANUFACTURER

The superbike World Championships were first held in 1988. Since that time, Ducati has won a record 235 World Championship races, 1988–2004. Pictured is Carlos Checa (Spain).

NASCAR

MOST CONSECUTIVE CHAMPIONSHIP WINS

Eight drivers have won back-to-back NASCAR – National Association for Stock Car Auto Racing – Championships, but Cale Yarborough (USA) has won three consecutively, from 1976 to 1978.

★ MOST TITLES BY AN OWNER

Richard Petty (USA) won six titles between 1964 and 1979, as did Junior Johnson (USA) in 1976–85, and Richard Childress (USA) in 1986–94.

MOST TITLES BY A DRIVER

Richard Petty (USA) won seven times,1964–79. Dale Earnhardt (USA) equalled this feat, 1980–94.

MOST WINS IN A SEASON

Richard Petty (USA) won 27 races in the 1967 NASCAR season, when he also set the mark for the **most consecutive wins**, with 10.

MOST DAKAR RALLY WINS

Ari Vatanen (Finland) has won the Dakar Rally a record four times, first in 1987 and then on three more occasions between 1989 and 1991. Vatanen is pictured near Barcelona, Spain, on 31 December 2004.

★ MOST TITLES BY A CAR MAKE

Chevrolet (USA) provided the winning car for the NASCAR champion 21 times between 1957 and 2001.

MOST NASCAR POLE POSITIONS IN A CAREER

Richard Petty (USA) achieved pole position 126 times, 1958–92.

RALLYING

★ MOST DAKAR RALLY TRUCK CATEGORY WINS

Karel Loprais (Czech Republic) won six times in the truck category of the Dakar rally (1988, 1994–95, 1998–99 and 2001).

MOST DAKAR RALLY BIKE CATEGORY WINS

Stéphane Peterhansel (France) won six times in the bike category of the Dakar rally (1991–93, 1995 and 1997–98).

YOUNGEST RALLY WORLD CHAMPIONSHIP DRIVER

Jari-Matti Latvala (Finland) was 18 years 61 days when he drove in the 50th Acropolis Rally, Athens, Greece, from 6 to 8 June 2003.

★ MOST WORLD CHAMPIONSHIP RACE WINS

Between 1990 and 2004, Carlos Sainz (Spain) won 26 World Championship races.

MOST WORLD CHAMPIONSHIP WINS BY A MANUFACTURER

Lancia (Italy) won the rally World Championships 11 times between 1972 and 1992.

MOST WORLD CHAMPIONSHIP TITLE WINS

Juha Kankkunen and Tommi Makinen (both Finland) have four title wins each, the former for the championships in 1986–87, 1991 and 1993; the latter for the championships in 1996–99.

★ LONGEST RALLY

The Singapore Airlines London–Sydney Rally covers 31,107 km (19,329 miles). The rally was won on 28 September 1977 by Andrew Cowan, Colin Malkin and Michael Broad (all UK) in a Mercedes 280E.

HIGHEST EARNINGS IN A NASCAR CAREER

Jeff Gordon (USA) won a record $66,956,249 (£35,512,172) during his NASCAR career from 1992 to 2005.

←

SUPERBIKE

MOST POLE POSITIONS BY A MANUFACTURER

Ducati (Italy) achieved 126 pole positions in superbike World Championship races between 1988 and 2005.

MOST SUPERBIKE WORLD TITLE WINS

The most titles won is four by Carl Fogarty (UK) in 1994, 1995, 1998 and 1999.

★ MOST TITLES WON BY A MANUFACTURER

Ducati have won 13 titles, in 1991–96 and 1998–2004.

MISCELLANEOUS

★ YOUNGEST STOCK CAR DRIVER

At just 12 years old, Amanda 'A K' Stroud (USA, b. 21 March 1989) was a regular competitor in the Papa John's Pizza Pro-Cup racing division at Hickory Motor Speedway, North Carolina, USA, during the 2001 racing season.

★ OLDEST RACING DRIVER

On 5–6 February 2005, the actor Paul Newman (USA,

b. 26 January 1925) competed in a Pixar/Newman Prod/ Silverstone Racing/Ford Crawford car during the Rolex 24 at the Daytona International Speedway, Florida, USA, aged 80 years 10 days.

★ MOST MOTOR RACES IN 24 HOURS

The most motor races driven by one racing driver in 24 hours is five by Fiona Leggate (UK) at Silverstone Circuit, Northamptonshire, UK, on 25 July 2004. The races were part of the MG Car Club Silverstone MG 80 Race Meeting, and Leggate won the last race.

MOST CART CHAMPIONSHIP TITLES WON

The most wins in the National Championship – formerly the AAA (American Automobile

Association, 1909–55), USAC (US Auto Club, 1956–78), CART (Championship Auto Racing Teams, 1979–91), IndyCar (1992–97) and currently the FedEx Series Championship – is seven by A J Foyt Jr (USA) in 1960–61, 1963–64, 1967, 1975 and 1979.

MOST WINS IN THE INDIANAPOLIS 500

The most Indianapolis 500 wins is four and is shared by A J Foyt Jr (USA; 1961, 1964, 1967, 1977); Al Unser Sr (USA; 1970–71, 1978, 1987); and Rick Mears (USA; 1979, 1984, 1988 and 1991).

→ HOW POWERFUL IS THE WORLD'S MOST POWERFUL PRODUCTION MOTORCYCLE? FIND OUT ON P.188

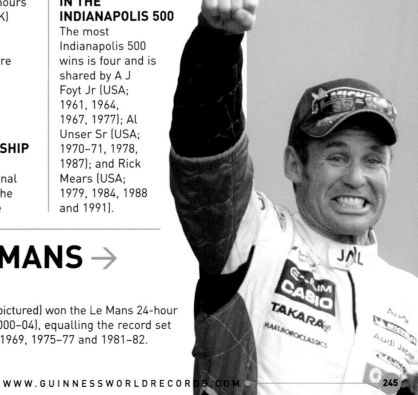

MOST LE MANS →
RACE WINS

Tom Kristensen (Denmark, pictured) won the Le Mans 24-hour race six times (1997 and 2000–04), equalling the record set by Jacky Ickx (Belgium) in 1969, 1975–77 and 1981–82.

← MOST MEDALS
WON AT A WINTER OLYMPIC GAMES (COUNTRY)

Germany won 35 medals at the XIX Winter Games held in Salt Lake City, Utah, USA, in 2002. Pictured left is Stephan Hocke, a member of Germany's gold medal-winning ski-jumping team.

INDIVIDUALS

THE INTERCALATED GAMES

Intended as an interim tournament to be held in Athens every four years, the Intercalated Games of 1906 were the only ones ever held.

The Intercalated Games were due to fit neatly into the gaps between the regular Olympics (1904, 1908, 1912, etc., the four-year span known as an Olympiad) but scheduling problems meant that the tournament was abandoned. Medals won in the 1906 Games are no longer recognized by the International Olympic Committee (IOC).

(The only other Olympics to be cancelled were the 1916, 1940 and 1944 Games, owing to the World Wars.)

MOST MEDALS WON

Gymnast Larisa Latynina (USSR, now Ukraine) won a total of nine gold, five silver and four bronze medals between 1956 and 1964, a total of 18 medals.

The **most Olympic medals won by a man** is 15, by gymnast Nikolay Andrianov (USSR), who collected seven gold, five silver and three bronze medals between 1972 and 1980.

MOST GOLD MEDALS WON

Three men have won nine gold medals at the Olympic Games. Paavo Nurmi (Finland) won three in 1920, five in 1924 and one in 1928 for athletics; Mark Spitz (USA) won two in 1968 and seven in 1972 for swimming; and Carl Lewis (USA) won four in

1984, two in 1988, two in 1992 and one in 1996 for athletics.

If the Intercalated Games of 1906 are included, the record is 10, by Raymond Ewry (USA), who won three in 1900, three in 1904, two in 1906 and two in 1908. He competed in standing high, standing long and standing triple jumps, all of which were dropped from the Olympic programme after 1912.

Larisa Latynina (USSR, now Ukraine) holds the record for **most gold medals won by a woman**, with nine for gymnastics: four in 1956, three in 1960 and two in 1964.

MOST CONSECUTIVE GOLD MEDALS WON

The only Olympians to win four consecutive individual titles in the same event are Al Oerter (USA), discus 1956–68, and Carl Lewis (USA), long jump 1984–96. However, Raymond Ewry (USA) won

both the standing long jump and the standing high jump at four games in succession (1900, 1904, 1906 and 1908) – if the Intercalated Games of 1906, which were staged officially by the IOC, are included. Also, Paul Elvstrøm (Denmark) won four successive gold medals at monotype yachting events, 1948–60, but there was a class change (1948 Firefly class, 1952–60 Finn class).

★ MOST CONSECUTIVE INDIVIDUAL EVENT MEDALS

George Hackl (Germany) won a medal in luge at five consecutive Olympic Games (1988–2002).

LONGEST SPAN AS AN OLYMPIC COMPETITOR

The longest span of an Olympic competitor is 40 years. The record is shared by: Dr Ivan Joseph Martin Osiier (Denmark) in fencing, 1908–32 and 1948; Magnus Andreas Thulstrup Clasen Konow (Norway) in yachting, 1908–20, 1928 and 1936–48; Paul Elvstrøm (Denmark) in yachting, 1948–60,

← ★ MOST GOLD MEDALS WON AT THE GAMES (COUNTRY)

The USA has won 976 gold medals at the Winter and Summer Olympic Games, from 1896 to 2004. Pictured from left to right are Tina Thompson, Tamika Catchings, Lisa Leslie and Ruth Riley, shown after receiving the gold medal for women's basketball on 28 August 2004 during the Summer Olympic Games at Athens that year.

1968–72 and 1984–88; and Durward Randolph Knowles (GB 1948, then The Bahamas) in yachting, 1948–72 and 1988.

The **longest span as a female Olympic competitor** is 28 years by Anne Jessica Ransehousen (née Newberry, USA) in dressage (1960, 1964 and 1988) and Christilot Hanson-Boylen (Canada), also in dressage (1964–76, 1984 and 1992).

YOUNGEST GOLD MEDALLIST

Kim Yun-mi (South Korea, b. 1 December 1980) was aged 13 years 85 days when she became champion in the 1994 women's 3,000 m short-track speedskating relay event.

COUNTRIES

MOST GOLD MEDALS WON AT A SUMMER GAMES

The USA won 83 gold medals at the XXIII Olympic Games in Los Angeles, California, USA, in 1984.

The USA also holds the overall records for the ★ **most gold medals won at the Summer Games** (907), the ★ **most medals won at the Games** (2,399) and the ★ **most medals won at the Summer Games** (2,215).

★ MOST GOLD MEDAL-WINNING COUNTRIES AT A SUMMER GAMES

An unprecedented 57 countries took home at least one

gold medal from the XXVIII Olympiad held in Athens, Greece, in 2004. During the same Games, a total of 931 medals (comprising 303 gold, 301 silver and 327 bronze) were awarded – the ★ **most medals awarded at one Games**.

★ MOST GOLD MEDAL-WINNING COUNTRIES AT A WINTER GAMES

Eighteen countries took home at least one gold medal from the XIX Olympic Winter Games held in Salt Lake City, Utah, USA, in 2002.

The **most countries to win a medal at a single Winter Games** is 25 in 2002 in Salt Lake City, Utah, USA.

MOST MEDALS WON AT THE WINTER GAMES

Norway has won 263 medals in the history of the Winter Games.

MISCELLANEOUS

★ MOST EVENTS FEATURED AT A GAMES

A total of 301 events were on the programme at the XXVIII Olympiad held in Athens, Greece, in 2004.

GREATEST ATTENDANCE

The overall spectator attendance at the Olympic Games held in Los Angeles, California, USA, in 1984 was given as 5,797,923 people.

MOST PARTICIPANTS AT A SUMMER GAMES

The Games in Sydney, Australia, in 2000 featured a total of 10,651 athletes (4,069 of them women).

MOST PARTICIPANTS AT A WINTER GAMES

The Games in Salt Lake City, Utah, USA, in 2002 drew 2,550 competitors from 77 countries.

MOST COUNTRIES TO PARTICIPATE IN THE SUMMER OLYMPIC GAMES

A total of 201 countries' NOCs (National Olympic Committees) participated in the Summer Olympic Games held in Athens, Greece, between 13 and 29 August 2004.

← ★ MOST SWIMMING MEDALS WON BY A MAN (SINGLE GAMES)

Michael Phelps (USA) won six gold medals (100 m and 200 m butterfly, 200 m and 400 m medley, 4 x 200 m freestyle and 4 x 100 m medley) and two bronze medals (200 m freestyle and 4 x 100 m freestyle) at the Athens Olympics in 2004.

RACKET SPORTS

★ MOST MEN'S TABLE TENNIS TEAM WORLD WINS →

Instituted in 1926, the most men's team titles for the Swaythling Cup is 14 by China (1961, 1963, 1965, 1971, 1975, 1977, 1981, 1983, 1985, 1987, 1995, 1997, 2001 and 2004, pictured).

→ WHO HAS THE FASTEST TENNIS SERVE IN THE WORLD? FIND OUT ON P.254

BADMINTON

MOST WORLD CHAMPIONSHIPS SINGLES TITLES
Four Chinese players have each won two individual world titles: the men's singles title was won by Yang Yang in 1987 and 1989; the women's singles title was won by Li Lingwei in 1983 and 1989; Han Aiping in 1985 and 1987; and Ye Zhaoying in 1995 and 1997.

MOST THOMAS CUP WINS
The most wins at the men's team badminton World Championships for the Thomas Cup is 13 by Indonesia (1958, 1961, 1964, 1970, 1973, 1976, 1979, 1984, 1994, 1996, 1998, 2000 and 2002).

MOST SUDIRMAN CUP WINS
The most wins at the mixed team World Championships for the Sudirman Cup is four by China (1995, 1997, 1999 and 2001).

MOST WORLD CUP WOMEN'S SINGLES WON
Susi Susanti (Indonesia) won five women's singles tournaments (1989, 1993–94 and 1996–97).

SHORTEST MATCH
On 19 May 1996, Ra Kyung-min (South Korea) beat Julia Mann (England) 11-2, 11-1 in 6 minutes during the Uber Cup in Hong Kong.

← FASTEST SHUTTLECOCK SPEED OFF A BADMINTON RACKET
In tests at Warwickshire Racquets and Health Club on 5 November 1996, Simon Archer (UK, pictured near left) hit a shuttlecock at a speed of 260 km/h (162 mph).

RACQUETBALL

★ MOST WOMEN'S DOUBLES WORLD CHAMPIONSHIPS BY AN INDIVIDUAL
Jackie Paraiso (USA) won six racquetball World Championships between 1990 and 2004.

★ MOST WOMEN'S WORLD CHAMPIONSHIPS BY AN INDIVIDUAL
The record of three championships is shared by two women. Michelle Gould (USA) won in 1992, 1994 and 1996; and Cheryl Gudinas (USA) won in 2000, 2002 and 2004.

★ MOST MEN'S DOUBLES WORLD CHAMPIONSHIPS BY A PAIR
Doug Ganim and Dan Obremski (both USA) won in 1988 and 1990. The record was equalled by Adam Karp and Bill Sell (both USA) after winning the championships in 1996 and 1998.

★ MOST MEN'S WORLD CHAMPIONSHIP WINS
Three people share this record – Egan Inoue (USA) won in 1986 and 1990; Sherman Greenfeld (Canada) in 1994 and 1998; and Jack Huczek (USA) in 2002 and 2004.

Badminton is played with a shuttlecock on a court with a high net. As with tennis, it is contested in five events: men's singles, women's singles, men's doubles, women's doubles and mixed doubles.

Racquetball is played mainly in the USA with rackets and a hollow rubber ball on an indoor court, with walls, floor and ceiling inbounds.

Real tennis (pictured) is the original racket sport from which lawn tennis is descended. It is played with a ball, handmade from cork or felt and wrapped in cloth, on a specialized court with walls on all sides, three of which have sloping roofs.

Squash, similar to racquetball, is played with slightly bigger rackets and a softer hollow rubber ball on an indoor court.

Table tennis, also known as ping pong, is played on a rectangular table with small rubber-coated wooden bats and a cellulose ball.

REAL TENNIS

MOST WOMEN'S WORLD CHAMPIONSHIPS

Instituted in 1985, the women's World Championships have been won six times by Penny Lumley (neé Fellows, UK), in 1989, 1991, 1995, 1997, 1999 and 2003.

★ MOST WOMEN'S DOUBLES WORLD CHAMPIONSHIPS BY A PAIR

Penny Lumley and Sue Haswell (both UK) won the women's doubles real tennis World Championships three times (1995, 1997 and 1999).

MOST MEN'S WORLD CHAMPIONSHIP WINS

Pierre Etchebaster (France) successfully defended the championship title eight times between 1928 and 1952.

Jacques Edmond Barre (France) had the **longest Real Tennis world championship career**. Although, at the time, the championships were not held every year, he was world champion over a period of 33 years (1829–62).

★ LARGEST PRIZE MONEY FOR A TOURNAMENT

Rob Fahey (Australia) was awarded $57,400 (£32,201) when he won the real tennis World Championships held at Newport, Rhode Island, USA, on 20 May 2004.

SQUASH

MOST WORLD CHAMPIONSHIP WINS BY A MEN'S TEAM

Australia have won an unprecedented eight men's world team titles, in 1967, 1969, 1971, 1973, 1989, 1991, 2001 and 2003.

MOST WORLD CHAMPIONSHIP WINS BY A WOMAN

Sarah Fitzgerald (Australia) won five World Open titles in 1996–98 and 2001–02.

★ MOST WORLD CHAMPIONSHIP WINS BY A WOMEN'S TEAM

The women's title has been won eight times by Australia in 1981, 1983, 1992, 1994, 1996, 1998, 2002 and 2004.

MOST WORLD OPEN TITLES

Jansher Khan (Pakistan) has won a record eight World Open titles in 1987, 1989, 1990 and 1992–96.

MOST UBER CUP WINS (BADMINTON) →

The most wins at the women's team badminton World Championships for the Uber Cup is nine by China, between 1984 and 2004. Pictured is Dai Yun (China) holding the Uber Cup trophy on 20 May 2000.

TABLE TENNIS

★ MOST WOMEN'S TEAM WORLD CHAMPIONSHIPS

Instituted in 1926, the Corbillon Cup has been won by China a record 16 times – 1965, 1971, 1975–89 (eight successive, every two years), 1993, 1995, 1997, 2000, 2001 and 2004.

★ LONGEST RALLY

Leif Alexis (Sweden) and Mat Hand (UK) achieved a 5 hr 8 min 22 sec rally at the Bonington Gallery, Nottingham, UK, on 9 December 2003.

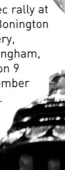

★ MOST IRB SEVENS SERIES TITLES →

The International Rugby Board Sevens series, which began in 1999, has been won five times (and every year) by New Zealand. The series is a competition comprising between seven and 11 separate Sevens tournaments, played around the world each season. New Zealand's captain Orene Ai'i is pictured performing the traditional Maori dance called the *haka* to celebrate their 34–5 defeat of Argentina in the final of the Los Angeles tournament in Carson, California, USA, on 13 February 2005.

RUGBY LEAGUE

MOST NRL TITLES

The National Rugby League is Australia's premier rugby league competition. The Brisbane Broncos have won two titles, in 1998 and 2000.

MOST CHALLENGE CUP WINS

The UK's rugby league Challenge Cup has been won 17 times by Wigan (1924, 1929, 1948, 1951, 1958–59, 1965, 1985, 1988–95 and 2002).

MOST SUPER LEAGUE TITLES

The Super League is the UK's premier rugby league competition, instituted in 1996. The most titles won by a team is four by St Helens (1996, 1999, 2000 and 2002).

MOST WORLD CUPS WON

The World Cup competition was first held in 1954. Australia have won eight times (1957, 1968, 1970, 1977, 1988, 1992, 1995 and 2000), and also won the International Championship of 1975.

FASTEST HAT-TRICK

The fastest hat-trick of tries scored from the start of a match is 6 min 54 sec by Chris Thorman (UK) playing for Huddersfield Giants against Doncaster Dragons in the semi-final of the Buddies National League Cup at Doncaster, South Yorkshire, UK, on 19 May 2002.

HIGHEST SCORE IN AN INTERNATIONAL MATCH

Australia beat Russia 110-4 in a rugby league World Cup match at Hull, East Riding of Yorkshire, UK, on 4 November 2000.

RUGBY UNION

★ YOUNGEST RUGBY UNION INTERNATIONAL

Edinburgh Academy pupils Ninian Jamieson Finlay (1858–1936) and Charles Reid (1864–1909) were both 17 years 36 days old when they played for Scotland v. England in 1875 and 1881 respectively. However, as Finlay had one less leap year in his lifetime up to his first cap, the record must be credited to him. Semi Taupeaafe (Tonga) was reportedly aged 16 when he played in a 1989 Test for Tonga v. Western Samoa.

★ OLDEST RUGBY UNION COMPETITION

The United Hospitals Cup was first played in 1875 between teams representing hospitals in England.

← ★ MOST STATE OF ORIGIN SERIES WINS

New South Wales have won Australia's rugby league State of Origin series 11 times between 1980 and 2004. Pictured left is New South Wales captain Brad Fittler (Australia).

BIGGEST RUGBY WORLD CUP MATCH WIN

The largest winning margin recorded in rugby union World Cup matches is 142 points, a feat achieved when host nation Australia beat Namibia 142-0 in Adelaide, Australia, on 25 October 2003.

★ MOST TRI-NATIONS TITLES

The Tri-Nations – an international competition inaugurated in 1996 and played annually between Australia, New Zealand and South Africa – has been won a record five times by New Zealand (1996–97, 1999 and 2002–03). Australia have won it twice (2000–01), as have South Africa (1998 and 2004).

MOST SIX NATIONS CHAMPIONSHIPS

The Six Nations replaced the Five Nations in 2000 when Italy were invited to join the historic competition. England have won three Six Nations Championships – more than any other country – in 2000–01 (when they failed to complete the grand slam in either year) and in 2003 (when they achieved the clean sweep of victories).

★ MOST SUPER 12 TITLES

The Super 12 is an annual tournament contested by teams from Australia, South Africa and New Zealand. The most Super 12 tournament victories by a team is four by the Canterbury Crusaders (New Zealand) from 1998 to 2000 and 2002.

FASTEST WORLD CUP TRY

Elton Flatley scored a try after only 18 seconds on 18 October 2003, playing for Australia against Romania at the Suncorp Stadium, Brisbane, Queensland, Australia.

MOST TRIES IN AN INTERNATIONAL CAREER

David Campese scored 64 tries in 101 internationals for Australia between 1982 and 1996.

MOST INTERNATIONAL APPEARANCES FOR BRITISH AND IRISH LIONS

William James 'Willie John' McBride (Ireland) made a record 17 test appearances for the British Isles, as well as 63 for Ireland.

MOST INTERNATIONAL APPEARANCES

Jason Leonard (UK) appeared 114 times for England between 1990 and 2004.

MOST POINTS IN AN INTERNATIONAL CAREER

In all internationals, Neil Jenkins (UK) has scored 1,049 points in 87 matches for Wales (1,008 points in 83 matches) and the British Lions (41 points in four matches), between 1991 and March 2001.

IRB SEVENS

★ MOST INDIVIDUAL IRB SEVENS TOURNAMENT APPEARANCES

Shane Thompson (Canada) appeared 46 times in International Rugby Board Sevens tournaments between 1999 and 2005.

★ MOST POINTS SCORED BY AN INDIVIDUAL IN IRB SEVENS TOURNAMENTS

Ben Gollings (UK) scored 1,120 points for England between 1999 and 2005.

★ MOST TRIES SCORED BY AN INDIVIDUAL IN IRB SEVENS TOURNAMENTS

Karl Te'Nana (New Zealand) scored 113 tries in IRB Sevens tournaments between 1999 and 2004.

← ★ MOST HEINEKEN CUP TITLES

Inaugurated in 1995, European club rugby's premier competition, the Heineken Cup, has been won twice by two teams: Toulouse (France) in 1996 and 2003, and Leicester Tigers (UK) in 2001 and 2002. Pictured left is Martin Johnson (UK), the Leicester captain.

MOST GOALS KICKED IN SIX NATIONS

Jonny Wilkinson (UK) kicked a record 13 goals – nine conversions and four penalty goals – for England during their match against Italy at Twickenham, London, UK, on 17 February 2001. Wilkinson also holds the record for the **most points scored by an individual in a season**, with 78 points (12 conversions and 18 penalty goals) in the five games of the 2000 International Championship series.

FARTHEST ARROW
SHOT USING FEET

Claudia Gomez (Argentina) shot an arrow into a target at a distance of 5.5 m (18.04 ft) using only her feet on the set of *El Show de los Récord*, Madrid, Spain, on 15 November 2001.

★ MOST BULL'S-EYES IN 90 SECONDS

Jeremie Masson (France) scored three bull's-eyes in 90 seconds, from a distance of 18 m (59 ft) from the target, in Argeles Gazost, France, on 15 July 2004.

HIGHEST SCORE IN 24 HOURS

Michael Howson and Stephen Howard (both UK) scored 26,064 points at Oakbank Sports College, Keighley, West Yorkshire, UK, on 11–12 November 2000.

MOST CROSSBOWS TRIGGERED – ARROW RELAY

The most arrows triggered by a single crossbow shot, with the final arrow hitting a marked target, is nine. Ross and Elisa Hartzell performed the feat on 18 December 1998, on the set of *Guinness World Records: Primetime* in Los Angeles, California, USA.

CROQUET

MOST NATIONAL TITLES

Bob Jackson (New Zealand) won the New Zealand Open Championship Singles title 14 times, in 1975, 1978, 1982–84, 1989, 1991–92, 1995, 1997–99 and 2002–03.

MOST WORLD CHAMPIONSHIP WINS BY AN INDIVIDUAL

The most wins by an individual is five by Robert Fulford (UK) in 1990, 1992, 1994, 1997 and 2002.

DARTS

YOUNGEST PLAYER IN A COMPETITIVE TOURNAMENT

Nick Stoekenbroek (Netherlands, b. 11 May 1989) played in the Dutch Open, Veldhoven, the Netherlands, on 5–7 February 2002, at the age of 12.

★ HIGHEST SCORE BY INNER AND OUTER BULL'S-EYES IN TWO MINUTES

Josette Kerdraon and Yannick Geay (both France) achieved a record with a score of 475 (15 x 25 and 2 x 50) on 5 August 2004 on the set of *L'Été De Tous Les Records* in Bénodet, France.

★ LARGEST ELECTRONIC DARTS TOURNAMENT

A tournament took place in Barcelona, Spain, between 26 and 28 March 2004 that featured 5,099 individual players.

LEAST DARTS 100,001

A total of 100,001 was achieved in 3,579 darts by Chris Gray (UK) at the Dolphin, Cromer, Norfolk, UK, on 27 April 1993.

ARCHERY

→ FOR A LIST OF ARCHERY WORLD RECORDS RECOGNIZED BY THE FÉDÉRATION INTERNATIONALE DE TIR À L'ARC (FITA), TURN TO THE SPORTS REFERENCE SECTION ON P.266

★ HEAVIEST LONGBOW DRAW WEIGHT

Mark Stretton (UK) drew a longbow to the maximum draw weight of 90 kg (200 lb) on an arrow of 82.5 cm (32.5 in) at The Bath Archers, Somerset, UK, on 15 August 2004.

SHOOTING RIFLE
← 50 M PRONE (MEN)

Numerous competitors have scored the maximum 600 points in this discipline, but this is without 'finals', which are points awarded in a final round. (The top eight shooters advance to a 10-shot final; the final is scored in tenths of a point and added to the match score to determine winners.) The record score of 704.8 points with finals was set by Christian Klees (Germany) at the 1996 Olympic Games in Atlanta.

← FASTEST 147
IN A PROFESSIONAL SNOOKER TOURNAMENT

Ronnie O'Sullivan (UK) achieved a 147 in 5 min 20 sec during the World Championships in Sheffield, South Yorkshire, UK, on 21 April 1997.

ISSF

Shooting with a **rifle, pistol or shotgun** has been included in the Olympic Games since 1896 and is monitored by the International Shooting Sport Federation (ISSF). The governing body administers records for both men and women as well as teams.

For **rifle, pistol and running target events**, shooters fire at round black aiming areas displayed on white backgrounds. The targets are divided into 10 concentric scoring zones or rings. Targets are electronic and a computer system instantly scores each shot.

For **shotgun events**, each time the shooter fires and hits the target so that at least one visible piece is broken, it is scored as a hit and counts as one point.

→ **FOR A LIST OF INDIVIDUAL EVENTS AND DISCIPLINES THAT THE ISSF MONITOR AT OLYMPIC LEVEL, TURN TO THE SPORTS REFERENCE SECTION ON P.273**

POOL

★ MOST WORLD TITLES
Ralph Greenleaf (USA) won the world professional pool title 19 times between 1919 and 1937.

SPEED POTTING ON ONE US TABLE (MEN)
Dave Pearson (UK) potted all 15 balls on a table in 26.5 seconds at Pepper's Bar and Grill, Windsor, Ontario, Canada, on 4 April 1997.

★ SPEED POTTING ON TWO US TABLES (MEN)
On 14 October 2002, Dave Pearson (UK) potted two consecutive racks of 15 pool balls in 1 min 22 sec in Natick, Massachusetts, USA.

★ SPEED POTTING ON 10 US TABLES (MEN)
Dave Pearson (UK) cleared 10 tables of 15 balls in 8 min 57 sec on 12 October 2002 in Natick, Massachusetts, USA.

SNOOKER

HIGHEST BREAK
Wally West (UK) made a break of 151 in a match at the Hounslow Lucania, Middlesex, UK, in October 1976. The break involved a free ball, which therefore created an 'extra' red, when all 15 reds were still on the table. In these very exceptional circumstances, the maximum break is 155.

YOUNGEST WORLD CHAMPION
On 29 April 1990, Stephen Hendry (UK, b. 13 January 1969) became world professional snooker champion at 21 years 106 days.

YOUNGEST PLAYER TO SCORE 147
Ronnie O'Sullivan (UK, b. 5 December 1975) scored a competitive maximum of 147 at the age of 15 years 98 days during the English Amateur Championship at Aldershot, Hampshire, UK, on 13 March 1991.

FASTEST COLOURS CLEAR
Ken Doherty (Ireland) potted all of the colours in sequence on a snooker table in 23.4 seconds at The Chase Centre, Staffordshire, UK, on 29 August 1997.

MISCELLANEOUS

★ CASTING – MOST WORLD TITLES (WOMEN)
Jana Maisel (Germany) won 36 gold medals at the International Casting Sport Federation World Championships from 1990 to 2002. In total, she has won 46 World medals (36 gold) and 42 European medals (30 gold).

★ MOST CASTS MADE IN 24 HOURS
Brent Olgers (USA) made 6,358 casts in 24 hours on Lake Michigan at Chicago, Illinois, USA, on 9–10 July 1999.

★ FASTEST TIME TO SHOOT 25 CLAY PIGEON TARGETS
Jose Lopes (France) shot 25 clay pigeon sporting targets in 1 min 11 sec on the set of *L'Été De Tous Les Records* in Argeles Gazost, France, on 12 July 2004.

★ HIGHEST TENPIN BOWLING PINFALL IN 24 HOURS USING ONE LANE
Twelve bowlers achieved a pinfall of 37,129 at REVS Bowling & Entertainment Centre, Burnaby, British Columbia, in 24 hours on 20–21 February 2004.

★ MOST TENPIN BOWLING STRIKES IN A MINUTE
Tomas Leandersson (Sweden) achieved six tenpin bowling strikes in a minute at Sundbybergs Bowling Hall, Sweden, on 24 October 2001.

MOST DARTS WORLD CHAMPIONSHIP TITLES →

The most World Championship titles won is 12 by Phil Taylor (UK): with the World Darts Organization (WDO) in 1990 and 1992, and the Professional Darts Council (PDC) in 1995–2002 and 2004–2005.

TENNIS

ROGER FEDERER

The men's tennis No.1 seed – and winner of a record 16 consecutive tournaments – talks about his world-beating achievements.

Who inspired you as a child?
I looked up to two athletes. One was Michael Jordan and the other was Björn Borg.

What do you think your greatest achievement in tennis is?
It has to be winning three grand slam tournaments, the Masters Cup, plus six additional events and only losing six matches throughout the year ... all in one year [2004].

What are your future goals?
Stay No.1 ... and Wimbledon is always a goal! I'd also like to do charity work. I set up the Roger Federer Foundation to promote sport for young people and fund projects for disadvantaged children, which I'd like to do more work with. I'd definitely like to stay in sports in some capacity.

What advice would you give to young sportsmen and women?
You're going to go through ups and downs, but you learn a lot during the down periods. You have to keep to your long-term goals and love what you're doing. You also need a lot of support around you, from parents and family.

★ MOST CONSECUTIVE FINALS WINS

Between October 2003 and February 2005, Roger Federer (Switzerland) won 16 consecutive Open finals: Vienna, Houston Masters, Australian Open, Dubai, Indian Wells Masters, Hamburg Masters, Halle, Wimbledon, Gstaad, Canadian Masters, US Open, Bangkok, Houston Masters, Qatar Open, Rotterdam and Dubai Open.

GRAND SLAM TOURNAMENTS

MOST TOURNAMENTS WONS (SINGLES)
Margaret Court (Australia) won 24 grand slam tournament singles titles between 1960 and 1973.

MOST TOURNAMENTS WON (DOUBLES)
Two women's partnerships have won 20 grand slam tournaments: Althea Louise Brough and Margaret Evelyn Du Pont (both USA) from 1942 to 1957; and Pam Shriver and Martina Navratilova (both USA) from 1981 to 1989.

The **most grand slam wins by a men's doubles partnership** is 12, by John Newcombe and Tony Roche (both Australia) between 1965 and 1976.

★ LONGEST MATCH
In 2004, Fabrice Santoro and Arnaud Clément (both France) played for a total of 6 hr 33 min in the first round of the French Open.

MOST WIMBLEDON SINGLES TITLES WON
Pete Sampras (USA) won seven Wimbledon singles titles in 1993–95 and 1997–2000.

The **most Wimbledon singles titles won by a woman** is nine by Martina Navratilova (USA) in 1978–79, 1982–87 and 1990.

★ MOST WIMBLEDON DOUBLES TITLES WON
Todd Woodbridge (Australia) won nine Wimbledon men's doubles tennis titles between 1993 and 2004. He won the first six playing with Mark Woodforde (Australia) and the last three with Jonas Bjorkman (Sweden).

FASTEST SERVE

The **fastest service by a woman** (measured by modern equipment) is 205 km/h (127.4 mph) by Venus Williams (USA) at Zurich, Switzerland, on 16 October 1998. The **fastest service by a man** is 246.2 km/h (153 mph) by Andy Roddick (USA) at the Queen's Club, London, UK, on 11 June 2004.

MOST US OPEN SINGLES TITLES

Three men have won a record seven US Open singles titles: Bill Tilden (USA) in 1920–25 and 1929; Richard Sears (USA) in 1881–87; and William Larned (USA) in 1901, 1902 and 1907–11.

The **most US Open singles titles won by a woman** is eight by Molla Mallory (née Bjurstedt, Norway) in 1915–18, 1920–22 and 1926.

MOST FRENCH OPEN SINGLES TITLES

Björn Borg (Sweden) won six French Open singles titles in 1974–75 and 1978–81. The **most French Open singles titles won by a woman** is seven by Chris Evert (USA) in 1974, 1975, 1979, 1980, 1983, 1985 and 1986.

MOST AUSTRALIAN OPEN SINGLES TITLES

Roy Emerson (Australia) won the Australian Open singles tennis title six times (1961 and 1963–67). The **most Australian Open singles titles won by a woman** is 11 by Margaret Court (Australia) in 1960–66, 1969–71 and 1973.

DAVIS CUP

MOST DAVIS CUP WINS

The most wins in the Davis Cup – the men's international team championship – is 31 by the USA between 1900 and 1995.

OLDEST DAVIS CUP PLAYER

Yaka-Garonfin Koptigan (Togo) was aged 59 years 147 days on 27 May 2001 when playing against Mauritius.

The world's **oldest tennis player** is José Guadalupe Leal Lemus (Mexico, b. 13 December 1902), who began playing tennis in 1925 and was still playing regularly at the age of 102.

YOUNGEST DAVIS CUP PLAYER

Kenny Banzer (Liechtenstein) was 14 years 5 days old on 16 February 2000 when playing against Algeria.

YOUNGEST WIMBLEDON WINNERS

NAME	COUNTRY	AGE	YEAR
Gentlemen			
Boris Becker	Germany	17 years 227 days	1985
Wilfred Baddely	UK	19 years 174 days	1891
Sidney Wood	USA	19 years 245 days	1931
Björn Borg	Sweden	20 years 22 days	1976
Ellsworth Vines	USA	20 years 278 days	1932
Ladies			
Charlotte Dod	UK	15 years 285 days	1887
Martina Hingis	Switzerland	16 years 278 days	1997
Maria Sharapova *(right)*	Russia	17 years 75 days	2004
Maureen Connolly	USA	17 years 292 days	1952
May Sutton	USA	18 years 286 days	1905

MISCELLANEOUS

LONGEST COMPETITIVE SINGLES MATCH

Christian Albrecht Barschel and Hauke Daene (both Germany) played a match lasting 25 hr 25 min on 12–13 September 2003 at Mölln Tennis Club, Mölln, Germany. The pair played a total of 36 sets.

★ LONGEST COMPETITIVE DOUBLES MATCH

The longest competitive doubles tennis match, by one pair playing against all comers, lasted 33 hr 33 min 33 sec and was played by Christian Albrecht Barschel and Hauke Daene (both Germany), from 13 to 15 August 2004 at Mölln Tennis Club, Germany.

LONGEST COACHING MARATHON

Butch Heffernan (Australia) coached tennis for 52 hours on 23–25 November 2001 at the Next Generation Club in Brierley Hill, Dudley, West Midlands, UK.

★ MOST PEOPLE BOUNCING TENNIS BALLS ON RACKETS

The most people to bounce tennis balls on tennis rackets simultaneously in one place is 258 at Devonport Tennis Club, Devonport, Tasmania, Australia, on 11 March 2004.

MOST TENNIS BALLS HELD IN THE HAND

Francisco Peinado Toledo (Spain) held 18 tennis balls in his left hand for 10 seconds at Valencia, Spain, on 18 September 2003.

OLDEST BALL BOY

Manny Hershkowitz (USA) worked on court at the US Open at Flushing Meadow, New York, USA, in September 1999, aged 82.

TENNIS 'GRAND SLAMS'

The term 'grand slam' was first used in 1933 to describe winning the four major tennis tournaments in the year:

Australian Open (Melbourne, Australia): inaugurated 1905, hardcourt, January

Tournoi de Roland-Garros (French Open) (Paris, France): inaugurated 1891, red clay, May/June

Wimbledon (London, UK): inaugurated 1877, played on grass, June/July

US Open (New York City, USA): inaugurated 1881, hardcourt, August/September

★ MOST CLUB → CHAMPIONSHIPS WON

The ★ **most club championships won by an individual** at the same club is 16 (including a record 10 consecutively) by Stuart Foster (UK, pictured) at Leverstock Green Lawn Tennis Club in Hemel Hempstead, UK, between 1987 and 2004.

Foster also holds records for the ★ **most club doubles championships won as a pair**, with 17 victories from 1988 to 2004 with partner Graham Fish (UK), and the ★ **most mixed doubles won** – 11 – with various partners between 1985 and 2001.

FASTEST → COAL-BAG CARRYING

David Jones (UK) holds the record for the fastest coal carrying Championship race on 1 April 1991 at Gawthorpe, West Yorkshire, UK, carrying a 50-kg (110-lb) bag over the 1,012.5-m (3,322-ft) course in 4 min 6 sec – the fastest by a man.

At the 2002 Championship on 6 April, Ruth Clegg (UK) carried a 20-kg (44-lb) bag over the same distance in 5 min 4 sec, winning the record of **fastest coal-bag carrying by a woman**.

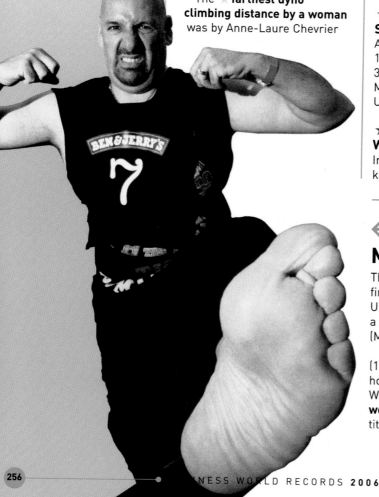

FARTHEST DYNO CLIMBING DISTANCE

In dyno climbing, participants launch from one set of handholds on a climbing wall to a higher set with no intermediate holds. Matt Heason (UK) achieved 2.60 m (8.61 ft) at the Edge Climbing Centre, Sheffield, UK, on 20 April 2002.

The ★ **farthest dyno climbing distance by a woman** was by Anne-Laure Chevrier (France), who dyno-ed 1.95 m (6.45 ft) in Benodet, France, on 5 August 2004.

★ MOST ELEPHANT POLO WORLD CHAMPIONSHIPS

The Tiger Top Tuskers (Nepal) have won the championships a record eight times (1983–85, 1987, 1992, 1998, 2000 and 2003).

★ FASTEST 100 M ON A SPACEHOPPER BY A MAN

Ashrita Furman (USA) travelled 100 m on a spacehopper in 30.2 seconds at Flushing Meadow Park, New York City, USA, on 16 November 2004.

★ MOST KABADDI WORLD CUP WINS

Inaugurated in 2004, the only kabaddi World Cup contested so far was won by India, who beat Iran 55-27 in the final, played at South Kanara Sports Club, Mumbai, India, on 21 November 2004.

★ MOST CONSECUTIVE FOOTBAG KICKS WITH TWO FOOTBAGS

Juha-Matti Rytilahti (Finland) achieved 68 footbag kicks with one foot, using two footbags, at the Turku Fair Centre, Turku, Finland, on 30 September 2001.

★ MOST ENTRANTS AT A BOG SNORKELLING WORLD CHAMPIONSHIPS

The bog snorkelling World Championships held on 30 August 2004 at Waen Rhydd peat bog, Llanwrtyd Wells, Powys, UK, saw a record 146 entries.

← TOE WRESTLING – MOST WORLD CHAMPIONSHIP WINS

The toe wrestling World Championships are held annually on the first Saturday in June at Ye Olde Royal Oak, Wetton, Staffordshire, UK. Contestants must push an opponent's foot to the other side of a specially constructed ring called a 'toerack' using only their toes. (Mixed matches are not allowed because of the danger of 'myxomatoesis'.)

In the men's category, Alan Nash (UK) won five championships (1994, 1996–97, 2000 and 2002). Nash, nicknamed 'Nasty', also has the honour of being knighted by His Majesty King Leo 1st of Redonda in the West Indies. The record for **most toe wrestling World Championships won by a woman** is held by Karen Davies (UK), who won a record four titles (1999–2002).

★ BOG →
SNORKELLING – MOST CONSECUTIVE WORLD CHAMPIONSHIPS

Two competitors have held the coveted bog snorkelling World Championship title three times in successive years: Steve Griffiths (UK) from 1985 to 1987; and Philip John (UK, pictured) from 2002 to 2004.

★ MOST HORSESHOE PITCHING WORLD CHAMPIONSHIPS WON

The horseshoe pitching World Championships have historically been played at irregular intervals, but have been held every year since 1946. The record for most titles in the men's category is 10, shared by Ted Allen (USA) in 1933–40 (competition not held in consecutive years), 1946, 1953, 1955–57 and 1959; and Alan Francis (USA) in 1989, 1993, 1995–99, 2001 and 2003–04.

★ GREATEST DISTANCE ROWED ON LAND

Rob Bryant (USA) rowed 5,278.5 km (3,280 miles) on a specially built land rowing machine. He left Los Angeles, California, USA, on 2 April 1990, and reached Washington DC on 30 July 1990.

★ MOST ROTATIONS IN TABLE WRESTLING

Table wrestling involves participants climbing 360° around a table top without touching the ground. The most rotations of a table in one minute is 11 by Chris Sturman (UK) on 10 July 1999.

★ FASTEST UNDERWATER ARCHERY

The fastest time to complete three circuits of an underwater archery course is 1 min 21 sec, set by Nicolas Rizzo (France) in Port Leucate, France, on 23 July 2004.

★ LONGEST SHAFT USED → TO COMPLETE A ROTATION IN KIIKING

Andrus Aasamäe (Estonia) used a 7.02-m (23-ft) shaft to successfully complete a kiiking rotation in Haapsalu, Estonia, on 21 August 2004. The women's record is held by Kätlin Kink (Estonia), who used a 5.93-m (19-ft 5-in) staff at Palmse, Estonia, on 19 July 2003.

★ MOST CROSSBRED LAMBS SHORN IN EIGHT HOURS

Trevor Bacon (Australia) sheared 471 crossbred lambs – in accordance with World Shearing Record Committee rules – on 7 October 2002 at Walla Brook Farm, Frances, Australia.

★ LONGEST GAME OF HUMAN TABLE FOOTBALL

A game at Foz do Arelho Beach, Caldas de Rainha, Portugal, on 12 August 2004 was played for 24 hours.

← PEA SHOOTING – MOST WORLD CHAMPIONSHIP WINS

The pea shooting World Championships are held every year in Witcham, Cambridgeshire, UK. The skill is to shoot at a target, the size of a dartboard and smeared with putty, gaining five points for the inner, three for the middle and one for the outer circle, from a distance of 3.2 m (10 ft 6 in). The pea shooter should be no longer than 30.48 cm (12 in). Mike Fordham (UK) has won seven championships (1977–78, 1981, 1983–85 and 1992). He also holds the record for **most consecutive pea shooting World Championships**, 1983 to 1985. David Hollis (UK, pictured) equalled the record (1999–2001) and was also the **youngest world champion**, aged just 13 when he first scooped the title.

What is kiiking?
Kiiking is a sport that originated in Baltic and Scandinavian countries. The aim is to complete a 360° revolution on an enormous swing. As the record is based on the length of the shafts for the swing, the longer the shafts the higher the score.

★ HIGHEST HYDROFOIL JUMP →

Billy Rossini (USA, right) reached a height of 7.01 m (23 ft) on a hydrofoil at Lake Norman, North Carolina, USA, on 1 August 2004. A hydrofoil consists of a long fin attached beneath a board on which the rider sits in a raised chair. The ★ **tallest hydrofoil ridden** was a 3.28-m tall (10-ft 9.1-in) example created by William Blair (UK).

lifesavers
The Royal Life Saving Society UK

↑
MOST LIFE-SAVING AWARDS

The greatest number of awards gained by a member of the Royal Life Saving Society is 250 by Eric Deakin of Hightown, Merseyside, UK, between 1954 and 2004.

AQUABIKING

★ MOST BARREL ROLLS IN TWO MINUTES

Fred Guerreiro (France) achieved a total of 10 barrel rolls on his aquabike in two minutes for *L'Été De Tous Les Records* at Argeles Gazost, France, on 15 July 2004.

HIGHEST SPEED

Forrest Smith (USA) achieved a speed of 122.79 km/h (76.17 mph) on a modified Yamaha GP1200R aquabike (PWC) over a measured kilometre in Savannah, Georgia, USA, on 5 July 2002.

CANOEING

MOST WORLD AND OLYMPIC TITLES

Birgit Fischer (GDR/Germany) won a total of 37 titles from 1979 to 1998: eight Olympic titles and 29 world titles.

Three men have each won a record 13 titles: Gert Fredriksson (Sweden) from 1948 to 1960; Rüdiger Helm (GDR) from 1976 to 1983; and Ivan Patzaichin (Romania) from 1968 to 1984.

MOST OLYMPIC GOLD MEDALS (MEN)

Gert Fredriksson (Sweden) won six gold medals from 1948 to 1960. He added a silver and a bronze for a record eight medals.

LONGEST RACE

The Canadian Government Centennial Voyageur Canoe Pageant and Race from Rocky Mountain House, Alberta, to the Expo 67 site at Montreal, Quebec, was 5,283 km (3,283 miles). Ten canoes represented Canadian provinces and territories. The winner of the race, which took place from 24 May to 4 September 1967, was the Province of Manitoba canoe *Radisson*.

LONGEST HUMAN-POWERED JOURNEY WITH PORTAGES

Verlen Kruger and Steven Landick (both USA) travelled 45,129 km (28,043 miles), starting from Red Rock, Montana, USA, and finishing at Lansing, Michigan, USA, from 29 April 1980 to 15 December 1983. All portages (i.e. carrying the canoe) were human-powered.

LONGEST WATERFALL DESCENT

Tao Berman (USA) descended 30 m (98.4 ft) in 2.4 seconds at the Upper Johnstone Canyon Falls in Banff National Park, Alberta, Canada, on 23 August 1999.

MOST →
CONSECUTIVE DAYS SPENT SURFING

Dale Webster (USA) has gone surfing every day since 2 September 1975, passing his 10,407th consecutive day of surfing on 29 February 2004. Webster set himself the condition that 'a surf' consists of catching at least three waves to shore each time.

MOST OLYMPIC GOLD →
CANOEING MEDALS (WOMEN)

The most golds won by a woman is eight by Birgit Fischer (née Birgit Schmidt, GDR/Germany), from 1980 to 2004. She also won four silvers for a record total of 12 medals.

FASTEST NORTH ATLANTIC CROSSING IN A KAYAK (SOLO)
Peter Bray (UK) crossed the Atlantic by sea kayak, solo and unsupported, in 76 days from 22 June to 5 September 2001.

FASTEST 100 ESKIMO ROLLS
Ray Hudspith (UK) completed 100 eskimo rolls in 3 min 7.25 sec at Killingworth Leisure Centre, Tyne and Wear, UK, on 3 March 1991.

★ MOST ESKIMO ROLLS IN TANDEM
Three teams have performed 26 eskimo rolls in a tandem canoe with paddles in a time of one minute. Bernard Bregeon and Richard Vezzoli (both France) first achieved the feat in Biscarrosse, France, on 30 June 2004. Marc Girardin and Frederic Lascourreges (both France) equalled the record at Argeles Gazost, France, on 15 July 2004. Finally, Yann Hascoet and Emmanuel Baclet (both France) equalled the feat in Bénodet on 2 August 2004. All records were achieved on the set of *L'Été De Tous Les Records*, the French Guinness World Records TV show.

★ MOST INDIVIDUAL WORLD CHAMPIONSHIP TITLES (MEN)
Vladimir Vala and Jaroslav Slucik (both Slovakia) won four titles at the International Canoe Foundation (ICF) wildwater racing World Championships. They took the C2 events in 1996 and 2000, and two titles in 2004.

★ MOST TEAM WORLD CHAMPIONSHIP TITLES (MEN)
Germany have won three titles (K1 in 1996 and C2 in 1996 and 2004) at the ICF World Championships.

DIVING

MOST OLYMPIC MEDALS
Klaus Dibiasi (Austria) won five medals for Italy (three gold, two silver) from 1964 to 1976; Gregory Efthimios Louganis (USA) also won five (four golds, one silver) over the 1976, 1984 and 1988 Games. Two divers have won the highboard and springboard doubles at two Games: Patricia Joan McCormick (née Keller, USA) in 1952 and 1956; and Greg Louganis in 1984 and 1988.

★ MOST HIGH-DIVING WORLD CHAMPIONSHIPS
Orlando Duque (Colombia) has won the World High Diving Federation World Championships a record three times – in 2000, 2001 and 2002.

★ HIGHEST-SCORED DIVE
In 2000, during the Cliff-Diving World Championships in Kaunolu, Hawaii, USA, Orlando Duque (Colombia) performed a double back somersault with four twists from a height of 24.40 m (80 ft). For this dive, he earned a perfect 10 from all seven judges and scored 159.00 points.

→ HOW BIG IS THE LARGEST SURFBOARD EVER MADE? FIND OUT ON P.160

HIGHEST →
HEAD-FIRST
DIVES

Professional divers from La Quebrada (meaning 'the break in the rocks') in Acapulco, Mexico, regularly perform head-first dives from a height of 35 m (115 ft) into 3.65 m (12 ft) of water. The base rocks, which project 6.4 m (21 ft) from the take-off, require a leap out of 8.22 m (27 ft).

★ WAKEBOARD –
LONGEST RAMP JUMP

A wakeboard is a short, broad ski on which a skier is dragged along behind a motorboat. The farthest that anyone has ramp-jumped on a wakeboard is 15 m (49.2 ft) by Jerome MacQuart (France) on the set of *L'Été De Tous Les Records* in Argeles Gazost, France, on 14 July 2004.

ROWING

MOST OLYMPIC GOLD MEDALS WON

Steve Redgrave (GB) won five gold medals: coxed fours (1984), coxless pairs (1988, 1992 and 1996) and coxless fours (2000).

Elisabeta Lipa (Romania) won five gold medals from 1984 to 2004, the ★ **most women's rowing gold medals won**.

SWIMMING

FARTHEST DISTANCE SWUM BY A 20-STRONG RELAY TEAM IN 24 HOURS

New Zealand's national relay team swam 182.807 km (113.59 miles) in Lower Hutt, New Zealand, in 24 hours, passing 160 km (100 miles) in 20 hr 47 min 13 sec, on 9–10 December 1983.

FASTEST TIME TO SWIM THE CHANNEL

The official Channel Swimming Association (founded 1927) record

is 7 hr 17 min by Chad Hundeby (USA), from Shakespeare Beach, Dover, UK, to Cap Gris-Nez, France, on 27 September 1994.

The **fastest France-to-England time** is 8 hr 5 min by Richard Davey (UK) in 1988. The **fastest crossing by a relay team** is 6 hr 52 min (England to France) by the US National Swim Team on 1 August 1990. They then completed the **fastest two-way relay** in 14 hr 18 min.

LARGEST RACE IN OPEN WATER

The most participants in an open-sea race was 3,070 for The Pier to Pub Swim, Lorne, Victoria, Australia, on 10 January 1998.

LONGEST OCEAN SWIM

Susie Maroney (Australia) swam 197 km (122 miles) from Mexico to Cuba – the **longest distance ever swum without flippers in open sea** – in 38 hr 33 min. She arrived in Cuba on 1 June 1998.

MOST WORLD CHAMPIONSHIP MEDALS WON

Michael Gross (West Germany) won 13 medals – five gold, five silver and three bronze – between 1982 and 1990. The **most World Championship medals won by a woman** is 10, by Kornelia Ender

(GDR, now Germany) – eight gold and two silver in 1973 and 1975.

The **most World Championship medals at a single championship** is seven by Matt Biondi (USA) – three gold, one silver, three bronze – in 1986. The **most World Championship gold medals won by a man** is eight by Ian Thorpe (Australia) in 1998 and 2001.

MOST CONSECUTIVE OLYMPIC GOLD MEDALS

Two swimmers have won the same event three times – Dawn Fraser (Australia), for the 100 m freestyle in 1956, 1960 and 1964; and Krisztina Egerszegi (Hungary), for the 200 m backstroke in 1988, 1992 and 1996.

WAKEBOARDING

★ MOST WAKEBOARDING WORLD TITLES (MEN)

Darin Shapiro (USA) has won three men's World Championship titles in 1999, 2001 and 2002.

The record for the **most women's wakeboarding World Championship titles** is shared between Tara Hamilton (USA), who won the title in 1998 and 2002, and Meghan Major (USA), who won in 1999 and 2000.

THE ENGLISH CHANNEL

The English Channel is an area of the Atlantic Ocean between France and the UK approximately 550 km (350 miles) long. At its narrowest, between Dover (England) and Cap Griz-Nez (France), it measures 34 km (21 miles).

Many swimmers have endeavoured to traverse this famous stretch of water. The **first to swim the English Channel from shore to shore (without a life jacket)** was Merchant Navy captain Matthew Webb (1848–83), who swam an estimated 61 km (38 miles) to make the 34-km (21-mile) crossing in 21 hr 45 min on 24–25 August 1875.

The **first woman** to succeed was Gertrude Caroline Ederle (USA), who swam from France to England on 6 August 1926 in the then overall record time of 14 hr 39 min, earning her a ticker-tape parade on her return to New York City, USA.

★ OLDEST →
CHANNEL SWIMMER

George Brunstad (USA, b. 25 August 1934) was 70 years 4 days old when he swam from Dover, UK, to Sangatte, France, in 15 hr 59 min on 29 August 2004. The **oldest woman to swim the Channel** was Susan Fraenkel (South Africa, b. 22 April 1948), aged 46 years 103 days on 24 July 1994, with a time of 12 hr 5 min.

MOST PRO SURFING WORLD CHAMPIONSHIPS (WOMEN)

Layne Beachley (Australia) won six ASP (Association of Surfing Professionals) Tour World Championship titles between 1998 and 2003.

☆ OLDEST BAREFOOT WATER SKIER

George Blair, aka 'Banana George' (USA, b. 22 January 1915), waterskied barefoot on Lake Florence, Winter Haven, Florida, USA, aged 90 years 29 days on 20 February 2005.

WHITEWATER RAFTING

MOST WORLD CHAMPIONSHIPS (MEN)

The World Rafting Challenge Championship has been held since 1995. Slovenia has won five times from 1995 to 1999.

★ MOST WORLD CHAMPIONSHIPS (WOMEN)

New Zealand have won three times, in 1999, 2000 and 2003.

☆ BAREFOOT WATER SKIING WORLD CHAMPION (MEN)

The most titles won by a man is four by Ron Scarpa (USA), who won in 1992, 1996, 1998 and 2000.

WATER POLO

☆ MOST OLYMPIC WINS (MEN)

Hungary has won the Olympic tournament most often, with eight wins in 1932, 1936, 1952, 1956, 1964, 1976, 2000 and 2004.

Since women's water polo was introduced at the 2000 Games, the winners have been Australia in 2000 and Italy in 2004.

☆ MOST WORLD CHAMPIONSHIP TITLES

The first water polo World Championships were held in 1973, and the most wins is three by the USSR, who took the title in 1975, 1982 and 2002 (as Russia).

Since it was introduced in 1986, the women's water polo World Championships have been won twice by Italy, in 1998 and 2001.

MOST INTERNATIONAL WATER POLO GOALS

The greatest number of goals scored by an individual in an international is 13 by Debbie Handley for Australia (16) v. Canada (10) at the World Championships in Guayaquil, Ecuador, in 1982.

LONGEST WATER POLO MARATHON

Rapido 82 Haarlem at the De Planeet pool in Haarlem, the Netherlands, played a water polo marathon lasting 24 hours from 30 April to 1 May 1999.

WATER SKIING (BAREFOOT)

☆ MOST WORLD CHAMPIONSHIPS (TEAM)

The team title has been won a total of nine times by the USA between 1988 and 2004.

MOST WORLD CHAMPIONSHIPS (WOMEN)

Two competitors have won the barefoot World Championship four times each: Kim Lampard (Australia) in 1980, 1982, 1985, 1986, and Jennifer Calleri (USA) in 1990, 1992, 1994 and 1996.

★ CURLING –
MOST WORLD CHAMPIONSHIP MEDALS (INDIVIDUAL)

Dordi Nordby (Norway) won 10 curling medals from 1989 to 2004 – two gold, three silver and five bronze. The ★ **most medals by a man** is nine: Eigil Ramsfjell (Norway) won three gold, two silver and four bronze medals from 1978 to 1991.

CRESTA RUN

The Cresta Run is a hazardously steep and winding channel of ice carved into the natural contours of the Cresta Valley in St Moritz, Switzerland, each year. The run is 1,212 m (3,977 ft) long and has a total drop of 157 m (514 ft). Racers can reach a top speed of 129 km/h (80 mph), and can control their lightweight toboggans by using rakes on their boots as a brake.

There are two starting points on the Cresta Run. The full course is run from the 'Top', and only experienced riders are permitted to ride from this point. The other starting point – the 'Junction' – is one third of the way down the course.

BOBSLEIGHING

★ MOST WORLD CHAMPIONSHIPS BY A WOMEN'S TEAM

Since the women's World Championships was introduced in 2000 and debuted at the 2002 Winter Olympic Games, Germany has won the title three times (2000, 2003 and 2004).

MOST INDIVIDUAL WORLD CHAMPIONSHIP TITLES

Eugenio Monti (Italy) won 11 titles between 1957 and 1968. He did this by winning eight two-man titles and three four-man titles.

FASTEST CRESTA RUN COMPLETION TIME

The Cresta run course is 1,212 m (3,977 ft) long with a drop of 157 m (514 ft). The record – 50.09 seconds (average speed 87.11 km/h; 54.13 mph) – was achieved by James Sunley (UK) on 13 February 1999.

FASTEST CRESTA RUN TIME FROM JUNCTION

On 17 January 1999, Johannes Badrutt (Switzerland) set a time of 41.02 seconds to travel 890 m (2,921 ft) on the Cresta Run, starting from Junction.

CURLING

LARGEST BONSPIEL

At the 1988 Bonspiel in Winnipeg, Canada, there were 1,424 teams of four men, a total of 5,696 curlers, using 187 sheets of curling ice. 'Bonspiel' means 'league game'.

★ MOST MEN'S WORLD CHAMPIONSHIP TITLES

Canada has won the men's World Championships a total of 28 times, from 1959 to 2003.

DOG SLEDDING

OLDEST SLED DOG RACING TRAIL

The oldest established sled dog trail is the 1,688-km (1,049-mile) Iditarod Trail from Anchorage to Nome, Alaska, USA, which has existed since 1910 and has been the course of an annual race since 1967.

LONGEST TRAIL

The longest race is the 2,000-km (1,243-mile) Berengia Trail from Esso to Markovo, Russia, which started as a 250-km (155-mile) route in April 1990. Now established as an annual event, the fastest time to complete the trail was achieved in 1991 by Pavel Lazarev (Russia) in 10 days 18 hr 17 min 56 sec – an average rate of 8 km/h (5 mph).

← ★ SPEED SKATING – LOWEST WORLD CHAMPIONSHIP SCORE

The lowest, and therefore best, World Championship speed skating score achieved by a man is 150.478 points by Chad Hedrick (USA) for the overall title in Hamar, Norway, on 7–8 February 2004. The **lowest women's score** is 161.479 points, set by Gunda Niemann-Stirnemann (Germany) at Hamar, Norway, on 6–7 February 1999.

★ CURLING – MOST WORLD CHAMPIONSHIP TITLES (WOMEN) →

The Canadian women's team has accumulated 13 World Championships in curling (1980, 1984–87, 1989, 1993–94, 1996–97, 2000–01, 2004).

The **most ice dance titles** (instituted 1952) won is six by Lyudmila Alekseyevna Pakhomova (1946–86) and her husband Aleksandr Georgiyevich Gorshkov (both USSR) in 1970–74 and 1976. The couple also won the first ever Olympic ice dance title in 1976.

HIGHEST MARKS
Donald George Jackson (Canada) scored a total of seven perfect 6.0s in the men's World Championship in Prague, Czechoslovakia (now Czech Republic), in 1962.

Midori Ito (Japan) is the **highest scoring woman** with seven perfect 6.0s awarded at the 1989 figure skating World Championships held in Paris, France.

YOUNGEST WORLD CHAMPION
Tara Lipinski (USA, b. 10 June 1982) was 14 years 286 days when she won the individual title on 22 March 1997.

FIGURE SKATING – MOST WORLD CHAMPIONSHIP TITLES ↑

The **most World Championship titles by a woman** is held by Sonja Henie (Norway), pictured, who won 10 championships between 1927 and 1936.

Ulrich Salchow (Sweden) won 10 individual figure skating world titles in 1901–05 and 1907–11, the **most World Championship titles by a man**.

SKATING – FIGURE

MOST PAIRS WORLD CHAMPIONSHIP TITLES
Irina Rodnina won 10 pairs titles (instituted 1908), four with Aleksey Nikolayevich Ulanov in 1969–72 and six with her husband Aleksandr Gennadyevich Zaitsev (all USSR) in 1973–78.

SKATING – SPEED

MOST WORLD CHAMPIONSHIP SPRINT WINS BY A MAN
Igor Zhelezovskiy (USSR/Belarus) has won six men's sprint overall titles (1985–86, 1989 and 1991–93).

MOST WORLD CHAMPIONSHIP TITLES
Two speed skaters have won five titles each: Oscar Mathisen (Norway) won in 1908–09 and 1912–14; Clas Thunberg (Sweden) won in 1923, 1925, 1928–29 and 1931.

→ WHICH COUNTRY HAS WON THE MOST MEDALS AT THE WINTER OLYMPIC GAMES? FIND OUT ON P.247

← BOBSLEIGHING – MOST CRESTA RUN GRAND NATIONAL WINS

The most wins in the Grand National (instituted 1885) is eight by the 1948 Olympic champion Nino Bibbia (Italy), 1960–1973; and by Franco Gansser (Switzerland), 1981–1991.

SKIING – →
MOST WORLD CUP WINS IN A SEASON

The men's record is held jointly by Ingemar Stenmark (Sweden) with 13 wins in the 1978/79 season and Hermann Maier (Austria, pictured) with 13 wins in the 2000/01 season.

The women's record is held by Vreni Schneider (Switzerland), who won 13 events (and a combined) including all seven slalom events in the 1988/89 season.

SKIING – ALPINE

LONGEST RACE

The Inferno in Switzerland stretches over 15.8 km (9.8 miles) from the top of the Schilthorn to Lauterbrunnen.

The **fastest time to complete the course** is 13 min 53.40 sec by Urs von Allmen (Switzerland) in 1992. The women's record is 17 min 8.42 sec by Christine Sonderegger (Switzerland), also in 1992.

The ★ **greatest number of entries for the race** was 1,611 in 2004.

MOST WORLD CUP RACE WINS BY A MAN

The World Cup for Alpine events was introduced in 1967. The most individual event wins is 86 (46 giant slalom, 40 slalom from a total of 287 races) by Ingemar Stenmark (Sweden) in 1974–89, including an unprecedented 14 successive giant slalom wins from 18 March 1978, his 22nd birthday, to 21 January 1980.

MOST ALPINE SKIING WORLD CUP RACE WINS BY A WOMAN

Annemarie Moser (née Pröll, Austria) achieved a women's record 62 individual event wins (1970–79). She had a record 11 consecutive downhill wins from December 1972 to January 1974 and has also claimed the World Cup overall champion (downhill and slalom events combined) title a record six times since the tour began in 1967.

SKIING – FREESTYLE

MOST WORLD CUP TITLES BY A MAN

Eric Laboureix (France) won five titles (1986–88 and 1990–91).

Connie Kissling (Switzerland) won 10 titles from 1983 to 1992, the **most World Cup titles by a woman**.

← ★ # SNOWBOARDING –
MOST WORLD CUP TITLES

Karine Ruby (France) has won an unsurpassed 20 titles: overall (1996–98, 2001–02 and 2003), slalom/parallel slalom (1996–98 and 2002), giant slalom (1995–98 and 2001), snowboard cross (1997, 2001 and 2003–04) and big air (2004).

The **most men's titles won** is six by Mathieu Bozzetto (France): overall (1999–2000) and slalom/parallel slalom (1999–2002).

MOST SOMERSAULT AND TWIST COMBINATION FREESTYLE AERIAL JUMPS

Matt Chojnacki (USA) successfully completed a quadruple-twisting quadruple backflip at Winter Park Resort, Colorado, USA, on 4 April 2001.

SKIING – NORDIC

MOST SUCCESSFUL WORLD CHAMPION

The first World Nordic Championships were those of the 1924 Winter Olympics in Chamonix, France. The most titles (including Olympics) won is 17 by Bjørn Dæhlie (Norway, b. 19 June 1967) – 12 individual and five relay, 1991–98. Dæhlie has won a record 29 medals in total from 1991 to 1999.

MOST SUCCESSFUL NORDIC SKIING BY A WOMAN

Yelena Välbe (Russia) won an unprecedented 10 individual and seven relay titles from 1989 to 1998. With an additional seven medals, her total of 24 is also a record.

MOST SUCCESSFUL INDIVIDUAL IN WORLD CHAMPIONSHIPS JUMPING

The most titles won by a jumper is five by Birger Ruud (Norway) in 1931–32 and 1935–37.

★ LONGEST → COMPETITIVE SKI-JUMP BY A MAN

Matti Hautamaeki (Finland) successfully landed a ski-jump measuring 231 m (757.8 ft) at Planica, Slovenia, on 23 March 2003. Hautamaeki is pictured here competing in the 2002 Winter Olympics at Salt Lake City, USA.

GREATEST DISTANCE SKIED IN 24 HOURS (MEN)

The men's record for the greatest distance travelled in 24 hours by a cross-country skier belongs to Seppo-Juhani Savolainen (Finland), who covered 415.5 km (258.2 miles) at Saariselk, Finland, on 8–9 April 1988.

The **greatest distance skied in 24 hours by a woman** is 333 km (206.91 miles) by Kamila Horakova (Czech Republic) between 12 and 13 April 2000 at the Canmore Nordic Centre, Alberta, Canada.

LONGEST RACE

The annual Vasaloppet Race covers a distance of 89 km (55.3 miles).

The fastest time to complete the race is 3 hr 48 min 55 sec, by Bengt Hassis (Sweden) on 2 March 1986.

SKI-JUMPING

LONGEST COMPETITIVE SKI-JUMP BY A WOMAN

The farthest distance achieved by a female ski-jumper is 127.5 m (418 ft 4 in) and was set by Anette Sagen (Norway) at Oslo, Norway, on 14 March 2004.

★ LONGEST SKI-JUMP ON A DRY SLOPE

Veli-Matti Lindstroem (Finland) jumped a distance of 148 m (485 ft 6 in) at a dry ski slope at Kuusamo, Finland, on 4 August 2001.

SNOWBOARDING

★ MOST WORLD CHAMPIONSHIP TITLES

Karine Ruby (France) won a total of seven World Championship titles – the giant slalom in 1996, snowboard cross in 1997, Olympic gold in 1998, giant slalom, parallel slalom and snowboard cross in 2001 and snowboard cross in 2003.

HIGHEST SPEED

The highest speed recorded by a snowboarder is 201.907 km/h (125.459 mph) by Darren Powell (Australia) at Les Arcs, France, on 2 May 1999.

SKIING TERMINOLOGY

Aerial = mid-air tricks and jumps, judged on individual merit

Alpine = downhill speed racing

Mogul = a large bump of snow, off which a skier performs jumps or turns. A patch of bumps is called a 'mogul field'

Nordic = cross country skiing

← SKIING (FREESTYLE) – MOST WORLD CHAMPIONSHIP TITLES

The first skiing World Championships were held at Tignes, France, in 1986, with titles awarded in ballet, moguls, aerials and combined categories. Edgar Grospiron (France) has won a record three titles in moguls (1989 and 1991) and aerials (1995). He has also won an Olympic title in 1992.

The **most world titles won by a woman** is also three, held by Candice Gilg (France) for moguls in 1993, 1995 and 1997.

→ WHAT WAS THE HIGHEST EVER SCORE IN AN ICE HOCKEY MATCH? FIND OUT ON P.241

SPORTS REFERENCE

ARCHERY

Jang Yong-ho (South Korea) on his way to setting a world record with a score of 337 at 90 m during the 42nd World Archery Outdoor Championships on 16 June 2003.

ARCHERY – OUTDOOR

MEN (RECURVE)	RECORD	NAME & NATIONALITY	PLACE	DATE
FITA Round	1,379	Oh Kyo-moon (South Korea)	Wonju, South Korea	1 November 2000
90 m	337	Jang Yong-ho (South Korea)	New York City, USA	16 June 2003
70 m	347	Choi Young-kwang (South Korea)	Hongseong, South Korea	20 August 2002
50 m	351	Kim Kyung-ho (South Korea)	Wonju, South Korea	1 September 1997
30 m	360/17	Kye Dong-hyun (South Korea)	Cheongju, South Korea	1 September 1997
Team Round	4,074	South Korea (Jang Yong-ho, Choi Young-kwang and Im Dong-hyun)	New York City, USA	16 July 2003

WOMEN (RECURVE)	RECORD	NAME & NATIONALITY	PLACE	DATE
★ FITA Round	1,405	Park Sung-hyun (South Korea)	Cheongju, South Korea	10 October 2004
★ 70 m	351	Park Sung-hyun (South Korea)	Cheongju, South Korea	9 October 2004
★ 60 m	351	Kim Yu-mi (South Korea)	Cheongju, South Korea	27 August 2004
50 m	350	Park Sung-hyun (South Korea)	Yecheon, South Korea	12 March 2003
★ 30 m	360/15	Yun Mi-jin (South Korea)	Yecheon, South Korea	27 October 2004
Team Round	4,094	South Korea (Cho Youn-jeong, Kim Soo-nyung and Lee Eun-kyung)	Barcelona, Spain	1 August 1992

ATHLETICS – INDOOR FIELD EVENTS

MEN	RECORD	NAME & NATIONALITY	PLACE	DATE		
High jump	2.43 m (7 ft 11.5 in)	Javier Sotomayor (Cuba)	Budapest, Hungary	4 March 1989	*60 m	6.67 sec
Pole vault	6.15 m (20 ft 2 in)	Sergei Bubka (Ukraine)	Donets'k, Ukraine	21 February 1993	Long jump	7.84 m
Long jump	8.79 m (28 ft 10.25 in)	Carl Lewis (USA)	New York City, USA	27 January 1984	Shot	16.02 m
Triple jump	17.83 m (58 ft 6 in)	Aliecer Urrutia (Cuba)	Sindelfingen, Germany	1 March 1997	High jump	2.13 m
Shot	22.66 m (74 ft 4.5 in)	Randy Barnes (USA)	Los Angeles, USA	20 January 1989	60 m hurdles	7.85 sec
Heptathlon*	6,476 points	Dan O'Brien (USA)	Toronto, Canada	13–14 March 1993	Pole vault	5.20 m
					1,000 m	2 min 57.96 sec

WOMEN	RECORD	NAME & NATIONALITY	PLACE	DATE		
High jump	2.07 m (6 ft 9.5 in)	Heike Henkel (Germany)	Karlsruhe, Germany	9 February 1992	†60 m hurdles	8.22 sec
★ Pole vault	4.90 m (16 ft 1 in)	Yelena Isinbayeva (Russia)	Madrid, Spain	6 March 2005	High jump	1.93 m
Long jump	7.37 m (24 ft 2.25 in)	Heike Drechsler (GDR)	Vienna, Austria	13 February 1988	Shot	13.25 m
★ Triple jump	15.36 m (50 ft 4.75 in)	Tatyana Lebedeva (Russia)	Budapest, Hungary	6 March 2004	Long jump	6.67 m
Shot	22.50 m (73 ft 10 in)	Helena Fibingerov (Czechoslovakia)	Jablonec, Czechoslovakia	19 February 1977	800 m	2 min 10.26 sec
Pentathlon†	4,991 points	Irina Belova (Russia)	Berlin, Germany	14–15 February 1992		

ATHLETICS – OUTDOOR FIELD EVENTS

MEN	RECORD	NAME & NATIONALITY	PLACE	DATE		
High jump	2.45 m (8 ft 0.25 in)	Javier Sotomayor (Cuba)	Salamanca, Spain	27 July 1993	*100 m	10.64 sec
Pole vault	6.14 m (20 ft 1.75 in)	Sergei Bubka (Ukraine)	Sestriere, Italy	31 July 1994	Long jump	8.11 m
Long jump	8.95 m (29 ft 4.5 in)	Mike Powell (USA)	Tokyo, Japan	30 August 1991	Shot	15.33 m
Triple jump	18.29 m (60 ft 0.25 in)	Jonathan Edwards (GB)	Gothenburg, Sweden	7 August 1995	High jump	2.12 m
Shot	23.12 m (75 ft 10.25 in)	Randy Barnes (USA)	Los Angeles, USA	20 May 1990	400 m	47.79 sec
Discus	74.08 m (243 ft)	Jürgen Schult (GDR)	Neubrandenburg, Germany	6 June 1986	110 m hurdles	13.92 sec
Hammer	86.74 m (284 ft 7 in)	Yuriy Sedykh (USSR)	Stuttgart, Germany	30 August 1986	Discus	47.92 m
Javelin	98.48 m (323 ft 1 in)	Jan Zelezny (Czech Republic)	Jena, Germany	25 May 1996	Pole vault	4.80 m
Decathlon*	9,026 points	Roman Sebrle (Czech Republic)	Gotzis, Austria	26–27 May 2001	Javelin	70.16 m
					1,500 m	4 min 21.98 sec

WOMEN	RECORD	NAME & NATIONALITY	PLACE	DATE		
High jump	2.09 m (6 ft 10.25 in)	Stefka Kostadinova (Bulgaria)	Rome, Italy	30 August 1987	†100 m hurdles	12.69 sec
★ Pole vault	4.92 m (16 ft 1.6 in)	Yelena Isinbayeva (Russia)	Brussels, Belgium	3 September 2004	High jump	1.86 m
Long jump	7.52 m (24 ft 8.25 in)	Galina Chistyakova (USSR)	St Petersburg, Russia	1 June 1988	Shot	15.80 m
Triple jump	15.50 m (50 ft 10.25 in)	Inessa Kravets (Ukraine)	Gothenburg, Sweden	10 August 1995	200 m	22.56 sec
Shot	22.63 m (74 ft 3 in)	Natalya Lisovskaya (USSR)	Moscow, Russia	7 June 1987	Long jump	7.27 m
Discus	76.80 m (252 ft)	Gabriele Reinsch (GDR)	Neubrandenburg, Germany	9 July 1988	Javelin	45.66 m
Javelin	71.54 m (234 ft 8 in)	Osleidys Menédez (Cuba)	Rethymno, Greece	1 July 2001	800 m	2 min 8.51 sec
Heptathlon†	7,291 points	Jacqueline Joyner-Kersee (USA)	Seoul, South Korea	23–24 September 1988		

★ NEW RECORD   ★ UPDATED RECORD

MEN'S 5,000 M →

Kenenisa Bekele (Ethiopia) celebrates breaking the world 5,000 m record during the Norwich Union Grand Prix at the Birmingham National Indoor Arena (NIA) on 20 February 2004 in Birmingham, UK.

ATHLETICS – INDOOR TRACK EVENTS

MEN	TIME	NAME & NATIONALITY	PLACE	DATE
50 m	5.56	Donovan Bailey (Canada)	Reno, USA	9 February 1996
		Maurice Greene (USA)	Los Angeles, USA	3 February 1999
60 m	6.39	Maurice Greene (USA)	Madrid, Spain	3 February 1998.
		Maurice Greene (USA)	Atlanta, USA	3 March 2001
200 m	19.92	Frank Fredericks (Namibia)	Lievin, France,	18 February 1996
400 m	44.57	Kerron Clement (USA)	Fayetteville, USA	12 March 1995
800 m	1:42.67	Wilson Kipketer (Denmark)	Paris, France	9 March 1997
1,000 m	2:14.96	Wilson Kipketer (Denmark)	Birmingham, UK	20 February 2000
1,500 m	3:31.18	Hicham El Guerrouj (Morocco)	Stuttgart, Germany	2 February 1997
1 mile	3:48.45	Hicham El Guerrouj (Morocco)	Ghent, Belgium	12 February 1997
3,000 m	7:24.90	Daniel Komen (Kenya)	Budapest, Hungary	6 February 1998
5,000 m	12:49.60	Kenenisa Bekele (Ethiopia)	Birmingham, UK	20 February 2004
50 m hurdles	6.25	Mark McCoy (Canada)	Kobe, Japan	5 March 1986
60 m hurdles	7.30	Colin Jackson (GB)	Sindelfingen, Germany	6 March 1994
4 x 200 m relay	1:22.11	Great Britain (Linford Christie, Darren Braithwaite, Ade Mafe, John Regis)	Glasgow, UK	3 March 1991
4 x 400 m relay	3:02.83	USA (Andre Morris, Dameon Johnson, Deon Minor, Milton Campbell)	Maebashi, Japan	7 March 1999
5,000 m walk	18:07.08	Mikhail Shchennikov (Russia)	Moscow, Russia	14 February 1995

WOMEN	TIME	NAME & NATIONALITY	PLACE	DATE
50 m	5.96	Irina Privalova (Russia)	Madrid, Spain	9 February 1995
60 m	6.92	Irina Privalova (Russia)	Madrid, Spain	11 February 1993 9 February 1995
200 m	21.87	Merlene Ottey (Jamaica)	Lievin, France	13 February 1993
400 m	49.59	Jarmila Kratochvílová (Czechoslovakia)	Milan, Italy	7 March 1982
800 m	1:55.82	Jolanda Ceplak (Slovenia)	Vienna, Austria	3 March 2002
1,000 m	2:30.94	Maria Mutola (Mozambique)	Stockholm, Sweden	25 February 1999
1,500 m	3:59.98	Regina Jacobs (USA)	Boston, USA	2 February 2003
1 mile	4:17.14	Doina Melinte (Romania)	East Rutherford, USA	9 February 1990
3,000 m	8:29.15	Berhane Adere (Ethiopia)	Stuttgart, Germany	3 February 2002
★ 5,000 m	14:32.93	Tirunesh Dibaba (Ethiopia)	Boston, USA	29 January 2005
50 m hurdles	6.58	Cornelia Oschkenat (GDR)	Berlin, Germany	20 February 1988
60 m hurdles	7.69	Lyudmila Engquist (Russia)	Chelyabinsk, Russia	4 February 1993
★ 4 x 200 m relay	1:32.41	Russia (Yekaterina Kondratyeva, Irina Khabarova, Yuliva Pechonkina, Julia Gushchina)	Glasgow, UK	29 January 2005
★ 4 x 400 m relay	3:23.88	Russia (Olesya Krasnomovets, Olga Kotlyarova, Tatyana Levina, Natalya Nazarova)	Budapest, Romania	7 March 2004
3,000 m walk	11:40.33	Claudia Iovan (Romania)	Bucharest, Romania	30 January 1999

MEN'S 200 M ↗

Frank Fredericks (Namibia) pictured after smashing the world record for the 200 m during the Vittel Du Pas Calais meeting in Lievin, France, on 18 February 1996.

← WOMEN'S 3,000 M

Berhane Adere (Ethiopia) in the 3,000 m women's event, which she completed in 8 min 29.15 sec on 3 February 2002 at the International Light Athletic meeting in the Schleyer-Halle in Stuttgart, Germany.

WOMEN'S 200 M →

Merlene Ottey (Jamaica), holder of the indoor 200 m world record, at the 1996 Centennial Olympic Games in Atlanta, Georgia, USA.

SPORTS REFERENCE

↗

MEN'S 100 M

Tim Montgomery (USA) completes the men's 100 m race in 9.78 seconds on 14 September 2002 at the IAAF Grand-Prix Final in Paris, France.

↑

WOMEN'S 5,000 M

Elvan Abeylegesse (Turkey) on her way to winning the women's 5,000 m race at the IAAF Bergen Bislett games held on 11 June 2004 in Bergen, Norway.

ATHLETICS – OUTDOOR TRACK EVENTS

MEN	TIME	NAME & NATIONALITY	PLACE	DATE
100 m	9.78	Tim Montgomery (USA)	Paris, France	14 September 2002
200 m	19.32	Michael Johnson (USA)	Atlanta, USA	1 August 1996
400 m	43.18	Michael Johnson (USA)	Seville, Spain	26 August 1999
800 m	1:41.11	Wilson Kipketer (Denmark)	Cologne, Germany	24 August 1997
1,000 m	2:11.96	Noah Ngeny (Kenya)	Rieti, Italy	5 September 1999
1,500 m	3:26.00	Hicham El Guerrouj (Morocco)	Rome, Italy	14 July 1998
1 mile	3:43.13	Hicham El Guerrouj (Morocco)	Rome, Italy	7 July 1999
2,000 m	4:44.79	Hicham El Guerrouj (Morocco)	Berlin, Germany	7 September 1999
3,000 m	7:20.67	Daniel Komen (Kenya)	Rieti, Italy	1 September 1996
★ 5,000 m	12:37.35	Kenenisa Bekele (Ethiopia)	Hengelo, Netherlands	31 May 2004
★ 10,000 m	26:20.31	Kenenisa Bekele (Ethiopia)	Ostrava, Czech Republic	8 June 2004
20,000 m	56:55.60	Arturo Barrios (Mexico, now USA)	La Flèche, France	30 March 1991
25,000 m	1:13:55.80	Toshihiko Seko (Japan)	Christchurch, New Zealand	22 March 1981
30,000 m	1:29:18.80	Toshihiko Seko (Japan)	Christchurch, New Zealand	22 March 1981
1 hour	21,101 m	Arturo Barrios (Mexico, now USA)	La Flèche, France	30 March 1991
110 m hurdles	12.91	Colin Jackson (GB)	Stuttgart, Germany	20 August 1993
400 m hurdles	46.78	Kevin Young (USA)	Barcelona, Spain	6 August 1992
★ 3,000 m steeplechase	7:53.63	Saif Saaeed Shaheen (Qatar)	Brussels, Belgium	3 September 2004
4 x 100 m relay	37.40	USA (Michael Marsh, Leroy Burrell, Dennis Mitchell, Carl Lewis)	Barcelona, Spain	8 August 1992
		USA (John Drummond Jr, Andre Cason, Dennis Mitchell, Leroy Burrell)	Stuttgart, Germany	21 August 1993
4 x 200 m relay	1:18.68	Santa Monica Track Club, USA (Michael Marsh, Leroy Burrell, Floyd Heard, Carl Lewis)	Walnut, USA	17 April 1994
4 x 400 m relay	2:54.20	USA (Jerome Young, Antonio Pettigrew, Tyree Washington, Michael Johnson)	New York City, USA	23 July 1998
4 x 800 m relay	7:03.89	Great Britain (Peter Elliott, Garry Cook, Steve Cram, Sebastian Coe)	London, UK	30 August 1982
4 x 1,500 m relay	14:38.8	West Germany (Thomas Wessinghage, Harald Hudak, Michael Lederer, Karl Fleschen)	Cologne, Germany	17 August 1977
STOP PRESS: 100 m	**9.77**	**Asafa Powell (Jamaica)**	**Athens, Greece**	**14 June 2005**

WOMEN	TIME	NAME & NATIONALITY	PLACE	DATE
100 m	10.49	Florence Griffith-Joyner (USA)	Indianapolis, USA	16 July 1988
200 m	21.34	Florence Griffith-Joyner (USA)	Seoul, South Korea	29 September 1988
400 m	47.6	Marita Koch (GDR)	Canberra, Australia	6 October 1985
800 m	1:53.28	Jarmila Kratochvílová (Czechoslovakia)	Munich, Germany	26 July 1983
1,000 m	2:28.98	Svetlana Masterkova (Russia)	Brussels, Belgium	23 August 1996
1,500 m	3:50.46	Qu Yunxia (China)	Beijing, China	11 September 1993
1 mile	4:12.56	Svetlana Masterkova (Russia)	Zürich, Switzerland	14 August 1996
2,000 m	5:25.36	Sonia O'Sullivan (Ireland)	Edinburgh, UK	8 July 1994
3,000 m	8:06.11	Wang Junxia (China)	Beijing, China	13 September 1993
★ 5,000 m	14:24.68	Elvan Abeylegesse (Turkey)	Bergen, Norway	11 June 2004
10,000 m	29:31.78	Wang Junxia (China)	Beijing, China	8 September 1993
20,000 m	1:05:26.6	Tegla Loroupe (Kenya)	Borgholzhausen, Germany	3 September 2000
25,000 m	1:27:05.9	Tegla Loroupe (Kenya)	Megerkirchen, Germany	21 September 2002
30,000 m	1:45:50.0	Tegla Loroupe (Kenya)	Warstein, Germany	6 June 2003
1 hour	18,340 m	Tegla Loroupe (Kenya)	Borgholzhausen, Germany	7 August 1998
100 m hurdles	12.21	Yordanka Donkova (Bulgaria)	Stara Zagora, Bulgaria	20 August 1988
400 m hurdles	52.34	Yuliya Pechonkina (Russia)	Tula, Russia	8 August 2003
★ 3,000 m steeplechase	9:01.59	Gulnara Samitova (Russia)	Iraklio, Greece	4 July 2004
4 x 100 m relay	41.37	GDR (Silke Gladisch, Sabine Rieger, Ingrid Auerswald, Marlies Göhr)	Canberra, Australia	6 October 1985
4 x 200 m relay	1:27.46	United States 'Blue' (Latasha Jenkins, LaTasha Colander-Richardson, Nanceen Perry, Marion Jones)	Philadelphia, USA	29 April 2000
4 x 400 m relay	3:15.17	USSR (Tatyana Ledovskaya, Olga Nazarova, Maria Pinigina, Olga Bryzgina)	Seoul, South Korea	1 October 1988
4 x 800 m relay	7:50.17	USSR (Nadezhda Olizarenko, Lyubov Gurina, Lyudmila Borisova, Irina Podyalovskaya)	Moscow, Russia	5 August 1984

ATHLETICS – ROAD RACE

MEN	TIME	NAME & NATIONALITY	PLACE	DATE
10 km	27:02	Haile Gebrselassie (Ethiopia)	Doha, Qatar	11 December 2002
15 km	41:29	Felix Limo (Kenya)	Nijmegen, Netherlands	11 November 2001
20 km	56:18	Paul Tergat (Kenya)	Milan, Italy	4 April 1998
Half marathon	59:17	Paul Tergat (Kenya)	Milan, Italy	4 April 1998
★ 25 km	1:12:45	Paul Kosgei (Kenya)	Berlin, Germany	09 May 2004
★ 30 km	1:28:00	Takayuki Matsumiya (Japan)	Kumamoto, Japan	27 February 2005
Marathon	2:04:55	Paul Tergat (Kenya)	Berlin, Germany	28 September 2003
100 km	6:13:33	Takahiro Sunada (Japan)	Yubetsu, Japan	21 June 1998

WOMEN	TIME	NAME & NATIONALITY	PLACE	DATE
10 km	30:21	Paula Radcliffe (UK)	San Juan, Puerto Rico	23 February 2003
15 km	46:57	Elana Meyer (South Africa)	Cape Town, South Africa	2 November 1991
20 km	1:03:26	Paula Radcliffe (UK)	Bristol, UK	6 October 2001
Half marathon	1:06:44	Elana Meyer (South Africa)	Tokyo, Japan	15 January 1999
25 km	1:22:31	Naoko Takahashi (Japan)	Berlin, Germany	30 September 2001
30 km	1:39:02	Naoko Takahashi (Japan)	Berlin, Germany	30 September 2001
Marathon	2:15:25	Paula Radcliffe (UK)	London, UK	13 April 2003
100 km	6:33:11	Tomoe Abe (Japan)	Yufutsu, Japan	25 June 2000

ATHLETICS – ULTRA LONG DISTANCE

MEN	TIME/DISTANCE	NAME & NATIONALITY	PLACE	DATE
100 km	6:10:20	Don Ritchie (GB)	London, UK	28 October 1978
★ 100 miles	11:28:03	Oleg Kharitonov (Russia)	London, UK	2 October 2002
1,000 miles	11 days 13:54:58	Piotr Silikin (Lithuania)	Nanango, Australia	11–23 March 1998
24 hours	303.5 km (188.6 miles)	Yiannis Kouros (Australia)	Adelaide, Australia	4–5 October 1997
6 days	1,022.0 km (635.0 miles)	Yiannis Kouros (Greece)	New York, USA	2–8 July 1984

WOMEN	TIME/DISTANCE	NAME & NATIONALITY	PLACE	DATE
★ 100 km	7:14:05	Norimi Sakurai (Japan)	Verona, Italy	27 September 2003
★ 100 miles	14:25:45	Edit Berces (Hungary)	Verona, Italy	21–22 September 2002
1,000 miles	13 days 01:54:02	Eleanor Robinson (GB)	Nanango, Australia	11–24 March 1998
★ 24 hours	250.1 km (155.4 miles)	Edit Berces (Hungary)	Verona, Italy	21–22 September 2002
6 days	883.6 km (549 miles)	Sandra Barwick (NZ)	Campbelltown, Australia	18–24 November 1990

FREEDIVING APNEA

DEPTH DISCIPLINES	DEPTH	NAME & NATIONALITY	PLACE	DATE
★ Men – constant weight	103 m (337 ft 10 in)	Martin Stepanek (Czech Republic)	Spetses Island, Greece	10 September 2004
★ Women – constant weight	78 m (255 ft 10 in)	Mandy-Rae Cruickshank (Canada)	Grand Cayman, Cayman Islands	21 March 2004
★ Men (without fins) – constant weight	80 m (262 ft 5 in)	Martin Stepanek (Czech Republic)	Grand Cayman, Cayman Islands	9 April 2005
★ Women (without fins) – constant weight	50 m (164 ft)	Mandy-Rae Cruickshank (Canada)	Grand Cayman, Cayman Islands	8 April 2005
★ Men – variable weight	136 m (446 ft 2 in)	Martin Stepanek (Czech Republic)	Grand Cayman, Cayman Islands	14 April 2005
Women – variable weight	122 m (400 ft 3 in)	Tanya Streeter (UK)	Turks and Caicos	21 July 2003
★ Men – no limits	171 m (561 ft)	Loic Leferme (France)	Nice, France	30 October 2004
Women – no limits	160 m (524 ft 11 in)	Tanya Streeter (USA)	Turks and Caicos	17 August 2002
★ Men – free immersion	102 m (334 ft 7 in)	Martin Stepanek (Czech Republic)	Grand Cayman, Cayman Islands	23 March 2004
★ Women – free immersion	74 m (242 ft 9 in)	Mandy-Rae Cruickshank (Canada)	Grand Cayman, Cayman Islands	11 April 2005

DYNAMIC APNEA	DEPTH	NAME & NATIONALITY	PLACE	DATE
Men	200 m (656 ft 1 in)	Peter Pedersen (Denmark)	Randers, Denmark	18 July 2003
★ Women	158 m (518 ft 3 in)	Johanna Nordblad (Finland)	Limassol, Cyprus	14 June 2004
★ Men (without fins)	166 m (544 ft 7 in)	Stig Aavail Severinsen (Denmark)	Aarhus, Denmark	19 July 2003
★ Women (without fins)	104 m (341 ft 2 in)	Renate De Bruyn (Netherlands)	Huy, Belgium	25 April 2004

STATIC APNEA	TIME	NAME & NATIONALITY	PLACE	DATE
★ Men (without fins, duration)	8 min 58 sec	Tom Sietas (Germany)	Eindhoven, Netherlands	12 December 2004
★ Women (without fins, duration)	6 min 31 sec	Lotta Ericson (Sweden)	Limassol, Cyprus	19 June 2004

WOMEN'S 10 KM

Paula Radcliffe (UK) in training for her record-breaking 10 km, which she finished in 30 min 21 sec in February 2003. She also holds the record for the women's 20 km.

MEN'S NO LIMITS

Loic Leferme (France) breaks the apnea world record by reaching a depth of 171 m (561 ft) on 30 October 2004, near Nice, France.

★ NEW RECORD   ★ UPDATED RECORD

WOMEN'S SINGLE SCULLS

Roumiana Neykova (Bulgaria) celebrates gold in the single sculls during the FISA Rowing World Championships in Seville, Spain, on 21 September 2002.

ROWING

MEN	TIME	ROWER(S)/COUNTRY	REGATTA	YEAR
Single sculls	6:36.33	Marcel Hacker (Germany)	Seville, Spain	2002
Double sculls	6:04.37	Luka Spik, Iztok Cop (Slovenia)	St Catharines, Canada	1999
Quadruple sculls	5:37.68	Italy	Indianapolis, USA	1994
Coxless pairs	6:14.27	Matthew Pinsent, James Cracknell (GB)	Seville, Spain	2002
Coxless fours	5:41.35	Germany	Seville, Spain	2002
Coxed pairs*	6:42.16	Igor Boraska, Tihomir Frankovic, Milan Razov (Croatia)	Indianapolis, USA	1994
Coxed fours*	5:58.96	Germany	Vienna, Austria	1991
Coxed eights	5:19.85	USA	Athens, Greece	2004

WOMEN	TIME	ROWER(S)/COUNTRY	REGATTA	YEAR
Single sculls	7:07.71	Roumiana Neykova (Bulgaria)	Seville, Spain	2002
Double sculls	6:38.78	Georgina and Caroline Evers-Swindell	Seville, Spain	2002
Quadruple sculls	6:10.80	Germany	Duisburg, Germany	1996
Coxless pairs	6:53.80	Georgeta Andrunache, Viorica Susanu (Romania)	Seville, Spain	2002
Coxless fours*	6:25.47	Canada	Vienna, Austria	1991
Coxed eights	5:56.55	USA	Athens, Greece	2004

MEN (LIGHTWEIGHT)	TIME	ROWER(S)/COUNTRY	REGATTA	YEAR
Single sculls*	6:47.97	Karsten Nielsen (Denmark)	St Catharines, Canada	1999
Double sculls	6:10.80	Elia Luini, Leonardo Pettinari (Italy)	Seville, Spain	2002
Quadruple sculls*	5:45.18	Italy	Montreal, Canada	1992
Coxless pairs*	6:29.97	Christian Yantani Garces, Miguel Cerda Silva (Chile)	Seville, Spain	2002
Coxless fours	5:45.60	Denmark	Lucerne, Switzerland	1999
Coxed eights*	5:30.24	Germany	Montreal, Canada	1992

WOMEN (LIGHTWEIGHT)	TIME	ROWER(S)/COUNTRY	REGATTA	YEAR
Single sculls*	7:15.88	Marit van Eupen (Netherlands)	Lucerne, Switzerland	1999
Double sculls	6:49.90	Sally Newmarch, Amber Halliday (Australia)	Athens, Greece	2004
Quadruple sculls*	6:29.55	Australia	Seville, Spain	2002
Coxless pairs*	7:18.32	Eliza Blair, Justine Joyce (Australia)	Aiguebelette, France	1997

*Denotes non-Olympic boat classes

→ **WHAT'S THE FARTHEST DISTANCE ANYONE HAS EVER ROWED ON LAND? FIND OUT ON P.257**

MEN'S SINGLE SCULLS

↙ Marcel Hacker (Germany) wins the men's single sculls during the Zurich Rowing World Cup event in Munich, Germany, on 3 August 2002.

www.marcelhacker.com GER ZURICH

★ NEW RECORD ⋆ UPDATED RECORD

MEN'S 10,000 M SPEED SKATING

Jochem Uytdehaage (Netherlands) on his way to beating countryman Gianni Romme's world record in 12 min 58.92 sec in the men's 10,000 m speed skating race at the Utah Olympic Oval, USA, on 22 February 2002.

SPEED SKATING – LONG TRACK

MEN	TIME	NAME & NATIONALITY	PLACE	DATE
500 m	34.32	Hiroyasu Shimizu (Japan)	Salt Lake City, USA	10 March 2001
1,000 m	1:07.18	Gerard van Velde (Netherlands)	Salt Lake City, USA	16 February 2002
⋆ 1,500 m	1:43.33	Shani Davis (USA)	Salt Lake City, USA	9 January 2005
⋆ 3,000 m	3:39.02	Chad Hendrick (USA)	Calgary, Canada	10 March 2005
5,000 m	6:14.66	Jochem Uytdehaage (Netherlands)	Salt Lake City, USA	9 February 2002
10,000 m	12:58.92	Jochem Uytdehaage (Netherlands)	Salt Lake City, USA	22 February 2002

WOMEN	TIME	NAME & NATIONALITY	PLACE	DATE
500 m	37.22	Catriona LeMay Doan (Canada)	Calgary, Canada	9 December 2001
1,000 m	1:13.83	Christine Witty (USA)	Salt Lake City, USA	17 February 2002
⋆ 1,500 m	1:53.87	Cindy Klassen (Canada)	Salt Lake City, USA	9 January 2005
3,000 m	3:57.70	Claudia Pechstein (Germany)	Salt Lake City, USA	10 February 2002
5,000 m	6:46.91	Claudia Pechstein (Germany)	Salt Lake City, USA	23 February 2002

SPEED SKATING – SHORT TRACK

MEN	TIME	NAME & NATIONALITY	PLACE	DATE
500 m	41.184	Jean-François Monette (Canada)	Calgary, Canada	18 October 2003
1,000 m	1:24.674	Jiajun Li (China)	Bormio, Italy	14 February 2004
1,500 m	2:10.639	Ahn Hyun-soo (South Korea)	Marquette, USA	24 October 2003
3,000 m	4:32.646	Ahn Hyun-soo (South Korea)	Beijing, China	7 December 2003
⋆ 5,000 m relay	6:39.990	Canada (Charles Hamelin, Steve Robillard, François-Louis Tremblay, Mathieu Turcotte)	Beijing, China	13 March 2005

WOMEN	TIME	NAME & NATIONALITY	PLACE	DATE
500 m	43.671	Evgenia Radanova (Bulgaria)	Calgary, Canada	19 October 2001
1,000 m	1:30.483	Byun Chun-sa (South Korea)	Budapest, Hungary	3 February 2002
1,500 m	2:18.861	Jung Eun-ju (South Korea)	Beijing, China	11 January 2004
3,000 m	5:01.976	Choi Eun-kyung (South Korea)	Calgary, Canada	22 October 2000
⋆ 3,000 m relay	4:11.742	South Korea (Choi Eun-kyung, Kim Min-jee, Byun Chun-sa and Ko Gi-hyun)	Calgary, Canada	19 October 2003

MEN'S 1,000 M SPEED SKATING

Gold medallist and new World and Olympic record holder Gerard Van Velde (Netherlands) in the men's 1,000 m speed skating event during the Winter Olympic Games at the Utah Olympic Oval in Salt Lake City, Utah, USA, on 16 February 2002.

WOMEN'S 5,000 M SPEED SKATING

Claudia Pechstein (Germany) skates to victory and a new world record time of 6:46.91 in the women's 5,000 m speed skating event during the Winter Olympic Games at the Utah Olympic Oval in Salt Lake City, Utah, USA, on 23 February 2002.

SPORTS REFERENCE

LONGEST SPORT MARATHONS

SPORT	TIME	NAME & NATIONALITY	PLACE	DATE
★Basketball	30 hr 12 min	Beatrice Hoops Basketball Organization (USA)	Beatrice, USA	6–7 August 2004
Billiards, individual	181 hr 8 min	Pierre De Coster (Belgium)	Kampenhout, Belgium	3–10 June 2003
Billiards, pair	45 hr 10 min	Arie Hermans and Jeff Fijneman (Netherlands)	Oosterhout, Netherlands	12–14 February 2004
★Bowling, tenpin	60 hr 15 min	Giancarlo Tolu (Italy)	St George's Bay, Malta	17–19 September 2004
Bowls, indoor	36 hours	Arnos Bowling Club (UK)	Southgate, UK	20–21 April 2002
★Bowls, outdoor	80 hr 25 min	South Grafton Bowling, Sport and Recreation Club (Australia)	South Grafton, Australia	1–4 October 2004
Cricket	26 hr 13 min	Cricket Club des Ormes (France)	Dol de Bretagne, France	21–22 June 2003
★Curling	30 hr 7 min	Wheat City Curling Club (Canada)	Brandon, Canada	13–14 March 2004
Darts, individual	72 hours	G Hofstee, AJ Amerongen and E Mol (Netherlands)	Borculo, Netherlands	22–25 April 2004
★Football	25 hr 35 min	Trevor McDonald XI and Elstead Village Idiots (UK)	Reading, UK	25–26 September 2004
Futsal	25 hr 10 min	Ayuntamiento de Almodóvar del Campo (Spain)	Puertollano, Spain	28–29 June 2003
Handball	70 hours	HV Mighty/Stevo (Netherlands)	Tubbergen, Netherlands	30 August–2 September 2001
★Ice hockey	203 hours	Sudbury Angels (Canada)	Azilda, Canada	3–11 April 2004
Hockey, indoor	24 hours	Mandel Bloomfield AZA (Canada)	Edmonton, Canada	28–29 February 2004
Hockey, inline	24 hours	8K Roller Hockey League (USA)	Eastpointe, USA	13–14 September 2002
★Hockey, street	30 hours	Conroy Ross Partners (Canada)	Edmonton, Canada	17–18 September 2004
Korfball	26 hr 2 min	Korfball Club de Vinken (Netherlands)	Vinkeveen, Netherlands	23–24 May 2001
Netball	54 hr 15 min	Castle View School (UK)	Canvey Island, UK	22–24 March 2002
Parasailing	24 hr 10 min	Berne Persson (Sweden)	Lake Graningesjön, Sweden	19–20 July 2002
★Pétanque	27 hr 30 min	Newcastle Pétanque Club (Australia)	Newcastle, Australia	24–25 January 2004
Pool, individual	75 hr 19 min	Raf Goossens (Belgium)	Kampenhout, Belgium	19–22 February 2003
★Pool, team	144 hours	Bell Hotel (UK)	Driffield, UK	2–8 August 2004
★Punchbag	36 hr 3 min	Ron Sarchian (USA)	Encino, USA	15–17 June 2004
Rifle shooting, team	26 hours	St Sebastianus Schützenbruderchaft (Germany)	Ettringen, Germany	20–21 September 2003
Skiing	168 hours	Christian Flühr (Germany)	Tyrol, Austria	8–15 March 2003
★Snowboarding	180 hr 34 min	Bernhard Mair (Austria)	Bad Kleinkirchheim, Austria	9–16 January 2004
★Softball	55 hr 11 min	Ronan's and Burns Blues (Ireland)	Dublin, Ireland	30 April–2 May 2004
Tennis, singles	25 hr 25 min	Christian Barschel and Hauke Daene (Germany)	Molln, Germany	12–13 September 2003
Tennis, doubles	48 hr 6 min	Kadzielewski, Siupka, Zatorsk, Milian (Poland)	Giliwice, Poland	30 August–1 September 2002
★Tennis, doubles, one pair	33 hr 33 min	Christian Barschel and Hauke Daene (Germany)	Molln Tennis Club, Germany	13–15 August 2004
Tennis, individual	52 hours	Butch Heffernan (Australia)	Dudley, UK	23–25 November 2001
Volleyball	24 hr 10 min	Torgau Vocational School (Germany)	Torgau, Germany	30 September–1 October 2002
Water polo	24 hours	Rapido 82 Haarlem (Netherlands)	Haarlem, Netherlands	30 April–1 May 1999
Windsurfing	71 hr 30 min	Sergiy Naidych (Ukraine)	Simerferopol, Ukraine	6–9 June 2003

All of the above records were set using guidelines established after 1998

MARATHON CRICKET ↘

The longest cricket marathon is 26 hr 13 min, set by Cricket Club des Ormes (France) at Dol de Bretagne, France, on 21–22 June 2003.

←WOMEN'S
300 M SHOOTING – INDIVIDUAL

Charlotte Jakobsen (Denmark), holder of the world record in the women's 300 m rifle prone competition, competes at the World Shooting Championships in Lahti, Finland, in 2002. Jakobsen set her world record (594) in the competition and took the gold medal.

SHOOTING (ISSF)

MEN	SCORE	NAME & NATIONALITY	PLACE	DATE
10 m running target mixed	391	Manfred Kurzer (Germany)	Pontevedra, Spain	14 March 2001
300 m rifle three positions	1,178	Thomas Jerabek (Czech Republic)	Lahti, Finland	13 July 2002
300 m rifle prone	600	Harald Stenvaag (Norway)	Moscow, USSR	15 August 1990
	600	Bernd Ruecker (Germany)	Tolmezzo, Italy	31 July 1994
300 m standard rifle 3x20	589	Trond Kjoell (Norway)	Boden, Sweden	7 July 1995
	589	Marcel Buerge (Switzerland)	Lahti, Finland	16 July 2002
50 m running target	596	Nicolai Lapin (USSR)	Lahti, Finland	25 July 1987
50 m running target mixed	398	Lubos Racansky (Czech Republic)	Milan, Italy	4 August 1994
10 m air pistol	593	Sergei Pyzhianov (USSR)	Munich, West Germany	13 October 1989
10 m air rifle	600	Tevarit Majchacheeap (Thailand)	Langkawi, Thailand	27 January 2000
25 m centre fire pistol	590	Afanasijs Kuzmins (USSR)	Zagreb, Yugoslavia	15 July 1989
	590	Sergei Pyzhianov (USSR)	Moscow, USSR	5 August 1990
	590	Mikhail Nestruev (Russia)	Kouvola, Finland	1 July 1997
	590	Park Byung-taek (South Korea)	Lahti, Finland	14 July 2002
Double trap	147	Michael Diamond (Australia)	Barcelona, Spain	19 July 1998
50 m pistol	581	Alexsander Melentiev (USSR)	Moscow, USSR	20 July 1980
50 m rifle three positions	1,186	Rajmond Debevec (Slovenia)	Munich, West Germany	29 August 1992
50 m rifle prone	600	Numerous competitors have achieved this score		
25 m standard pistol	584	Erich Buljung (USA)	Caracas, Venezuela	20 August 1983
Trap	125	Giovanni Pellielo (Italy)	Nicosia, Sicily, Italy	1 April 1994
	125	Ray Ycong (USA)	Lahti, Finland	9 June 1995
	125	Marcello Tittarelli (Italy)	Suhl, Germany	11 June 1996
	125	Lance Bade (USA)	Barcelona, Spain	23 July 1998
★25 m rapid fire pistol	583	Dongming Yang (China)	Changwon, South Korea	14 April 2005
	583	Emil Milev (Bulgaria)	Ft Benning, USA	14 May 2005
★Skeet	124	Vincent Hancock (USA)	Changwon, South Korea	16 April 2005

WOMEN	SCORE	NAME & NATIONALITY	PLACE	DATE
10 m running target	391	Wu Xuan (China)	Lahti, Finland	6 July 2002
10 m running target mixed	390	Audrey Soquet (France)	Lahti, Finland	9 July 2002
300 m rifle three positions	588	Charlotte Jakobsen (Denmark)	Lahti, Finland	12 July 2002
300 m rifle prone	597	Marie Enquist (Sweden)	Plzen, Czech Republic	22 July 2003
10 m air pistol	393	Svetlana Smirnova (Russia)	Munich, Germany	23 May 1998
10 m air rifle	400	numerous competitors have achieved this score		
25 m pistol	594	Diana Iorgova (Bulgaria)	Milan, Italy	31 May 1994
	594	Tao Luna (China)	Munich, Germany	23 August 2002
50 m rifle three positions	592	Vesela Letcheva (Bulgaria)	Munich, Germany	15 June 1995
	592	Shan Hong (China)	Milan, Italy	28 May 1999
50 m rifle prone	597	Marina Bobkova (Russia)	Barcelona, Spain	19 July 1998
	597	Olga Dovgun (Kazakhstan)	Lahti, Finland	4 July 2002
	597	Olga Dovgun (Kazakhstan)	Busan, Phillipines	4 October 2002
Trap	74	Victoria Chuyko (Ukraine)	Nicosia, Sicily	23 July 1998
★Skeet	71	Christine Brinker (Germany)	Changwon, Korea	15 April 2005
	71	Haley Dunn (USA)	Changwon, Korea	15 April 2005
	71	Cristina Vitali (Italy)	Changwon, Korea	15 April 2005
	71	Ning Wei (China)	Changwon, Korea	15 April 2005

★ NEW RECORD   ☆ UPDATED RECORD

SPORTS REFERENCE

MEN'S 50 M BUTTERFLY

Ian Crocker (USA) takes the lead in the qualifying heat for the men's 50 m butterfly during the FINA World Swimming Championships on 9 October 2004 in Indianapolis, USA. He went on to win the event the following day.

WOMEN'S 4 x 100 M FREESTYLE

Australian team members Petria Thomas (left), Lisbeth Lenton (centre) and Alice Mills (right) cheer their teammate Jodie Henry on their way to winning gold in the women's 4 x 100 m longcourse freestyle relay final on 14 August 2004 during the Summer Olympic Games in Athens, Greece.

SWIMMING – SHORTCOURSE

MEN	TIME	NAME & NATIONALITY	PLACE	DATE
★50 m freestyle	21.10	Fred Bousquet (France)	New York City, USA	25 March 2004
★100 m freestyle	46.25	Ian Crocker (USA)	New York City, USA	27 March 2004
200 m freestyle	1:41.10	Ian Thorpe (Australia)	Berlin, Germany	6 February 2000
400 m freestyle	3:34.58	Grant Hackett (Australia)	Sydney, Australia	18 July 2002
800 m freestyle	7:25.28	Grant Hackett (Australia)	Perth, Australia	3 August 2001
1,500 m freestyle	14:10.10	Grant Hackett (Australia)	Perth, Australia	7 August 2001
4 x 50 m freestyle	1:25.55	Netherlands (Mark Veens, Johan Kenkhuis, Gijs Damen, Pieter van den Hoogenband)	Dublin, Ireland	14 December 2003
4 x 100 m freestyle	3:09.57	Sweden (Johan Nyström, Lars Frolander, Mattias Ohlin, Stefan Nystrand)	Athens, Greece	16 March 2000
4 x 200 m freestyle	6:56.41	Australia (William Kirby, Ian Thorpe, Michael Klim, Grant Hackett)	Perth, Australia	7 August 2001
★50 m butterfly	22.71	Ian Crocker (USA)	Indianapolis, USA	10 October 2004
★100 m butterfly	49.07	Ian Crocker (USA)	New York City, USA	26 March 2004
200 m butterfly	1:50.73	Frank Esposito (France)	Antibes, France	8 December 2002
50 m backstroke	23.31	Matthew Welsh (Australia)	Melbourne, Australia	2 September 2002
★100 m backstroke	50.32	Peter Marshall (USA)	New York City, USA	26 March 2004
★200 m backstroke	1:50.52	Aaron Peirsol (USA)	Indianapolis, USA	11 October 2004
50 m breaststroke	26.20	Oleg Lissogor (Ukraine)	Berlin, Germany	26 January 2002
100 m breaststroke	57.47	Ed Moses (USA)	Stockholm, Sweden	23 January 2002
200 m breaststroke	2:02.92	Ed Moses (USA)	Berlin, Germany	17 January 2004
★100 m medley	52.51	Roland Schoeman (South Africa)	Stockholm, Sweden	18 January 2005
★200 m medley	1:53.93	George Bovell (Trinidad)	New York City, USA	25 March 2004
400 m medley	4:02.72	Brian Johns (Canada)	Victoria, Canada	21 February 2003
4 x 50 m medley	1:34.46	Germany (Thomas Rupprath, Mark Warnecke, Fabian Freidrich, Carstein Dehmlow)	Dublin, Ireland	11 December 2003
★4 x 100 m medley	3:25.09	USA (Aaron Peirsol, Brendan Hansen, Ian Crocker, Jason Lezak)	Indianapolis, USA	11 October 2004

WOMEN	TIME	NAME & NATIONALITY	PLACE	DATE
50 m freestyle	23.59	Therese Alshammar (Sweden)	Athens, Greece	18 March 2000
100 m freestyle	52.17	Therese Alshammar (Sweden)	Athens, Greece	17 March 2000
200 m freestyle	1:54.04	Lindsay Benko (USA)	Moscow, Russia	7 April 2002
400 m freestyle	3:59.53	Lindsay Benko (USA)	Berlin, Germany	26 January 2003
800 m freestyle	8:13.35	Sachiko Yamada (Japan)	Nishinomya-shi, Japan	24 January 2004
★1,500 m freestyle	15:42.39	Laure Manaudou (France)	La Roche sur Yon, France	9 November 2004
4 x 50 m freestyle	1:37.27	USA (Kara Lynn Joyce, Neka Mabry, Paige Kearns, Andrea Georoff)	Texas, USA	18 March 2004
4 x 100 m freestyle	3:34.55	China (Le Jingyi, Na Chao, Shan Ying, Nian Yin)	Gothenburg, Sweden	19 April 1997
4 x 200 m freestyle	7:46.30	China (Xu Yanvei, Zhu Yingven, Tang Jingzhi, Yang Yu)	Moscow, Russia	3 April 2002
50 m butterfly	25.36	Anne-Karin Kammerling (Sweden)	Stockholm, Sweden	25 January 2001
100 m butterfly	56.34	Natalie Coughlin (USA)	New York, USA	22 November 2002
200 m butterfly	2:04.04	Yu Yang (China)	Berlin, Germany	18 January 2004
50 m backstroke	26.83	Hui Li (China)	Shanghai, China	2 December 2001
100 m backstroke	56.71	Natalie Coughlin (USA)	New York City, USA	23 November 2002
200 m backstroke	2:03.62	Natalie Coughlin (USA)	New York City, USA	27 November 2001
50 m breaststroke	29.96	Emma Igelstrom (Sweden)	Moscow, Russia	4 April 2002
★100 m breaststroke	1:04.79	Tara Kirk (USA)	Texas, USA	19 March 2004
200 m breaststroke	2:17.75	Leisel Jones (Australia)	Melbourne, Australia	29 November 2003
100 m medley	58.80	Natalie Coughlin (USA)	New York City, USA	23 November 2003
200 m medley	2:07.79	Allison Wagner (USA)	Palma de Mallorca, Spain	5 December 1993
400 m medley	4:27.83	Yana Klochkova (Ukraine)	Paris, France	19 January 2002
4 x 50 m medley	1:48.31	Sweden (Therese Alshammar, Emma Igelström, Anna-Karin Kammerling, Johanna Sjöberg)	Valencia, Spain	16 December 2000
★4 x 100 m medley	3:54.95	Australia (Sophie Edington, Brooke Hanson, Jessica Schipper, Lisbeth Lenton)	Indianapolis, USA	9 October 2004

SWIMMING – LONGCOURSE (50-M POOL)

MEN	TIME	NAME & NATIONALITY	PLACE	DATE
50 m freestyle	21.64	Alexander Popov (Russia)	Moscow, Russia	16 June 2000
100 m freestyle	47.84	Pieter van den Hoogenband (Netherlands)	Sydney, Australia	19 September 2000
200 m freestyle	1:44.06	Ian Thorpe (Australia)	Fukuoka, Japan	25 July 2001
400 m freestyle	3:40.08	Ian Thorpe (Australia)	Manchester, UK	30 July 2002
800 m freestyle	7:39.16	Ian Thorpe (Australia)	Fukuoka, Japan	24 July 2001
1,500 m freestyle	14:34.56	Grant Hackett (Australia)	Fukuoka, Japan	29 July 2001
☆ 4 x 100 m freestyle relay	3:13.17	South Africa (Roland Schoeman, Lydon Ferns, Darian Townsend, Ryk Neethling)	Athens, Greece	15 August 2004
4 x 200 m freestyle relay	7:04.66	Australia (Grant Hackett, Michael Klim, William Kirby, Ian Thorpe)	Fukuoka, Japan	27 July 2001
☆ 50 m butterfly	23.30	Ian Crocker (USA)	Austin, USA	29 February 2004
☆ 100 m butterfly	50.76	Ian Crocker (USA)	Long Beach, USA	13 July 2004
☆ 200 m butterfly	1:53.93	Michael Phelps (USA)	Barcelona, Spain	22 July 2003
☆ 50 m backstroke	24.80	Thomas Rupprath (Germany)	Barcelona, Spain	27 July 2003
☆ 100 m backstroke	53.45	Aaron Peirsol (USA)	Athens, Greece	21 August 2004
☆ 200 m backstroke	1:54.74	Aaron Peirsol (USA)	Long Beach, USA	12 July 2004
50 m breaststroke	27.18	Oleg Lisogor (Ukraine)	Berlin, Germany	2 August 2002
☆ 100 m breaststroke	59.30	Brendan Hansen (USA)	Long Beach, USA	8 July 2004
☆ 200 m breaststroke	2:09.04	Brendan Hansen (USA)	Long Beach, USA	11 July 2004
200 m medley	1:55.94	Michael Phelps (USA)	Maryland, USA	9 August 2003
☆ 400 m medley	4:08.26	Michael Phelps (USA)	Athens, Greece	14 August 2004
☆ 4 x 100 m medley relay	3:30.68	USA (Aaron Peirsol, Brendon Hanson, Ian Crocker, Jason Lezak)	Athens, Greece	21 August 2004

WOMEN	TIME	NAME & NATIONALITY	PLACE	DATE
50 m freestyle	24.13	Inge de Bruijn (Netherlands)	Sydney, Australia	22 September 2000
☆ 100 m freestyle	53.52	Jodie Henry (Australia)	Athens, Greece	18 August 2004
200 m freestyle	1:56.64	Franziska van Almsick (Germany)	Berlin, Germany	3 August 2002
400 m freestyle	4:03.85	Janet Evans (USA)	Seoul, South Korea	22 September 1988
800 m freestyle	8:16.22	Janet Evans (USA)	Tokyo, Japan	20 August 1989
1,500 m freestyle	15:52.10	Janet Evans (USA)	Orlando, USA	26 March 1988
☆ 4 x 100 m freestyle relay	3:35.94	Australia (Alice Mills, Lisbeth Lenton, Petria Thomas, Jodie Henry)	Athens, Greece	14 August 2004
☆ 4 x 200 m freestyle relay	7:53.42	USA (Natalie Coughlin, Carly Piper, Dana Vollmer, Kaitlin Sandeno)	Athens, Greece	18 August 2004
50 m butterfly	25.57	Anna-Karin Kammerling (Sweden)	Berlin, Germany	31 July 2000
100 m butterfly	56.61	Inge de Bruijn (Netherlands)	Sydney, Australia	17 September 2000
200 m butterfly	2:05.78	Otylia Jedrejczak (Poland)	Berlin, Germany	2 August 2002
50 m backstroke	28.25	Sandra Voelker (Germany)	Berlin, Germany	17 June 2000
100 m backstroke	59.58	Natalie Coughlin (USA)	Fort Lauderdale, USA	13 August 2002
200 m backstroke	2:06.62	Krisztina Egerszegi (Hungary)	Athens, Greece	25 August 1991
50 m breaststroke	30.57	Zoe Baker (UK)	Manchester, UK	30 July 2002
100 m breaststroke	1:06.37	Jones Liesel (Australia)	Barcelona, Spain	21 July 2003
☆ 200 m breaststroke	2:22.44	Amanda Beard (USA)	Long Beach, USA	12 July 2004
200 m medley	2:09.72	Wu Yanyan (China)	Shanghai, China	17 October 1997
400 m medley	4:33.59	Yana Klochkova (Ukraine)	Sydney, Australia	16 September 2000
☆ 4 x 100 m medley relay	3:57.32	Australia (Giaan Rooney, Leisel Jones, Petria Thomas, Jodie Henry)	Athens, Greece	21 August 2004

↑

MEN'S 200 M BACKSTROKE

Aaron Peirsol (USA) swims to victory in the men's 200 m at the 2004 US Olympic Team Trials in Long Beach, California, USA, on 12 July 2004.

WOMEN'S
4 x 200 M FREESTYLE →

Carly Piper (left), Natalie Coughlin (centre) and Dana Vollmer (right) of the US women's 4 x 200 m longcourse freestyle relay team celebrate their victory after winning the gold medal at the Olympic Games in Athens, Greece, on 18 August 2004. Kaitlin Sandeno, the fourth member of the team, is out of shot.

WATER SKIING

MEN	RECORD	NAME & NATIONALITY	PLACE	DATE
Slalom	1 buoy/9.75-m line	Jeff Rogers (USA)	Charleston, USA	31 August 1997
		Andy Mapple (GB)	Miami, USA	4 October 1998
		Jamie Beauchesne (USA)	Charleston, USA	6 July 2003
Tricks	12,320 points	Nicolas Le Forestier (France)	Chaugey, France	13 July 2003
Ski fly	91.1 m (298 ft 10 in)	Jaret Llewellyn (Canada)	Orlando, USA	4 May 2000
Jump	71.9 m (235 ft 9 in)	Jimmy Siemers (USA)	Lago Santa Fe, USA	10 August 2003
Overall	2,818.01 points	Jaret Llewelyn (Canada)	Seffner, USA	29 September 2002

WOMEN	RECORD	NAME & NATIONALITY	PLACE	DATE
Slalom	1 buoy/10.25-m line	Kristi Overton Johnson (USA)	West Palm Beach, USA	14 September 1996
Tricks	8,630 points	Tawn Larsen Hahn (USA)	Wilmington, USA	11 July 1999
Ski fly	69.4 m (227 ft 7 in)	Elena Milakova (Russia)	Pine Mountain, USA	26 May 2002
Jump	56.6 m (186 ft)	Elena Milakova (Russia)	Rio Linda, USA	27 July 2002
★ Overall	2,903.43 points	Clementine Lucine (France)	Mauzac, France	8 August 2004

★ MOTO X

Brian Deegan (USA) has won an unsurpassed nine medals in moto X. He is pictured below riding in the first round of the Moto X Freestyle event in the ESPN X Games VIII on 15 August 2002 at First Union Center in Philadelphia, Pennsylvania, USA.

↓

WATER SKIING – BAREFOOT

MEN	RECORD	NAME & NATIONALITY	PLACE	DATE
Jump	27.4 m (89.8 ft)	David Small (GB)	New South Wales, Australia	8 February 2004
Slalom	20.5 crossings of wake in 15 sec	Brian Fuchs (USA)	New South Wales, Australia	April 1994
Tricks	9,550 points	David Small (GB)	New South Wales, Australia	5 February 2004

WOMEN	RECORD	NAME & NATIONALITY	PLACE	DATE
Jump	20.6 m (67.58 ft)	Nadine de Villiers (South Africa)	Roodeplaat Dam, South Africa	4 March 2000
Slalom	17.0 crossings of wake in 15 sec	Nadine de Villiers (South Africa)	Wolwekrans, South Africa	5 January 2001
Tricks	4,400 points	Nadine de Villiers (South Africa)	Wolwekrans, South Africa	5 January 2001

X GAMES – WINTER

MEN	MEDALS	HOLDER & NATIONALITY
★ Overall	10	Barrett Christy (USA)
★ Skiing (overall)	8	Jon Olsson (Sweden)
★ Snowboard (overall)	10	Barrett Christy (USA)
★ Snocross	7	Blair Morgan (Canada)
★ Ultracross	3	Peter Lind (Sweden) and Xavier de le Rue (France)
★ Moto X	2	Tommy Clowers, Mike Jones, Mike Metzger, Caleb Wyatt (all USA)

★ AGGRESSIVE INLINE SKATING

Fabiola da Silva (Brazil) – holder of the most inline skating medals record – performs at the launch of the X Games Xperience at Disney's California Adventure at Disneyland on 1 July 2003 in Anaheim, California, USA.

↓

X GAMES – SUMMER

DISCIPLINE	MEDALS	HOLDER & NATIONALITY
★ Overall	18	Dave Mirra (USA)
★ Bike stunt	18	Dave Mirra (USA)
★ Moto X	9	Brian Deegan (USA)
★ Skateboard	16	Tony Hawk (USA)
★ Aggressive inline skate	8	Fabiola da Silva (Brazil)
★ Wakeboard	6	Darin Shapiro (USA)

WEIGHTLIFTING WORLD RECORDS

MEN	CATEGORY	WEIGHT LIFTED	NAME & NATIONALITY	PLACE	DATE
56 kg	Clean & jerk	168 kg	Halil Mutlu (Turkey)	Trencín, Slovakia	24 April 2001
	Snatch	138.5 kg	Halil Mutlu (Turkey)	Antalya, Turkey	4 November 2001
	Total	305.0 kg	Halil Mutlu (Turkey)	Sydney, Australia	16 September 2000
62 kg	Clean & jerk	182.5 kg	Maosheng Le (China)	Busan, Korea	2 October 2002
	Snatch	153 kg	Zhiyong Shi (China)	Izmir, Turkey	28 June 2002
	Total	325 kg	World Standard*		
69 kg	Clean & jerk	197.5 kg	Guozheng Zhang (China)	Qinhuangdao, China	11 September 2003
	Snatch	165 kg	Georgi Markov (Bulgaria)	Sydney, Australia	20 September 2000
	Total	357.5 kg	Galabin Boevski (Bulgaria)	Athens, Greece	24 November 1999
77 kg	Clean & jerk	210 kg	Oleg Perepetchenov (Russia)	Trencín, Slovakia	27 April 2001
☆	Snatch	173.5 kg	Sergey Filimonov (Kazakhstan)	Almaty, Kazakhstan	9 April 2004
	Total	377.5 kg	Plamen Zhelyazkov (Bulgaria)	Doha, Qatar	27 March 2002
85 kg	Clean & jerk	218 kg	Zhang Yong (China)	Tel Aviv, Israel	25 April 1998
	Snatch	182.5 kg	Andrei Ribakov (Bulgaria)	Havirov, Czech Republic	2 June 2002
	Total	395 kg	World Standard*		
94 kg	Clean & jerk	232.5 kg	Szymon Kolecki (Poland)	Sofia, Bulgaria	29 April 2000
	Snatch	188 kg	Akakios Kakiashvilis (Greece)	Athens, Greece	27 November 1999
	Total	417 kg	World Standard*		
105 kg	Clean & jerk	242 kg	World Standard*		
	Snatch	198.5 kg	Marcin Dolega (Poland)	Havirov, Czech Republic	4 June 2002
	Total	440 kg	World Standard*		
☆ +105 kg	Clean & jerk	263.5 kg	Hossein Rezazadeh (Iran)	Athens, Greece	25 August 2004
	Snatch	213.0 kg	Hossein Rezazadeh (Iran)	Qinhuangdao, China	14 September 2003
	Total	472.5 kg	Hossein Rezazadeh (Iran)	Sydney, Australia	26 September 2000

WOMEN	CATEGORY	WEIGHT LIFTED	NAME & NATIONALITY	PLACE	DATE
48 kg	Clean & jerk	116.5 kg	Zhuo Li (China)	Qinhuangdao, China	10 September 2003
☆	Snatch	97.5 kg	Nurcan Taylan (Turkey)	Athens, Greece	14 August 2004
☆	Total	210 kg	Nurcan Taylan (Turkey)	Athens, Greece	14 August 2004
53 kg	Clean & jerk	127.5 kg	Xueju Li (China)	Busan, South Korea	20 November 2002
	Snatch	102.5 kg	Ri Song Hui (North Korea)	Warsaw, Poland	1 October 2002
	Total	225 kg	Yang Xia (China)	Sydney, Australia	18 September 2000
58 kg	Clean & jerk	133 kg	Caiyan Sun (China)	Izmir, Turkey	28 June 2002
	Snatch	110 kg	Li Wang (China)	Bali, Indonesia	10 August 2003
	Total	240 kg	Li Wang (China)	Bali, Indonesia	10 August 2003
63 kg	Clean & jerk	138 kg	Natalia Skakun (Ukraine)	Vancouver, Canada	18 November 2003
☆	Snatch	115 kg	Anna Batsiushka (Belarus)	Athens, Greece	18 August 2004
	Total	247.5 kg	Xia Liu (China)	Qinhuangdao, China	12 September 2003
☆ 69 kg	Clean & jerk	153 kg	Chunhong Liu (China)	Athens, Greece	19 August 2004
☆	Snatch	122.5 kg	Chunhong Liu (China)	Athens, Greece	19 August 2004
☆	Total	275 kg	Chunhong Liu (China)	Athens, Greece	19 August 2004
75 kg	Clean & jerk	152.5 kg	Ruiping Sun (China)	Busan, South Korea	7 October 2002
☆	Snatch	125 kg	Natalia Zaboloynaia (Russia)	Athens, Greece	20 August 2004
☆	Total	272.5 kg	Natalia Zaboloynaia (Russia)	Athens, Greece	20 August 2004
+75 kg	Clean & jerk	182.5 kg	Gonghong Tang (China)	Athens, Greece	21 August 2004
	Snatch	137.5 kg	Meiyuan Ding (China)	Vancouver, Canada	21 November 2003
☆	Total	305 kg	Gonghong Tang (China)	Athens, Greece	21 August 2004

WEIGHTLIFTING MEN'S +105 KG CLEAN AND JERK

Hossein Rezazadeh (Iran) celebrates his gold medal in the men's super heavyweight +105 kg Olympic weight lifting competition in Athens, Greece, on 25 August 2004. Rezazadeh won the gold medal with a world-record-breaking display in the clean and jerk of 263.5 kg, beating his own previous record of 263 kg.

* From 1 January 1998, the International Weightlifting Federation (IWF) introduced modified bodyweight categories, thereby making the then world records redundant. This is the new listing with the world standards for the new bodyweight categories. Results achieved at IWF-approved competitions exceeding the world standards by 0.5 kg for snatch or clean and jerk, or by 2.5 kg for the total, will be recognized as world records.

WEIGHTLIFTING – MEN'S 56 KG →

Halil Mutlu (Turkey) in action while winning the gold medal in the 56 kg snatch event at the Sydney Convention and Exhibition Centre during the 2000 Olympic Games in Sydney, Australia. He currently holds all records in the category.

This year's index is organized into two parts: by subject and by superlative. **Bold** entries in the subject index indicate a main entry on a topic, and entries in CAPS indicate an entire chapter. Neither index lists personal names.

SUBJECT

ACKNOWLEDGMENTS

The 2006 book team would like to thank the following people for their help during the production of this year's edition:

Laura Baker; Laura Barrett; Jim Booth; Nicky Boxall; James Bradley; Nadine Causey; Ann Collins; Sam Fay; Marco Frigatti; Lisa Gibbs; Simon Gold; Nick Hanbridge; James Herbert; Mary Hill; Sam Knights; Peter Laker; Joyce Lee; Anthony Liu; Simon McKeown; Laura McTurk; Rob Molloy; Yeung Poon; Christopher Reinke; Alistair Richards; David Roberts; Paul Rouse; Nicola Savage; Malcolm Smith; Nicola Shanks; Amanda Sprague; Ryan Tunstall; Nicholas Watson; Kate White.

The team also wishes to give special thanks to the following individuals and organizations:

Faisa Abdi; Ernest Adams; Dr Leslie Aiello; Stan Allen; Roy Allon; Dr Martyn Amos; Jorgen Vaaben Andersen; David Anderson; Anritsu; Aqua Hotel South Beach Miami; Lance Armstrong; Vic Armstrong; Augie; Aussie Man & Van; Ron Baalke; John Bain; Bank of England; Dr Peter Barham; BBC; BBC Wildlife Magazine; Capt. Alan Bean; Guenter Bechly; Thomas Blackthorne; Chris Bishop; Richard Boatfield; Jim Booth; Dr Richard Bourgerie; Professor John Brown Bernie Barker; BP; Laura Bradley; Sir Richard Branson; British Academy of Film & Television Arts; British Antarctic Survey; British Board of Film Classification; British Museum; British National Space Centre; Tim Brostom; BT; Cambridge University; Caida; Caltech; Dr Robert Carney; Cassella CEL, Inc; Alan Cassidy; Dr Kenneth Catania; Michael Motsa, British High Commission, Swaziland; CERN; Dr Hubert Chanson; Professor Phil Charles; Charlotte Street Hotel; Franklin Chang-Diaz; Edd China; Christie's; CIA World Fact Book; Cinderella May A Holly Grey; Isabelle Clark; Admiral Roy Clare; Richard Clark; CMR/TNS Media Intelligence; Competitive Media Reporting/TNS Media; Kathleen Conroy; David Copperfield; Dr Mike Coughlan; Warren Cowan; Dr Paul Craddock; Neil Cresswell; Professor Mike

Cruise; Jack Cruwys-Finnigan; Dr Pam Dalton; Davy's at Regent's Place; Elaine Davidson; Professor Kris Davidson; Dr Ashley Davies; Jim DeMerritt; Dr David Dilcher; Discovery News; Martin Dodge; Tracy Eberts; *The Economist*; Lourdes Edlin; Dr Joan Edwards; EETimes; Brad Ekman; Dr Farouk El-Baz; Elysium; Dr John Emsley; Louis Epstein; Dr Cynan Ellis-Evans; Exeter University; Xiaohui Fan; Adam Fenton; Keo Films; Sarah Finney; Forbes; Brian Ford; Steve Fossett; Arran Frood; Tim Furniss; Drew Gardner; Michael Galbe; Martin Gedny; Geographical Magazine; Geological Society of London; Dr Richard Ghail; Mauricio Giuliani; Stephanie Gordon; Donald Gorske; Dr Robert Angus Buchanan; Professor John Guest; Dr Jim Gunson; Mary Hanson; Andy Harris; Colin Hart; Fiona Hartley; Russell Harrington; Harvard-Smithsonian Center for Astrophysics; David Hasselhoff; Tony Hawk; Jeff Hecht; Stuart Hendry; Mark Higgins; Dr Paul Hillyard; Ron Hildebrant; His Majesty King Mswati III of Swaziland; Shannon Holt; Dr David Horne; Graham Hudson; Paul Hughes; Amanda Hunter; David Huxley; Intel; Intelligence; International Energy Agency; International Jugglers' Association; Imperial College London; Institute of Nanotechnology; Steve Irwin; Professor Steve Jones; Iggy Jovanovic; JoAnn Kaeding; Emily Kao; Judy Katz; David Keys; Dr Nichol Keith; Taig Khris; Paul Kieve; Professor Joseph Kirschvink; Jamie & Ryan Knowles; Sir John Kreb; Panama J. Kubecka; Lancaster University; Dr Rolf Landua; Dr Roger Launius; Alain Leger; John Lee; Tony Lloyd; Kate Long; Los Alamos National Laboratories; Robert Loss; Mr & Mrs Michel Lotito (Mr Mangetout); Louisiana State University; Dr Karl Lyons; Ranald Mackechnie; Klaus Madengruber; R Aidan Martin, Director - ReefQuest Centre for Shark Research; Ludivine Maitre; Simone Mangaroo; Professor Giles Marion; Lockheed Martin; Brian Marsden; Jenny Marshall; Dr Jim Marshall; Dave McAleer; McDonald's Family Restaurant, Mont Fort, Dallas, Texas; Matthew McGrory; Paul McKain; Dr Alan McNaught; The Met Office; Erin Mick; Microsoft;

Lauren Miller; Lucy Millington; Andy Milroy; Robert Milton; Edgar Mitchell; Dr Sir Patrick Moore; Professor Jon Morse; Derek Musso; Munich Re; Martin Munt; Michael Murphy; National Academy of Sciences; National Federation of Window Cleaners; National Geographic; Natural History Museum; National Physical Laboratory; National Maritime Museum; National Science Foundation; NASA; the Nelson; NetNames; Ted Nield; NOAA; Barry Norman; NT gaming clan; Nua.com; Oracle; Oxford University; Alan Paige; Ed Parsons; Stephen & Morag Paskins; Conoco Phillips; PPARC; Qantas; Qinetiq; Professor Sir Martin Rees; Regional Planetary Image Facility, University College London; Brian Reinert; Greg Rice; John Rice; Ian Ridpath; Dr Mervyn Rose; Cory Ross; Sally Roth; Royal Astronomical Society; Royal Geographical Society with the Institute of British Geographers; Royal Horticultural Society's *Dictionary of Gardening*; The Royal Institution; Royal Philips Electronics; Royal Society of Chemistry; Rutherford Appleton Laboratory; Ryan Sampson; Amy Saunders; Franz Schreiber; Score on Lincoln, Ali Scrivens; The Science Museum, London; Search Engine Watch; Istvan Sebestyen; Dr Paul Selden; Prof Dick Selley; Jordi Serra; SETI Institute; Kit Shah; Kiran Shah; Chris Sheedy; Dr Seth Shostak; Schumacher West Palm Beach; Dr Martin Siegert; Siemens; Sotheby's; Speed Stacks Inc; Lara Speicher; Stapleford Airport; Dirk Steiner; Natalie Stormer; Danny Sullivan; SuperHire; Sword Swallowers Association International; Greg Swift; Carolyn Syangbo; Sydney Kingsford Smith Airport; Charlie Taylor; Telegeography; Gary Thuerk; Heather Tinsley; T J Graphics; Garry Turner; Twin Galaxies; UK Planetary Forum; Professor Martin Uman; United Nations; University of Bath; University of Birmingham; University of Boston; University of Colorado; University of Dundee; University of Florida; University of Greenwich; University of Hertfordshire; University of Oklahoma; University of Southampton; Professor Martin Uman; Emily Voigt; Juhani Virola; Ryan Wallace; Dr David Wark;

Professor Kevin Warwick; Bryony Watts; Danny Way; Isabel Way; Andy Weintraub; James Withers; Richard Winter; Dr Richard Wiseman; Greg Wood; World Bank; World Flying Disc Federation; World Footbag Association; World Meteorological Organisation; Professor Joshua Wurman; Dr David Wynn-Williams; www.nationmaster.com; Robert Young.

END PAPERS

Front: Most scheduled flight journeys within 30 days; Longest motorcycle ride (distance); heaviest carrot; furthest mallee root tossing - male; largest snow cone; most participants in a golf lesson; largest marching band; longest bean; heaviest deadlift with the little finger; largest recorder ensemble; longest beard - living male; smallest telephone; most roller coasters ridden in 24 hours; greatest amount of corn harvested by a single combine harvester in eight hours; largest private collection of Ford vehicles; most car lifts in an hour; largest fountain pen; longest golf carry at altitude lower than 1000 m; longest backwards unicycle ride; largest sandwich; longest car; side-wheelying, (car, distance); most push-ups in an hour; largest wasp nest; largest shamisen ensemble; youngest person to score a century, snooker; largest artificial Christmas tree; lowest vocal note by a male; largest tortoise.

Back: Fastest Seven Summit ascent; largest collection of royal memorabilia; Mah Jongg marathon; longest painting; greatest distance skipping on a rolling globe; most successful international show dog; tinned pea eating - most in 3 minutes; largest bonfire; largest box of popcorn; fastest 10km run wearing a pantomime costume (2 person); longest solo motorcycle ride by a woman; largest incense stick; largest saxophone ensemble; largest carpet of flowers; largest puppet; largest cowbell; longest throw - no tail; largest golf cart parade; largest stir-fry; most people crammed into a Citroen 2CV; largest piggy bank; youngest sports commentator; largest sandal; most expensive draught horse; largest simultaneous tea party; largest bag of chips (fries); largest seafood display; largest bonfire.

PICTURE CREDITS

4-5: Getty Images(5) GWR (2)
4: ASIMO Honda; © 2001-2005 Lionhead Studios Limited All Rights Reserved; Ardea; Courtesy of Apple
5: Getty Images; © Ranald Mackechnie/GWR
6: Andy Catterall/HIT Entertainment Ltd; © Ranald Mackechnie/ GWR; Rex Features
7: Jonny Greene/ Taylor Herring; Taylor Herring/GWR
8: c/o Fox Broadcasting(5); c/o Mike Howard; c/o Seven Network Australia (2)
9: © ITV (3); © Drew Gardner/GWR; c/o *L'Été de Tous Les Records* (2); Rob Molloy
10: Taylor Herring/GWR (2); c/o Deira City Centre shopping mall; Julian Camilleri
11: Andy Roberts; c/o Rocketbuster Boots; Laura Barrett
12: National Geographic Kids; Nickelodeon Australia (3)
13: c/o Dante Lamb; Corbis; c/o Adám Lörincz
14-15: © Drew Gardner/GWR
16-17 : GWR (5)
16: Empics; c/o Coffey family
17: Getty Images; Gamma
18: Paul Hughes/GWR; c/o John Prestwich; c/o Alexander Stone (2)
19: c/o Kolyo Tanev Kolov (2); c/o Brett House
20: © Drew Gardner/GWR (3)
21: c/o Flossie Bennett; Ana Venegas; c/o Beverly Allen
22: © Drew Gardner/GWR; c/o Flaherty family (2)
23: c/o Laura Shelley; c/o Caroline Cargado; Jay L. Clendenin/Polaris
24-25: © Ranald Makechnie/GWR; Alamy; © Drew Gardner/GWR; c/o Radhakant Bajpai; Alamy; Corbis; Alamy; c/o Tribhuwan and Triloki Yadav ; c/o Daniel Valdes
26-27: © Ranald Mackechnie/GWR
28-29: GWR (6)
28: c/o Rick Hansen; Corbis
29: c/o David Dyson; c/o David Abrutat
30: c/o Rainer Zietlow & Ronald Bormann; Corbis
31: c/o Matty McNair; c/o Tina Sjögren
32: Corbis; Getty Images
33: Getty Images (2)
34: © Ranald Mackechnie/GWR
35: Getty Images; © David Anderson/GWR
36: c/o Ricki Lake Show; c/o Heart Health Hop
37: © Drew Gardner/GWR
38: Getty Images; © Paul Hughes/GWR; c/o Sentosa Leisure Management
39: c/o Brian Spotts; c/o Maverick Marketing & Communications
40: Empics/PA; © Paul Hughes/GWR; Reuters
41: c/o East Lansing High School; Benny Schmidt
42: © Drew Gardner/GWR; © Fotostudio Huber André/GWR
43: Paul Hughes/GWR; c/o Deafblind UK; Jonny Greene/GWR
44: c/o Gary Duschl; © Paul Hughes/GWR; © Ranald Mackechnie/GWR
45: © Ranald Mackechnie/GWR; © Drew Gardner/GWR
46: Rex Features; © Paul Hughes/GWR (2)
47: c/o Great East Asia Surveyors & Consultants Co. Ltd; © Paul Hughes/GWR; c/o Domino Day 2004
48: c/o Chinese YMCA; Empics/AP; © Paul Hughes/GWR
49: © Paul Hughes/GWR (2); c/o Youlia Bereznitskiaia
50: Getty Images; Brad Barket/GWR
51: c/o Pretoria University; Jeff Day/Splash News
52/53/54: Rex Features (2); Science Photo Library; c/o Cindy Jackson (2); Rex Features; c/o Kam Ma; © Ranald Mackechnie/GWR; © Drew Gardner/GWR; Alamy; Corbis; c/o Fulvia Celica Siguas Sandoval; Corbis
55-58: Natural History Museum Picture Library; Science Photo Library; Corbis (3); OSF; Science Photo Library; Corbis (2); NHPA; Corbis
59-61: c/o Igor Kvetko; c/o Marina Merne; © Matthew Pontin/GWR; c/o Paulette Keller; Rex Features; © Drew Gardner/GWR; Corinna Atkinson; c/o Cathy Smith; c/o Mokumoku Tedsukuri Farm; c/o Bill Pierfert; c/o Waymon and Margaret Nipper; © Drew Gardner/GWR
62: © Drew Gardner/GWR; c/o Salil Wilson (3); © Paul Hughes/GWR
63: c/o Anita Cash; c/o Henry Shelford
64: © Drew Gardner/GWR; c/o Kevin Cook; Zuma Press; Will & Deni McIntyre/Photo Researchers, Inc.; © Paul Hughes/GWR
66-67: Getty Images
68-69: Getty Images (5) Carol Kane
68: NASA; Corbis
69: Getty Images; Corbis
70: Corbis; BAS/EPICA
71: Corbis; Jacques Descloitres, MODIS Land Rapid Response Team, NASA/GSFC
72: Science Photo Library; National Geographic Images
73: USGS x 3
74: National Geographic Images; Getty Images
75: Corbis (2)
76: Science Photo Library (2); Corbis
77: Science Photo Library; Cliff Tan; Ian Bull
78: Brad Seibel; Getty Images
79: c/o JAMSTEC; SeaPics
80: Ardea; Getty Images
81: SeaPics; Ardea
82: Taylor Herring/GWR; Reuters; c/o Chengdu Research Base; Barcroft Media
84: Alamy; c/o Vanderbilt Education
85: Alamy
86: Corbis; SeaPics
87: OSF; SeaPics
88: OSF; c/o Steve Bird/Birdseekers
89: OSF (2)
90: Rex Features; Getty Images; Corbis
91: Corbis; Topham Picturepoint
92: Science Photo Library; c/o Dr Neil Clark
93: Science Photo Library; c/o The Heyuan Museum; Corbis
94: Science Photo Library (2)
95: Empics/AP; Corbis
96: OSF (2)
97: Corbis; OSF
98: c/o Norm Craven; c/o Scott Robb
99: Forest Service, an agency of DARD Northern Ireland
100: Getty
101: Corbis; USGS Eros Data Center, based on data provided by the Landsat Science team (3); c/o Senna Tree Company
102-103: Getty Images
104-105: Getty Images (5) GWR
104: NASA/LMSAL; NASA/JPL; ESA/NASA/University of Arizona; NASA/JSC/Cornell; Science Photo Library
105: NASA/JPL/SSI
106: ESA/NASA, the AVO project and Paolo Padovani; ESA
107: NASA/ESA and The Hubble Heritage Team (STScI/AURA); NASA, ESA and H.E Bond (STScI) (5)
108: Corbis; Getty Images
109: Corbis; Getty Images
110: c/o Complan Medien GmbH; Getty Images
111: NASA-HQ-GRIN; c/o Arecibo
112: DefCon Wi-Fi Shootout; TNO TPD
113: c/o Gary Thuerk; Test image for the PICA project from CCETT in France (2); Getty Images; c/o Martin Dodge/ www.cybergeography.com
114: © Paul Hughes/GWR; EFDA-JET (2); Corbis; c/o Edison International
116: Don Harley; NASA - KSC; c/o Cornell University
117: NASA ; Getty Images
118: UC Berkeley; OQO
119: NASA; ASIMO Honda (3)
120-121: Getty Images
122-123: Getty Images (6)
122: c/o Christa Rasanayagam; c/o Suresh Arulanantham
123: c/o Tadao & Minoru Watanabe; Getty Images
124: Corbis (2)
125: Corbis (2)
126: Getty Images; Alamy
127: c/o Maurizio Giuliano; Alamy
128: Getty Images; Paul Hughes/GWR; c/o Fellsmere Frog Leg Festival
129: Corbis; Rex Features
130: Getty Images (3)
131: Getty Images (2)
132: Corbis; Empics
133: Corbis
134: Getty Images; c/o Ran Gorenstein
135: Christie's Images; Empics/AP
136-137: Rex Features/ © 2004 Disney Enterprises, Inc./Pixar Animation Studios
138-139: Getty Images (5) GWR (2)
138: c/o Michael Carmichael; c/o Bev Kirk
139: Getty Images/ © Succession Picasso / DACS 2005; c/o Universal Press Syndicate; c/o Maesa Elephant Camp (2)
140: c/o Bon Prix; Rex Features
141: Alamy; © Rankin
142: Getty Images
143: Colleen Manassa; Corbis
144: NewsPix; Alamy
145: Getty Images; c/o Cinema Dei Piccoli
146: Corbis
147: Rex Features/ Photograph from the motion picture "Shrek 2" TM & © 2004 DreamWorks L.L.C. and PDI, reprinted with permission by DreamWorks Animation; Rex Features; Getty Images (2) ; Rex Features (3); The Ronald Grant Archive
148: c/o Sony (3); Getty Images
149: Getty Images
150: THE POLAR EXPRESS © 2004 Warner Bros. Entertainment Inc. All Rights Reserved; © Ranald Mackechnie/GWR
151: Empics/AP; © Ranald Mackechnie/GWR; Moviestore Collection
152: Getty Images; © Ranald Mackechnie/GWR
153: Rex Features (2); Getty Images; Rex Features (3); Getty Images (2)
154: © BBC Archive; Getty Images
155: Corbis; © BBC Archive (2); Jonny Greene/Taylor Herring; Getty Images
156: Getty Images; Comic Relief UK
157: Courtesy of Apple (2); Archos; Getty Images
158: Getty Images (3)
159: Getty Images (3)
160-162: c/o Laura Hughes; c/o Truly Nolen; c/o Mike Stephenson; c/o Foundation Skateboards; © Drew Gardner/GWR; Rex Features; c/o HARIBO GmbH & Co KG; Discovery Channel BIG!; Getty Images
163-166: Corbis; c/o Residents of Bethel; Empics/AP; Getty Images; Getty Images; c/o 101 Tower; Building Illustrations by Cliff Tan
167-169: Buzz Pictures; Getty Images (2) ; Action Plus (2); Buzz Pictures; Getty Images (3)
170: Getty Images (2)
171: c/o Yahir Othön Parra; Getty Images
172: c/o The Grand Boys; c/o George Barbar
173: Getty Images
174: Rex Features; Cylla von Tiedemann © Kevin Wallace Ltd. 2005
175: Getty Images (3)
176: c/o Cirque du Soleil; © Paul Hughes/GWR; Rick Diamond/Cirque de Soleil (2)
177: c/o Paul-Erik Lillholm; © Ranald Mackechnie/GWR
178: Royal Mail (2) ; Christie's Images; Showtime 2003; Corbis; Ramon Torra; c/o Galllup Extreme Productions
180: © 2001-2005 Lionhead Studios Limited All Rights Reserved; c/o David Storey
181: Namco; Rockstar Games (2) ; Courtesy of Computer History Museum; © Bluth Group LTD
182-183: Corbis
184-185: Getty Images (4) GWR (2)
184: c/o MAN TAKRAF Fördertechnik GmbH; c/o Jonathan Reeves (2)
185: c/o Autostadt GmbH (2); c/o Stephen McGill
186: c/o Koenigsegg CCR; c/o Team FANCY CAROL-NOK
187: c/o Ken O'Hara; Corbis; c/o International 7300 CTX
188: c/o MTT; c/o Roger LeBlanc
189: Getty Images; c/o Bobby Root
190: c/o Great Southern Railway; Corbis
191: Corbis; c/o Holloman High Speed Test Track
192: Getty Images
193: Reuters (2)
194: AirTeamImages.com; The Flight Collection; Jan Lidestrand
195: Corbis
196: Richard Hunt; U.S. Navy
197: Defence Picture Library; Corbis
198: Getty Images (2) ; c/o Lockheed Martin
199: c/o APOPO; Corbis
200: Ian Stirling
200-201: © Paul Hughes/GWR; c/o Angus Robson (9)
201: Tim Barnsley/Armidale Express
202: Getty Images; Corbis; Alamy
204: c/o Sportschallengers; Corbis
205: Corbis (2)
206: Mollison Communications/Luna Park Melbourne; c/o The Holy Land Experience
207: c/o Kristin Siebeneicher PR; Corbis
208-209: Getty Images
210-211: Getty Images (7)
210: c/o The Echo Trust; Corbis
211: c/o Paraclub Flevo; c/o Thomas S. Nielsen; c/o Jay Stokes
212: Getty Images (2)
213: Getty Images (3)
214: c/o Mad Cow Entertainment P/L (5); Getty Images
215: Getty Images (2)
216: Getty Images (2)
217: Getty Images (2)
218: Getty Images (2)
219: Getty Images (2)
220: Getty Images; Newspix
221: Getty Images; Empics
222: Getty Images; Corbis
223: Empics; Reuters; Getty Images
224: Getty Images; c/o Joe Pfeiffer
225: Getty Images (2)
226: NBA/Getty Images (2)
227: NBA/Getty Images; Getty Images
228: Empics; Getty Images; c/o Mongolian Wrestling Tournament; Corbis
230: Getty Images (2)
231: Getty Images (2)
232: Getty Images (2)
233: Getty Images (2)
234: c/o Eric Kirchner and Patrick Herresthal ; c/o Mission Hills
235: Getty Images
236: Empics; Getty Images
237: Empics; Getty Images
238: Getty Images (3); Empics; Getty Images; Corbis
240: Getty Images (2)
241: Getty Images (2)
242: Getty Images (2)
243: Getty Images (2)
244: Getty Images (2)
245: Sporting Pictures; Empics
246: Corbis; Getty Images
247: Getty Images (2)
248: Getty Images (2)
249: Getty Images (2)
250: Getty Images (2)
251: Getty Images (2)
252: c/o El Show de los Récord (4); Getty Images; © Paul Hughes/GWR
253: Getty Images (2) ; Ian Bull/ISSF
254: Getty Images (2)
255: Getty Images; c/o Stuart Foster
256: Ross Parry Picture Agency; c/o Ben & Jerry's
257: c/o Ben & Jerry's ; c/o George Hollis; c/o Ene Laansalu
258: Getty Images (2); Getty Images
259: Time Life/Getty Images; Getty Images (2)
260: Getty Images (2)
261: Getty Images (2)
262: Royal Lifesaving Society; c/o Billy Rossini; Getty Images
263: Getty Images; Empics/AP
264: Buzz Pictures; Empics/PA
265: Buzz Pictures; c/o Ror Scarpa
266: Getty Images (2)
267: Getty Images (3); Empics/PA
268: Empics/PA; Getty Images
269: Getty Images (2)
270: Getty Images (2)
271: Getty Images (3)
272: c/o Cricket Club des Ormes
273: Empics/PA
274: Getty Images (2)
275: Corbis; Getty Images
276: Getty Images (2)
277: Getty Images (2)
288: © Paul Hughes/GWR; COURTESY OF LUCASFILM LTD. Star Wars: Episode III - Revenge of the Sith © 2005 Lucasfilm Ltd. & TM. All rights reserved; c/o Fan Yang; Jason Lindsey/GWR
All other illustrations by Ian Bull

STOP PRESS

★ LARGEST ↑ ELVIS GATHERING

A record total of 77 Elvis impersonators gathered at Selfridges' London store, UK, on 17 April 2005 to sing 'Viva Las Vegas'. Each Elvis wore an appropriate outfit from a period of the King's career, including GI uniforms and jump suits.

★ DRIVING TO THE HIGHEST ALTITUDE BY CAR

Matthias Jeschke (Germany) drove a Toyota Land Cruiser 90 to an altitude of 6,358 m (20,860 ft) on the slopes of the volcano Ojos del Salado on the Chile–Argentina border on 4 March 2005.

★ LARGEST MILITARY AIR SHOW

The annual Royal International Air Tattoo at RAF Fairford, Gloucestershire, UK, is the world's largest in terms of participating aircraft. An average of 350 static and flying aircraft attend each year, with a record total of 535 aircraft at the 2003 show.

★ HIGHEST BOX OFFICE GROSS – → OPENING DAY

Star Wars: Episode III – Revenge of the Sith (USA, 2005) took a record $50,013,859 (£27,395,847) on its opening day in the USA on 19 May 2005 from a total of 3,661 cinemas. The movie was also given the ★ **largest print run** of any film in history, with 9,000, and the ★ **largest simultaneous premiere**, opening in 115 countries.

★ LONGEST MARRIAGE – LIVING COUPLE

Percy and Florence Arrowsmith (both UK) celebrated 80 years of marriage on 1 June 2005. They are also the ★ **oldest living married couple**, with an aggregate age 205 years 293 days.

★ MOST CONCERTS BY A SYMPHONY ORCHESTRA

The New York Philharmonic (USA) has played 14,000 concerts over the last 162 years. The orchestra's archive has the first performance on 7 December 1842 and the 14,000th on 18 December 2004.

★ LARGEST COMPANY MASCOT

Duracell Latin America created a giant version of the Duracell Bunny measuring 12.6 m (40 ft 2 in) tall. The mascot was completed and measured in Los Angeles, California, USA, on 20 April 2005.

★ HIGHEST ATTENDANCE FOR A BASEBALL FRANCHISE

The highest cumulative attendance for a baseball franchise is 165,770,718 by the Los Angeles Dodgers (USA) between 1901 and 2004.

★ LARGEST BANK ROBBERY

The largest bank robbery was an estimated £26.5 million ($51.46 million) stolen from the Northern Bank, Belfast, UK, between 19 December and 20 December 2004.

★ LONGEST DOG EARS

Tigger the bloodhound – owned by Bryan and Christina Flessner of St Joseph, Illinois, USA – has ears measuring 34.9 cm (13.75 in) and 34.2 cm (13.5 in) for his right and left ears respectively.

★ MOST PEOPLE ← INSIDE A SOAP BUBBLE

Fan Yang (Canada) blew a soap bubble large enough to enclose 18 adults – all no shorter than 1.52 m (5 ft) tall – at the Toys "R" Us store in Times Square, New York City, USA, on 19 March 2005.